Acclaim for *Diverse Gashes*

"The 1648 murder of four-year-old Martha Clarke, by her own mother, is perhaps Plymouth Colony's most notorious but least studied community tragedy. In *Diverse Gashes*, Donna Watkins has masterfully pieced together the stories of family, witnesses, and magistrates, and placed the horrendous event in its social and historical contexts." - Caleb Johnson, author, historian, and creator of http://mayflowerhistory.com

"Ms. Watkins provides the reader with an informative backstory into the lives of the Pilgrims before, during and after their arrival in the New World in 1620. In this compelling and fascinating account, Watkins explores in depth the circumstances of Alice's heinous crime as well as the many unanswered questions brought forth as a result of her actions." - Christine Cook, genealogist and Mayflower Descendant.

"In *Diverse Gashes*, Watkins focuses on the details leading up to the event and goes on to explain the social and religious stresses within the colony that were major contributory factors in Alice's actions. The picture Donna has drawn of life in Plymouth Colony goes well beyond other historic reading I have done in this area. I recommend this book to anyone interested in the history of the Pilgrims, particularly those with ancestral lines back to Alice Bishop." - Dennis Sutton, creator of "Home Grown in the Garden State," http://www.njsuttonfamily.org.

"Watkins' epic historical story, *Diverse Gashes*, gives an insightful glimpse into the Plymouth Pilgrims' lives, their struggles, trials, and achievements against the odds. The murder of Martha Clarke by her mother, Alice Bishop, the investigation, and subsequent trial, leaves the reader with a true appreciation of modern-day justice." - Michal Marshall, descendant of Alice Bishop.

"The 1648 death of four-year-old Martha Clarke at the hands of her mother, Alice Bishop, has haunted Alice's descendants for centuries. Using primary documentation and hundreds of sources, Donna Watkins carefully investigates the murder and trial, as well as the key characters involved in this tragic story. As much a history of the Pilgrims as it is of Alice Bishop, *Diverse Gashes* explores the culture of "control and watchfulness" that pervaded Plymouth Colony, providing the context that family historians have long sought." - Erin Taylor and Kristin Luce, co-authors of *Alice Martin Bishop: Motherhood & Murder in Plymouth Colony*, http://www.alicemartinbishop.com

"What women suffered in New England, in the so-called name of justice, is a dark stain that should not be hidden under the rug of history. I congratulate Donna Watkins on her fearless handling of this subject." - Sue Allan, author and historian

Diverse Gashes

ALSO BY DONNA A. WATKINS

Weaker Vessels: The Women and Children of Plymouth Colony

Diverse Gashes

Governor William Bradford,
Alice Bishop,
and the
Murder of Martha Clarke,
Plymouth Colony, 1648

Donna A. Watkins

American History Press
Staunton Virginia

Copyright © 2020 Donna A. Watkins

All rights reserved. No part of this book may be transmitted in any form by any means electronic, mechanical or otherwise using devices now existing or yet to be invented without prior written permission from the publisher and copyright holder.

Staunton, Virginia
(888) 521-1789

Visit us on the Internet at:

www.Americanhistorypress.com

First Printing March 2020

To schedule an event with the author or to inquire about bulk discount sales please contact American History Press.

Library of Congress Cataloging-in-Publication Data

Names: Watkins, Donna A., author.
Title: Diverse gashes : Governor William Bradford, Alice Bishop, and the murder of Martha Clarke, Plymouth Colony, 1648 / Donna A. Watkins.
Description: Staunton, Virginia : American History Press, [2019] | Includes bibliographical references and index.
Identifiers: LCCN 2019003763 | ISBN 9781939995315 (pbk. : alk. paper)
Subjects: LCSH: Bishop, Alice, 1616-1648. | Clarke, Martha, 1644-1648. | Bradford, William, 1590-1657. | Women murderers--Massachusetts--Biography.
 | Children--Crimes against--Massachusetts--History. | Massachusetts--History--New Plymouth, 1620-1691--Biography.
Classification: LCC HV6248.B58 W38 2019 | DDC 364.152/3092--dc23 LC record available at   https://lccn.loc.gov/2019003763

Manufactured in the United States of America on acid-free paper.
This book exceeds all ANSO standards for archival quality.

DEDICATION

*To the descendants of
Damaris Bishop Sutton,
because I made a promise to Alice.*

AUTHOR'S NOTE

In most cases the language of the original records has been modernized for clarification. I standardized the spelling of personal and place names using Eugene Aubrey Stratton's *Plymouth Colony: Its History & People, 1620-1691* as my primary guide.

The Pilgrims used the Julian calendar (Old Style or O.S.), with each year beginning on March 25, Conception Day. For the sake of clarity, I have chosen to cite dates using the modern Gregorian calendar (New Style or N.S.), with January 1 starting the new year.

I will readily admit to a bias in the case of the murder of Martha Clarke. I am Alice Bishop's eighth great granddaughter through her grandson Richard Sutton. While there is little doubt that Alice committed the crime and that her hanging was justified within the Pilgrim's justice system, I believe she deserves a defense and an attempt to explain the circumstances of the event.

CONTENTS

Foreword	*viii*
1 – Execution and Burial	1
2 – William Bradford and the Separatists	8
3 – Alice Martin	26
4 – The Pilgrims in Holland	37
5 – Leaving Leiden on the *Mayflower*	51
6 – George Clarke	72
7 – Arriving at New Plymouth	88
8 – Alice Clarke, Wife and Mother	106
9 – Building the Colony	119
10 – The Clarke Family in Plymouth	136
11 – Growth and Change	145
12 – Richard Bishop	160
13 – Dispersion and Disappointment	167
14 – The Great Migration Begins	176
15 – A Murder in Playne Dealing	187
16 – Behind the Court Records	191
17 – Investigation of the Crime Scene	202
18 – The Trial and the Verdict	212
19 – Moving On	222
20 – William Bradford and the Decline of Plymouth	235
21 – Why Did Alice Do It?	245
22 – Plymouth's Legacy and Its Secret	260
Afterword	*268*
Appendix – Plymouth Colony Court Records	*269*
Acknowledgments	*274*
Source Notes	*278*
Bibliography	*310*
Index	*335*

FOREWORD

It has been a pleasure to watch Donna Watkins' *Diverse Gashes* come into full and impressive shape over the four years since she first contacted me in October of 2015. She had just come across an online announcement of a talk I had delivered a few months earlier at the University of Cambridge, in which I had presented some discoveries that I had made in the notebooks of Plymouth Governor William Bradford, currently housed in the Massachusetts Historical Society. While I had to disappoint Donna's hope that these writings might cast some light on the inner life of the man who presided over the trial of her ancestor, Alice Bishop, her query nonetheless proved to be the beginning of an electronic friendship that cross-fertilized and enriched both our ongoing book projects on Plymouth Colony.

Both of us came to write books on the Plymouth Separatists through a long and circuitous route. Donna's professional career was that of a public librarian, followed by the earning of a Master's Degree in American Studies at the University of California, Irvine. My career was in the field of Classics, teaching Greek, Latin, and Greco-Roman culture at the university level for over three decades. Our happy convergence in seventeenth-century New England was the result of both scholarly and personal curiosity. My investigations were natural northward extensions of work I had published on Greco-Roman influences on colonial Latin America, though my interest in early New England surely also owed something to a curiosity about my maternal ancestors in Plymouth and Massachusetts Colonies. Donna's personal connection to Plymouth Colony acted as a more powerful motivation for her exploration of that lost world. Indeed, her project has throughout been an act of justice, an attempt to restore a voice to an ancestor who committed a seemingly inexplicable crime—a classical scholar like myself is bound to recall Medea—and paid for it in the humiliating ceremony of a public execution.

While Donna Watkins' determination—indeed, her mission—to understand her ancestor and to give her a voice persistently informs and energizes *Diverse Gashes,* she has at the same time shown herself fully and energetically committed to researching and composing a work of serious scholarship. Her book gives deeper meaning and resonance to the story of Alice Bishop by embedding it securely in overlapping historical and social contexts: English Puritanism, the Separatist community in England, Holland, and Plymouth, and the lives of women and children in mid-seventeenth century Plymouth village and nearby Duxbury. For this task, her career as a librarian and her graduate training in American Studies have served as a sound foundation.

Especially admirable is Donna's mastery of primary sources. Two species of such sources are especially on display here. First is her skillful exploitation of the rich but scattered evidence offered by the Plymouth Court Records. Inevitably, these provided her with the only direct evidence of the crime and punishment of Alice Bishop, evidence that she has interpreted expertly and imaginatively. But her use of the court records extends far beyond this particular case, for she has used her wide and perceptive reading of these records to help reconstruct the wider experience of the colony's inhabitants, especially its women. Indeed, it came as little surprise to me that the discoveries she made in the court records while researching this book inspired her to launch forth upon a second book, a more broadly conceived companion volume to this one: *Weaker Vessels: The Women and Children of Plymouth Colony,* soon to appear with this same press.

Another kind of primary source that informs and deepens Donna's account of Alice Bishop is the array of books and pamphlets known to have been present in Plymouth Colony's personal libraries and likely to have been read and shared by its more literate inhabitants. For example, William Gouge's *Of Domestical Duties,* first published in London in 1622, offered the Pilgrim paterfamilias a handy set of guidelines for managing his household and its denizens—wife, children, and servants. William

Lambarde's *Eirenarcha*, an "idiot's guide" for justices of the peace first published in 1581 and many times reprinted, supplied a deeper understanding of the administration of justice in Plymouth Colony. I was also pleased to discover that Donna made excellent use of a book of essays by the Pilgrims' Leiden pastor John Robinson, his *Observations Divine and Morall,* first published in 1625, the year of his death, and owned by both Brewster and Bradford. I had myself been drawn to these 62 elegant essays in which Pastor Robinson made apt and extensive use of classical sources, alongside more expected biblical and patristic quotations. Donna's excellent exploitation of this volume was quite different from my own—a testimony to the variety and richness of this relatively under-utilized source of intellectual, spiritual, and practical guidance for Plymouth Colony's leaders.

In addition to its skillful engagement with primary sources, *Diverse Gashes* also displays a wide and judicious familiarity with the vast scholarly literature on Plymouth Colony and early colonial New England. No less impressively, Donna has brought all this together in a lucid and accessible style to produce a book that is a compelling experience for the reader.

David A. Lupher
Professor of Classics, Emeritus
University of Puget Sound
Tacoma, Washington

Cover illustration from A Pittilesse Mother, a 17th century book by Margaret Vincent.

It is not with us as with other men whom small things can discourage, or small discontentments cause to wish themselves at home again....We are well weaned from the delicate milk of our mother country, and inured to the difficulties of a strange and hard land, which yet in a great part we have by patience overcome.

-William Brewster and John Robinson,
in a letter to Sir Edwin Sandys (1617)

Chapter One

Execution and Burial
Plymouth Colony 1648

The two-day Duxbury Fair was over, but before the colonists packed up their purchases and unsold wares, and prior to saying goodbye to one another, there was a disturbing piece of community business to deal with: the hanging of Alice Bishop. From the Pilgrim point of view, the more people who witnessed it the better. But unlike similar executions in the seventeenth century, this hanging would not be a festive affair, but would be conducted with sadness and solemnity. As Pastor Robinson had written, just as rewards are bestowed with joy and gladness, "punishments must be administered with sorrow and commiseration." There would be no taunting or cheering coming from the crowd, since this was a sad duty, not an entertainment.[1]

There had been plenty of time for the community to make its peace with the murder. After Alice had been jailed ten weeks earlier, Sunday sermons had probably focused on various aspects of the crime, and had centered on God's judgment and mercy for the unfortunate woman. Clearly, she was sorry for killing her own daughter. She had said so the day of the crime and had continued to say so ever since. In the Pilgrim mind, since she had admitted her guilt and expressed regret, she had redeemed herself in the eyes of God. Though there is no record of it, the colony's ministers probably would have visited Alice Bishop during her incarceration. There can be little doubt that she would have expressed her remorse and repentance, and been assured of God's "forgiveness to sinners, when so ever they repent." Even so, according to the laws of God and man, she must hang.[2]

Exercising the death penalty would serve the colony in several ways. It would satisfy the need for justice by making Alice pay for the crime with her own life, and it would discourage others from engaging in criminal behavior. It would also remove any danger that Alice Bishop might pose to Plymouth Colony in the future. Retribution, deterrence, and prevention were the weighty ideals that justified the capital punishment that would be inflicted on Alice, but no matter how warranted the death penalty might have been, in 1648 it was still not easy to hang a woman.

Preparations

Hanging was the preferred method of execution in Plymouth since it was considered the most humane way to put a criminal to death in the seventeenth century. Compared to the gruesome variety of punishments commonly employed in Europe, such as being drawn and quartered, it was compassionate and quick. It was economical, too, requiring only a strong rope and a tree branch thick enough to bear the condemned person's weight.

Plymouth law required that elected constables carry out the rulings of the courts, and "safely keep such prisoners as are committed to your custody and inflict or execute such sentence as shall be awarded." Thomas Heyward Sr. was chosen to be constable of Duxbury at the June 7, 1648, meeting of the General Court, when the annual election of colony officers was held. There is no record of Thomas Heyward having had any experience with public executions, but there was another Pilgrim who did have some expertise in taking a life.[3,4]

Myles (Miles) Standish, Captain of the Guard, was a professional soldier, and was probably the only Pilgrim who had any proficiency in killing another human being. Not only did he have the skill, but he also had the nerve and daring to undertake the task. In 1623 Standish had carried out a brutal attack in nearby Wessagusset that resulted in several deaths. He may have also been in charge of the execution of John Billington for murder in 1630. As the Plymouth community stood watching, and with Heyward's assistance, Standish doubtless took charge of Alice Bishop's hanging. No one wanted there to be any mistakes.

The technical aspects of early colonial hangings were simple. Generally, a ladder was placed against a large tree with sturdy branches. A rope tied into a noose was thrown over the strongest branch and draped around the prisoner's neck, whose hands had been bound together. The loose end of the rope was pulled tight and tied to the tree's trunk. The condemned was directed to climb up the ladder, and when everything was in place, ordered to "step off." He or she would swing in space until death occurred.

Death by hanging is essentially execution by strangulation. Once the air supply is cut off by the rope, unconsciousness usually occurs within two to four minutes and death within ten. Depending on how far the body is dropped, the person remains either conscious or unconscious during the ordeal. Ideally, the form thought most humane is for the person to drop far and fast, with enough force to break the bones in their neck, which immediately severs the spinal cord and renders them unconscious.

For the execution to be both quick and merciful, the prisoner must drop from the proper height. For example, to hang a man (or a woman) of 120 pounds humanely, the drop distance must be slightly over eight feet. If the drop is too short, he will remain fully conscious and suffer during the strangulation phase; if the drop is too long, he will be decapitated. Done properly, the prisoner will experience only a brief instant of pain.

Colonial hangings in the seventeenth century were not handled so scientifically, and a lot could go wrong, especially if the prisoner were a woman. Executioners during this time period had far more experience hanging men than hanging women, and they often failed to consider that a woman weighed less than a man and that the drop distance must be longer.

Surely Capt. Standish would have been aware of the case of Dorothy Talby, who was hanged in Salem in 1638 for the murder of her three-year-old daughter. Dorothy fought the executioner until the gruesome end. She even reached up and pulled the hood off her face, and once she had stepped off and "had a swing or two," she remained fully conscious, and even reached back for the ladder. Hers must have been an agonizing death, slowly strangling after her hands were peeled from the rungs and she was forced to hang freely.[5]

Standish would also have known about the execution of Mary Martin, who was sentenced to hang in Boston in 1646 for murdering her newborn child. Like Alice Bishop, she was very penitent during her incarceration and subsequent execution but was "turned off the ladder" twice before she died. After the first swing, she hung in the air, apparently unaffected by the tight rope around her neck. After "she hung a space, she spoke, and asked what they did mean to do? Then some[one] stepped up, and turned the knot of the rope backward, and then she soon died."[6]

Standish would have planned carefully for the hanging of Alice Bishop by choosing a large, strong tree or perhaps building a simple wooden scaffold. He would have boiled the rope so it would not stretch and rubbed the noose knot with soap or wax so it would slide smoothly. He would have also gathered a hood to cover Alice's face, and ropes to bind her hands and her legs.

A Hanging in Duxbury

Although no specific details of Alice Bishop's hanging were recorded, other contemporary records describe a typical hanging in colonial New England in the middle of the seventeenth century. We can presume that Alice Bishop's hanging was similar.

Setting aside the recent merriments of the Duxbury Fair, everyone would have gathered quietly at the site of execution. This was a formal ritual, solemn and dramatic, designed to make a deep and lasting impression on all those in attendance. It was a powerful statement of the colony's condemnation of wrongdoing, and the entire community played a role by serving as somber witnesses to the event.

Alice would have been washed and dressed at the jail in clean simple clothes, and then led outdoors to meet a group of local officials who were waiting for her. These included the governor and his assistants, all of whom would be dressed in their dark Sabbath suits with full flowing cloaks. All would assemble into a solemn procession leading from the jail to the place of execution, with a drummer in the lead playing a funereal beat. A clergyman would be present, probably Reverend Ralph Partridge, pastor of the Duxbury church, who would have been accompanied by his deacons. A uniformed Capt. Standish would be in the procession, along with Constable Heyward. Alice's coffin, if one could be afforded, would have preceded her, and she may have even worn the heavy hanging noose around her neck. As the procession neared the gallows, the attending clergymen would have prayed aloud for Alice.

Once they reached the hanging tree or scaffold, the death warrant would be read out loud for everyone to hear, citing Alice's crime and her sentence. She would be directed to climb the ladder. Then the minister would have prayed and preached a sermon, perhaps citing Alice's sorrow and regret and her promised redemption, and certainly reminding those gathered to be watchful over one another and constantly alert to the Devil's presence among them.

Alice may have been given an opportunity to make a statement to the crowd. If so, she probably repeated that she was repentant for her crime, and perhaps added that she had been praying with the ministers. She may have spoken to her husband and two daughters, who very likely would have been in the crowd. All gathered may have sung a solemn hymn.

A hood would have been pulled over Alice's face, and the rope adjusted around her neck with the knot settled behind her left ear. Her hands and feet would have been tied against her body to prevent her reaching back for the ladder. Capt. Standish then would have ordered Alice Bishop to step off the ladder. No need to ask twice; as a good Separatist wife, she would have obeyed immediately.

Alice may have died quickly and painlessly, with a merciful snap of her neck as her spinal cord was severed. Perhaps things went badly, and she died slowly, strangling and struggling to breathe as the rope crushed her windpipe. Either way, it would have taken several minutes for her to die. Once it was presumed that Alice Bishop was dead, the rope would be released and her limp body examined to confirm her death. A formal announcement would be made and her body prepared for burial.

Burial

After Alice Bishop had been declared dead, the crowd would have gathered their belongings, disbursed, and headed for home. It was not the custom of the Pilgrims to pray at a burial. To pray for the dead was to recognize the doctrine of purgatory, in which they did not believe.

Family and friends must have prepared Alice's body for burial. Burial expenses were the responsibility of the grieving Richard Bishop and they may have influenced his decisions. Court costs were two shillings, six pence; digging the grave cost three shillings. Alice's body may have been wrapped in the traditional five-yard length of winding sheet, but at a cost of eight shillings, five pence, Richard may have opted to bind her in a simple blanket. A coffin would have cost another eight shillings, so she may have been laid to rest without one.[7]

After she was prepared for internment, Constable Heyward would have hauled her body to the burial place in an ox cart, where a fresh grave was already dug and waiting for her. While we don't know for certain, Alice's body was probably buried near Harden Hill. A convicted murderer, even a repentant and forgiven one, would not have been laid to rest in the community cemetery. Harden Hill is in the southeast section of Duxbury, directly east of the meeting house. Today the area boasts million-dollar mansions, many with their own tennis courts and sparkling swimming pools, but in 1648 it was a remote place of sand dunes with no public road. It was the preferred place to bury the remains of those who were deemed unfit to be included in Duxbury's hallowed burying ground.[8]

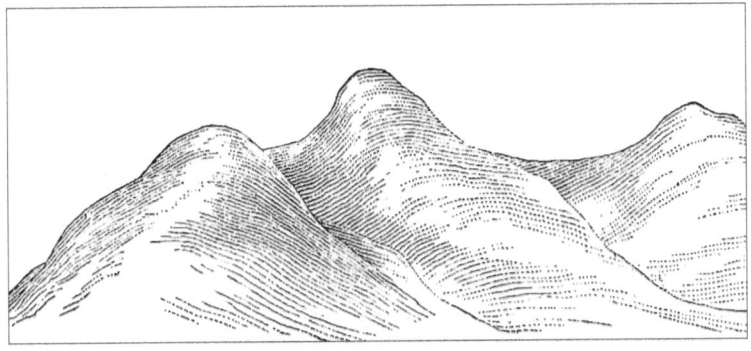

Harden Hill, a desolate burial ground.

The Duxbury Fair was over, Alice Bishop was buried, and justice had been served. The community had dealt with the murder of Martha Clarke in accordance with the colony's laws regarding capital crimes. There had been a full and complete investigation, and Alice had been tried and found guilty of the capital crime of murder. She was hanged in accordance with Plymouth law.

The murder had disrupted the order of Plymouth society, and this was a community that took pride in self-control. Alice had created chaos in the colony when she cut her own daughter's throat, but through her repentance and execution, order had been restored. The Pilgrims had shown their disapproval of the crime, yet had shown forgiveness at the same time, just as God would have desired.

They could be assured that God's blessings were restored on Plymouth and eventually all would once again be normal and under control. Everyone would be in his or her place. Governor Bradford and his assistants would see to it. It was the Separatist way, and it all began in Austerfield, England, nearly forty years earlier.

Chapter Two

William Bradford and the Separatists

Austerfield, England 1590

On March 19, 1590, William and Alice Bradford brought their newborn son, William, to St. Helena's, Austerfield's parish church, to be baptized. This was the third child the couple had carried to the church for the rite. Margaret, born in 1586, had been baptized on March 8 and was buried the very next day. Their daughter Alice had been baptized in 1587.[1]

It was a short walk to St Helena's, less than 200 yards south of the Bradford's home. The church was almost 500 years old, built by the Normans in 1080 out of stones ferried up the Ryton and Idle Rivers and hauled to the site by horse and cart. Atop the west façade was an open bell gable, its twin bells hung in two arched openings visible from the Bradford farm.

When the congregants entered the church from the south porch, the ancient baptismal font, made of stone with a lead liner, was straight ahead. Behind it and through a large stone arch hung Queen Elizabeth's Coat of Arms, reminding the parishioners of the union between the church and the crown. To the east, in front of another archway, stood the tall pulpit where the vicar read prayers and preached sermons. Behind the pulpit and through another stone arch was the chancel, an area separated from the congregation and reserved for the clergy and choir. Against the east wall, behind a railing, stood the altar.

This was a Protestant church, as were all in England at the time. It followed the prescribed Book of Common Prayer for each of its

St. Helena's Church in Austerfield.

services, the 1559 edition on this occasion. Baptisms were held on Sundays or holy days, so that the "most number of people may come together," and "every man present may be put in remembrance of his own profession made to God in his Baptism." The ritual was to be conducted in English, for the same reason. Parents were responsible for requesting a baptism the night before so the curate could prepare for the event. On the day of the baptism, "the Godfathers, Godmothers, and people, with the children must be ready at the font" immediately after the last lesson of either the morning or evening prayers.[2]

With everyone gathered, the priest in his holy vestments would begin the prescribed prayer, "Dearly Beloved, forasmuch as all men be conceived and born in sin, and that our Savior Christ said, none can enter into the kingdom of God, except he be regenerate and born anew of water and of the Holy Ghost..., that [this child] may be baptized with water and the holy Ghost, and received into Christ's holy Church." William may have slept in his godmother's arms, as the prayers were being read over him. Surely he cried out when the priest "dipped" him in the water on that chilly March day, no matter how "discretely and warily done," while saying, "William, I baptize thee in the Name of the Father, and of the Son, and of the Holy Ghost. Amen."[3]

At the end of the ceremony the minister reminded the godparents of their responsibilities, "that these children may be virtuously brought up, to lead a godly and a Christian life." The minister added that the child should be brought to the bishop for confirmation as soon as he was able to recite the Articles of Faith, the Lord's Prayer, and the Ten Commandments, and after he had received some Catechism instruction.[4]

Who could have imagined that tiny boy child, still damp from baptism, would grow to publicly reject the Church of England, the Book of Common Prayer, the priests and ministers, and all they stood for? William Bradford would grow up to join the Separatist movement, leave his family, leave England, travel across the sea, and help establish a successful British colony in Plymouth.

William Bradford in Austerfield, Yorkshire

William Bradford was born into one of the more prosperous families in Austerfield, a tiny and remote farming village of about twenty-five households in the south of Yorkshire County some 170 miles north of the heart of London. His father, also named William, had chosen Alice Hanson, daughter of John Hanson and Margaret Gresham, for his wife. The Hanson family was second only to the Bradfords in wealth and importance in the hamlet of Austerfield. Alice was twenty-two when they married on June 21, 1584, thus uniting the two most influential families in the area.

Stands of oak and beech trees still shade the large ferns and grasses that grow abundantly in this rainy region. Hedgerows from Bradford's time still exist there today, thick barricades of holly, hawthorn, and blackberry vines marking the boundaries of properties. In the sixteenth century, the thin and sandy soil was mainly suitable for growing rye and peas. The farmers and field hands in the area raised cattle, sheep, and pigs, and their diet consisted mostly of rye bread, pea soup, pork, and weak beer.

Bradford's family were landowners, and therefore enjoyed some standing in the community. Their home, a solid two-story Tudor-style yeoman's house, was half-timbered, with inside and outside frames constructed of dark squared oak timbers. These were filled in between with white wattle and daub, a plaster-like mixture of straw, wet soil, clay and sand. The house had a steep winding staircase to an upper floor, where it is said that William Bradford was born. A cellar, where perishables were stored, was accessible by circular stone steps.[5]

William Bradford's home in Austerfield, still standing today.

The younger William was privileged in many ways, and it was assumed that he would take over the Bradford lands someday and become a yeoman farmer like most of his ancestors before him. But events did not proceed exactly as they had been planned. Before young William was two years old, in July of 1591, his father, the elder William Bradford, died. By the time he was four, on September 23, 1593, his mother had married Robert Briggs. Alice and Robert had two children, Agnes, baptized September 22, 1594, and Robert, baptized on May 8, 1596, both at St. Helena's. Alice died two weeks after Robert's birth, on May 23, 1596, perhaps as a result of trauma from the delivery.[6]

It was not unusual at the time, especially among the relatively prosperous, that upon his father's death and his mother's remarriage, a male child was sent to live with his biological father's family, therefore preserving the family's estate. That may be why William was put into the care of his grandfather, William Bradford (the eldest William). In 1594 his grandfather died, and the future Pilgrim William was sent to live with his uncle, Robert Bradford. Robert, also a yeoman, owned eleven acres of land in Austerfield and rented another twenty-three from the Crown. He was well-respected in the community and even served as church warden in 1601, 1602, and 1608.[7,8]

Uncle Robert had married Alice Waingate on January 31, 1585, and had a family of his own when William Bradford, about six years old, came to live with them in 1595. Bradford never wrote of the earliest years of his life, so his feelings about losing his parents at such a young and impressionable age remain unknown. Whatever the cause might be, William developed an independent and somewhat rebellious spirit as he grew older.[9]

Bradford was set to inherit his father's property at the age of twenty-one, which would have made him financially independent. His family, community, and local tradition presumed that he would maintain the Bradford family's position and preserve their land holdings. His Uncle Robert was especially determined to prepare the boy for the life of a yeoman farmer. But things did not go well, since William did not seem suited to the affairs and rigors of husbandry.

Perhaps that was one of the causes of William's apparent physical breakdown, described as "a long sickness," that weakened him and left him too ill to work outdoors. Whatever the affliction that incapacitated him, Bradford would later write that it was actually a blessing that "kept him from the vanities of youth." He began to do what came naturally to him—reading books and educating himself.[10]

Robert's situation became even more challenging when his wife Alice died in 1600, leaving him with his own young children and the sickly William. Robert eventually decided to make the best of it. His nephew would receive an education. If he couldn't work the fields, his uncle reasoned, he could keep the family's accounts in order. He would become the Bradford family scholar, dedicated to literary pursuits. Accordingly, a tutor may have been engaged to guide his studies, and surely William was found to be a quick learner. His future seemed to be on track, but this plan, too, would backfire before long.[11,12,13]

Reading and studying the Scriptures was a part of every young man's education at the time, but William Bradford became more interested in them than most, spending hours poring over the passages and pondering their meanings. Cotton Mather wrote that when Bradford was around twelve years old (1602), "the reading of the Scriptures began to cause great impressions upon him." Most likely young Bradford was studying from an English translation of the Bible; perhaps it was a Geneva Bible, first published in 1560, that so transfixed him.[14]

The availability of a Bible in the English language would eventually challenge everything that was accepted about religion in England. William Tyndale made the first English translation of the New Testament in 1534, working from scholarly Greek and Hebrew editions. The Geneva Bible, favored by the Dissenters, was based on Tyndale's work. It was the first to contain extensive marginal notations, study guides to the scriptures and numbered verse citations, making it possible to cross-reference verses. This vernacular Bible was a direct challenge to the authority of the Church of England, since it made the scriptures accessible to anyone who could read, without the interpretation and influence of the clergy. It cut out the middleman, so to speak.

While the Geneva Bible provided one element that nurtured the dissenting movement, other factors contributed to a general dissatisfaction within the English populace, especially the system of a national mandatory religion.

Sources of the Dissenting Movement

King Henry VIII had been born a Roman Catholic, as had many English monarchs before him, and as he began his reign this was the established church. However, a difference of opinion over his divorce from Catherine of Aragon led him to separate from the Holy See and Rome in 1534. He then created the Church of England with himself as its head, but still maintained many Catholic doctrines and practices, many of which the Protestant reformers wanted to change. After Henry's death in 1547, his nine-year old son Edward was crowned. During Edward's reign, for both political and religious reasons, the Church of England took on more of a Protestant flavor, and the last vestiges of the Catholic Church were nearly destroyed. It was during his reign that Protestantism was firmly established as the state religion. When Edward became ill at the age of fifteen in 1553, he named his cousin, Lady Jane Grey, as his successor to prevent the country from reverting to Catholicism after his death. Lady Jane Grey was deposed and later executed, and so Mary, Henry's daughter and a devout Catholic, became queen.

Queen Mary declared that Catholicism was once again the state religion. She was an intolerant ruler who forbade all disagreement and became widely known for her bloody persecution of Protestants. Under her authority nearly 300 Protestants were put to death, many "worthy martyrs and confessors," burned alive in the "fiery flames" at the stake. When Mary died in 1558, her half-sister Elizabeth took the throne. Elizabeth quickly restored Protestantism and required conformity to the Book of Common Prayer. However, many believed that Elizabeth's church had too many Catholic carry-overs from Mary's reign and began to advocate for reforms to "purify" the church from that influence; hence the name Puritans.[15]

In response, in 1593, Elizabeth enacted the Act Against Seditious Sectaries, or the Religion Act of 1593. This act was aimed directly at the Puritans and required that all persons above the age of sixteen attend "some church, chapel, or usual place of common prayer, to hear divine service established by her majesty's laws and statutes...." Puritanism was made an official offense against the crown. Those who did not comply and those who persuaded others not to comply "shall be committed to prison, there to remain without bail...until they shall conform...to her majesty's laws and statutes aforesaid, and to make such open submission and declaration of their said conformity...." In effect, during the later years of Elizabeth's reign, any dissention against the established church—the Protestant Church of England—was against the law.[16]

It was in this unsettled environment that William Bradford first began to question how the practices of the Church of England measured up against the scriptural teachings that he was reading in his English-language Bible. He became interested in the dissenting movement, whose members were proposing drastic reform in the English Church. Dissenters believed—and Bradford was coming to agree—that the true Church should be modeled strictly on the teachings of the Scriptures.

Bradford began to attend the meetings of Richard Clyfton, a minister in nearby Babworth who was preaching a nonconformist message. William would make the long 12-mile walk southward along the Great North Road, essentially a simple horse trail shaded by sycamores and yews. Clyfton was well educated, a graduate of Cambridge University, a hotbed of the dissenting movement. He was known as a "forward preacher," or a reformist, and since Babworth was a backwater farming village with a small population, he was largely ignored by the royal authorities.

It was against the crown's law to attend another church outside of your own parish, since the local parish church was considered the center of community life, and its cultural, social, and religious heart. For men to seek out a specific preacher in another neighborhood would have threatened the cohesiveness of the village—and the power of the church. William's uncle Robert Bradford undoubtedly began to worry about his nephew. It was against the law to dissent against the Church of England, and by attending Clyfton's meetings young William was putting himself, his family, and the entire community in danger.

William was enthralled with Clyfton's sermons. He had finally found someone who understood his doubts and questions about the established church and how it compared to the biblical example. While attending a church outside your own village was unlawful, Bradford was never cited by the church warden at St. Helena's and fined the proscribed twenty pounds. Robert

Bradford, William's uncle, was the warden, and whether it was out of a protective affection for his nephew or dissenting sympathies on his own part, Robert never reported the boy missing.

Understandably, family, friends, and neighbors pressured the young man to stop such foolishness, return to the family farm, and take up his responsibilities as God had intended. But William had found a cause that aroused his energy and engaged his passion. The more his family and community objected, "the more fixed he was in his purpose to seek the ordinances of the gospel."[17]

Bradford would later speak of his family's objections when he wrote:

> [To] keep a good conscience and walk in such a way as God has prescribed in his Word, is a thing which I must prefer before you all, and above life itself. Wherefore, since 'tis for a good cause that I am like to suffer the disasters which you lay before me, you have no cause to be either angry with me or sorry for me; yea, I am not only willing to part with everything that is dear to me in this world for this cause, but I am also thankful that God has given me a heart to do [so], and will accept me so to suffer for him.[18]

In 1603 Queen Elizabeth died, and James of Scotland succeeded her. James believed in the divine right of kings, the doctrine that asserts that a monarch derives his authority directly from God and need not be responsible to the will of the people. As a youth, James had seen Separatists proselytizing in Scotland and carried a very poor opinion of them. In his treatise on government, the *Basilikon Doron* (Greek for "royal gift"), he advised his son Henry, the presumed heir to the throne, that the Dissenters are "not worthy to enjoy the benefit of breathing," because, among other things, they "make the Scriptures to be ruled by their conscience and not their consciences to be ruled by the Scriptures." Punish the Separatists, James advised his son, "in case they refuse to obey the law and will not cease to stir up a rebellion."[19]

Under James, "their former afflictions were but as flea-bitings in comparison [to] these which now came upon them," wrote Bradford. Still, he was not to be deterred. The dissenting movement would give the teenage William Bradford a meaningful purpose in life. It would also give him a surrogate father, another William: William Brewster.[20]

William Brewster and the Scrooby Separatists

Approximately three miles south of Austerfield, also on the Great North Road, sat the village of Scrooby, the seat of the Archbishop of York, and the location of his manor house. The rural village itself was tiny, "a village of two furlongs," or about a quarter mile, consisting of a road lined with cottages. In 1603, the population was about one hundred and thirty adults. In contrast to the hamlet's humble cottages, the medieval manor house was grand.[21] In 1538, John Leland, King Henry VIII's historian, described it as "a great Manor Place, standing within the moat, and [be]longing to the Archbishop of York, built in two Courts, where of the first is very ample." The archiepiscopal mansion was originally built in the black and white half-timber style, but extensive decorative brick work was added to the front of the building in the early 1500s. There were several outbuildings and courtyards added through the years as needs required. The property included a vast fenced deer park and several stocked ponds, providing hunting and fishing activities for the recreation of the archbishop and his guests, and fresh meat and fish for is table.[22,23,24]

The Archbishop of York was second in importance and power only to the Archbishop of Canterbury. When visiting Scrooby he would arrive with an entourage of aides and servants, along with his own furniture, linens, and table settings. A flurry of activity ensued, which would only die down when His Grace departed with all his belongings and staff.

In 1575 the elder William Brewster was appointed as Receiver and Bailiff of the Archbishop Edmund Grindal's properties in Scrooby. This meant that he was responsible for managing the estate, which included

The Manor House in Scrooby.

maintaining order, settling disputes, and collecting rents from tenants who farmed properties they rented from the archbishop. A life-long appointment, it was a position of great responsibility and high status.

The "very ample" Scrooby Manor House, located on the Great North Road, served the crown as the twelfth official coach stop between London and Berwick in Scotland. Under Queen Elizabeth's reign, the elder William Brewster was also appointed Master of the Queen's Post at Scrooby. As such he was responsible for ensuring that dignitaries and documents continued quickly and safely along their way. Brewster kept a stable of fresh horses ready for couriers; he also maintained clean and comfortable lodgings and a well-stocked pantry for those boarding overnight.

By the early 1600s the main building of Scrooby Manor was, as King James I noted, in a sad state of disrepair. However, it continued to serve as a relay station with William Brewster the Elder in charge. Brewster's official positions at Scrooby made him wealthy enough to send his son, also named William, to Cambridge University to become a clergyman. During his brief studies at Peterhouse College, Cambridge, the younger Brewster would learn the theology of the Church of England. He would also be exposed to the dissenting movement against it.

There was widespread dissatisfaction at the university with the

Church of England and the leftovers of Catholicism that permeated its practices. Brewster and his classmates would debate the differences between the word of God as presented in the Bible against the Church of England's interpretation. Those lively discussions would affect William deeply.

After a brief stint of service in the Court of Queen Elizabeth as a diplomatic assistant, William Brewster returned to Scrooby and was appointed Master of the Post upon his father's death in 1590. The younger Brewster's position as postmaster was an enviable one, since Scrooby still served as an inn and relay station for travelers heading north and south on the Old North Road. Brewster earned a comfortable salary providing for their needs, and also had access to the latest news, as travelers shared gossip and reports of recent events while enjoying delicious meals at the long tables in the great hall of the manor. Brewster quickly became one of the most important and well-connected men in Scrooby. In about 1591 he married, and his wife Mary delivered their first child, Jonathan, in 1593.

Still pursuing his religious studies after his return to Scrooby, Brewster developed a close friendship with Richard Clyfton of Babworth, the same preacher whom young William Bradford had been visiting. Brewster was also acquainted with John Smyth, who was preaching even more radical non-conformist notions at nearby Gainsborough. At Brewster's invitation, Clyfton and Smyth began to meet with him informally at Scrooby Manor, perhaps in one of the small dining rooms upstairs, where they would discuss and debate the ideas originating from the dissenting movement. One day Richard Clyfton invited William Bradford to join them.

What started as lively discussions in Scrooby Manor over discontent with the Church of England developed in time into a belief that the only way to practice God's truths, as presented in the Bible, was for individuals to join the Separatist movement and remove themselves completely from the established state church. God's truth did lay in the Scriptures, Separatists believed, but not as interpreted by priests or bishops. Accordingly, God spoke directly to each man, and his word was available to all without priestly intermediaries. The Bible was open to individual interpretation. As Pilgrim pastor John

Robinson would later put it, "the scriptures are as well mine, as any other man's." Furthermore, God wasn't finished. There were divine revelations still to come, because "the Lord ha[s] more truth and light yet to break forth out of his holy word." Separatists were confident that by sharing and discussing what they felt in their hearts, new biblical truths would be revealed. They called this activity *prophesying*. An unintended side effect of their preliminary conversations was that the Separatists became very skilled at the art of debate and persuasion, which would serve them well over time. [25]

Like the Puritans, the Separatists believed in predestination, but with a significant difference. The Puritans believed that there was nothing a man could do to save himself because God had already decided who would be saved. The Separatists reasoned that God would not have chosen those who lived wicked lives for redemption, but that "those that receive this his grace, by faith in his Son, them, in this his eternal predestination he elected." In other words, it was those who demonstrated godliness and believed in Christ who were assumed to be among the saved.[26]

Theirs was a movement which was considered dangerously radical by the majority of the populace. The Scrooby community in particular resented having Dissenters among them. This was a conservative farming village, and its inhabitants were dependent on one another for survival. It was a threat to everyone's welfare when one of their leaders, namely William Brewster, began to resist and challenge the status quo.

To strengthen their bond, and perhaps their resolve, the little group of Scrooby Separatists entered into a formal and sacred covenant in 1602. This was considered a contract between themselves and God. In his name, they solemnly promised each other to "walk with God, and one with another, in the enjoyment of the Ordinances of God, according to the Primitive Pattern in the Word of God." This was a radical act. They believed that they had a divine right to bind themselves together—with God—in a solemn promise that was beyond the control of king or bishops. They affirmed that just as Noah, Abraham, and Moses had made covenants with God in the Bible, they could too. They would honor this promise, in a loose sense, for the rest of their lives.[27]

All of this was very appealing to young William Bradford. The movement offered him many of the things he must have longed for, including male role models, intellectual stimulation, and deep religious conviction. It also offered him a choice, an opportunity for a life very different from the one his Uncle Robert envisioned for him. In short, the dissenting movement offered Bradford a chance to take control of his own destiny. And perhaps enjoy a little adventure too, though he was not likely to admit it.

When traveling from Austerfield to Babworth along the Old North Road, Bradford would have passed through Bawtry. At that time, Bawtry was an important port on the River Idle, an tributary of the Trent. Its location inland made it the preferred route for imports into Yorkshire and for the export of outbound Yorkshire products. Since the thirteenth century, it had been a market town, a busy place of trade to and from London and ports abroad. Perhaps a sense and longing for adventure had lodged in Bradford's mind, a young man bored with the yeoman's life. As he walked through Bawtry, he would have seen ships sail into the port from far-away places the young man could hardly imagine. As it turned out, it would be on such a merchant ship that Bradford would sail to the New World.

Sometime during this early period, Bradford left behind his Uncle Robert's household and Austerfield. He moved in with the Brewsters at Scrooby Manor House and committed himself to the goals and ideals of Separatism. The Bradfords still living in Austerfield must have been very disappointed in him, since they were depending on him and his ample inheritance to keep the family lands productive. This was a society that practiced primogeniture, and William was an only son, the scion who had responsibilities to his family. It seems evident that in William Brewster, Bradford found the father he'd never had, and Mary Brewster was there to become the mother he surely longed for, one who was supportive and provided a stable home. She would become his model for the ideal Separatist wife. As a bonus, Bradford suddenly had Brewster "brothers" and "sisters."

In about 1606, John Robinson joined the Scrooby congregation. He was a former student at Cambridge who became an assistant clergyman at Norwich but was later removed for preaching against the established church. Robinson would eventually rise in the ranks of the Scrooby group to become their teacher and one of William Bradford's beloved mentors. Robinson's writings would become the template for daily life in Plymouth Colony.

Persecution of the Separatists

In 1604 King James held a conference at Hampton Court royal palace, about twelve miles from London, to address the merits of Puritan requests for church reforms. Some agreements were reached, including James commissioning an authorized English language version of the Bible, which became known as the now-familiar King James Version. Overall, however, things did not bode well for dissidents. At the Hampton Court Conference, King James had a few words of warning for the non-conformists: "I shall make them conform themselves, or I will harry them out of the land, or else do worse."[28]

It wasn't long before ministers were asked to sign a pledge of conformity, and those who refused lost their appointments, and thus their livelihoods. Richard Clyfton, for example, was dismissed from his position as vicar at Babworth, and John Robinson lost his position as assistant pastor at St. Andrew's in Norwich. Most of the detached clerics continued to preach, although this was an unlawful practice. Clyfton was found to be illegally preaching at Bawtry and was subsequently excommunicated.[29]

The king and his bishops were determined "to imprison, fine, or banish all dissidents from the dominant Church." Bradford would later write that the Separatists "were hunted and persecuted on every side.... For some were taken and clapped up in prison, others had their houses beset and watched night and day...." Things were heating up for any who held dissenting views.[30,31]

The Separatists continued to meet in Scrooby for about a year, but in secret, "their meetings every Sabbath in one place or other." However, the pressure was on, not only from the crown, but from their own consciences. They were in very real danger of execution or imprisonment, which could be a death sentence of its own given the condition of English prisons at the time. Even more important, they believed their very souls to be in jeopardy. The Pilgrims, as Bradford later called them, were certain that God had spoken directly to them and called them to live on the model of scriptural values. They believed that to ignore this truth was to provoke God's anger and risk damnation for themselves and their families.[32]

On September 15, 1607, William Brewster, among others, was cited for being a Brownist and a follower of Robert Browne, an early leader of the Separatist movement. Richard Bancroft, Archbishop of Canterbury, ordered that he be apprehended. Brewster and others went into hiding, and the deputy sent to arrest him had to admit that "he cannot find them, nor understand where they are." By September 30 Brewster had lost his job, and a replacement was soon named as Scrooby Postmaster and Bailiff. On December 1, the King's Court officially announced that Brewster was "disobedient in matters of religion."[33]

It is not known who first proposed the idea of leaving England, but "by a joint consent," the congregation decided that it was too dangerous to continue their lives in Scrooby. "They resolved," Bradford wrote, "to go into the Low Countries [the Netherlands], where they heard [there] was freedom of religion for all men."[34]

According to biblical teaching, wives and children were expected to comply with their husbands' decisions and to follow them wherever they went. Literally. Perhaps some of the Separatist wives agreed with their husbands and accepted their religious beliefs; perhaps some did not. Nonetheless, dissent within the family was not tolerated. Wives, John Robinson wrote, were expected "to patiently bear the burden of obedience."[35]

To understand more fully the "burden of obedience," consider the words of Susanna Bell, a woman faced with the decision of leaving England for the colonies:

> Some troubles being here, many of the people of God went for New England and among them my husband desired to go, but I and my friends were very averse unto it. I having one child, and being big with another, thought it to be very difficult to

cross the seas with two small children, some of my neighbors advising me to the contrary, living so well as I did. But I told them that what the Lord would have me to do, that I would willingly do; and then it pleased the Lord to bring that Scripture to my mind, Eph, 5, 22, 'Wives submit yourself unto your own Husbands, as unto the Lord.' And then my heart was brought off to a quiet submission.[36]

Susanna's hesitation would not go unpunished, as she further explained:

But after this, I being well delivered, and the child well; it pleased the Lord soon after to take my child to himself. Now upon this, so far as it pleased the Lord to help a poor wretch, I begged earnestly to him, to know why he took away my child, and it was given in to me, that it was because I would not go to New England."[37]

Completely chastised, Susanna surrendered her will:

Upon this the Lord took away all fears from my spirit, and then I told my husband that I was willing to go with him. For the Lord had made my way clear to me against any that should oppose. And then my husband went presently upon the work to fit to go. And the Lord was pleased to carry us as upon Eagles wings, according to that Deut. 32, 10-11."[38]

The Scrooby congregation was quietly preparing to leave England, although some were perhaps more enthusiastic about the move than others.

※※※※※

Alice Martin was not part of the early Scrooby congregation, but she was a Plymouth colonist and as such would have been trained to submit, just as the other Separatist wives were expected to do. We first meet her on her wedding day in 1639.

Chapter Three

Alice Martin

1639

Prior to 1648 there was nothing remarkable or unusual written in the colony's records about Alice Martin Clarke Bishop— no record of her appearing before the courts for "unseemly behavior," or any other indication of what would lead to her subsequent actions. Most likely she was very much like other Pilgrim women, brought up to be a Separatist wife and mother, and known only by that designation.

"George Clarke & Alice Martin marryed Ye 22nd of January 1638."

The earliest evidence of Alice Bishop's actual existence in Plymouth is a marriage record: "George Clarke & Alice Martin [were] married the 22nd of January, 1638." (Note that the record is in the Old Style of dating; in the New Style the year would be 1639.) Who—or even where—Alice was before she showed up at Plymouth is pure conjecture. Martin may have been her maiden name, but speculation that she was the daughter of *Mayflower* passenger Christopher Martin are not supported. William Bradford, in his "Passengers in the *Mayflower*" appendix to his classic *Of Plymouth*

Plantation, clearly states that "Mr. Martin, he and all his died in the first infection, not long after the arrival." It is also possible that she had been previously married, and that Martin was her married name, leaving her maiden name unknown, but no evidence has yet been discovered confirming this possibility. Perhaps she was related to the Martin family that settled in Hingham, Rehoboth, and Plymouth, all villages which were part of the colony. These included Robert, Isaac, Abraham, and Elizabeth, and their families. If so, they were an inconspicuous family, since Alice's marriage record is the first time the name "Martin" is mentioned in the colony's court records.[1,2,3]

Even though very little is known about Alice Martin personally, no matter where she came from or who her parents were, once she arrived in Plymouth Colony, she would have had to comply with the Separatists' expectations for women. Before her marriage she would have been a part of someone's family, the responsibility of a husband, a parent, or a master who was answerable for her care, training, and behavior.

Plymouth was a very homogeneous community, a place with little cultural diversity. Any deviation from the community's expectations would have been swiftly quashed. Therefore, it is within Separatism and its values, especially in the family and home, that we will find the ideal of the Plymouth woman, the model Alice would have endeavored to emulate.

Women in Separatism

In Separatist families women were considered the "weaker vessel," and authority was seated at the head of the family, that is, the husband. John Robinson, the Pilgrims' teacher in Scrooby and later their pastor in Leiden, made that clear when he wrote, "Many common graces and good things are requisite both for husband and wife: but more especially the Lord requires in the man love and wisdom; and in the woman subjection." Separatist theology did recognize that women had free will and had their own innate desires and passions, but the religion required its women to suppress any inborn inclination to make choices for themselves. Women, Robinson instructed, "must bear patiently the burden" of obedience, "which God Hath laid upon the daughters of Eve."[4]

William Gouge was not a Separatist, but his advice book Domesticall Duties (1622) was in William Bradford's personal library in Plymouth, so we can assume that Bradford was familiar and most likely in agreement with his teachings. Gouge warned that a wife who imagines "that she herself is not inferior to her husband, ariseth from monstrous self-conceit, and intolerable arrogancy, as if she herself were above her own sex, and more than a woman." She must submit, Gouge wrote, even if her husband be a man "of lewd and beastly conditions, as a drunkard, a glutton, a profane swaggerer, an impious swearer, and blasphemer."[5,6]

Gouge felt that a woman's surrender must be complete and so internalized that it naturally affected "the ordering of her countenance, gesture, and whole carriage before her husband." She must manifest a "pleasingness to him, and a contentedness and willingness to be under him and ruled by him. ... Contrary to this mildness is a frowning brow, a lowering eye, a sullen look, a pouting lip, a swelling face, a deriding mouth, a scornful cast of the arms and hands, a disdainful turning of this side and that side of the body, and a fretful flinging out of her husband's presence."

It is to her own peril that a wife disrespects her husband in this manner, says Gouge: This type of behavior can "oft stir up much passion in the man, and bring much mischief upon the wife herself."[7]

This is not to say that heads of households were permitted to be tyrants; the relationship between husband and wife was to be based on love, "holy for quality, and great for quantity." Submission must not be imposed, Robinson advised, but freely given: "The woman in innocence was to be subject to the man: but this should have been without all wrong on his part, or grief on hers."[8]

And yet, Robinson continued, it is desirable that a wife be somewhat less intelligent, less enlightened, than her husband. It is not enough, he says, that "the husband walk with his wife as a man of love." He should also walk before her "as a man of understanding," so that he can "guide and go before her, as a fellow heir of eternal life with him." Anything else is fraught with danger. "Experience teacheth," he warns, "how inconvenient it is, if the woman have but a little more understanding...than her husband hath." And, even if she had a bit more "understanding" than her husband, she must endeavor, adds Gouge, "to bring her judgment and will to her husband's,...to suspect her judgement when it [is] contrary to her husband's."[9,10]

When conflicts arose in Separatist households and a decision needed to be made, the wife was expected to acquiesce to her husband. "One must give way," Robinson wrote, and "this God and nature layeth upon the woman, rather than upon the man." Simply put, according to Robinson, in the Separatist family, "it is monstrous if the head stands where the feet should be."[11]

There was a special station for women within the Separatist church hierarchy: the office of deaconess. John Robinson described five offices of ministry in the church, the pastor, the teacher, the governing elder, the deacon, and "the widow or deaconess, who is to attend the sick and impotent with compassion and cheerfulness." While there is no evidence of a deaconess serving in the church in Plymouth, there was one in the church in Holland, an old woman, an "ancient widow, well past sixty, who...visited the old and the sick and collected alms for the needy." During the church services on Sundays, she would sit "in a convenient place...with a little birchen rod in her hand, and kept little children in great awe, from disturbing the congregation."[12,13]

It was also technically permissible for women to prophesize during church meetings, that is, to share aloud their insights into the biblical readings with the entire congregation. On this point, John Robinson disagreed with St. Paul's teaching which required that women observe "deep silence in this church exercise, not permitting them at all to speak." Robinson argued that God had furnished some women with "extraordinary gifts and endowments of prophecy," citing the Bible's "Miriam, Deborah, Huldah, Anna, as also even in Jezebel herself," as examples. The practice dated back to the ancient Jewish church, according to Robinson, "where liberty both for teaching and disputing publicly..., in the temple and synagogue, was freely given to all gifted accordingly, without respect had to any office." Nonetheless, there is no record of any Separatist woman having an official office or speaking aloud in the Plymouth Church.[14]

There is also no record of any woman ever holding an official office in the government of Plymouth. In 1623 Governor Bradford and Isaac Allerton wrote a letter to their investors in England making that point very clear: "Touching on government you are mistaken if you think we admit women and children to have to do in the same, for they are excluded, as both reason and nature teacheth they should be." However, in 1679, there was the exceptional occurrence of women serving on the jury in a case of child abuse. The five "matrons" may have been chosen for their expertise in childcare.[15,16]

Women and the Pilgrim Work Ethic

One of the most important of the Pilgrim values was that everyone should be industrious. John Robinson wrote that "it is a shame for a man not to work and exercise himself in some one or other lawful vocation....[God] would have none of his sinful posterity lead their life in idleness." Hard work was hardwired into the Pilgrims. Nothing in their experience or their beliefs promised or condoned an easy life. Committed to their holy purpose, they expected to have to work diligently and live plainly.[17]

Plymouth Colony law stated that the grand jurymen of each town had the power to identify those who "are suspected to live idly and loosely, and to require an account of them how they live." If they were found to be "delinquents," they would be brought before the Court of Assistants and "in the wisdom of the Government shall be adjudged just and equal."[18]

Within this cultural value of productiveness was the concept of a division of labor based on gender. Generally speaking, a woman's place was in the home. Maintaining the household and her family was both her obligation and responsibility. She grew and prepared food, fabricated, repaired, and cleaned clothing, and kept up the house. But it went further than that. She was expected to imbue all her home-making activities with an attitude of cheerful caring, with love and devotion to her family. Her meals were required to be not only nutritious, but also prepared with her family's preferences in mind. Most important, it was her holy responsibility to instill these gendered expectations in her children, to train them to assume their assigned roles in this society.

Educating and Training the Women of Plymouth

A woman in Plymouth Colony was expected to marry and have a family. Her education, therefore, was purely a practical one, focusing on the skills she would need as a homemaker. She would be trained by her mother, who had been in turn trained by her mother. Beginning at six or seven years old, she would be taught how to cook, to tend the kitchen garden, to spin wool into yarn, to weave yarn into cloth, to sew clothes and linens, to launder, to make candles and perform

Women doing laundry.

other domestic chores. In fact, all primary learning occurred in the home as values and manners were passed from one generation to the next.

Not everyone could read and write in Plymouth. There were no formal schools in the colony during the early years. It wasn't until 1670 that the issue was even raised, when John Morton offered "to teach the children and youth of the town to read and write and cast accounts on reasonable considerations."[19]

As a result, most of the women were illiterate. The only handwritten records Plymouth women left were their signatures or "markes" on formal documents, and the ability to sign one's name is the only evidence we have indicating some level of literacy. While being able to write her name does not in itself prove that she could read, it does assume some education beyond training in housekeeping. Many of the colony's men could sign their names, but this was true of very few of the women. Mary Winslow, for example, signed her last will and testament in 1633 with "her marke." Eleanor Billington also signed official documents in a similar manner. Later in the colony's history, women had been able to achieve a slightly higher level of literacy. In 1686, Elizabeth Howland signed her last will and testament with her initials rather than with a mark, indicating some familiarity with the alphabet.[20,21,22]

Families who took in children as servants had the same responsibilities as parents to teach and train them. Boys were more likely to learn to read from their masters than girls, however. When Alice Grinder went into service to Isaac Allerton in 1633, Isaac was required to furnish only food and clothing for the five-year term. But in 1636, when Benjamin Eaton went into the service of the widow Bridget Fuller for fourteen years, she was required for two of those years "to keep him at school."[23,24]

Whether raised by parents or masters, or whether taught to read or not, along with the practical training all children received they were most certainly taught to be virtuous. It was, after all, not only against the rules of the church to stray off the moral path, it was also against the laws of Plymouth Colony.

Stringent Laws and Ordinances

By 1639, when Alice Martin's name first appeared in the Plymouth Colony records, there were laws in place governing the sexual activity of the colony's residents, men and women alike. Punishments varied, but breaches of the laws were taken very seriously. Isaack de Rasieres commented in 1628 that the Pilgrims "have made stringent laws and ordinances upon the subject of fornication and adultery, which laws they maintain and enforce very strictly indeed, even among the tribes which live amongst them."[25]

The founding generation believed it was their responsibility to maintain the biblical values upon which the colony was established. Expectations needed to be clear, and anyone of weak character needed to be punished to prevent the corruption of the entire society. Any aberrant behavior, it was believed, was clear justification for quick and severe punishment. The reasoning behind this was not only religious, but practical too. Children born out of wedlock placed a financial burden on the whole colony. "Unclean carriages," or fornication before marriage, was considered a criminal offense. Each case was carefully evaluated by the governor and his assistants, and punishment was decided "at the discretion of the Magistrates according to the nature thereof."[26]

Women and their behavior were especially suspicious. The Bible story of Eve's transgression in the Garden of Eden had been interpreted by the Pilgrims to imply that women were inherently corrupt. They could not be fully trusted and must be carefully and continually monitored.

The obvious evidence of sexual relations before marriage was an untimely pregnancy. It was believed that it was exactly nine months between conception and the birth of a child who had "come to full perfection." If a full-term child was born before the nine-month period from the date of marriage, both the husband and the wife were punished. For example, in April, 1633, "John Hewes & Joan his wife [were] adjudged to sit in the stocks because the said Joan conceived with child by him before they were publicly married."[27,28]

Women and Pilgrim Watchfulness

Cases of fornication and sexual misbehavior came before the courts because some resident was counting the days between marriage and childbirth. Neighbors in Plymouth Colony kept a close watch over each other, and this was not always a good thing. It was the Pilgrims' practice of watchfulness that permitted and encouraged them to snoop. "It is required of every member of the church in his place, to watch for the good of the whole," wrote John Robinson. In fact, congregations were deliberately kept small so that "members then can conveniently watch over one another...."[29,30]

In theory, Plymouth's citizens were scrutinizing each other for any spiritual missteps. But in practice, no matter the intentions behind this code of behavior, submission to constant judgment must have made for a very stressful society. Both the Pilgrims' religious system and their government allowed and encouraged tattling among them. With so few people living in daily contact with one another, it was impossible to hide anything for long. It was with a smug satisfaction that another's affairs were watched, judged, and reported.

It can be safely speculated that the women of Plymouth had a special role to play in the principle of watchfulness, especially when the transgressor was another woman. The home was their particular sphere, and child rearing was more than their occupation; it was their very purpose in life. Who better to judge a woman's behavior than another woman? For example, women attended each other during childbirth, and perhaps it was in this most intimate of situations that women betrayed one another to the authorities. This appears to be the case of John Ellis and his wife.

In 1644, John and Elizabeth Ellis were charged with fornication before marriage. Jonathan, Mary, and Nathaniel Fish, Jane Wood, Rose Holly, the wives of Richard Kerby and Michael Turn, and the widow Joan Swift were all called as witnesses, "to give evidence in John Ellis & his wife's case." A guilty verdict was rendered, and John was whipped at the post, with Elizabeth forced to stand by. John was further fined five pounds "for his long and tedious delays, occasioning much trouble [and] charge to the country, for that he would not confess the truth until this present." It may be confidently assumed that the wives who were called to testify in this case had attended Elizabeth in childbirth and could confirm the delivery date of the child and reveal any comments the mother may have made under the stress of labor.[31]

Women participated in the system of watchfulness within their own culture and in their own way. Through daily interactions, they could observe, judge, and report another woman's behavior. Gossip among themselves was a major element of social control at Plymouth because a woman's reputation identified and categorized her in this society. In this small remote community, women—out of necessity—depended on each other. Anyone singled out for bad behavior would suffer the consequences.

Dress and Demeanor

Women, and men, too, to a certain extent, were judged by the way they dressed. A woman's clothing was to be simple and practical, and constructed of separate pieces which she had fashioned herself. Traditional colors of the English yeoman class—muted russets, browns, and creams—were the only acceptable shades. Several calf-length layers of heavy linen or wool covered her womanly curves and folds, and her legs were covered with stockings. Even in the privacy of her home a woman would have dressed modestly, her hair covered with a linen cap. In a word, her dress was all very simple with no embellishment. As John Robinson wrote, a husband's virtues could be "measured by their wives' homeliness in attire."[32]

A woman was also judged by her demeanor, the way in which she presented herself to others. Robinson advised that modesty is the most graceful of all the virtues, referring not only to modesty in dress but also in bearing. Facial expressions, body language, and all those delicate and unspoken aspects of a woman's deportment had to be learned and incorporated into a woman's behavior in order for her to fit in. In this culture women were discouraged from appearing too bold or saucy, and were encouraged instead to cultivate feminine, constrained gestures. Women would have been taught to carry themselves with a soft posture, chin tilted downward, in modesty and humility. Blushing in embarrassment was considered an enhancement of a woman's beauty, an adornment of "a comely countenance."[33]

Given human nature, there were probably some Pilgrim women who were considered pleasing in appearance, but any acknowledgement of a woman's beauty would have been soundly discouraged. The official Separatist position was that acknowledging physical beauty was deceitful and "a vain thing" and that "vanity…is everywhere evil."[34,35]

☙❧☙❧☙❧

Everything about a woman's behavior and appearance reflected her role in Plymouth society; she was a woman, and gender roles were strictly enforced. Men were in charge, and women were to be submissive. However, apart from the men of Plymouth, women participated in a culture all their own, one based in the home and within their roles as wives and mothers. Men took that role for granted, and women were expected to perform their duties with virtue and godliness. But among the women themselves there were subtle values and meanings that influenced their daily lives. As a wife and mother, Alice was a member of this subculture and inescapably subject to its stresses.

It had been that way as long as anyone cared to remember, even when they lived in Holland.

Chapter Four

The Pilgrims in Holland
Leiden 1608

The Scrooby Separatists were not the first Dissenters to look to the Netherlands for religious asylum and freedom. Others, "sundry from London and other parts of the land [who] had been exiled and persecuted for the same cause," had already settled in Amsterdam and started churches, paving the way for the Scrooby congregation.[1]

One of those congregations was led by John Smyth, former member of the Scrooby group and leader of the Gainsborough Separatists. Smyth had been financed by some of their wealthier members, among them Thomas Helwys, a solicitor. The Scrooby Separatists must have had similar financial support, for "to get over into Holland" was certainly a costly endeavor. It is not known for certain who provided the funds for the move or who intervened to shelter the Pilgrims during this time; more than once, however, they had required a protector.[2,3]

The First Leaving
Scrooby to Amsterdam, 1607 and 1608

Some of the members of the Scrooby congregation had lived in other places, but for the majority of them this would be their first time out of the region. They were leaving their homes, their land, their families and friends—all that was dear and familiar. The presumption was that they would never return, so they had sold many of their personal belongings. "It was much," wrote Bradford, "and thought marvelous by many." Indeed it was.[4]

The Separatists leaders meant it to be a quick and permanent move, but things did not work out that way. The first attempt to leave Scrooby for Amsterdam was in 1607, and it was a complete disaster. The plan was to leave England from a secret location near Boston, Lincolnshire, perhaps on the River Witham, a tidal estuary. A ship and her captain had been covertly and unlawfully engaged by the Separatists to transport them and their belongings to Amsterdam.

It was a long, arduous walk of more than sixty miles across the countryside to Boston. The "large companie" of Pilgrims—men, women, and children—finally all gathered together and settled in for at least three months before all their plans were finalized. It was a "long waiting," and the Pilgrims incurred unexpected expenses before the ship finally did arrive. At the appointed hour, under protection of darkness, the captain quickly loaded everyone and all their possessions on board. However, he had a cruel surprise in store. The captain "having beforehand complotted with the searchers and other officers," betrayed his passengers and turned them over to the authorities. It was against the law to leave the country without the Crown's permission. Their skipper had betrayed them, probably in anticipation of a nice reward.[5,6]

The now terrified Dissenters were forcefully removed from the ship and put into open boats. Once ashore they were searched by the officers, the men "to their shirts for money," and "...even the women further than became modesty." It was against the law not only to leave England but to take any money out of the country without written permission. The group was transported back to Boston, marched through town, and "made a spectacle and wonder to the multitude, which came flocking on all sides to behold them." "Stripped of their money, books and much other goods," they were taken to appear before the magistrates, interrogated, and jailed. Word was soon sent to the Privy Council in London of their arrest.[7]

Bradford notes that they were well-treated in Boston, but the local magistrates could not authorize their release until word came from the Lords of the Privy Council to do so. After a month in prison, "the greatest part" was dismissed "and sent to the places from whence they came," but seven men, among them William Brewster and Richard Clyfton, were kept until the Court of Assizes would meet in Boston.[8]

The Pilgrims had been directed to return to "whence they came," but it is not clear where they went or even if they left Boston. Presumably, they could not return to their villages because they had sold most of what they owned. Not only that, the local authorities would have been alerted to double their efforts to watch over them and monitor their activities. It may be that they had sympathetic friends of means and position who provided hiding places and financial support, but who those persons may have been remains a secret to this day. It wasn't William Bradford's sister Alice, for she had died and was buried on January 30, 1607. His Uncle Robert Bradford, who died in April 1609, had his own family to care for in 1607. Robert's will did not mention William, and he left his entire estate to his own four underage children: Robert, Mary, Elizabeth, and Margaret.[9,10]

The Scrooby Separatists made another attempt to leave England a few months later, in the spring of 1608. How this trip was financed also remains a mystery. Having been betrayed by one of their own countrymen, the Pilgrims cautiously approached a Dutchman who owned his own ship. A deal was made, and a meeting place was agreed upon, an out of the way location, "a large common a good way distant from any town." It was between Grimsby and Hull, on the River Humber, somewhere near Killingholme Creek (today known as Immingham), and about fifty miles east of Scrooby.[11]

This time the women and children of the Pilgrims travelled separately from the men to the designated meeting spot. They, and all their remaining goods, sailed along the waterways (perhaps from Gainsborough on the River Trent) to the River Humber in a small bark, a sailing ship with perhaps one or two masts, a voyage of about seventy miles. As they neared their destination a day ahead of schedule the waters became turbulent. The mothers and their children became frightened and many experienced seasickness. The women convinced the master to "put into a creek hard (by)" to give them a respite. It was a serious mistake—the ship became grounded when the tide receded.[12]

There was more trouble ahead. True to his word, the Dutch master arrived at the prescribed location and time near Killingholme Creek. However, since the bark with the women and children on board was grounded fast, it could not sail until the tide rolled in at about noon. According to Bradford, the master of the Dutch boat, aware of the grounded bark with its women, children, and cargo, and "perceiving how the matter was," felt it best to begin loading the men who were waiting on shore while he waited for the tide to come in and release the other ship.[13]

The master sent a small boat to retrieve the men waiting on shore. After they boarded, he sent the boat back to pick up more, when "the master espied a great company, both horse and foot, with bills, and guns, and other weapons; for the country was raised to take them." Once again, the long arm of the king's law had stopped the Pilgrims from leaving England—or at least their families would not be departing.[14]

Seeing the king's men bearing down on them, "[the] Dutchman swore his country's oath, Sacremente!; and having the wind fair, weighed his anchor, hoisted sails, and away!" He was breaking the law by transporting Dissenters. Fearing for his life and livelihood, he made a quick decision and set sail for the open sea. The men on board "were in great distress for their wives and children," for they could only watch helplessly from a distance as their families were taken into custody while they were powerless to help. "It drew tears from their eyes," Bradford noted.[15]

Their wives were in tears, too. They had been abandoned to the authorities and were terrified for themselves and their children. The few men left on shore stayed with the women, but the others fled. It was a terrible scene, women "weeping and crying on every side! Some for their husbands that were carried away in the ship,…others not knowing what should become of them and their little ones. Others again melted in tears, seeing their poor little ones hanging about them; crying for fear and quaking with cold."[16]

Attempted flight of the Pilgrims from England in 1608.

The women and children were once again in the hands of the authorities, who were faced with the perplexing question of what to do with them. They had no homes to go to, and, as Bradford commented, "to imprison so many women and innocent children for no other cause (many of them) but that they must go with their husbands, seemed to be unreasonable and all would cry out [for] them."[17]

Cry out they did. The presence of terrified women and shivering children in the court of the local magistrate must have presented him with a very uncomfortable political situation. His solution was to pass the pathetic group on to the neighboring magistrate, who did likewise, on to the next. After "they had been thus turmoiled a good while," the women, children, and their baggage were finally released, as the magistrates "were wearied and tired with them."[18]

After their release, "some few shrunk at these first conflicts" and abandoned their plans to escape to Holland. Others who were not involved in the escape at all were so impressed by the Separatists' patience, perseverance, their "godly carriage and Christian behavior," that they up and joined the movement themselves. But, in the meantime, where did they go? Bradford admits "they had no homes to go to, for they had either sold or otherwise disposed of their houses and livings." Again, there must have been someone with money and power who provided hiding places and financial help until the wives and children could attain safe passage to Holland to rejoin their husbands.[19]

Meanwhile, the men on the Dutch ship crossing the North Sea to Amsterdam had serious problems of their own. They "endured a fearful storm," and for the next two weeks were in daily fear of losing their lives. Bradford remarks that only the "Lord's power and mercy" saved them, for when "water ran into their mouths and ears and the mariners cried out, 'We sink, we sink!,'" the faithful prayed, "Yet Lord Thou canst save!"[20]

Their prayers were answered, the storm began to subside, and then "the Lord filled their afflicted minds with such comforts as everyone cannot understand, and in the end brought them to their desired haven." Once the men arrived safely in Amsterdam, "people came flocking, admiring their deliverance; the storm having been so long and sore, in which much hurt had been done, as the master's friends related unto him in their congratulations." Relieved to be safe, surely their thoughts turned to their families.[21]

Bradford leaves out the details, probably to protect those who provided shelter and safety for the abandoned women and children, but he reports that eventually they all made it to Amsterdam, "some at one time and some at another, and some in one place and some in another, and met together again according to their desires, with no small rejoicing." Undoubtedly that sentence glosses over what must have been a harrowing experience for those women in their efforts to escape England and reunite with their husbands. All in all, there were about 125 Separatists from the Scrooby congregation who ended up in Amsterdam, including Richard Clyfton, John Robinson, William Brewster, and William Bradford.[22]

Women in the Separatist Movement

When William Bradford wrote that "women must go with their husbands," he was commenting not only on the attempted escape from England, but also on the position women held in Separatism. As would be the case in Plymouth Colony, English society was built upon the family unit, with the father as its head. Likewise, the family was the fundamental element at the foundation of order within the Church. The head of the family, the master, reigned as both king and priest within his family and household. While the Separatists believed in women being spiritually equal to men, it was generally accepted beyond question that women were by their very nature inferior and weaker, and each one had a destiny to marry and bear children.[23]

Yet, women were a significant part of the Separatist movement. Many attended services led by Dissenters alongside their husbands. As early as 1598, William Brewster's wife and family were cited along with him for attending services outside their parish church to hear a dissenting sermon. No doubt, Mary Brewster then taught those principles to their children during the activities of the day. In the Geneva Bible, it notes that alongside the father, "it is the mother's duty also to instruct her children."[24,25]

Women also provided hospitality in their homes. Mary Brewster surely saw to it that food and drink were served at Scrooby Manor during her husband's gatherings of Separatists. Another example is that of Lady Isobel Bowes, of Coventry, who hosted a meeting of deposed clergy at her home in 1606, among them Richard Clyfton, John Smyth, and John Robinson, to discuss their precarious situation.[26]

Furthermore, women were subject to the same laws and punishments as men. Couples who married "irregularly," that is, who married in the simple Separatist manner rather than in the Church of England form, were liable for prosecution, and women were cited along with their husbands.

It is not known, however, how women took part in Sabbath meetings in Scrooby. There is no record that any women joined the spirited religious discussions around the blazing hearth at Scrooby Manor, nor any evidence that they were invited to join in the sacred covenant. When William Bradford, for instance, says that "by a joint consent they resolved to go into the Low Countries," it is not clear who he means by "they." It is not known how, or even if, women were participants in the decision.²⁷

And then there is William Bradford's statement to consider. When the Separatist wives and children were apprehended in Killingholme, Bradford reflects that "to imprison so many women and innocent children for no other cause (many of them) but that they must go with their husbands, seemed to be unreasonable and all would cry out [for] them." Apparently, "many of them" were not necessarily Separatist in their own right. This statement hints that wives may have been conscripted into the undertaking simply because their husbands made the decision for them.²⁸

These women did what their husbands told them to do. They were considered fully under their husband's authority. Can it be assumed that they shared their husbands' religious beliefs? Were the wives Dissenters too? Many of their marriages were arranged by their parents and most likely they were between like-minded couples. While the record is silent on the wives' enthusiasm for the venture, it is not unreasonable to conclude that "many of them"—if given the choice—would have stayed in England. Nonetheless, the husband's authority would have prevailed.

The Scrooby Separatists in Amsterdam

The Scrooby Separatists knew Amsterdam only "by hearsay," as Bradford wrote. They "had only been used to a plain country life and the innocent trade of husbandry," and now these countryfolk had to learn skills and trades which suited them for life in this mostly mercantile city. "Many [of the congregation] thought [this] an adventure almost desperate; a case intolerable and a misery worse than death," he added. The language to their ears was "strange and uncouth," the manners and customs "with their strange fashions and attires," were so different from what they were used to that "it seemed they were come into a new world."²⁹,³⁰

At first they joined with the "Ancient Brethren," a congregation in Amsterdam of earlier English Dissenters that was formed in the

1590s. The Ancient Brethren and their leader, Francis Johnson, no doubt helped the newcomers settle in the city, but that group was plagued with internal squabbling and scandal, and the Scrooby congregation was hesitant to affiliate themselves with such an unstable assembly. "Such things were thought on," wrote Bradford, "as were necessary for their settling and best ordering of the church affairs."[31]

Once again, the Pilgrims, now under John Robinson's leadership, chose to relocate. They had taken a sacred oath in the manor house at Scrooby, an oath among themselves, "to walk in all his ways" and, again, they believed they could do that only in isolation, away from outside influences. They decided to move to Leiden.[32]

The Second Leaving
Amsterdam to Leiden, Holland

Leiden, "a fair and beautiful city of a sweet situation" located about twenty miles southwest of Amsterdam, was their choice, and they moved there in 1609. This second move so soon after the first would further drain their resources and force them to find immediate employment, but it seemed worth the trouble. Leiden's residents took pride in their city and boasted of clean rivers and canals and healthy air. The original city of Leiden was surrounded by a protective wall that was expanded as the population grew. Outside the walls were gardens, vineyards, grazing meadows and orchards.[33]

When the Pilgrims arrived, Leiden was a busy and dense city of about 18,000 residents. Undoubtedly intimidating and disorienting to rural folk, it was not very large and could be walked end-to-end in half an hour. The largest buildings in Leiden, the town hall and St. Pieterskerk and St. Pancraeskerk Churches, provided landmarks that likely helped residents find their way around.

Things went well in Leiden. Bradford wrote that "they continued many years in a comfortable condition, enjoying much sweet and delightful society and spiritual comfort together in the ways of God, under the able ministry and prudent government of Mr. John Robinson and Mr. William Brewster...." The Pilgrims were able to

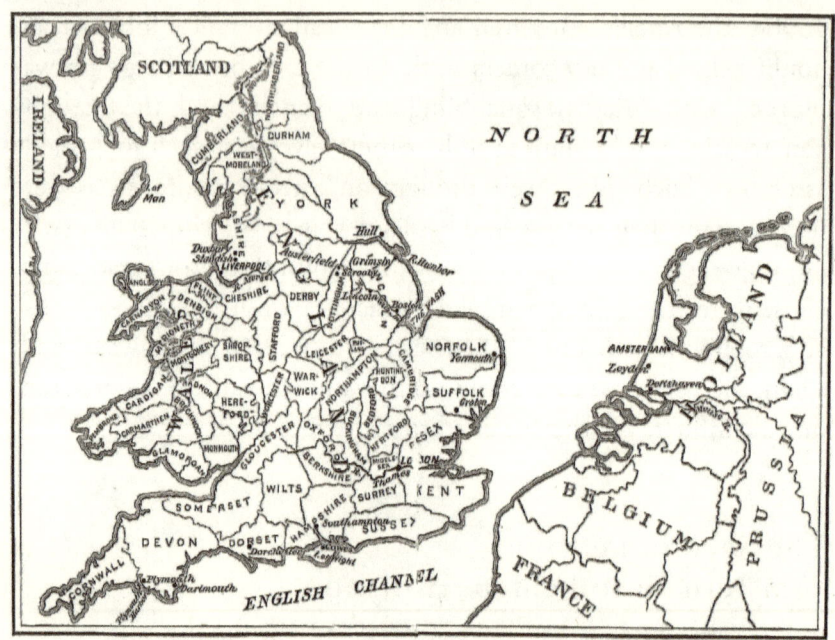

Map showing England and Holland.

attract other Separatists from England to join them, but if there was any dissent within this group of Dissenters, it was "nipped in the head," and "the church purged off those that were incurable and incorrigible." Ironically, within this group of non-conformists, non-conformity would not be tolerated. Nonetheless, the congregation appeared to be very happy. Committed to each other and to their love of God, they believed that "they came as near the primitive pattern of the first churches as any other church of these later times have done."[34]

In 1611, the congregation bought a large house to use as a meeting place. Robinson and his family lived upstairs, and church meetings were held downstairs. Homes and businesses in Leiden did not have street addresses but were known by names, and John Robinson's home was called "The Green Close."

The Pilgrims had been farmers, used to laboring in the fields and caring for animals, but Leiden was a commercial city with a flourishing textile industry and many of the Pilgrims eventually found work in the trades. Bradford was a maker of "fustian," a type of corduroy cloth, and Jonathan Brewster made ribbon. Whatever their employment, they all worked long hours for wages that barely afforded them a decent living. In 1612 William Bradford, at twenty-three, took out Leiden citizenship papers. As a citizen, he could join a guild and earn a higher salary. He was ready to marry and hoped to better his situation. His intended was Dorothy May, the daughter of Henry May, an elder in one of the original Separatist congregations in Amsterdam. Little is known of their courtship, but he asked her to join him in Leiden, and they were married on December 10, 1613. Two years later a child was born to them, a son they named John, perhaps after John Robinson.[35]

Daily life for the Pilgrims in Leiden was pleasant but routine. If the husband was a wool comber, weaver or tailor, he would work out of his house while his wife and children helped him prepare materials. Women spun yarn at home, looms were set up for weaving, and children assisted in knitting and sewing. Children did not normally work a full day, so they had free time to play with toys and enjoy games. Attesting to their contentment in Leiden, many of the Separatists courted, married, and started their families in that city. While there, the Separatists adopted the Dutch custom of civil marriage instead of marriage as a religious service as practiced by the Church of England.

As pleasant as things may have been, over time it became evident that life in Leiden was not fully what the Pilgrims had hoped for. Bradford never wrote about his wife and son in Leiden, but he did reflect on the difficulties of supporting a family: "At length they came to raise a competent and comfortable living, but with hard and continual labor." Workdays were often twelve to fifteen hours. Older children were reluctantly put to work, and watching their children become "decrepit in their early youth, the vigor of nature being consumed in the very bud," distressed them all. By about 1617, once again some of the group began to grow restless and to entertain "thoughts of removing themselves to America."[36,37]

Their reasons were "weighty and solid," not "out of any newfangledness or other such like giddy humor," Bradford explained.

It wasn't only the work situation that was bothering them. The Separatists were worried, too, that with the passage of time "their posterity would...become Dutch, and so lose interest in the English nation." Evidently, they still thought of themselves and their children as English at heart. Also, the congregation was not growing as they had expected. Those who did come from England to join the Leiden congregation, "by reason of the hardness of the country, soon spent their estates, and were forced either to return back to England, or to live very meanly."[38,39]

In addition, the Twelve Years' Truce between Spain and the Netherlands, signed in 1609, was nearing its end, and war with Spain was always a possibility. William Bradford remarked that "the Spaniard might prove as cruel as the savages of America, and the famine and pestilence as sore here as there." Lastly and rather unconvincingly, they expressed hope that by settling in America they could "lay...some good foundation, or at least to make some way thereunto, for the propagating and advancing [of] the gospel of the kingdom of Christ in the remote parts of the world; yea, though they should be but even as stepping stones unto others for the performing of so great a work."[40]

But, "of all sorrows [the] most heavy to be borne...[was] that the great licentiousness of youth in that country, and the manifold temptations of the place [had] drawn [their children] away by evil examples into extravagant and dangerous courses, getting the reins on their necks, and departing from their parents." Six days a week the Separatist children worked, and on the Sabbath, while the Dutch youth were free to enjoy themselves, the Separatist children were in the meeting house. The temptations were too great, and the Separatists were losing control over their children.[41]

What William Bradford did not write about was perhaps the most compelling reason the Separatists had for leaving Leiden. They had run into trouble with King James I, this time thanks to William Brewster and his printing press. In about 1617 Brewster began publishing books and pamphlets in a room off the back of his house. It was harmless enough on the surface; none of the books dealt with controversies, and none were aimed at an English audience. But it was not as innocent an enterprise as it seemed. Other books were surreptitiously published by Brewster, books not intended for sale in Holland but written in English and intended for underground distribution in England by sympathetic Separatists and Puritans. These were the types of books, critical of the king and his church, that had been banned by the Crown. Brewster was breaking English law and endangering everyone.

The books were traced back to the Pilgrim press in Leiden and before long the English ambassador to The Hague began to complain about Brewster's activities. The book he found most offensive was *The Perth Assembly* by the Scottish Puritan David Calderwood, a book that attacked King James I and his bishops for forcing the Scots to adopt the king's religion. Copies of the book were packed into wine vats and smuggled into Scotland, where they were circulated in secret. After William Brewster was identified as the publisher, the king demanded that Brewster be seized by the Dutch authorities and brought to justice. Brewster went into hiding and would not be seen again until he turned up on the deck of the *Mayflower* some three years later.

Once again, even though they had brought at least some of the trouble onto themselves, the outside world threatened the autonomy of the Scrooby Separatists. It was only in complete isolation, the Pilgrims decided, that they could avoid the interference of the government, the church, and the society in which they lived, and create for themselves the biblical way of life they believed was their sacred destiny. The idea of moving again was "debated first in private, and thought weighty." It was then brought up to the congregation and "raised many variable opinions amongst men and caused many fears and doubts amongst themselves." Some of the Separatists were concerned about the dangers of the voyage, the "miseries of the land" in America where they might be subject to famine and disease, and the threat of "the savage people, who are cruel, barbarous and most treacherous."[42,43]

All of these worries, Bradford argued, "through the help of God, by fortitude and patience, might either be borne or overcome." After all, he added, "their condition was not ordinary, their ends were good and honorable, their calling lawful and urgent; and therefore they might expect the blessing of God in their proceeding." In other words, Bradford argued, God was on their side.[44]

Even though the Scrooby congregation was, on balance, "at peace, and in rest at this time, [and they] quietly and sweetly enjoyed their church liberties" in Holland, the arguments in favor of a change were compelling to many. "After solemn days of humiliation observed both in public and private, it was agreed that part of the church should go before their brethren into America, to prepare for the rest." They decided to move again to "dislodge betimes to some place of better advantage and less danger, if any could be found."[45,46]

The Pilgrims were going to America.

Chapter Five

Leaving Leiden on the *Mayflower* 1620

The Pilgrims had grand plans for their settlement in America. They fancied themselves an investment opportunity; anyone who provided the funds necessary for the voyage and the initial planting of a colony would reap significant financial rewards. John Robinson assured prospective investors that he could induce "four hundred families to accompany him thither, both out of this country [Holland] and England." Those colonists would be hard workers, he promised, and would make the settlement a profitable one.[1]

What the Pilgrims wanted was full financial backing for the venture, which would include passage to America and funding to build the new colony. Furthermore, they wanted complete authority over the operation of the colony, with no objections to their religious beliefs and practices. They wanted full autonomy and total control. In return the Pilgrims would establish a fishing industry. They would bring a second ship to America, one that would enable them to fish the coastal waters, and would produce their own salt to cure the fish for shipment back to England.

On paper the plan made some sense. Yet the Pilgrims had absolutely no experience in fishing or harvesting salt—or even sailing, for that matter. Not only that, it had been eleven years since they left England and their former lives as yeoman farmers. During that time, they lived and worked in an industrial society and bought their groceries at the markets. It had been years since most of them had worked the soil and harvested their own food. Who or what made them think they could succeed, besides their unwavering faith in the sanctity of their venture? Stephen Vincent Benét called it "the humble, stupendous arrogance of men who are quite sure God is with them." They were not the only ones being lured to America. Under the influence of Capt. John Smith and his book, *A Description of New England*, published in 1616, many were tempted to take the chance. That book was with the passengers of the *Mayflower*, and most likely they had read it while living in Leiden, passing it around and sharing it among themselves.[2,3]

Capt. Smith was an adventurer; among his many travels was a voyage to the Massachusetts coast in 1614. Based on that visit, Smith wrote his *Description* in an attempt to attract colonists to "New England," as he was the first to call the region. His enthusiasm for colonizing the area bordered on propaganda and puffery. While he warned, "It is not a work for everyone, to manage such an affair as makes a discovery and plants a colony: it requires all the best parts of art, judgement, courage, honesty, constancy, diligence and industry...," he was still effusive in the benefits of such an undertaking. And his words spoke directly to those ideals the Separatists held most dear.[4]

"So freely hath God and his Majesty bestowed those blessings on thee that will attempt to obtain them," Smith wrote, that in New England "every man may be master and owner of his own labor and land." And, what a land it is, "a most excellent place, both for health and fertility." The ground is so fertile that "it is capable of producing any grain, fruits, or seeds you will sow or plant."[5]

Fishing can make it all possible: "The main staple...is fish." The fish are so abundant that "a little boy might take of [fish] at the ship's stern, more than six or ten can eat in a day; but with a casting-net...." An adult must be "a very bad fisher," says Smith, "[who] cannot kill in one day with his hook and line one, two, or three hundred cods." Preserving the fish for transport back to England is no problem because, according to Smith, "Salt upon salt may assuredly be made."[6]

Beyond the financial aspects of colonizing in New England, there are other reasons to venture abroad, wrote Smith. Of special interest to the Pilgrims must have been this passage: "If he have any grain of faith or zeal in religion, what can he do less hurtful to any; or more agreeable to God, then to seek to convert those poor savages to know Christ...." If they needed any more convincing, Smith offered these words: "Planting and discovering these north parts of America... serves our God, our King, our Country, and ourselves."[7]

Smith, ever the promotor, promised that a colonist could "fish an hour a day and make more than [he] can eat in a week," but as things turned out, the Pilgrims must have looked back on their gullibility with as much sorrow as regret.[8]

Financing Plymouth

Not only did the Pilgrims need help financing the venture, they needed official permission from the crown. Historical records are sparse and confusing on exactly how this was accomplished, but we do know that in 1617, with the help of Thomas Weston, an ironmonger, the Pilgrims made a deal with the Virginia Company in London. The company managed to obtain a patent for land in the northern part of the Virginia colony. This patent, or charter, was in the name of John Wyncop, who died shortly thereafter, thus negating that deal.

The Dutch then came forward with an offer of their own. Their New Netherlands Company would provide free transportation, and would also provide each family with cattle, if they would settle in the Dutch colony of New Netherland. If they agreed, the Separatists would be assured of religious independence. But the Dutch could not provide armed ships to protect the Pilgrims during their voyage, and so that offer was refused. Influencing that decision might have been the Pilgrims' self-identification as Englishmen; they wanted their settlement to retain its "Englishness" at all cost.

Thomas Weston appeared in Leiden with yet another offer. After thinking it over, he decided that he could put a deal together himself. His merchant friends in London, he pledged, would finance the Pilgrims' venture. He was brimming with exciting promises, and he must have been very convincing. The small congregation abandoned all other possibilities and drew up a contract with Weston, who immediately returned to London and began raising money.

Weston managed to obtain a patent from the Virginia Company on February 2, 1620, in the name of one of his associates, John Peirce. It was this patent the Pilgrims trusted as their authority to build a plantation in the New World. But the Virginia Company suffered financial difficulties and was being reorganized into the Council of New England. Although of little consequence in 1620, this would cause problems for Plymouth Colony in the future.[9,10]

Weston convinced about seventy investors to participate in the joint stock company that would finance the Pilgrim colony. While the Merchant Adventurers, as they were known, were men of Puritan sympathies, they were mainly interested in the large profits promised by the cunning Weston. An agreement was now firmly in place, or so everyone thought.

The Separatists Prepare to Move Yet Again

In Leiden, meanwhile, there was a great deal of discussion and debate among the congregation about who would go to America. The deal with Thomas Weston and the Merchant Adventurers made it advantageous for the Pilgrims to bring family members with them. Every man who brought his wife, children, and servants as a family unit would, at the end of seven years, be awarded a single share in the joint stock company for each person over sixteen years of age. Children between ten and sixteen years of age would each receive half a share, and children under ten would get "fifty acres of un-manured land." It was, therefore, beneficial for each male head of a family to bring along as many people as possible. On the other hand, there was very real danger in this undertaking.[11]

An earlier attempt by another group of Separatists to colonize America had ended in tragedy. In the fall of 1618, Francis Blackwell, an elder in Francis Johnson's Ancient Brethren congregation in Amsterdam, had split with that group. Differences in religious beliefs led him and his followers to part from Johnson, "in a woeful manner, which brought so great dishonor to God, scandal to the truth, and outward ruin to themselves in this world." Blackwell organized a venture for a group of Separatists to sail to America and build themselves a colony in Virginia. Captain Maggner and 180 persons set sail on the *William and Thomas*, but strong fall winds blew their ship off course. The crew and passengers were then struck with "the flux [dysentery]." The captain and six of the crew died, leaving no one on board with any sailing experience. After "long seeking and beating about," they somehow made their way to Virginia, to Jamestown in the Chesapeake Bay. "Mr. Blackwell is dead," wrote Robert Cushman, "and [Capt.] Maggner.... Yea, there are dead...130 persons." Of the 180 passengers who left England, only fifty were still alive. The survivors, no doubt feeling fortunate just to have lived through the voyage, scattered into anonymity throughout the Virginia Colony, abandoning all their goals of building a Separatist religious colony.[12]

While Robert Cushman, a Leiden Separatist who was instrumental in planning the voyage, called the tragedy "heavy news," he added that "I see none here [in London] discouraged much." It was overcrowding that doomed that voyage, Cushman theorized, because "they were packed together like herrings."

The Leiden group assured themselves that their experience would be different. They would "learn to beware by other men's harms and to amend that wherein they have failed." They seemed to have an answer for everything, but many in the congregation were unconvinced and understandably fearful of the perils of the voyage, and of the possibility of "casualties of the sea." Bradford wrote of their concerns: Would women, with their "weak bodies," the elderly, and those "worn out with age and travail" be able to survive the long voyage? Once they arrived, would the "miseries of the land" be their undoing, "consume and utterly...ruinate them"? They would be "liable to famine and nakedness and the want...of all things." Not to mention "the change of air, diet, and drinking of water would infect their bodies with sore sicknesses and grievous diseases."[13,14]

And then there were the Indians, as the Pilgrims called the indigenous inhabitants, "the savage people, who are cruel, barbarous and most treacherous, being most furious in their rage and merciless where they overcome; not being content only to kill and take away life, but delight to torment men in the most bloody manner that may be."[15]

After all was considered, when the final vote was taken at Pastor Robinson's house, less than half the congregation volunteered to go. Some felt the whole adventure too dangerous. Some were too weary and too poor to consider moving again, and they simply opted out. They had suffered huge financial losses when they left England and moved to Holland. Truth be told, many were simply quite comfortable in Leiden. It had been their home for eleven years, they knew their way around, they had jobs, and their families and friends were nearby. And they had their church. To them a risky move seemed unnecessary and ill-advised.

The larger portion of the congregation, no doubt including William Bradford, were more enthusiastic about the adventure. Of those who volunteered to go, not everyone was considered fit for the rigors of the undertaking, at least for the first sailing. After talking it over, the leaders decided that a smaller group of the youngest and strongest would go first. They would be responsible for establishing the settlement, setting up a government, dealing with the Indians, launching a profitable fishing industry, building homes and planting gardens, in essence all that was necessary to create a colony in the wilderness. The rest, it was promised, "if the Lord gave them life and means, and opportunity," would join them as soon as possible.[16]

How did each man make the decision to volunteer to leave Leiden? Was he motivated by the novelty of the adventure, the "newfangledness," or was he truly one of those men who believed he was called by God to undertake a sacred task, even if it cost him his life? This is impossible to determine. Impossible, too, to know if the women of the congregation had any say in the decision. A Separatist wife was expected to go with her husband and unquestionably abide by his decisions—wives "must go with their husbands." However, many of the men who eventually sailed on the *Mayflower* did leave wives and children in Holland, as the Bradfords did their son, but whether that was each man's preference or his wife's is unknown.[17]

The first group that was set to leave Leiden began to prepare for the departure, deciding what would be necessary to bring and what to leave behind. Space was limited, and choices must have been difficult. Funds were pooled for the larger purchases. The most important investment, of course, was a ship, one that would remain with them in America. They bought the *Speedwell*, a sixty-ton decommissioned pinnacle, a light sailing ship, which had been used to fight against the Spanish Armada in 1588. The plan was that this ship would not only transport them to America, but would be the basis of the colony's economy, their fishing industry.

Thomas Weston in England

While the Pilgrims were busy preparing for their voyage, Thomas Weston was equally busy in London angling for investors. To attract more backers for the venture, he made some alterations to his original contract with the Pilgrims—without telling them.

The original agreement had stated that in exchange for the investors' funding the venture, the Pilgrims would be in partnership with them for a period of seven years. During that time, they would work four days each week for the profit of the investors and two for their own interests, and they would save the Sabbath for worship. They would build their own houses and cultivate their own gardens, which they would own at the end of seven years.

The new agreement, however, had two differences that vastly changed the contract. First, the houses and gardens that the colonists built would be "equally divided betwixt the Adventurers and Planters." They would not own their own properties. Second, that the two days set aside "for their own private employment, for the more comfort of themselves and their families, especially such as had families," had been eliminated.[18]

When presented with the altered agreement, Robert Cushman protested, but Weston responded by threatening to pull away all support unless the modified pact was accepted. Since the first group of Leiden Pilgrims to make the voyage had already sold their property and belongings in preparation, Cushman felt that it was too late to pull out of the agreement. Seeing "that all was like to be dashed and the opportunity lost," he reluctantly agreed to the changes, but chose not to tell the Leiden congregation what he had done on their behalf.[19]

When John Robinson found out what Cushman had agreed to, he was understandably furious. Robert Cushman, he wrote, was "a good man…yet most unfit to deal with other men by reason of his singularity and too great indifferency for any conditions." In other words, Cushman was outmatched when it came to negotiating with a man like Weston.[20]

To further add to the Separatists' frustrations, a new man was added to the venture. Christopher Martin was hired by the investors to not only join the voyage, but to purchase the necessary provisions. Martin, a Puritan but not a Separatist, was known as a headstrong man with a strong temper. He began buying supplies without anyone's approval or agreement, belligerently refusing to account to the Pilgrims for his expenditures and incurring debt well beyond his authority.

The Separatists' dream of an independent religious colony under their complete control was already slipping out of their hands.

A Tearful Farewell

In Leiden, 125 members of the congregation, about a third of the entire group, were preparing to sail to America. Necessities were listed and gathered. Women collected kitchen utensils, according to the list, which included a great iron pot, a copper kettle, and two smaller ones, large and small frying pans, two skillets, a brass mortar, a spit and an iron grid, along with wooden platters, dishes, and spoons.[21]

Many families had decided to divide themselves, with some wives and younger children staying in Holland while their husbands went ahead. The remaining Separatists who wanted to go would follow later. The larger share of the congregation that continued to live in Holland requested that Pastor Robinson stay with them as their spiritual leader. The departing colonists invited William Brewster, then in his fifties and in hiding in England, to accompany them as their religious leader. Brewster was not ordained but was considered by the assembly as an elder or teacher among them. Affairs were settled and "all things were got ready and provided."[22]

On July 21, 1620, the day of departure, the whole congregation met at Pastor Robinson's home. William Bradford recalled that they had a day of "solemn humiliation," spent "in pouring out prayers to the Lord with great fervency, mixed with [an] abundance of tears." Edward Winslow remembered the feast, "where we refreshed ourselves after our tears, with singing of Psalms, making joyful melody in our hearts, as well as with the voice, there being many of the Congregation very expert in music."[23,24]

Leaving Leiden.

The first leg of the adventure took place on Dutch canal boats. The barges were likely moored near John Robinson's home at Nuns Bridge, over the Rapenburg Canal in Leiden. After prayers and the farewell gathering, belongings and supplies were loaded onto the boats, and everyone boarded the barges for the trip to Delfshaven, extending their time together just a little longer. The barges would float quietly south in the Rapenburg Canal to the Vliet Canal, then to the Schie, and finally into the Delfshaven Canal. Slowly passing through a series of sluice gates, the barges were gradually elevated to higher waters, where the *Speedwell* awaited them.

It was in Delfshaven where they met Capt. Myles Standish, whom they hired to be the new colony's military expert, and his wife, Rose. Standish was already known to John Robinson and was most likely a common English soldier fighting for the Dutch, not an officer. His rank as "captain" was probably a colonial title signifying that he held a position of authority over citizen soldiers.[25]

Undoubtedly too soon for some, it was time to say goodbye and set sail. All the cargo was loaded onto the *Speedwell*, accommodations were assigned, and bearings set for the Maas River and on into the North Sea. Farewells were heartbreaking. They were "not able to speak one to another for the abundance of sorrow to part." On July 22, 1620, the *Speedwell* pulled away from the shore; those on board fired off "three pieces of Ordinance" in a volley of farewell. And, "so lifting up our hands to each other, and our hearts for each other to the Lord our God, we departed."[26]

Reflecting on leaving Leiden, William Bradford later wrote, "that goodly and pleasant city," had just been a resting place. "They knew they were pilgrims," he continued, journeying to a holy place, "and looked not much on those things [like leaving Leiden], but lifted up their eyes to the heavens, their dearest country, and quieted their spirits." Whether or not their spirits were entirely "quieted" is open to debate. No doubt there was more than a little anxiety aboard the *Speedwell*, as well as on shore, as they all considered the risks at hand and the sad prospect that they might not ever see their loved ones again.[27]

The *Mayflower* and the Strangers

On July 26, 1620, the *Speedwell* arrived in Southampton, and the Pilgrims got their first look at the *Mayflower*, the ship that Thomas Weston had hired to join the voyage. They also got their first look at "the rest of their company." Without discussing it with the Pilgrims, Weston and the London investors had determined that there were not enough colonists from Leiden to make the venture sufficiently profitable, so they had recruited others in London to join them. Religious affiliation was not a requirement, just a desire for a better life and a willingness to work. They were common folk, chosen because they were willing to risk their lives for the opportunity to labor hard for seven years so they could own a piece of land, then an impossible dream for the underclass in England.[28]

No doubt the Pilgrims were shocked. This was not what they expected or wanted. To the Separatists this was their sacred endeavor, commissioned to them alone by God Himself, not an economic adventure. Nonetheless, an effort was made to welcome the newcomers. Bradford says that there was a "joyful welcome and mutual congratulations, with other friendly entertainments," at their first meeting. While there may have been lots of smiling and backslapping, the Pilgrims surely were already planning how to deal with these folks they called "The Strangers" and reestablish full control.[29]

The original plan was for both ships to make the voyage to America. The *Speedwell* was to stay with them and the *Mayflower*, hired only for the one-way transport, would then return to England. Remembering Francis Blackwell's tragic overcrowded voyage, the Pilgrims believed that the two ships would allow sufficient room for all. The presence of the extra colonists, the Strangers, changed everything. The Pilgrims, who had already stored all their belongings on the *Speedwell*, may have stayed on that ship; the Strangers perhaps were settled on the *Mayflower*; Bradford doesn't say. Both ships were more crowded than intended. In any case, before too long, fate would join most of them together.

Before the Pilgrims set sail, a letter arrived from John Robinson. The Separatist pastor had written to give them one final dose of fatherly advice before they left, "if not because you need it,...[but] because I owe it in love and duty." The letter was read aloud to the entire company. First, he wrote, repent daily, "especially for our sins known, and generally for our unknown sins and trespasses." Furthermore, he added, get along with each other, and be patient. "You are many of you strangers," he added, not only to other individuals, but also to their human shortcomings. There will be problems, he warned, but keep your goal in mind and work for the common good. Set up your own government, he advised, a "body politic." Choose your leaders carefully, and "let your wisdom and godliness appear not only in choosing such persons [who] entirely love and will diligently promote the common good." Once they are selected, he advised, "yield...unto them all due honor and obedience in their lawful administrations."[30]

The letter was well received, William Bradford reported, and they applied Robinson's advice straight away. They "chose a governor and two or three assistants for each ship, to order the people by the way, and see to the disposing of their provisions and such like affairs." Robert Cushman was elected to lead the Separatists on the *Speedwell*, Christopher Martin as leader on the *Mayflower*. Both ships set sail from Southampton on August 5, 1620. Hopes were high, and excitement was in every heart. Finally, they were underway—only to be disappointed once again.[31]

The Loss of the *Speedwell*

Three days out to sea, after sailing about 130 nautical miles, the *Speedwell* developed leaks, and it was decided that both ships must return to land. Barely a week into the adventure, the *Mayflower* and the *Speedwell* put in at Dartmouth. After repairs were made to the *Speedwell*, both ships sailed again on August 23. Again the *Speedwell* began to leak, and both ships returned to shore on August 26, but this time in Plymouth, England.

On August 28, after lengthy discussions among the would-be colonists, it was decided that the *Speedwell* would be too unreliable for a trans-Atlantic voyage. The party would be reduced in number, supplies and belongings would be sorted and thinned out, and those who remained would sail on the *Mayflower*. About twenty of the Pilgrims decided to go back to London. Some of the others were asked to depart, as Bradford wrote, "in regard of their own weakness and charge of many young children, [they] were thought least useful and most unfit to bear the brunt of this hard adventure."[32]

Robert Cushman, who recorded that he felt as if "a bundle of lead, as it were, [was] crushing my heart," had enough of the whole business and was among those who quit. Bradford commented that even though Cushman's body was with them, by this point "his heart and courage was gone...." Later, in a letter to his friend Edward Southworth, Cushman made a very candid evaluation of the venture: "Friend," he wrote, "if ever we make a plantation, God works a miracle, especially considering how scant we shall be of victuals, and most of all un-united amongst ourselves and devoid of good tutors [leaders] and regiment [discipline]."[33]

The loss of the *Speedwell* was a serious blow to the Pilgrims. They had counted on the ship as the cornerstone of their economy. They were planning to be fishermen and use their profits to pay off their mounting debts, but sailing without the *Speedwell* required drastic alterations to their plans.

When Separatists and Strangers together boarded the *Mayflower*, they chose a new governor of the ship for the long journey. Apparently, Christopher Martin's unpopularity with passengers and crew alike was his undoing, although he did remain treasurer of the venture. Careful planning and strategizing had paid off, and the Pilgrims had the votes they needed to elect their fellow Separatist John Carver as the new governor. He was one of the organizers of the enterprise, apparently one of the wealthiest, and he had "disbursed the greatest part of that considerable estate God had given him, for the carrying on the interest of the company." He had also brought along a staff of four indentured servants, including a "lady's maid" for his wife, Katherine.[34]

To the Sea at Last

On September 6, 1620, about six weeks after the Separatists had left Leiden, the *Mayflower* finally set sail from Plymouth, England. There were 102 passengers on the ship. The average age among the 50 men was about thirty-four. There were 19 women, 14 teenagers, and 19 children under twelve years of age. Of the total passengers, the Separatists from Leiden numbered only 44, and of those only William and Mary Brewster and William Bradford were from the original Scrooby congregation.

From the Leiden congregation of Separatists, in alphabetical order, came the following:[35,36]

- Isaac and Mary Allerton took their three young children, Bartholomew (seven or eight years old), Remember (age five or six), and Mary (age three or four). They brought John Hooke as a servant.
- William Bradford brought his wife, Dorothy, but left his four-year-old son, John, in Leiden.
- William and Mary Brewster brought two sons, Love (age nine) and Wrestling (age six), but left Jonathan, Patience, and Fear behind.
- John and Katherine Carver took along a ward, Desire Minter, about fifteen years old, and servants John Howland, William Latham, Roger Wilder, and a maidservant named Dorothy.
- James and Susanna Chilton were accompanied by their thirteen-year-old daughter, Mary.
- Francis Cooke, who had left his wife and other children in Leiden, brought his fifteen-year-old son, John.
- John Crackstone sailed with his namesake son, John, who was about eighteen.
- Moses Fletcher left his wife, Sarah, in Leiden.
- Edward Fuller was accompanied by his wife.
- Samuel Fuller, Sr. was the Pilgrims' "physition & chirurgeon" and was Edward's brother. He had a servant named William Butten.
- John Goodman left his wife behind but brought two dogs on the *Mayflower*.

- Dregory Priest also left his wife in Leiden.
- Thomas Rogers sailed with his son Joseph (about seventeen years old).
- Edward Tilley brought his wife, Ann, and her nephew, Henry Samson (sixteen years old), and niece, Humility Cooper (one-year-old).
- John and Joan Tilley brought their daughter, Elizabeth, who was about fifteen years old. John was Edward Tilley's brother.
- Thomas Tinker had his wife and son with him.
- John Turner, perhaps a widower, came with his two young sons, ages five and three years.
- William and Susanna White brought their son, Resolved, who was about five years old. A second son, Peregrine, would be born on the *Mayflower*. Their servants were William Holbeck and Edward Thompson.
- Thomas Williams traveled alone.
- Edward Winslow was accompanied by his wife, Elizabeth, and servants Elias Story and George Soule. His brother, Gilbert, was not of the Leiden congregation but may have joined the voyage in London.
- Ellen, Jasper, Richard, and Mary were known as the More (Moore) orphans. English gentleman, Samuel More, had learned that the children born to his wife were fathered by another man. When he discovered the deception, he disinherited the children and put them into the care of Thomas Weston, paying him one hundred pounds to make each child a full partner in the Separatist colony venture. These four orphans were placed with the Pilgrims. Ellen More, about eight years old, was bound to Edward Winslow. Jasper, who was about seven, was bound to John Carver. Richard, six years old, and Mary, who was about four, were bound to William Brewster.[37]

The Strangers, who were recruited by Weston and his investors, made up the majority of the party. Thomas Weston probably had handpicked some of them because they had skills that he felt would be useful in the new colony.

They were the following:[38,39]

- John Billington, thirty-eight, was accompanied by his wife, Eleanor, and their sons, John (age sixteen) and Francis (age fourteen).

- Richard Britteridge who was thirty-nine and traveled alone.
- Peter Brown was twenty and also alone.
- Richard Clarke traveled alone.
- Francis and Sarah Eaton brought their one-year-old son, Samuel.
- Richard Gardiner came alone.
- Stephen and Elizabeth Hopkins brought their three children, Constance (about thirteen or fourteen), Giles (eleven or twelve), and Damaris (age two). Another son, Oceanus, was born at sea. Edward Doty and Edward Leister came as servants of Stephen Hopkins.
- John Langmore was a servant to Christopher Martin.
- Edmund Margesson also came alone.
- Christopher Martin, who was treasurer of the venture, brought his wife, Mary, and her son Solomon Prower.
- William Mullins brought his wife, Alice, and their two children, Joseph, who was twenty-four, and Priscilla, who was seventeen years old, and a servant named Robert Carter, who was also a shoemaker.
- John Rigsdale brought his wife Alice.
- Richard Warren left his wife and five daughters in England.

Among the crew were:

- John Alden, twenty-one years old, who was a cooper, or barrel maker.
- John Allerton, hired by the colony for one year.
- Thomas English, hired to be master of the ship's shallop, the thirty foot open coastal boat the Pilgrims had disassembled and brought with them.
- William Trevor, a seaman, was hired to stay a year.
- Mr. Ely, a seaman, was also hired to stay one year.

Capt. Myles Standish and his wife, Rose, joined the group earlier in Delfshaven.

Although they were then in the minority, the Pilgrims still considered the entire undertaking their sacred mandate, assigned to them alone by God Himself. For them to be successful as a Separatist colony, to live as the Bible exemplified, and to remain in God's favor, however, they had to make sure that their religious beliefs dominated the colony and were adhered to by all. The Separatists were well prepared to enforce their convictions. Because of their practice of prophesying during their Sabbath meetings, they were experienced and clever at debate and public discourse, but as they may have surmised, it would take all their persuasive skills to convince the Strangers to accept their authority.

Their main challenge would be Christopher Martin, the representative of the investors and the company's treasurer. In addition to exceeding his charge and refusing to account for expenditures, he was arrogant toward other passengers, especially the Separatists. Robert Cushman wrote that Martin "so insulteth over our poor people, with such scorn and contempt, as if they were not good enough to wipe his shoes." Even the ship's crew had enough of his "ignorant boldness in meddling and controlling in things he knows not," so much so that they "threatened to mischief him." Christopher Martin posed a real threat to the Pilgrims' ultimate goals, and to the trip in general.[40]

The Voyage of the *Mayflower*

William Bradford devotes only two pages of his history to the *Mayflower*'s sixty-six-day "weighty" voyage across the Atlantic Ocean. Surely it was terrifying to be a passenger on that tiny ship, all alone on the vast sea, lurching in the waves at the whim of the ocean. There was a lifeboat of sorts, a small longboat stored on the upper deck, but it would accommodate only a few even if it could be launched fast enough in case of an emergency. It would take all their faith in God to quiet their anxieties.

Bradford does note that "many were afflicted with seasickness." That is not surprising considering their accommodations. The *Mayflower*, a vessel of 180 tons, was designed to haul cargo, not passengers. Before carrying Pilgrims she was employed in the Mediterranean wine trade. On this journey, instead of casks of wine, the passengers' provisions and equipment were stored in the hold.

The Mayflower.

The passengers occupied the lower deck, a space between the hold and the upper deck, a space that was normally reserved for storage and for the hammocks of the crew. This windowless "'tween deck" was about seventy-five feet long, less than twenty-five feet wide, and barely five feet high.[41]

Since she was a merchant ship, the *Mayflower* did not have separate passenger cabins, and the colonists had to fashion some privacy for themselves by sectioning the 'tween deck into "cabins" with wooden walls. These cabins, of which there may have been four on either side of a common area, were primarily designed as sleeping quarters for the women and children. Within the cabins were probably single berths stacked two high. The men would have slept in the common area, but there wasn't much room. On this deck was also stored some of the ship's equipment and the 30-foot shallop.

In hindsight such small cabins, although offering some privacy, might not have been the best possible arrangement for comfort. With little light and fresh air, it would have been dark and damp both in the tiny cubicles and the common area. Later when *Mayflower* passenger Edward Winslow wrote to his friend George Morton about sailing to New England aboard the *Anne,* he advised, "Build your cabins as open as possible."[42]

For the most part, meals were served cold and uncooked, including biscuits, cheese, dried fish, meats and fruits, pickled eggs, vegetables, and such. Likely there were regular distributions of foods from a common store to each family and the passengers probably ate together in the common area, getting to know each other and sharing stories. Having all their food in storage must have been a hardship for the passengers. Keep some of your food "close by" in your cabins, Winslow advised future colonists, as "it will much refresh you."[43,44]

The daily diet probably also included an assortment of fish caught by the sailors. Bonitos, or "Spanish dolphins," were delicious, according to John Josselyn, who made a similar voyage, and beautiful "with [an] admirable variety of glittering colors in the water." Shark, however, cooked by the crew, "proved very rough grained, [not] worthy of wholesome preferment."[45]

For sixty-six days, the colonists lived in the close quarters in the 'tween deck. The limited store of fresh water was saved for drinking, so there was only saltwater for bathing or laundry. Furthermore, the only sanitation on board were chamber pots or buckets. The constant roar of the wind must have frayed nerves which were already on edge. In fair weather, they doubtless spent time on the upper deck, walking about and enjoying the fresh air. Perhaps whales were sighted along the way, the great creatures terrifying to the Pilgrims. Josselyn remarked on seeing two whales, "the one spouted water through two great holes in her head into the air a great height and making a great noise with puffing and blowing." They raise out of the water, he explained, "and fall with such an extreme violence all whole together as one drop.... If they should light in any ship, she were in danger to presently sink down into the sea."[46]

During the arduous voyage, the men probably forged alliances and busied themselves with making plans for settlement in their new home. The women were engaged in taking care of the children, preparing meals, and in forming friendships of their own. They were also reproducing.

When the passengers boarded the *Mayflower*, three among the nineteen women were pregnant, which surely added to their anxiety of setting out to an unknown destination. Even under familiar conditions, medical care was primitive in the seventeenth century, and while at sea labor, and delivery was even more frightening and dangerous. Had the *Mayflower* sailed earlier in the year as originally planned, Elizabeth Hopkins' child would have been born in the New World. As it was, little Oceanus, aptly named and "surely a sign of God's mercies," was born at sea sometime between September 16 and November 11, 1620, probably in one of the tiny sleeping berths.[47]

A seaman would be the first person to die. Bradford wrote, "There was a proud and very profane young man, one of the seamen, of a lusty, able body, which made him the more haughty; he would always be condemning the poor people in their sickness and cursing them daily with grievous execrations; and...[told] them that he hoped to help to cast half of them overboard before they came to their journey's end, and to make merry with what they had." If any were to admonish him, "he would curse and swear most bitterly." At about mid-voyage, "it pleased God...to smite this man with a grievous disease, of which he died in a desperate manner, and so was himself the first that was thrown overboard." It was, Bradford wrote, "a special work of God's providence." But it was much too early in the venture to gloat over the death of a foe. It was all too possible, they must have thought, that they would be releasing one of their own to the cold depths of the ocean before the voyage had ended.[48]

Bradford reported that "they enjoyed fair winds and weather" at the beginning of the voyage. But then conditions turned on them. They "met with many fierce storms," which shook the ship badly and opened leaks. One of the main beams holding the ship together cracked from the stress, and some of the passengers met with the captain and crew to discuss "the sufficiency of the ship." There was talk of returning to England, but they were already past the halfway point, and that option wasn't a practical one. The master "affirmed... the ship to be strong and firm under water," and the crew used a "great iron screw," which one of the passengers had brought from Leiden, to raise and support the broken beam. Convincing themselves it was the best option when clearly they had no others, they carried on: "So they committed themselves to the will of God and resolved to proceed."[49,50]

After a month at sea, the constant swaying and pitching became familiar, if not pleasant. During one storm, John Howland, who was one of John Carver's servants, went to the upper deck and was thrown overboard as the *Mayflower* lurched in the stormy ocean waves. "But it pleased God," Bradford wrote, "that he caught hold of the topsail halyards which hung overboard." He was pulled from the sea and saved, "though he was something ill with it."[51]

There was one other death aboard the *Mayflower*. William Butten, who was Dr. Samuel Fuller's assistant, died on November 6, 1620. The cause of death was not recorded, and he was buried at sea, probably wrapped in sailcloth with a "bullet" or canon ball tied to his neck and another to his legs so his body would sink. It seems remarkable that more lives were not lost during the crossing, given that the passengers were unaccustomed to sea travel and were becoming more and more weary as the voyage progressed.[52]

George Clarke was not a *Mayflower* passenger; he came later to Plymouth. But his aspirations matched those of the first-comers, to have his own land, and his own family. Apparently, he had set his cap for Alice Martin.

Chapter Six

George Clarke
Plymouth Colony 1639

By the age of six or seven Alice Martin would have assumed many of the housekeeping responsibilities at home. As she grew older, the household tasks would have become more complex, training her for the day when she would have her own home and family. There was no word for, nor acknowledgement of, that difficult period of life we now call adolescence at Plymouth. There was no recognition of the point in a young person's development that marked the boundary between childhood and adulthood. Young people simply assumed adult roles as a natural part of their growing older and more capable.

In Plymouth Colony, Alice Martin was considered of marriageable age when she reached her early twenties. Under the watchful eyes of the entire community, young men might have noticed her and felt an attraction, but as with all things Pilgrim, many controlling factors were in place. The fitness of the match would have to be analyzed and approved before formal courtship could be initiated. One of the most important requirements was that the prospective groom be financially prepared to assume the responsibilities of a family.

Plymouth's Economy in the 1630s

By the 1630s, the Great Migration of Puritans into the Massachusetts Bay Colony affected Plymouth in many ways. Plymouth's economy changed from subsistence farming to cultivation for profit from trade with their new neighbors to the north. These exciting opportunities prompted the colonists to begin to move out of Plymouth proper and into the countryside, where they could have larger land holdings, grow more crops and raise more livestock to trade with the recent immigrants. The demand for land made it possible for the original Plymouth colonists to sell and trade their land grants among themselves, parlaying their smaller holdings into larger parcels of acreage.

Outsiders could purchase their way into Plymouth, too. For some it was the religious ideology that drew them, but living in a colony that was established, stable, and well organized was attractive to many. With hard work and a willingness to live within the Separatists' ideology, success at Plymouth could be had by just about anyone. But any person desiring admission to the colony was screened by the leadership, who controlled who was and was not allowed membership. The law stated, "No person or persons hereafter shall be admitted to live and inhabit within the Government of New Plymouth without the leave and liking of the governor and two of the assistants at least." Newcomers were required to take an "oath of fidelity" to the government of Plymouth and would have been asked to leave if they refused.[1]

All residents were expected to attend Sabbath services in their local meeting house. This may have been where George Clarke met Alice Martin. If so, George's interest in Alice would have been noticed immediately. Not even his shy glance towards Alice would have escaped the eyes of this watchful and controlling community. The fitness of the match was likely discussed and judged, possibly before George and Alice even realized their own interest in each other. While there are no details of their initial meeting, it is apparent that George Clarke was ambitious and determined. For such a man there were many opportunities in Plymouth Colony, but the first thing he needed was a plot of land.

George Clarke first appears in the Plymouth Colony records in March of 1637, regarding a land purchase. He was not a first-comer and was, therefore, not entitled to a land grant. If he wanted to own property in Plymouth, he would have to purchase it.[2]

Playne Dealing

The property George Clarke wanted was a 10-acre plot in a small seaside village within the township of Plymouth known as Playne Dealing. The original fortified settlement of Plymouth still served as the colony's seat of government, but by 1637 there were several new, small neighborhoods outside the palisade walls. These consisted of a few families with their homes and outbuildings constructed on small farm sites. Playne Dealing, about two miles north of the Town of Plymouth, was one of its first suburbs. Later the area became known as North Plymouth. Those living in Playne Dealing were members of the Plymouth Church and would have walked to the fenced town for Sabbath meetings, official business, and perhaps to gather with family and friends on market days.[3]

It is unclear where George Clarke came from before he appeared in the Plymouth court records. We do know that he was living in Playne Dealing in January 1637, likely under the authority of someone's family, since that was then the custom. It may have been Thurston Clarke's family, a speculation based on the fact that they shared a surname, and that the land George Clarke wanted in Playne Dealing was adjacent to Thurston's, "between Phineas Pratt and the widow Billington." It was quite common for families to buy adjacent properties, and although no evidence has yet surfaced tying the two men together, it is tempting to imagine they were related. Thurston Clarke came to Plymouth in 1634 aboard the *Francis*. He was then forty-four years of age, and brought his wife and daughter, both named Faith, with him. In January, 1635, Thurston's daughter married Edward Doty.[4,5,6]

Edward Doty, Ne'er-Do-Well

Unlike George Clarke, who must have been an independent man of some means, Edward Doty came to Plymouth as a servant. He was a passenger on the *Mayflower*, indentured to Stephen Hopkins. After completing his seven years of service to Hopkins, Doty would have been awarded a parcel of land, and by 1633 he was listed as a freeman, which gave him voting rights in the colony. A year later he was doing very well for himself. He owned property and had developed a business raising and trading pigs. He even had two servants of his own, John Smith and Peter Talbot.[7,8,9]

Though Doty came to Plymouth as a servant, he had a unique understanding of the opportunities Plymouth Colony provided to someone who was smart and enterprising. He figured out early that even a servant could attain financial success by working the system. Edward Doty became a master at buying and selling land, livestock, corn futures, and just about anything else, whether he lawfully owned it or not. His deals were so complicated and so close to bordering on illegal that he was constantly in court, either as a plaintiff or a defendant. Laws were in place to prevent fraud, but they did not stop Doty. He was amazingly tenacious—but so was George Clarke.

In March of 1637, George Clarke sued Edward Doty. Clarke had paid Doty eight pounds as down payment on a plot of land, the plot next to Thurston Clarke's farm in Playne Dealing, but Doty never completed the sale. The court ruled that Doty had made a "deceitful bargain" and ordered him to either give Clarke his eight pounds back or accept another four pounds and complete the deal. Doty was given until November to "assure the said lot of land [be transferred] unto the said George Clarke and his assignees forever." It turned out that Edward Doty had not been completely honest with George Clarke.[10]

On August 22, 1636, Peter Talbot, "the late servant of Edward Doty," appeared before the court. He had completed his indenture to Doty and, by their agreement, was due a portion of land. Talbot later sold the right to that land to James Skiff for six bushels of corn. Six months later, on January 14, 1637, the Court of Assistants granted to James Skiff five more acres, which along with the right to the five acres he bought from Peter Talbot gave him a ten-acre plot "lying next unto the lands granted to [Thurston] Clarke." The land officially belonged to James Skiff. Doty had accepted George Clarke's down payment on land that Doty did not rightfully own.[11]

By October of 1637, the matter had still not been settled, and Clarke sued Doty again, this time for twenty pounds sterling, "for denying him liberty to hold land for the term he had taken it for." The jury found in George Clarke's favor, awarding him the damages and directing Doty to pay court charges. The court may have been satisfied, but Doty was not, and he was a scrapper. Later that same day Clarke brought Doty back into court and sued him for assault and battery, "for striking the plaintiff," demanding five pounds sterling for the abuse. The jury found for the plaintiff but awarded Clarke only a small portion of his original claim, ordering twelve pence in damages and assessing Doty the court costs.[12]

George Clarke kept pressing the matter, and relations between the two men festered. Three months later Doty again attacked Clarke. On January 2, 1638, Doty was charged with "breaking the Kings peace, in assaulting George Clarke" and fined ten shillings.[13]

Finally, all the issues entangling the plot of land were worked out. In January of 1638, nearly two years after George Clarke made a down payment to Edward Doty, the sale was completed. Clarke and Skiff agreed that the price for the land would be eighty bushels of corn (the yield of about four and a half acres) and a goat, "to be the third choice of all [Clarke's] goats." Skiff had already started building a house on the land and agreed to finish it and make other improvements on the property as Clarke requested. This was to be George and Alice Clarke's honeymoon cottage, and George wanted it just right.[14]

The House of George Clarke

The house that James Skiff had started to build was probably of the earthfast or post-in-ground construction style, with walls attached to four large corner posts set directly into the soil. From what we know about other houses at Plymouth, it was likely around fifteen or twenty feet long on each side. George directed that the outside be covered with "boards" and that the inside be "clapboarded" to the ceiling of the main floor. This inside paneling was probably made of the same materials that covered the outside of the house. It would also have had a wooden floor.[15]

A typical Plymouth house.

Clarke directed Skiff to finish a full second floor, "a boarded chamber floor over the house," making the dimensions approximately 600 square feet, including the attic. There would be an opening at one end of the upper floor, probably nearest to the front door, to allow for upstairs access. The upper chamber was likely intended for sleeping or storage. Some dwellings in Plymouth had narrow staircases leading upstairs, but in this case there was only a ladder.[16]

Clarke wanted the main floor divided into two rooms, with a "partition to be made of clapboard through the middest." The fireplace was probably at one end of the house, in the main living room, and would have been huge by our standards. Seven feet in width was not uncommon. It was not only the home's source of heat, but also the main cooking area. The chimney stack was to be "daubed," that is, covered with a crude plaster mixture. The other first floor room, usually referred to as the "inner room," may have been used as a sleeping area.[17]

There were likely only a few small windows to admit light, openings in the walls simply covered with heavy paper coated with linseed oil or perhaps sliding wooden panels. The inside of the house would have been dark, but cozy when lit with candles and a fire blazing on the hearth. The roof was probably covered with boards or shingles in compliance with the law prohibiting "any kind of thatch, as straw, reed, etc.," as a safeguard against fire.[18]

While there was no mention of outbuildings in this court record, Clarke did give James Skiff careful instructions about how he was to prepare the fields. Clarke wanted three acres enclosed with "pallasadoes," a fence made of rows of posts set close vertically and pounded into the ground. This enclosed area would probably have held Clarke's goats and any other livestock. The fields at the "upper end" of the property were to be "hedged," as was the style in England. There, shrubbery hedges were used as permanent fences; they were attractive to look at, kept animals in or out as desired, and the overgrown branches could also be cut for fuel.[19]

After the last payment was made on November 15, 1638, George Clarke finally and officially owned his own farm, which meant that, while not a freeman, he had the official status of "inhabitant." He could not vote, but otherwise had civil and legal equality with the freemen; he would be required to pay taxes, attend church, participate in military service, and enjoy property ownership. He was also ready to get married.[20]

The Way of Marriage

Separatists believed that marriage was necessary "for the benefit of man's natural and spiritual life…." They believed that the purpose of marriage was the procreation of children, so that "our kind should be preserved and posterity propagated." Furthermore, marriage was necessary because it prevented "the most foul and filthy sin of adultery," and "is a medicine against uncleanness." In *Domesticall Duties*, Gouge wrote that another of the ends of marriage was that "man and wife might be a mutual help one to [the] other," not only in raising a family, but a help also "for well ordering prosperity and well bearing adversity, a help in health and sickness."[21,22]

The Pilgrims believed in marriages based on mutual affection and attraction, with Christ's love for his church as the model:

"The love of the husband to his wife must be like Christ's to his church; holy for quality, and great for quantity," wrote John Robinson. A husband must be gentle in his affections and faithful to their marriage bond. He also had the responsibility to guide his wife to eternal life.[23]

Arranged marriages were not the custom in Separatism or in Plymouth Colony. Young men and women were free to choose their own mates; the community, however, was to be involved in the decision. "In truth," wrote John Robinson, "is there anything wherein persons more need and less use reason, and true discretion, than in their marriage choice[?]" In choosing a spouse, "affection so far overrules reason in the most," that parents and friends were encouraged to become involved. Robinson advised parents to "do the duty" which God and nature has "laid upon them…in preventing two dangerous evils, uncleanness and unfit matching." Likewise, friends "should be officious and forth-putting" in offering advice. The community must also identify those who should not seek marriage, those "who are unable to perform the essential duties of marriage,…who are defective, or closed in their secret parts,…[or] they who are infected with such contagious disease…"[24,25]

Robinson advised that the more alike the couple, the better. "Fitness of years is requisite," he wrote, so that "an old head be not set upon young shoulders." "Fitness in estate," is important, "lest the excelling person despise the other." Matching dispositions and "agreement of affections" are a good thing, because "if the one be too fiery hot and suddenly moved, that the other can cast on the more cold water of forbearance."[26]

For all this good advice, in actuality there was not a very large pool of prospective mates for Plymouth's eligible young women and men to choose from. By the year 1630 approximately 350 to 400 people lived in Plymouth Colony. By 1643 the list of males between sixteen and sixty who were healthy enough to bear arms consisted of about 600 men, living throughout the colony in eight different towns, most of them already married. Despite this, George Clarke and Alice Martin somehow managed to find each other.[27,28]

Plymouth Law and Marriage

Plymouth Colony referred to many of Robinson's writings about marriage when writing their laws. Since the choice of a spouse was essential to the stability of the family, and family was the basis of religious and community authority, then the community—especially the parents of the couple—was required to be involved in those decisions. It was against the law to marry without parental approval: "None be allowed to marry that are under the covert of parents but by their consent [and] approbation."[29]

The official thinking behind these laws was the concern that some persons might be too young or too poor to enter into marriage, or that some innocent young woman might be taken advantage of and in need of protection from those "practicing the inveigling of men's daughters [or] maids under guardians, contrary to their [parents' or] guardians' liking." Some may have remembered their time in Leiden, when they were losing control over their children. Whatever the reasoning behind it, the law was clear: "If any shall make any motion of marriage to any man's daughter or maid servant not having first obtained leave and consent of the parent or master so to do, shall be punished either by fine or corporal punishment or both...." However, allowances could be made in special circumstances. If consent could not be had from parents or masters, the governor or one of his assistants who knew both parties could "see the marriage be fit before it be allowed by him."[30]

There was little in the way of formal courting rituals, such as dating, dances, and the like, at Plymouth Colony. Courtship mostly took place during the usual events of daily life as part of routine work and leisure activities. We can be sure, however, that George Clarke and Alice Martin got to know and care for each other under the watchful eyes of the community. As the relationship became more serious, George would have obtained the necessary permission from parents or guardians, asked Alice for her hand, and informed the authorities of their intentions. The next step was that the couple entered into a lawful contract or betrothal, similar to the modern custom of an engagement. With this formality, it was understood that there was "the mutual consent of two parties with the consent of parents or guardians, if there be any to be had, and a solemn promise of marriage in due time to each other before two competent witnesses."[31]

Plymouth law required that George and Alice's betrothal be "published" at town meetings three times "before the solemnizing of it," giving anyone in the community ample opportunity to challenge the couple's fitness for marriage. It was among the duties of the messenger, or constable, to "give warning of such marriages as shall be approved by authority."[32] As constable, Joshua Pratt, coincidently one of George Clarke's neighbors, would have had the honors.

Even with this official status, however, the couple was expected to remain chaste throughout their engagement. If they should have sexual relations before marriage, they would have been fined five pounds, imprisoned not more than three days, or, if they could not afford the fine, been publicly whipped.[33]

Preparations

The usual period of engagement in Plymouth was two to three months, which meant that George Clarke and Alice Martin would probably have entered into a formal agreement to marry around November 1638, about the same time Clarke made his final payment on his farm. During their engagement, the two sets of parents, or masters, if there were any, would have met and negotiated an agreement for furnishing the young couple with all they would need to set up housekeeping and commence farming or the practice of a trade.

The Plymouth custom of parents assisting a young couple in setting up an independent household was not based on birth order, since Plymouth did not practice primogeniture, a system in which the eldest son inherited the entire estate . All children were treated equally, and it was the custom that a son's marriage, not a father's death, was the occasion for the transfer of property from parent to child. It was quite common for a young man to receive his "portion" of his father's estate as an early inheritance, in the form of property and a house.

During the year leading up to his marriage to Alice Martin, George Clarke would have been busy gathering all the equipment needed to run a farm in Plymouth Colony in the 1630s. This was an agricultural community, and he would need to be prepared to grow or hunt food for himself and his family.

In the record of his land purchase from James Skiff, Clarke was referred to as a yeoman. While there is no record of his owning land in Plymouth before then, it is clear that he was an experienced farmer. We also know that he kept a herd of goats, which he used for trade, because part of his payment to James Skiff was "a goat to be the third choice of all his goats." Goats were prevalent and prized in the early years of the colony. The English considered them hardy enough to survive in situations where other types of livestock could not. In 1638 a milk goat was worth three or founds pounds, female kids thirty to forty shillings. Goats were multipurpose animals, kept both for their milk, which made good cheese, and for their meat. Their skins were also used for gloves, and in at least one case as a "coverlid," or coverlet. But goats presented problems.[34,35,36,37]

When George Clarke instructed that James Skiff build him some fenced pens, he must have had his goats in mind. Able to exist on native vegetation, Clarke's goats would otherwise have eaten their way through the hedges he used to enclose some of his land. They also were known to enjoy eating the bark off the native apple trees, whose fruit was used to make cider. The animals needed to be penned and not allowed to roam freely.

Beyond a house and animal paddocks, George Clarke needed to assemble the necessary equipment to run his own farm. Our best evidence of everyday life in Plymouth can be gleaned from wills and inventories, and a review of the items valued and bequeathed gives a good idea of what George Clarke would have required. To work the land, he would need the basics: a plow, a farm cart, and a collection of small tools such as scythes, sickles, shovels, dung forks, and hoes. Wooden spades were also common items mentioned in inventories.

A farmer could hire or borrow the larger equipment from a neighbor but would probably want his own smaller tools. The equipment was likely homemade, and thus would have been somewhat crude and rough. These tools were highly prized, though, and more than one individual was brought before the court for stealing a spade or other such tool, as we shall see later.[38]

Clarke may also have gathered an ax, a hatchet, and a saw, and perhaps some woodworking tools, such as an auger, hammer, chisel, plane, and vise. There were at least three professional carpenters in Plymouth in its early years, and most furniture was probably locally produced or imported from England on one of the ships that brought in new colonists. The Pilgrims may have constructed their own simple pieces, such as benches or chests. Pilgrim homes had no closets, so chests were used to store clothes and linens while also serving as chairs and tables.

Though many of the early colonists slept on mattresses on the floor, by 1637 more comfortable beds were desired. George Clarke likely furnished his new home with a bedstead, a simple corded bed made with rope laced back and forth on a wooden frame. Perhaps it had a headboard or even some posts from which bed curtains were hung.

The fireplace was the center of activity in any Plymouth home, and Clarke needed the equipment necessary for keeping a fire going and for preparing food. Secured across the mouth of the hearth was the lug pole, to which were attached several hooks of different sizes. Kettles and pots were hung on these hooks and were placed either closer or farther from the flames to control the cooking temperature. Andirons supported the logs burned in the fireplace, and shovels, tongs, and forks were used to control the fire and clean out the ashes.

One absolute necessity was a firearm. The Pilgrims wanted everyone to be prepared in case of an attack by the Native Americans, and by law every man was required to "have [a] piece, powder [and] shot, a sufficient musket or other serviceable piece for war with bandolero [cartridge belt], sword and other appurtenance for himself and each man servant he keeps able to bear Arms."[39]

Every man was required to be armed.

It was required by Plymouth Colony law that George Clarke be able to support himself and his wife. Men were considered unfit for marriage if they were too young or unable to work, "and also in regard to their weak estate." Whoever was helping him set up his own farm would have made sure he had animals, seeds, equipment, and the necessary know-how to run a successful homestead.[40]

Pilgrim Bride

The best information about what was in a Pilgrim bride's trousseau comes from the record of Damaris Hopkins' inheritance from her father's estate in 1644. The list of domestic items included a featherbed and bedding, tablecloths and napkins, plates, platters, pots, "one tin candlestick," various utensils, and a chamber pot.[41]

Alice had been preparing all her life for marriage, learning how to keep a house and raise a family. She may have made some bed and table linens and collected a few other items into a hope chest. During her betrothal period, she would likely have been sewing pillowcases—or "pillow beers," as they were called—hemming sheets, and sewing and mending her clothes in preparation for marriage.

It was the custom at this time, and it would be law by 1672, that only a magistrate could join any residents of Plymouth together in marriage. From the earliest day of the colony, when the first marriage occurred there, it had been established that marriage was a civil matter and not a religious one. This was a view they had picked up while in Leiden, "the laudable custom of the Low-Countries, in which they had lived." Marriage involved civil issues, such as inheritance, wrote Bradford, and, besides, nowhere in the Gospel was marriage to be "laid on the ministers as part of their office."[42]

The ceremony would have been very simple, probably held at the bride's home. There may have been a simple gathering afterward, for as Gouge wrote, "By a right celebrating of marriage, it is much honored: and man and wife with much honor are brought together." George Clarke and Alice Martin were married on January 22, 1639, and soon after they moved into their new home.[43]

Pilgrim Sexuality – Delightful Love

According to Plymouth law, a married couple had three basic obligations. First, they were required to live together. Only under unusual circumstances was a married person allowed to live apart from his or her spouse. This requirement assured the community that the family was under the control of the head of the household.

Second, they must live together in relative peace and harmony. Peace, wrote John Robinson, "is both pleasant and profitable… for all persons and societies," and this was a society that had little tolerance for displays of anger. Anger, Robinson said, was a blind thing: "there is nothing so sacred and precious which it will spare; but without difference it flieth, where the wings are not clipped, upon friends as well as foes; and upon unreasonable creatures, as well as upon men." When disagreements arose, according to Robinson, the wife must give in. "One must give way," he wrote, "and apply unto the other." The submissive role, wrote Robinson,

"God and nature layeth upon the woman, rather than upon the man." For wives to be rebellious against their husbands would be an affront "both against God and their husbands; which shall not escape unpunished from God."[44,45,46]

The third requirement for marriage was that the couple have a normal and exclusive sexual union. In order to encourage this, adultery was deemed a punishable offense. In 1641, for example, Anne Linceford was convicted of adultery and sentenced to be "severely whipped." She and her lover, Thomas Bray, who was also whipped, were both ordered to wear "two letters, viz AD, for Adulterers, daily, upon the outside of their uppermost garment[s]."[47]

Even under the sanction of marriage, Pilgrim couples were to use a measure of control over their passions. Husbands were warned by Pastor Robinson not to indulge themselves too frequently: "Both marriage and wine are of God, and good in themselves," he wrote, however, either can be abused: "As a man may surfeit at his own table or be drunken with his own drink; so may he play the adulterer with his own wife, both by inordinate affection and action."[48]

There was also an emphasis on women's pleasure during intercourse. In the seventeenth century it was widely accepted that the conception of a child was the result of the mixing of "seed" from both the male and the female. "The perfect mixing of the seed of both sexes is the beginning of conception," wrote midwife Jane Sharp in 1671. She explained that the woman emits her seed during intercourse when she experiences an orgasm: "By the stirring of the clitoris the imagination causeth the vessels to cast out that seed that lyeth deep in the body, for in this and the ligaments that fastened in it, lies the chief pleasure of love's delight in copulation; and indeed were not the pleasure transcendently ravishing us, a man or woman would hardly ever die for love."[49]

Following the logic of this model of procreation, the success of Plymouth Colony, which based its religious and social structure upon the nuclear family, depended on families producing children, which depended on the ability of husbands to "delightfully" pleasure their wives. How men were instructed to do this has been lost to history, but apparently George and Alice figured it out.

When the *Mayflower* arrived at Cape Cod in 1620, her passengers were beyond weary, probably much too tired and sick to even think of copulating. Three women boarded the ship already pregnant; one child was born during the crossing, one in Cape Cod, and one stillborn in Plymouth Harbor. When land was finally sighted in November 1620, surely their thoughts were focused on simple survival.

Chapter Seven

Arriving at New Plymouth
Cape Cod 1620

In the view of the Leiden Separatists, God had entrusted them alone to build a colony in America. It was a holy responsibility, a blessed undertaking to establish a community based on the biblical ideal in a wilderness across the sea. There they could live without the threat of interference, and there they would be in total control. Nowhere in their plan was there a provision for outsiders.

The Strangers who joined the venture in London must have been an unwelcome surprise to the Separatists. No matter how congenial Bradford claims that first meeting was, as soon as they met the rest of their party in London, the men from the Leiden congregation were undoubtedly thinking about how to regain full control.

The plan was to form a civil government as soon as they landed in America. It was still to be decided, however, who would fill the leadership positions. There was the possibility that Christopher Martin, their treasurer and representative of the investors, could be elected governor of the new colony. If that happened, the Pilgrims could hardly achieve their intended goal of creating a godly Separatist community.

As the *Mayflower* pitched and rolled in the rough Atlantic waters during the crossing, the Separatists were most certainly busy planning, plotting, and secretly setting events in motion that would culminate with the Mayflower Compact and the election of a governor—that is, the right governor—for Plymouth Colony.

Cape Cod Harbor

Early in the morning on November 9, William Bradford reported, "after long beating at sea," land was sighted, "that land which is called Cape Cod." They were on the outside of the Cape, east of the peninsula that reaches out into the Atlantic like the well-muscled arm of a bodybuilder. "They were not a little joyful," wrote Bradford in what must be one of history's great understatements. It had been sixty-six days since they had left England, and surely they were tired of the confines and disagreeable conditions on board the *Mayflower*.[1]

Cape Cod was not their intended destination. The Peirce Patent from the Virginia Company, believed to be a valid one at the time, was for land to the south, near the Hudson River. According to Bradford, they tried to sail southward "to find some place about the Hudson River for their habitation," but they sailed straight into dangerous rough seas that imperiled them all. They decided to "bear up again for the Cape and thought themselves happy to get out of those dangers before night overtook them." As a result, they sailed back toward Cape Cod.[2]

That decision opened a loophole in the agreement the Strangers had made individually with Thomas Weston, and they were poised to jump through it. Their agreement stipulated that they were to settle on land granted by the Virginia Company. If the party did not settle on that specific grant, the Strangers argued, then wasn't the entire agreement voided? And if the agreement was voided through no fault of their own, then what was there to stop them from going off and establishing their own colony, one with no debt to repay to London?

There was muttering and complaining, "discontented and mutinous speeches," among the Strangers, who were threatening to split from the Separatists and build their own colony. The Pilgrims were keen to what was going on, "observing some not well affected to unity and concord, but gave some appearance of faction." If the London group split off, not only would survival be more difficult, if not impossible, but the Pilgrims would be left owing the entire debt to the Merchant Adventurers. This issue needed to be settled before things got out of their control.[3,4]

The *Mayflower* sailed around the northern tip of Cape Cod and on November 11 anchored just inside the wrist of Cape Cod Bay, in what is now Provincetown Harbor. The Separatists gave thanks: "Being thus arrived in good harbor, and brought safe to land, they fell upon their knees and blessed the God of Heaven who had brought them over the vast and furious ocean, and delivered them from all the perils and miseries thereof, again to set their feet on the firm and stable earth, their proper element."[5]

Looking out from the bobbing deck of the *Mayflower*, Bradford finally realized the full impact of what was set in motion years before. What he saw was truly a wilderness, a "silent emptiness," and they were quite alone in it. He wrote, "being thus passed the vast ocean, and a sea of troubles before in their preparation,...they now had no friends to welcome them nor inns to entertain or refresh their weather-beaten bodies; no houses or much less towns to repair to, to seek for succor." Looking west he saw "a hideous and desolate wilderness, full of wild beasts and wild men.... For summer being done, all things stand upon them with a weather-beaten face, and the whole county, full of woods and thickets, represented a wild and savage hue." Looking towards the east he saw a "mighty ocean...a main bar and gulf to separate them from all the civil parts of the world." Ironically, these Separatists, who wanted to be alone, now stood in astonishment of the prospect.[6,7]

Some historians have argued that the Pilgrims had originally and covertly decided early on that the best place for their colony was New England, not Virginia. Bradford Smith, for example, in *Bradford of Plymouth* claimed that while in Leiden the Pilgrims "all agreed on New England." Perhaps they chaffed at the prospect of being under the jurisdiction of the Virginia Colony. But Bradford's own words refute Smith's statement: "[after landing at Cape Cod and] after some deliberation had amongst themselves and with the master of the ship, they tacked about and resolved to stand for the southward (the wind and weather being fair) to find some place about Hudson's River for their habitation."[8]

Nonetheless, New England was where they decided to stay.⁹

Their only home for the previous two months had been the *Mayflower*, "a ship to succor them," but Master Jones was eager to return to England. His job had been accomplished, and food for his crew was running low. He urged his passengers to decide on a place to settle so he could unload the passengers and all their belongings and set sail for home.¹⁰

The journey was over. It was time for the Pilgrims to get to work.

The Mayflower Compact

The Pilgrims had to act fast. They needed to bind everyone together under their religious rule in order to preserve their mission. Their first step was to establish a covenant amongst themselves, a compact, a promise to join together, form a government, elect leaders, and honor their authority. It was probably William Brewster who wrote the document, as it was clearly modeled on the church covenants, those sacred agreements already long in use by the Separatists. He may have started composing it when they first encountered the Strangers in London, in anticipation of formally uniting everyone.

The words of the Compact reflected the Separatist experience, their struggle for autonomy and self-government. But it was more than that. It was the first step towards Separatist dominance of the new colony. In the Compact, Brewster appealed to the Strangers on several levels—through their love of England, their love of God, and their need to stick together to survive. Propagating and advancing the gospel of the kingdom of Christ in those remote parts of the world," which had been listed last, but "which was not the least," of their reasons for leaving Leiden, had now moved to first place.¹¹

> In the name of God, Amen. We whose names are underwritten, the loyal subjects of our dread Sovereign Lord King James, by the Grace of God of Great Britain, France, and Ireland, King, Defender of the Faith, etc.

Having undertaken for the Glory of God and advancement of the Christian Faith and Honor of our King and Country, a Voyage to plant the First Colony in the Northern Parts of Virginia, do by these presents solemnly and mutually in the presence of God and one of another, Covenant and Combine ourselves together in a Civil Body Politic, for our better ordering and preservation and furtherance of the ends aforesaid; and by virtue hereof to enact, constitute and frame such just and equal Laws, Ordinances, Acts, Constitutions and Offices, from time to time, as shall be thought most meet and convenient for the general good of the Colony, unto which we promise all due submission and obedience.

In witness whereof we have hereunder subscribed our names at Cape Cod, the 11th of November, in the year of the reign of our Sovereign Lord King James, of England, France and Ireland the eighteenth, and of Scotland the fifty fourth, Anno Domini 1620.[12]

It may have taken some coaxing and persuading, but in the end all the men on board who were eligible to sign, those who were of legal age and who were free agents, forty-one in all, affixed their signatures or marks to the Mayflower Compact. The signers, in order, were John Carver, William Bradford, Edward Winslow, William Brewster, Isaac Allerton, Myles Standish, John Alden, Samuel Fuller, Christopher Martin, William Mullins, William White, Richard Warren, John Howland, Stephen Hopkins, Edward Tilley, John Tilley, Francis Cooke, Thomas Rogers, Thomas Tinker, John Rigsdale, Edward Fuller, John Turner, Francis Eaton, James Chilton, John Crackstone, John Billington, Moses Fletcher, John Goodman, Degory Priest, Thomas Williams, Gilbert Winslow, Edmund Margesson, Peter Brown, Richard Bitteridge, George Soule, Richard Clarke, Richard Gardiner, John Allerton, Thomas English, Edward Doty, and Edward Leister.[13,14]

In this document each signer, whether master or servant,

held an equal weight. However, there was a hierarchy among them—the first five to sign were Separatists and the last ones were Strangers and servants. Those males who did not sign were either under-age or bound by a servant's contract which did not permit them to do so.[15]

The *Mayflower* passengers were all from the lower classes. By signing the Compact they had participated in an act of self-government, most likely a first for most of them. They might be subjects of the king in faraway London, but here in America they answered only to each other. As remarkable and as revolutionary as this idea may seem, it must be remembered that the motives behind the Mayflower Compact were carefully calculated. The document was more about control than it was about freedom, for obtaining everyone's commitment to combine themselves into a cohesive group and to submit to the group's leadership was only the first step towards Separatist dominance of the colony. The leadership of the group was still to be determined. A governor had to be elected, and the choice would be crucial to the future of Plymouth as a Separatist colony.

Electing a Governor

The Separatists were in the minority, since they represented only forty percent of the voters. Their candidate for governor was John Carver, who was a Leiden Separatist, one of the organizers of the voyage, and the assumed leader of the Pilgrims. A deacon of the church and a successful merchant, Carver was the wealthiest of the colonists, with six servants. Christopher Martin, leader of the London group and treasurer of the whole enterprise, was likely the second candidate. Since Martin was so unpopular with the passengers, the Strangers may have proposed a third candidate, one of their own.

What the Separatists were counting on was their cohesiveness; they would vote as a bloc. The Strangers' votes would likely be split between their two candidates, but the Separatists still needed some of the Strangers' votes to gain majority control. The male servants of the Pilgrims who had signed the Compact were probably permitted to vote and were likely encouraged to join with their masters and cast their votes for Carver.

The strategy worked. After the vote was taken, William Bradford simply reported that "they chose, or rather confirmed, Mr. John Carver (a man godly and well approved amongst them) their governor for that year."[16]

Whatever the tally of votes, the choice of Carver was more important than Bradford's few words imply. His election meant that authority of the colony would be in the Pilgrims' hands. At long last, after all they had gone through, they had again regained control, to a certain extent, over their own futures. Plymouth would be a Separatist colony, and everyone in it would be subject to Separatist principles. There were still a few "discontents and murmurings" among them, Bradford reported, but they were overcome by the "wisdom, patience, and just and equal carriage of things, by the governor and better part, which clave faithfully together in the main."[17]

There may have been a sigh of relief, but the respite was short-lived; there would be much work and much heartbreak to come.

Venturing Ashore

After the signing of the agreement and the election of a governor, fifteen or sixteen men went ashore to fetch wood, "for we had none left." They brought bunches of juniper branches back on board the *Mayflower*, "which smelled very sweet," and must have been most welcome, especially in the crowded and sour 'tween deck. This trip to shore to fetch wood would be repeated every Saturday that the *Mayflower* was at anchor in New England, which would be longer than anyone could have anticipated.[18]

Sunday, November 12, was the Sabbath, so the entire group remained aboard the ship, worshipping God under Elder Brewster's direction. They held morning and afternoon meetings, individual and family prayer meetings, and both work and play were forbidden. It may have been on this day that the Separatists—surely with great diplomacy—first exercised their newly acquired authority, requiring all to attend religious services with them. One can only imagine what the Strangers felt when they realized what was in store for them.

On Monday, many of the passengers enjoyed their first day on land. After nearly seventy days living in the cramped and crowded 'tween deck, breathing foul air and eating cold food, they were doubtless eager for a change. Disoriented and weak from their long sea voyage, they wanted to feel land under their feet again, breathe fresh air, and explore their new homeland for themselves. What they viewed were woods, dense forests of "oaks, pines, sassafras, juniper, birch, holly, vines, some ash, [and] walnut," which must have been a welcome sight after so many days at sea.[19]

Those Separatists with imagination could envision a neat and tidy colony on a rise above the sea, its residents well fed and prosperous. All around them they saw natural riches, "the whales play about them and the greatest store of fowls they ever saw." The colony would be dedicated to the glory of God with everyone happily following scriptural principles. Such lofty thoughts may have comforted them, but they could not dwell on the future for long. They were a practical people, and there was much work ahead of them.[20]

The first job was to reassemble the shallop, the small open boat that had been cut in pieces and stowed aboard the *Mayflower* when they left London. They must have used the *Mayflower*'s longboat to haul the pieces closer to shore. In shallow water, they waded ashore, dragging the pieces of the shallop with them. Francis Eaton, a twenty-five-year-old carpenter, was probably put in charge of the project. He estimated that it would take sixteen or seventeen days to rebuild the boat.

A freshwater creek was discovered, and so, for the women, it was washday, "as they had great need," Bradford wryly noted. Some of the men obligingly cut wood and built fires to boil the wash water. The women spent the day doing laundry while the smaller children played around them, but the icy water and freezing winds "affecteth them with grievous colds and coughs." These ailments foretold that things were to get much, much worse.[21,22]

First chance to do laundry in several months.

Wash day aside, the first expedition on shore took place sometime between November 15 and 17. While the men were waiting for the shallop to be repaired, they decided to go exploring. The scouting party, led by Capt. Standish, included sixteen armed men, who walked about a mile along the coast in a single file. It was on this outing that they saw their first Native Americans, a group of "five or six…savages," who ran off into the woods upon seeing them.[23]

They camped on the beach that night, with three men at watch in case any of the local indigenous peoples returned. The next day they set out again and discovered a lush valley where they "found springs of fresh water, of which we were heartily glad, and sat us down and drunk our first New England water with as much delight as ever we drunk drink in all our lives." After refreshing themselves they marched southward where they found "a fine clear pond of fresh water, being about a musket shot broad and twice as long."[24]

Later that day they found the ruins of an Indian home site, "where some planks and a great kettle was remaining, and heaps of sand newly paddled [into a mound] with their hands." They found "new stubble, of which they had gotten corn this year, and many walnut trees full of nuts, and great store of strawberries, and some vines."

Being curious, they dug into the sandy mound and found a large, new woven basket filled with about three or four bushels of corn, "which was as much as two of us could lift up from the ground, and was very handsomely and cunningly made." They discussed what to do with the corn. "At length, after much consultation, we concluded to take the kettle and as much of the corn as we could carry away with us; and when our shallop came, if we could find any of the people, and come to parley with them, we would give them the kettle again, and satisfy them for their corn." They took all the ears, packed as much loose corn into the kettle as two men could carry, and also filled their pockets before returning to the ship. William Bradford called the find a "special providence of God." [25,26]

That night they returned to the freshwater pond, and set up camp for the night, again with three men on guard. The next morning, they continued to explore. The leader of the group came across a deer trap made of a bent and tied tree sapling. They admired the handiwork, even more so after William Bradford, bringing up the rear of the party, stepped into the trap and, "it gave a sudden jerk up, and [he] was immediately caught by the leg." "It was a very pretty device," they admitted after helping the no-doubt embarrassed Bradford out of the trap, but when Edward Winslow spotted three bucks close by, he added with amusement that "we had rather have had one of them."[27]

During the next week, "our people did make things as fitting as they could," but the shallop was still not repaired. During low tide many of the *Mayflower* passengers rowed the longboat away from the ship and then waded ashore. "Oftentimes they waded to the middle of the thigh, and oft to the knees, to go and come from land." The weather was cold, the water icy, and the chill of getting wet "brought to the most, if not to all, coughs and colds."[28]

The Second Expedition

On November 28, a second expedition set out. About thirty men struggled ashore this time, including Master Jones and several sailors, setting off in both the newly-repaired shallop and the *Mayflower*'s longboat. The wind was so strong that they were forced ashore, where it snowed all day and on into the night. It was their exposure on this freezing night that they later blamed as the cause of their "general sickness."

The next day they marched back to the place where they had found the buried corn and retrieved what remained. They searched the immediate area, found more mounds, and dug up yet more corn. In the end they had scavenged about ten bushels, "which will serve us sufficiently for seed." By the end of the day, Master Jones and some of the others were tired and wanted to reboard the *Mayflower*. "We sent home with him our weakest people, and some that were sick, and all the corn." The other eighteen stayed onshore and camped that night.[29]

The next day they continued surveying the area, and came upon "a place like a grave, but it was much bigger and longer than any we had yet seen." The ground was covered with snow. Nonetheless, curiosity overcame them, and they dug into the grave, finding the body of a man wrapped in canvas, "fine yellow hair" still on the skull. A smaller body was in the grave, "the bones and head of a little child." Strings of "fine white beads" were tied around the child's body, "and other odd knacks." With little reflection on what was obviously a sacred gravesite, they sifted through the mementos and "brought sundry of the prettiest things away with us, and covered the corpse up again."[30]

On this expedition, they came upon two well-built huts made of saplings, "bended with both ends stuck into the ground. They were made round, like unto an arbor, and covered down to the ground with thick and well-wrought mats, and the door was not over a yard high, made of a mat to open. The chimney was a wide-open hole in the top, for which they had a mat to cover it close when pleased. In the midst of them were four little trunches [stakes] knocked into the ground, and small sticks laid over, on which they hung their pots, and what they had to seethe [simmer or boil]." These practical dwellings may have served as models for the first shelters the Pilgrims themselves built.[31]

The explorers entered the houses, and even though they found fresh meat, a sign of current habitation, they sorted through the bowls, trays, dishes, baskets, dried acorns, fish, and seeds, and boldly helped themselves, reporting that "some of the best things we took away with us." They had intended to leave "some beads and other things," as a sign of peace and to indicate they were willing to trade, but neglected to do so.[32]

There was serious and lengthy discussion aboard the *Mayflower* that night. Some thought it best to stay in the wrist of Cape Cod. It seemed like a good place to start a colony, and besides many of the party were sick, "for scarce any of us were free from vehement coughs." Also, there was a second infant on board; Susanna White had given birth to a son, who was fittingly named Peregrine, the anglicized form of the Latin word peregrinus, which came to mean "pilgrim." Others wanted to explore further still. According to Winslow, a member of the crew, Master's Mate Robert Coppin, had been in the country before on a previous voyage and offered that there was a good site across the bay. It was decided that a third exploring party would set out.[33,34]

The pressure was on to establish a settlement and do so quickly. People were sick, and one had already died. On December 4, Edward Thompson, who was William White's servant, had passed. After services on board, a digging party was sent ashore on December 5 to bury his body, the first of the *Mayflower* Pilgrims to be buried in America. But certainly not the last.

The Third Expedition and Dorothy Bradford's Death

The third expedition set out on December 6. They didn't get away from the ship until the afternoon, after services had been conducted for seven-year-old Jasper More, who had died earlier that day. The Pilgrims sailed in their shallop, and the burying party followed in the *Mayflower*'s longboat.

The weather was bad and "it was very cold, for the water froze on our clothes and made them many times like coats of iron." As they got near the shore, the explorers sighted a group of Native Americans, who immediately fled into the woods. Shaken, the colonists established a camp on shore, constructed a quick barricade, gathered firewood, and set a schedule for guards throughout the night. The American Indians apparently did the same, for the Pilgrims could see their fires in the distance.[35]

The next day the party split into two groups, one to explore by sea in the shallop, the other to explore on land. More Native homes were found, as well as old corn fields, but no sign of the inhabitants. That night the two groups met on the shore at the mouth of the Herring River, where present-day Eastham is now located. They built a campsite and spent an uneasy night.

Early the next morning after prayers, while eating breakfast and preparing to load their belongings in the shallop, "all of a sudden, we heard a great and strange cry." A group of Indians rushed from the forests in attack, and Bradford reported that "their arrows came flying amongst them." The colonists fired their muskets and scared them away. Even as the Native Americans retreated, the colonists continued to shoot so that "they might see we were not afraid of them nor discouraged.... Thus it pleased God to vanquish our enemies and give us deliverance." They named the area First Encounter Beach, a name still in use today.[36,37]

Staying parallel to the shore, the expedition sailed along Cape Cod Bay in search of the site Robert Coppin had suggested. It began to snow and rain by afternoon, and the sea became so rough that it broke their rudder. They spotted the harbor, but the rough seas and wind broke their mast into three pieces, and the sail fell into the sea. They furiously rowed until they landed on a small island and camped there for two nights, resting and drying out their belongings. The passengers named the island Clarke's Island in honor of John Clarke, one of the *Mayflower*'s mates, who had piloted the shallop and brought it to safety; the name still stands. On Sunday, December 10, the group celebrated the Sabbath.

Bradford reported that on December 11, 1620, "they sounded the harbor and found it fit for shipping, and marched into the land and found divers cornfields and little running brooks, a place (as they supposed) fit for situation. At least it was the best they could

Celebrating the Sabbath on Clark's Island.

find, and the season and their present necessity made them glad to accept of it." This area seemed like the most likely settlement because it was already cleared, and the hill that sloped up from the harbor would make a good place to erect a fort. There was also clean, fresh, running water. No thought was given to who had cleared the land.[38]

The site had already been named "Plimouth," marked so on Captain John Smith's chart of 1616, and the Pilgrims likely knew that. They were familiar with Smith's *A Description of New England* and had read in his book that Plimouth was "an excellent good harbor, good land; and no want to anything, but industrious people...." They knew that Smith had noted that "Cape Cod [is an] excellent harbor of all weathers [where] the best and greatest fish [are] to be had, winter and summer, in all that country."[39,40]

The men returned to the *Mayflower* bringing "good news to the rest of our people, which did much comfort their hearts." But all was not well on board the ship. James Chilton had died on December 8, leaving a wife and thirteen-year-old daughter.[41,42]

But the most shocking news awaited William Bradford. His

wife, Dorothy May Bradford, had died while he was away from the ship. Years later Cotton Mather would explain that Dorothy, Bradford's "dearest consort accidentally falling overboard, was drowned in the harbor."[43]

To this day, Dorothy Bradford's death remains an intriguing mystery. That she would simply fall overboard while the *Mayflower* was at anchor in the bay seems questionable. During sixty-six days at sea, tossed by the waves and weather ("The winds were so fierce and the seas so high, as they could not bear a knot of sail."), only one passenger had fallen overboard. John Howland had been thrown into the sea during a storm but had been rescued. No one witnessed Dorothy Bradford's fall, but foul play was not suspected, and there was no investigation. Bradford recorded no explanation afterwards and never spoke of Dorothy again. Nonetheless, several historians have suggested that her death was a suicide.[44,45,46,47,48,49]

After five months that included a grueling open-sea voyage of more than two months' duration, Dorothy Bradford and all the other women and children were still living on board the *Mayflower* in the harbor. Their only easterly view was the empty, immeasurable Atlantic Ocean, and to the west the windy and barren sand dunes of Cape Cod. To add to their misery, it continued to be bitterly cold. Bradford later wrote that "it was winter, and they that know the winters of that country know them to be sharp and violent, and subject to cruel and fierce storms." It is not difficult to imagine that those who waited on the *Mayflower* might be filled with feelings of despair. Even William Bradford had to admit, "what could now sustain them but the Spirit of God and his grace?"[50]

God's grace may not have been enough to sustain Dorothy. Not only did the future look bleak, but she had been separated from her three-year-old son, John, who was left behind in Leiden. There were two infants aboard the *Mayflower*, Oceanus Hopkins and the newborn Peregrine White, constant reminders of her little boy. The death of young Jasper More may have been more than she could bear. Furthermore, her husband was preoccupied with exploration, and involved in all the important discussion, debates, and decisions.

Like the other wives, Dorothy was left to submissively wait with no say in her own future.

But there is another factor to consider—the debilitating effects of scurvy. Most, if not all, of the *Mayflower* passengers were most likely afflicted with scurvy by the time the ship dropped anchor in Cape Cod Harbor, as Bradford himself recorded. The Pilgrims had gone for months without fresh fruits and vegetables, and so their diets lacked many important vitamins and minerals, among them Vitamin C. A few years later immigrants would be advised to carry "juice of lemons well put up to cure or prevent the scurvy."[51,52]

One of the early symptoms of Vitamin C deficiency is fatigue and a "loss of all strength and spirit." Not surprisingly, considering all the other symptoms of scurvy—bleeding gums and loss of teeth, joint pain, and swelling of limbs to cite a few—deep depression may soon follow.[53]

Facing a very uncertain future, longing for all that has been left behind, and suffering from scurvy, it is plausible that Dorothy Bradford succumbed to despair and quietly climbed over the gunwale and slipped into the dark, cold waters of the Atlantic. If Bradford suspected that Dorothy's death was a suicide, he never expressed those feelings. Given his beliefs, he would have believed the act of suicide to be self-murder in God's eyes. However, it seems reasonable to assume that he may have felt some sense of responsibility and guilt because, as he admitted, wives "must go with their husbands." Bradford may have felt some anger, too, although he never would have admitted it. The plain fact was that the family unit was essential to the plan for Plymouth, and now Bradford was without a family.[54]

Whatever the cause of Dorothy's death, any excitement Bradford might have felt for the adventure must have been diminished as the reality and the enormity of what he had helped design became very clear. Putting his wife's death aside, he reacted as might be predicted by anyone who knew him. He became even more committed (if that were possible) to the Separatists' goals and beliefs, throwing himself completely into the building of the colony. Bradford's commitment would never waiver.

A Site Is Chosen

On December 16, the *Mayflower* sailed into Plymouth Harbor and dropped anchor. The bay, the Pilgrims remarked, "is a most hopeful place, full of delicious fowl, fish, mussels, crabs and lobsters." The next day was the Sabbath, so no work was permitted.[55]

On Monday, December 18, the male colonists went "a-land with the master of the ship and three or four of the sailors." They were delighted with what they found, including fruit trees and plenty of herbs. "Here is sand, gravel, and excellent clay, no better in the world," they crowed, "excellent for pots, and will wash like soap, and great store of stone, though somewhat soft, and the best water that ever we drank, and the brooks now begin to be full of fish." They spent the night back on the *Mayflower*, "being weary with marching."[56]

The next day, a group again went ashore to explore the land on foot, and along the shore with the shallop. After looking at a second site, three miles up the Jones River (named after the *Mayflower*'s Capt. Jones), they found that area "so full of wood as we could hardly clear so much as to serve us for corn." That night on the ship, they realized that they must make a decision soon because they were running low on supplies. The question arose, should they stay where they were, or look further? They had three sites to choose from: Plymouth, the mouth of the Jones River [today's Kingston], or Clarke's Island. True to their nature, there was undoubtedly much discussion.[57,58]

On the morning of December 20, "after we had called on God for direction, we came to this resolution; to go presently ashore again, and to take a better view of two places, which we thought most fitting for us, for we could not now take time for further search or consideration, our victuals being much spent, especially our beer."[59]

They finally chose the site "on the mainland, on the first place, on a high ground, where there is a great deal of land cleared, and hath been planted with corn three or four years ago, and there is a very sweet brook [that] runs under the hill side, and many delicate springs of as good water as can be drunk, and where we may harbor our shallops and boats exceeding well.... In one field is a great hill on which we point to make a platform and plant our ordnance, which will command all round about.... From thence we may see into the bay, and far into the sea, and we may see thence Cape Cod.... So, there we made our rendezvous and a place for some of our people, about twenty, resolving in the morning to come all ashore and to build houses."[60]

The Pilgrims named the place New Plymouth, and they believed that God had led them to this spot and that they had a divine right to the location. It was obvious that the land had already been farmed by local Native Americans, but any claim they had was ignored and dishonored. The indigenous people, as the Pilgrims saw them, were merely another obstacle set in their path that must be dealt with on their holy quest.

The Pilgrims were apparently unaware that they were not off to a good start with the American Indians. Already they had stolen corn, entered into their homes uninvited, and helped themselves to the owners' belongings. They had desecrated and robbed graves, one of them the grave of a child. They also had demonstrated the power of their weapons, weapons that were far superior to Native Americans' arms. While the Pilgrims assumed correctly that the Natives had been silently watching their every move, they had no idea that they were busy forming their own agenda, planning how they could use these settlers to their own advantage.

By the time Alice Martin and George Clarke were married in 1639, a treaty had been arranged between the Pilgrims and the local Natives. There was always the possibility that something might happen, but the agreement was a strong one and trust existed on both sides. It was peaceful in Plymouth, at least for the time being.

Chapter Eight

Alice Clarke, Wife and Mother
Plymouth Colony, 1643

George and Alice had married in January 1639. Along with settling into their new home, they now needed to prepare for the upcoming planting season. George would have made sure his farm equipment was in good repair and his fields fertilized. Seeds had to be prepared for spring planting: corn kernels scraped from the cobs, wheat and rye threshed and winnowed to separate out the seeds. Alice would have helped George with these tasks, but she also had the household to run. She would soon adopt the same day-to-day recurring routine as other Pilgrim wives. Perhaps in the beginning, in the blush of a new marriage, she would have delighted in her daily activities, performing each task for the first time in her cozy new home, but after a few months the chores would have lost any sense of novelty. Within each new season in Plymouth Colony, George's tasks would vary, while for Alice, every day was very much like the last.

Women and Daily Life in Plymouth

The Pilgrim home was the wife's domain, which she governed with both skill and authority, at least in the absence of her husband. She was responsible for childcare, meal preparation, keeping the home clean and safe, planting and maintaining the kitchen garden, sewing, repairing and cleaning clothes and linens, and much more.

Since there were no children yet in the Clarke household, many chores that would traditionally be assigned to children were likely done by Alice. For example, she would get up before dawn to restart the fire, using pine kindling and hardwood prepared by her husband. She would bring in pails of fresh water from a well or creek and begin to prepare breakfast.

Meanwhile, George would be at work outside, tending to the livestock. Upon returning indoors, he might read a Bible passage and ask for God's blessing on his new family. Their morning meal was probably hasty pudding, a hot cereal of cornmeal mush which was boiled in an iron pot and served with milk or molasses. Or perhaps Alice had made an oatmeal out of "naked oats," also called "silpee ," and boiled milk, sweetened with a little sugar and spice. Then George would head out to work in the fields or to cut wood, hunt deer, or go fishing.[1]

After breakfast Alice would begin to prepare dinner, which was served at around noon and was the principal meal of the day. She might set a stew to simmer over the fire, make some cornbread, and clean some berries. Pompions, or as we know them, pumpkins, were a common side dish. Diced and stewed all day in water over the open fire, they would break down into something resembling baked apples. Served with a little butter, vinegar, and spices, this dish was a nice accompaniment to fish or meat. Alice would then milk the cows or goats, feed the chickens, and work in her kitchen garden of vegetables, herbs and salad greens.[2]

George would come home for dinner and then head out again to work in the fields. Alice might spend her afternoon churning butter or making cheese. She might also be mending and laundering clothes or working in her garden. She knew how to spin and weave, for in 1639 every Plymouth family was required to plant a square rod (about 16'x16') of flax or hemp so they could spin their own yarn and weave it into fabric to make their own clothing. With no access to processed goods, she also needed to produce her own candles and soap.[3]

At the end of the day, supper was usually a light meal of leftovers from breakfast and lunch. After eating and cleaning up, one or both

An evening at home by the fireside.

of them might enjoy smoking tobacco in a clay pipe. Evenings were spent talking together, reading the Bible, or visiting with neighbors. Alice might have mending or embroidery to work on by candlelight. Then it was off to bed.

Surely Alice slept well. Her days were very demanding yet unchanging from one day to the next. Food preparation alone was quite time-consuming in this rural community. For example, corn was a major part of the Pilgrim diet. Housewives could grind the corn themselves, or if they could afford the cost, have it ground for them. In 1637 John Jenney was authorized by the courts to erect a mill, "for grinding and beating of corn." For each bushel he processed he was permitted to charge "a pottle of corn," or about two quarts. It was the wife's responsibility to make the ground corn into mush, bread, or pudding. She grew all their table vegetables in the kitchen garden, such as parsnips, onions, peas, cabbage, and carrots. Alice would make cheese, churn butter, preserve food with salt for storage, ferment ale or cider, and more.[4,5]

Meals were cooked over the hearth in large iron or copper kettles, some holding up to fifteen gallons of water which had to be hauled into the house. Of course, fire was a constant danger, and Alice would have kept a bucket full of water nearby to douse any flyaway sparks. Without indoor plumbing or electricity, doing laundry was a grueling task that took up an entire day. Water needed to be hauled and heated in huge kettles to boil the clothes. To remove stains, the clothes were pounded with mallets, then rinsed, wrung, and finally hung out to dry. Not only was the work physically exhausting, but housewives were also exposed to rough handmade soaps and harsh lye that burned their hands.

No household, however, was expected to be completely self-sufficient, and Plymouth housewives developed informal networks of trade and exchange within the colony. Since the women were engaged in many of the same tasks, they practiced a functional economy of mutual favors, a practical and neighborly female support system, and they visited each other throughout the day. One housewife might need to borrow some domestic item from a neighbor or ask advice for a sick child. Another might offer to swap some of the soap she made for candles her neighbor had crafted.

Visiting a neighbor also provided an opportunity for socializing, exchanging news, and a chance to get out of the house for a welcome break. Social visits also enabled women to monitor each other's behavior, which made for a subtle pressure to conform to community standards. It was each Pilgrim's responsibility to report unlawful behavior or "unclean carriages" to the authorities, and no doubt most of these reports came from concerned—or meddlesome, depending on one's point of view—neighbors who were in the habit of dropping in to borrow something or other.

Market Days and Fairs

Alice must have looked forward to Plymouth's weekly market day. By a law enacted in 1639, every Thursday was set aside for a farmer's market held inside the walls of the Town of Plymouth. Even though attending the market meant an hour's walk, it was a good opportunity for Alice to meet and visit the other colonists and get a break from her daily routines. Anyone who had something to trade or sell, be it eggs, butter, cheese, fish, or chicken, came to town on Thursdays. Someone might have some especially sweet strawberries or more squash than one family could eat. The Pilgrim economy was a barter economy for the most part, so actual coins seldom changed hands; the Pilgrims made informal trades among themselves. Local Native Americans sometimes came to market, bringing their handmade baskets and brooms to trade. Men could enjoy a beer or two together, and children would have the opportunity to play with one another.[6]

Twice a year, colony-wide fairs were held, the last Wednesday in May at the Town of Plymouth and the first Wednesday in October at Duxbury. These gatherings lasted several days and were large, lively affairs. Colonists came from all over Plymouth to trade with each other and to see what the peddlers from Boston had to offer. Goods for sale might be as small as a paper stuck through with pins and needles or as large as a herd of cattle. It was the constable's job to see that people behaved themselves and that no one got drunk or disorderly.[7]

Whenever the community got together, the courts took advantage of the opportunity to administer public punishments. Miscreants were locked into stocks or whipped on market days and, in at least one case, hanged at a harvest fair.

Sabbath in Plymouth Colony

The Pilgrim Sabbath commenced at sundown on Saturday and continued until sundown on Sunday. Sabbath meetings were held in the lower room of the fort, which also served as the courthouse. Usually there were two meetings on Sundays, with prayers and songs and a sermon lasting at least an hour. In prayer, the Separatists raised their heads and open eyes towards the heavens, and following the example of St. Timothy, lifted "up pure hands to God in every place." Ministers endeavored to make their long sermons interesting by using plain language, a moderated speaking style, and judicious hand gestures. They wore dignified dark suits with collars and cuffs of white linen, which drew attention to their faces and hands.[8,9]

Without an ordained minister, the Pilgrims had to do without the sacraments of baptism and the Lord's Supper at Plymouth for the first decade of the colony's existence. William Brewster served as a preacher and was widely loved and respected for his devotion and wisdom, but he was not ordained.[10]

When Governor Winthrop of the Massachusetts Bay Colony visited Plymouth in 1632, he described the services this way: "On the Lord's Day there was a sacrament which they did partake in, and, in the afternoon, Mr. Roger Williams (according to their custom) propounded a question, to which the pastor, Mr. Smith, spoke briefly; then Mr. Williams prophesized, and after the governor of Plymouth spoke to the question; after him the Elder; then some two or three more of the congregation. Then the Elder desired the governor of Massachusetts and Mr. Wilson to speak to it, which they did. When this was ended, the Deacon, Mr. Fuller, put the congregation in mind of their duty of contribution. Whereupon the governor and all the rest went down to the deacon's seat and put into the box, and then returned."[11]

Keeping the Sabbath meant that no work was done, including cooking, and everyone attended church services during the morning and the afternoons. Alice prepared the Sunday meal on Saturday evening, perhaps setting a pot of beans on the fire to bake. Unnecessary travel was restricted, drinking beer or liquor was limited to those who were ill, and "none might smoke within two miles of the meeting house." Breaking the Sabbath was a punishable offence in Plymouth. In June of 1638, Webb Adey was accused of "working upon the Lord's day in his garden . . . in breach of the Sabbath," and sentenced to sit in the stocks. A month later he was again brought before the court for continuing to "profane" the Lord's Day and this time "was censured to be severely whipped at the post."[12]

George Clarke Expands His Holdings

Alice had made a good match, for George Clarke was an ambitious man and a hard worker. Within a year of marriage, on December 15, 1639, he had enlarged his property holdings. Clarke purchased eight acres of land which adjoined his property from William Hoskins, a planter, for eight pounds sterling, payable in "money, corn, or cattle."[13]

This eight-acre plot was the piece formerly owned by Thurston Clarke. On April 2, 1638, the courts had decided that "the land formerly appointed to Thurston Clarke...are now granted to William Hodgkinson [Hoskins]." Apparently, three months earlier Thurston had received a new grant for forty acres "at the southwest end of Derby's Pond" in Playne Dealing. With the purchase of a plot adjacent to his farm, George Clarke was able to expand his property to eighteen acres.[14,15]

William Bradford may have believed that Plymouth Colony was a religious enterprise devoted to achieving the biblical ideal of a life well lived under God's guidance, but for many of its residents it was all about the land. The governor and his assistants continued to seek an official patent for Plymouth Colony and on January 13, 1630, the Earl of Warwick signed a patent that defined the boundaries of Plymouth Colony and conferred all those lands and the right to govern them to William Bradford personally. The details are murky, many documents are missing, and the legality of this grant has been questioned over the years. The earl had been president of the Council for New England, but it is unclear whether he was acting as a representative of the council when he granted this patent. What is clear is that the Warwick Patent, such as it was, granted the colony to William Bradford, which meant that he could have named himself Lord and Proprietor of Plymouth, entitled to full and private ownership of the entire Colony.

Still, the trustees made up a very powerful body, and by 1639 the freemen began to question the monopoly they held on the granting of land. Grumbling colonists took their complaints to the grand jury, who brought them to the attention of the court on March 5, 1639. "We desire," they demanded, "to be informed by what virtue and power the governor and assistants do give and dispose of lands either to particular persons or townships and plantations." They also wanted to know, they continued, what lands were still to be had, "or is reserved for the purchasers as hath been formerly agreed to in Court, too."[16]

The usual procedure for acquiring new land was to file an

application with the court for a large area, and if the application—and the applicant—was approved, the court would appoint a committee to purchase the land from the Native Americans and obtain a deed. The court would confirm the purchase, and the colony would assume ownership of the territory. The colonists would then apply to the court for grants of land from that purchase.

What the freemen were worried about was the fairness of the land grants. They felt that the original colonists were being favored over the next generation in the granting of land. Those born in Plymouth, they believed, should have lands set aside for them before any land was given to newcomers from England or anywhere else. Responding to the complaints, William Bradford agreed to surrender the authority granted to him under the Warwick Patent, relinquishing all his governing rights that were therein granted. But first he earmarked several huge tracts of land exclusively for the original purchasers, arguing that they were the real owners of the colony. He still believed, as he had stated years earlier, that the rank and file of Pilgrims could participate in the government "only in some weighty matters, when we think good." Control over the colony was still very much an issue, but it was becoming more evident that as the colony matured and expanded, the government needed to evolve with it.[17]

No matter how much land he owned, however, George Clarke's ultimate goal was to have children. This was, in fact, the goal of every Pilgrim family. "God, that made all things good, and blessed them," wrote John Robinson, "imparted expressly this blessing first to his creatures, capable thereof, that they should increase and multiply in their kind." As George and Alice Clarke went about the work of building and maintaining their farm and home, they waited eagerly for God to bless them with a child.[18]

Pilgrim Pregnancy

After about three years of marriage, Alice Clarke became pregnant. In Plymouth Colony the average time between marriage and the birth of the first child was about fifteen months, so it is possible that

Alice had an earlier pregnancy that failed, but there is no evidence to support this. Alice may have conceived in the spring because there seemed to be a seasonal rhythm to the arrival of children in the rural American colonies.

According to a seventeenth-century midwives' book, a woman could be fairly certain she had conceived if "she feel the womb shut close" after her husband's ejaculation, and "the pleasure she takes at that time is extraordinary." Other signs would be that "her monthly terms stop," "her breasts swell and grow round," and "she so much loatheth her victuals, that let her but exercise her body a little in motion, and she will cast off [vomit] what lieth upon her stomack."[19]

A married Pilgrim woman's pregnancy was typically a welcomed event. As her pregnancy progressed, she would begin to let out the drawstrings of her skirt and petticoat waists. Alice Clarke would have received lots of advice from her friends, who might tell her she must "observe some good rules beforehand, that when her time of delivery is at hand, she may more easily undergo it, and not so soon miscarry." She would be told that "fasting starves the child, [yet] too much eating and drinking will stifle it; great heats or baths, or stoves, [can cause] the child to press for a more free air, and great cold is not good for it, all immoderate exercises, passions, desires, longings, falls, strokes, and all violent running, leaping, coughing, lifting and such like" could bring about a miscarriage. It was believed that if a woman does not take "tender care over herself when she is with child," and a miscarriage occurs, she "makes [her] self guilty of that miscarriage."[20,21]

An expectant mother may have been advised to drink every morning "a good draught of Sage Ale [a type of strong beer], because it makes the uterus stronger. She also might eat "meats and drink such things as nourish well," including "roasted apples…with sugar in the morning" to keep "her body loose."[22]

As the time of her delivery became more imminent, Alice no doubt became most anxious. She had already witnessed many childbirths as part of her training and may have even seen a woman die during delivery. In Plymouth, approximately one birth in thirty resulted in the death of the mother. Because of the high birthrate, one woman out of five in Plymouth Colony would die in childbirth, and one in ten newborns would not survive.[23]

The religious culture also conditioned women to fear childbirth. Cotton Mather advised expectant women that they ought to know "your Death has entered into you, and you may have conceived that which determines but about nine months at the most, for you to live in the world. Preparation for death is that most reasonable and most seasonable thing, to which you must now apply yourself."[24] John Robinson, the Pilgrim pastor, warned that children "are a blessing great, but dangerous. ... [an infant's] first day of being in the world, being often her last in it."[25] The Massachusetts Bay poet, Anne Bradstreet, filled with dread about her upcoming delivery, wrote these words to her husband:

> How soon, my Dear, death may my steps attend,
> How soon't may be thy lot to lose thy friend.[26]

As was the custom at the time, Alice would choose the women she wished to attend her during her labor, those she most loved and trusted. There is no record of an official midwife at Plymouth at the time, but there may have been women particularly adept at delivering babies, perhaps an older woman who had many children of her own and had assisted others during their labors. Whomever Alice chose, no men would be included. They may have had authority over the church and the government, but the realm of childbirth belonged exclusively to women.

As soon as she felt the first cramps of labor, Alice would have sent her husband to gather her friends around her. She would have been advised to "walk easily in her Chamber, and then again lie down, keep herself warm, rest herself and then stir again, till she feels the waters coming down and the womb to open."[27]

She may have labored in the main room of the Clarke home, a room large enough to accommodate all the women who would be there to help during the delivery and Alice's lying-in. They would have built a fire in the fireplace, boiled water, wrapped Alice in warm blankets, and gathered together warm cloths and coverlets for the baby. Her friends no doubt prepared food and drink for Alice and themselves to keep up everyone's strength. Warm cloths might have been applied to her abdomen to ease the discomfort.

In a healthy delivery, a woman would have labored on her back, with pillows under her head and back and buttocks, "her thighs and knees wide open asunder, her legs must be bowed backwards toward her buttocks and drawn upwards, her heels and soles of her feet must be fixed against a board to that purpose laid cross her bed." Her attendants would lift her upper body as she pushed against the board during contractions, "that she may with more ease force the child forth." If the labor was especially long and tiring, the mother could be fed "some chickens broth or the yolk of a poached egg, with a little bread, or some wine, or strong water, but moderately taken." Her birth canal may have been greased, "anointed...with ducks grease, or oil of lilies, or sweet almonds, or such things as may smooth the passage and ease woman's labor."[28]

The women surrounding Alice would have been attentive and supportive. That was their role. According to *The Birth of Mankind* (first published in 1545), the role of the midwife was to "instruct and comfort the party, not only refreshing her with good meat and drink, but also with sweet words, giving her hope of a speedy deliverance, encouraging and enstomaking [instructing? comforting?] her to patience and tolerance, bidding her to hold in her breath so much as she may, also striking [stroking] gently with her hands her belly above the navel, for that helpeth to depress the birth downward."[29]

Alice Becomes a Mother

Alice Clarke delivered her first recorded child, whom she and George named Abigail, sometime in 1643. Abigail may have been born during the winter months, but the exact birthdate has been lost to history. The infant would have been carefully attended right after birth. John Robinson warned that children, "come into the world at first with danger...as passing sometimes from the womb to the grave." Abigail would have been examined and washed with warm wine. It was the custom to cut the "navel-string" immediately after birth. Afterward, the child would have been swaddled, making "sure that all parts be bound up in their due place and order gently, without any crookedness, or rugged folding; for infants are tender twigs, and as you use them, so they will grow straight or crooked." The child would be wrapped like this for about four months.[30,31,32,33]

After Abigail was born, Alice would have been washed carefully and her belly rubbed with oil and wrapped with linen bandages. Warm cloths would have been applied to her breasts, and she would have been fed a light meal of broth and perhaps given some spiced wine or ale.

The birth of Abigail Clarke must have been joyous, as both mother and child had survived, and Plymouth Colony had grown by one more resident. All women present would have celebrated a safe delivery with toasts and merrymaking and general relief that all had gone well.

Alice would have been expected to breastfeed her child, rather than put Abigail in the hands of a wet nurse, even if one were available. It was believed that, "children…nursed by their mothers prosper best. Mothers are most tender over them, and cannot endure to let them lie crying out, without taking them up and stilling them; as nurses will let them cry and cry again…."[34]

Baptisms usually took place on the next Sunday following the birth. Since Alice "by reason of her travail and delivery [was] weak," the responsibility to have Abigail baptized fell to George.[35] Alice's lying-in period with a daughter would be forty days; curiously, if she had delivered a son, it would have been thirty days. Her friends would have stayed on for a few days and then checked in on her for several more. They prepared food, performed household tasks, and supplied necessities.[36]

For Alice and her friends, a social childbirth gave them a break from their usual daily routines. With their help, Alice could stay in bed for three or four weeks while they took over running her household. She was, of course, expected to reciprocate when another woman gave birth. In the meantime, she could recuperate and nurse her newborn. Having this time to rest was highly valued. Colonial

Pilgrim mother and infant.

women typically breastfed their babies for at least a year. Should a woman's nipples become chapped during nursing, John Josslyn recommended a compound of "the ashes of the burnt shell [of the land turtle] and the whites of eggs," mixed and applied as needed. Nonetheless, it was believed unlikely that a woman would become pregnant while nursing. But no contraception was used in this society, so Pilgrim births usually occurred fifteen to twenty months apart and most Plyouth women spent their adult lives either pregnant or nursing.[37]

With a supportive husband and friends, a healthy new baby, and a comfortable home, Alice Clarke undoubtedly felt happy and secure in her position in Plymouth Colony. Tragically, all of that would change before too long.

༄༅༄༅༄༅༄

George and Alice Clarke lived in a settled and stable community governed by law and religion. Surely, they had been told of the trials of those who came first, decades earlier, the people who built the colony during that long, frigid first winter, when death had been a constant visitor. Their sacrifice was the fabric of Plymouth's history.

Chapter Nine

Building the Colony

Plymouth Colony, 1620

Getting to Cape Cod—as difficult as it had been—was only the first step in establishing a colony. Shelters had to be built, sources of food found, and peaceful relations with the Natives established. The Pilgrims were miserable, tired and sick, but still they worked. In the rain and snow and bitter cold they labored felling trees, gathering thatch, and hunting the forests for game.

The price paid for Plymouth Colony would be much greater than the debt owed to the London investors. Within a few months, half the Pilgrims would be dead—fifty lives lost, whole families wiped out, children orphaned, spouses widowed, and friends deceased. William Bradford wrote that "they had borne their sad affliction with [as] much patience and contentedness as I think any people could do." Still, it is not hard to imagine that memories of this "starving time" would haunt many of them for many years.[1]

December 1620

Because of the delays at the onset of their voyage, the Pilgrims arrived at Cape Cod just as winter was blowing in, and it was achingly cold. Once they had decided on a site, the immediate task was to begin to move the entire company off the *Mayflower* and onto the shore. Housing was the top priority. There were plenty of forests to provide building materials, but the weather made it impossible for the Pilgrims to get to shore on some days. The *Mayflower* was about a mile and a half out, and the rough, freezing waters made sailing in the shallop both difficult and dangerous.

Furthermore, the colonists, already weak from the long voyage, began to sicken in the wet and raw weather. They were, as Bradford wrote, "infected with the scurvy and other diseases which this long voyage and their inaccommodate condition had brought upon them," Saints (as the Pilgrims sometimes called themselves) and Strangers alike were stricken. "The first who dies in this harbor" was Richard Britteridge, who had joined the group in London. He died on December 21.[2] The next day, Isaac Allerton's wife, Mary, gave birth to a stillborn son, considered an ominous sign by many.[3,4,5,6]

On December 23 the weather quieted, and "so many of us as could, went on shore, felled and carried timber, to provide themselves stuff for building." The next day, while work continued on land, Solomon Martin, Christopher Martin's stepson, died aboard the *Mayflower*. "The first sickness," as William Bradford called it, was just beginning, and things would only get worse—much worse.[7,8]

There wasn't even a Christmas celebration to give them a cheerful break, since the Separatists did not celebrate Christmas. December 25 was just another workday on their calendar, and work they did: "Some [to] fell timber, some to saw, some to rive, and some to carry, so no man rested all that day."[9] Twenty men remained on shore at the construction site, while the rest returned to the *Mayflower*. Celebrating Christmas in his own way, Master Jones treated those on board to a rare ration of beer that night.[10]

On Wednesday, December 27, they "began to erect the first house for use to receive them and their goods." This "common house" was probably an earthfast building, with walls of tree trunks buried in the ground, interwoven with branches and cemented with clay. It was twenty feet square and would take them about two weeks to finish. The roof was made of a thick thatch of reeds and cattails. On December 28 some of the men started working on a wooden platform at the top of the hill. This was to be the site of the fort, where they would mount the cannons they brought with them for protection. That afternoon they laid out the town, one main street running toward the sea from the top of the hill, with houses on both sides.[11]

The family was established early on as the basic unit in the social structure of Plymouth Colony. To simplify things, the Pilgrims divided themselves into nineteen families with a male head-of-household for each, assigning "all single men that had no wives to join with some family, as they thought fit, that so we might build fewer houses." House sites were measured out depending on the size of each family, "to every person half a pole in breadth, and three in length [8.25' x 49.5']" They drew lots for each site, and the properties were staked out.[12]

Creating nineteen "families" was not only a practical solution, but a political one, too. Fewer houses would have to be built initially, and at the same time every colonist was placed under the authority of a male family head. The head of each household answered directly to the governor and his assistants for the behavior of those in his family. Control—that is, Separatist control—was carefully and deliberately instituted in the colony from the very beginning.

While all this planning was going on, the wives and children were still living on board the *Mayflower* and had no opportunity to take part in the decisions being made that would directly affect them. For example, while assigning single males into existing families was practical, having more men added to her household meant that each wife would have to take on extra work once they were all ashore and in their own houses. If the colony's leaders didn't realize the full effect of that decision initially, they soon would when they had—so unexpectedly—a revolt on their hands.

No work was done on December 29 or the next day because of the weather: "We fitted ourselves for our labor, but our people on shore were much troubled and discouraged with rain and wet, that day being very stormy and cold." Off in the distance they could see smoke from the Native American's fires. The colonists were being watched.[13]

January 1621

Early in January, the Pilgrims began to realize just how unprepared they were to build their colony. All along they had planned to support themselves by fishing, even though they lacked any experience in that industry. While the fish were plentiful, they discovered that the hooks they brought with them were too large to catch the smaller fish that filled the bay. Master Jones stepped in to help and set out with his crew on the shallop. They were able to catch three seals and a cod, "which did assure us that we should have plenty of fish shortly."[14]

Back on the *Mayflower*, more and more of the passengers began to "grow ill of grievous colds, from the great and many hardships they had endured." Next to die was Degory Priest, a forty-one-year-old hatter who had left a wife and two daughters in Leiden. On Saturday, January 6, Christopher Martin was near death, and Governor John Carver was brought back to the ship the next morning to speak with him about the accounts. The contentious Martin died two days later on January eighth.[15,16,17,18]

By January 9, the weather had cleared, and planning and building resumed. Before working on individual homes, the men worked on the "common house," which would be used as a storehouse by everyone for their belongings until the private houses were finished. It still needed plastering and more thatch for the roof, but due to the weather they could only work three or four days each week. Even though unfinished, the building was quickly put to use as a sick bay. William Bradford "was vehemently taken with a grief and pain…it was doubted that he would have instantly died." He grew better by night, "through God's mercy," but remained bedfast in the common house, suffering from a cold and pains in his ankles and "hucklebone" [hip bone].[19]

Bradford and John Carver were both sick and in bed in the common house when a spark from their small fire caught in the thatched roof, which quickly was engulfed with flames. The entire building was destroyed in a matter of minutes. While they escaped physical harm, they lost all their bedding and clothes, necessary and irreplaceable items. The loss of the common house and all the work which had gone into building it was a terrible blow to the Pilgrims. It was also terrifying for those aboard the *Mayflower* who saw the flames and feared the worst—that the Indians had attacked the men, killing them all and setting fire to everything.

Tuesday through Friday, January 16 through 18, "were very fair sunshiny days, as if it had been in April." and on Sunday, January 21, the colonists held their first Sabbath meeting on land at Plymouth Colony in their rebuilt little common house. When the Pilgrim women and children saw their new homes still under construction, there may have been some disappointment. The first homes were probably merely temporary huts with mud plastered over small saplings, crude dwellings designed for temporary residence.[20]

By the end of the month, in spite of the bone-chilling cold, the colonists were able to load some of their common goods into both the longboat and the shallop and haul them to shore. Work was progressing, but the weather was brutal, and anxiety ran high. American Indians were sighted "on the island near our ship," but no contact was made. Aboard the *Mayflower*, sickness continued to plague the Pilgrims. Rose Standish, the wife of Capt. Standish, succumbed to the sickness and died on January 29. In all, eight members of the party had died that month.[21]

February 1621

An immense storm hit Cape Cod Bay on Sabbath Day, February 4, "with the greatest gusts of wind that ever we had since we came forth." The gales endangered the *Mayflower* because most of the Pilgrims' belongings had been moved to shore and the ship was lighter and more buoyant. Without the weight of their supplies to stabilize her, she heaved and pitched in the winds, making things even more miserable for the sick Pilgrims still remaining on board. Things weren't much better on shore; some of the "daubing," the mud that was applied so carefully to the walls of the huts, had washed off in the storm.[22]

The presence of Natives watching them from their hiding places in the woods continued to concern the colonists. Attempts to make contact with them had been unsuccessful, and the anxious Pilgrims decided it was time to fortify the colony and "establish military orders among ourselves." Myles Standish was officially given command of military affairs. On February 21, the shipmaster and many of his sailors carried ashore a heavy cannon capable of firing a four-pound shot. All joined in to tug it to the top of the hill, and then three smaller cannons were installed at the bottom of the hill.[23]

The dying continued. Among the first features of Plymouth Plantation would be a cemetery. By the end of February, noted William Bradford, "seventeen of our number die." Among the dead was Mary Allerton, Isaac Allerton's wife, perhaps not having fully recovered since the still-birth two months earlier. The colonists' numbers had been reduced by nearly a third.[24]

March 1621

On March 3, the weather showed signs of spring: "the morning misty, but towards noon warm and fair...the birds sang in the woods most pleasantly." Yet "at one of the clock," as if to remind the colonists of their precarious situation, there were "strong and great claps" of thunder. Still, the Pilgrims were beginning to feel at home. They had found "the great ponds, which seem to be excellent fishing-places." Also, they began to put down roots, literally: "This day some garden seeds were sown."[25]

On March 16 the colonists were astonished to receive a visitor. A Native American appeared out of the woods and walked confidently into the colony: "There presented himself a savage, which caused an alarm. He very boldly came all alone, and along the houses straight to the rendezvous." His boldness may have surprised them, but the fact that he greeted them in English dumfounded them. Nearly naked, "only a leather about his waist, with a fringe about a span long, the "savage" declared "Welcome Englishmen!"[26,27]

His name was Samoset, and "he was not of these parts, but belonged to the eastern parts where some English ships came to fish, with whom he was acquainted and...amongst whom he had got his language." Actually Samoset was an Algonquian sagamore, a lesser tribal chief, from what is now the state of Maine. The colonists met with him, asking about "the people here, of their names, number and

Samoset's surprising visit.

strength, of their situation and distance from this place, and who was chief amongst them."[28]

Samoset "became profitable to them," Bradford noted, no doubt attributing the Native American's surprising appearance among them to God's Providence, and never doubting the remarkable coincidence. As much as they appreciated his help, they still regarded him as a savage: "Saturday, in the morning we dismissed the savage, and gave him a knife, a bracelet, and a ring."[29,30]

What the Pilgrims had not realized was that Samoset had been carefully selected by the Natives as an ambassador to open relations between them. Apparently, they felt that the meeting had been successful, for a few days later their "great Sachem, called Massasoit" came to visit Plymouth. Massasoit was the leader of the Wampanoag Tribe, who had been watching the Pilgrims since they arrived. Along with him came Squanto, another English-speaking Native. Gifts were exchanged, "friendly entertainment" was enjoyed, and—to everyone's credit—a peace agreement was approved.[31]

The terms of the agreement were four: First, that neither Massasoit nor any of his people would do harm to any of the colonists; second, that if anyone did harm them, Massasoit would see that the offender was turned over to the Pilgrims for punishment; third, that if anything was stolen by the colonists it would be returned, and the Native Americans would do likewise. The fourth and last term was probably what the Indians were after all along, an alliance based on protection against their enemies: "If any did unjustly war against him [Massasoit], they [the Pilgrims] would aid him; if any did war against them, he should aid them." The Wampanoag had learned very soon after the *Mayflower* arrived in Cape Cod that the colonists had powerful weapons that were superior to bows and arrows; thus, an alliance with the Pilgrims would give the tribe an advantage over their enemies.[32] The meeting and treaty with Massasoit may have been the first time the Pilgrims realized there were many distinct groups among the American Indians, many different tribes with their own leaders and objectives.

The treaty was a major achievement for the Pilgrims, but it could not stop the dying. On March 24, Elizabeth Winslow, wife of Edward Winslow, succumbed aboard the *Mayflower*. By now the illness had spread to the crew and would take half of them before they sailed back to England. One of the crew died cursing his wife, "saying if it had not been for her he had never come [on] this unlucky voyage." Calling this an "unlucky voyage" was an understatement. March had been a horrible month. "This month," wrote Nathaniel Morton, "thirteen of our number die." Nearly half of their party had been lost. On some days two or three persons died, and of the original hundred, "scarce fifty remained."[33,34]

Things were so bad that at one point there were only six or seven persons who were well enough to tend to the others, "fetched them wood, made them fires, dressed them meat, made their beds, washed their loathsome clothes, clothed and unclothed them. In a word, did all the homely and necessary offices for them which dainty and queasy stomachs cannot endure to hear named, and all this willingly and cheerfully." Bradford cites William Brewster and Myles Standish as among the caregivers, "unto whom myself and many others were much beholden in our low and sick condition." Not only were they caring for the sick, they were also burying the dead secretly at night so that the Indians would not realize how many of their number had been lost.[35]

Those losses were indeed significant. Of the original twenty-six heads of families, only twelve survived; only four of the unattached men remained; and all but a few of the single women died. Only five of the married women survived; only three married couples remained. Whole families had been wiped out. Three of the four More orphans had perished. Nonetheless, compared to adult deaths, losses among the children were slight. None of the Pilgrims' seven daughters died, and only three of the thirteen sons succumbed. Children who had lost their parents were assigned to new families.

Following the Old-Style calendar, the grieving colonists observed the beginning of the New Year on March 25, and the event caused William Bradford to pause, reflect on the past year and, ever optimistic and trusting in Divine Providence, speak to the future. "The spring now approaching, it pleased God the mortality began to cease amongst them, and the sick and lame recovered apace, which put as [it] were new life into them, and contentedness as I think any people could do. But it was the Lord which upheld them, and had beforehand prepared them; many having long borne the yoke, yea from their youth." They held elections, and John Carver was reelected governor for the New Year.[36]

April 1621

By April all of her passengers had finally disembarked from the *Mayflower*. It had been eight months since the ship had departed from Leiden. It had remained at Plymouth because of the bad weather and the lowly condition of the colonists. But concern for the well being of the Pilgrims was not the only reason the *Mayflower* had stayed for so long. The ship's crew had been hit with the same sickness that plagued the colonists, many of the "ablest of them" had died, and "of the rest many lay sick and weak." As Bradford put it, "The master durst not put to sea till he saw his men begin to recover, and the heart of winter over."[37,38]

Delaying its departure until the colonists were at least somewhat settled on shore, the *Mayflower* set sail for England on April 5, but undoubtedly not before gathering letters to deliver

Pilgrims watching the Mayflower *sail.*

to investors and friends. None of the colonists sailed back to England on the *Mayflower*. All who were left alive decided to stay. The *Mayflower* would make the crossing in only one month, arriving in England on May 6, 1621.

The ship had served not only as a transport to North America; it had been a floating home for the families of the men on shore and an infirmary for the sick and dying. For nearly seven months the women and children lived on board in close and damp conditions. How they kept the children entertained and out of mischief is nowhere recorded, but at least one prank almost sank the entire venture—literally.

On December 5, 1620, Francis Billington, who was about fourteen years old, had been relegated to living aboard the *Mayflower* while the colony was being laid out. He somehow escaped adult supervision and got hold of a musket, which he accidentally set off in his family's cabin. The blast nearly ignited a nearby barrel of gunpowder, which could have blown up the entire ship along with all on board. The Billingtons were already known as a contentious family—Bradford called them "one of the profanest families amongst them"— and this prank did nothing to endear them to their fellow colonists. Not surprisingly, Francis was immediately reassigned to the men on shore, where he could be carefully supervised.[39]

As they watched the *Mayflower* sail away, the Pilgrims had little time for sorrow, regret, sentimentality, or even reflection. There was still so much work to do. Their survival depended on moving forward, even if their hearts were heavy. With Squanto's help and advice, they planted the fields with corn, barley, and peas. Only the corn produced a successful crop, the other "came not to good, either by the badness of the seed or lateness of the season or both, or some other defect."[40]

The work was hard. After so much cold and wet weather, the days turned uncomfortably hot. In mid-April Governor John Carver "came out of the field very sick. …He complained very greatly of his head and lay down, and within a few hours his senses failed, so as he never spake more till he died, which was within a few days after." Governor Carver's death, probably due to sunstroke, was a huge loss to the group, and "was much lamented and caused a great heaviness amongst them." Within six weeks, his wife Katherine had also died.[41]

Shortly after Carver's burial, elections were held to replace him, and William Bradford was unanimously chosen governor. Bradford's commitment to the original Separatist ideals was solid and unwavering. He had been mentored by William Brewster and was one of the original members of the seminal Scrooby congregation. He had left his birth family and his home in England, had lost his wife to a mysterious death, which had left his son motherless and virtually fatherless, all in pursuit of the Separatist utopia. He was a widower and, with no children with him in Plymouth, a man whose focus would be the business of the colony, rather than family responsibilities. His election also meant that absolute leadership and power would stay with the Leiden Separatists, assuring that their goals would remain paramount. Bradford, however, was still ill, so Isaac Allerton was appointed as his assistant. Allerton was also a Separatist widower. He had two daughters: Mary, who was about five, and Remember, who was approximately seven years old.

The work of building a colony continued, and on May 12 the first wedding in Plymouth was celebrated: "The first marriage of this place is of Mr. Edward Winslow to Mrs. Susanna White." Mrs. Elizabeth Winslow had died only eight weeks before, on March 24; William White, Susanna's spouse, had died on February 21. Whether they married for love or companionable convenience is not known. As was the custom in Holland, the marriage was performed by the magistrate, perhaps William Bradford, "as being a civil thing, upon which many questions about inheritances do depend. . .and no where in the Gospel to be laid on the ministers as a part of their office."[42,43]

After all they had been through, it is not surprising that tempers would flare, and on June 18, Edward Doty and Edward Leister, both servants to Stephen Hopkins, fought "the first duel in New England." One armed with a sword and one with a dagger, both ended up injured, one in the hand and one in the thigh. The "whole company," desiring to quash dueling as a way to settle differences in Plymouth, decided they must be punished, bound head and feet together, "and so to lie for twenty-four hours, without meat or drink." However, they were released by the governor after only an hour, "because of their great pains, and their own master's humble request, upon promise of better carriage."[44]

At this time the plantation was governed informally and pragmatically. Bradford was their leader and made important decisions, but he consulted with others and took their advice. This system was both practical and fair, given their confidence in William Bradford and the small size of the community. Duels notwithstanding, by the summer season life had settled into a routine in Plymouth. Things were going well. After all the challenges and suffering of the winter and the gentle but uncertain promises of the spring, Bradford wrote with no little appreciation, "All the summer there was no want." It was time to strengthen relations with the Wampanoag.[45]

Summer 1621

In July, with Squanto as their guide, Edward Winslow and Stephen Hopkins set out to meet Massasoit and his people, who lived about forty miles from Plymouth. What they found was a "sad spectacle to behold." The Wampanoag had not yet recovered from a "wasting plague" that had killed thousands of them three years before. So weak were the people that bodies still had not been buried, "their skulls and bones were found in many places lying still above the ground where their houses and dwellings had been...."[46]

Winslow and Hopkins learned more about the Wampanoags on this visit. The Narragansett, who lived on the other side of the bay, were the enemies of Massasoit. They were "a strong people and many in number, living compact together, and had not been at all touched with this wasting plague." They also learned about a recent conference of the Indians called by Massasoit, a three-day meeting where "all the noted powaws [priests] in the country" got together. The Pilgrims assumed that the purpose of the gathering was to summon devils against them, but they believed that since they were under God's protection, the devils refused to cooperate, forcing the Native Americans to acknowledge that "that they could not hinder those people from their becoming the owners and masters of the country." "God had convinced [them]," the Pilgrims assumed, "that there was no enchantment or divination against such a people."[47,48]

However, considering the surprising coincidences of two English-speaking Natives appearing in Plymouth, this three-day meeting may have had a completely different agenda. It is possible that the various factions under Massasoit's leadership had gathered to discuss how to deal with the colonists, that is, how to turn this situation to their own advantage. The first step would have been to establish communication. It is most likely that both Samoset and Squanto had been summoned by Massasoit to serve as interpreters and diplomats. If so, their clever plan worked, as the last item in the treaty proves. Should the Narragansett attack them, Massasoit and his people would have allies armed with superior weapons.

Fences had been somewhat mended with the Nauset, a tribe of American Indians who lived south of Plymouth, the ones whose corn had been stolen during the first explorations of the cape. One day young John Billington, older brother of Francis (who nearly blew up the *Mayflower*), had wandered off from Plymouth and became lost. "At length he light on an Indian plantation twenty miles south of this place, called Manomet; they conveyed him further off, to Nauset among those people that had before set upon the English when they were coasting whilst the ship lay at the Cape."[49]

Massasoit led negotiations with the Nausets for John Billington's return. When the Nausets accompanied the boy back to Plymouth, the Pilgrims were able to make good on their promise and repay them for the corn they stole during their first expedition on land: They "gave full satisfaction to those whose corn they had found and taken when they were at Cape Cod." At least one of their debts had been repaid. Feeling very thankful for all they had accomplished, the Pilgrims planned a day of celebration.[50]

The First Thanksgiving

Bradford recorded that by the fall harvest in 1621 the colonists had "well recovered in health and strength and had all things in good plenty." Plymouth Colony was a tidy community of about fifty colonists, who lived in seven private houses. There were also four buildings for communal use. Twenty acres had been planted in "Indian corn," which, "God be praised," did very well. Six additional acres had been sowed with "barley and peas." They had plenty of fish and fowl. They also had a stable government and enjoyed good relations with the local tribes.[51,52]

After the crops were harvested, "our governor sent four men on fowling, that so we might…rejoice together after we had gathered the fruit of our labors." This was the simple plan for what turned out to be one of the most famous dinner parties in American history.[53]

During the gathering, according to Edward Winslow, the Pilgrims fired their weapons in celebration, "exercised our arms." The gunshots must have attracted the Wampanoag, "many of the Indians coming amongst us," who arrived to investigate the commotion. It was, after all, part of their peace agreement that should the Pilgrims be attacked, the Wampanoag would come to help fight, and the Pilgrims would do likewise. Seeing it was a celebration, however, the Wampanoag sent for "their greatest king Massasoit" to join the party,

Day of Thanksgiving.

as did ninety of his men. The guests stayed for three days. When the food ran low, the tribe's hunters "went out and killed five deer, which they brought to the plantation and bestowed on our governor, and upon the captain and others."[54]

It is not certain from either William Bradford's or Edward Winslow's records of the event whether the Wampanoag were invited to join in the celebration beforehand or after they arrived, attracted by the gunfire. Surely, Bradford would have considered it rude not to invite them once they appeared. This unanticipated increase in the number of guests (more than double) would have been handled with quiet courtesy and grace. Both Pilgrim men and women would have participated in providing hospitality. William Gouge wrote that both husband and wife should participate in "giving entertainment" to visitors. "It is more fit," he wrote, that the husband "take order for the provision of things without doors," leaving "the smaller things within doors" to the wife. The husbands would have taken charge of outdoor grilling, and the wives would have provided side dishes of fruits, nuts, and vegetables.[55]

Everyone was very optimistic about relations with the Wampanoag. "We have found the Indians very faithful in their covenant of peace with us, very loving and ready to pleasure us. ... We often go to them, and they come to us...." It was the Wampanoag who first sighted another ship on the horizon and alerted the Pilgrims.[56]

The Fortune Arrives

On November 9, 1621, the *Fortune* sailed into Plymouth harbor loaded with thirty-five passengers, all of whom were ready to become Plymouth's newest residents. Thomas Weston had sent them, hoping to increase the colony's population, and consequently his own profit. But these were not the kind of people the Pilgrims wanted in Plymouth, "for most of them were lusty young men and many of them wild enough." They were not religious-minded and there were only a few family groups among the lot. Furthermore, they came very poorly prepared, dressed in thin, cheap suits, and bringing "not so much as a biscuit-cake." On their first night in Plymouth, the Fortune's would-be colonists even managed to increase their number by one when the widow Ford gave birth to a son.[57,58]

Thomas Weston had sent the Pilgrims a letter on the *Fortune*, which was about as well received as the new recruits. In it he complained that the *Mayflower* had returned to England empty and that the merchants had not yet received any return on their investment in Plymouth Colony. He wrote, "I know your weakness was the cause of it," but added unkindly, "I believe more weakness of judgment than weakness of hands." Stung, Bradford wrote back, "to be greatly blamed for not freighting the [*Mayflower*] both indeed [does] go near us and much discourage us." He adds, "we were not negligent. But it pleased God to visit us then with death daily, and with so general a disease that the living were scarce able to bury the dead, and well not in any measure sufficient to tend the sick." Furthermore, he wrote, the people you sent on the *Fortune*, "would bring famine" among the Pilgrims if more supplies are not sent soon.[59]

This was not an exaggeration on Bradford's part. The newcomers were assigned to the existing family groups, into the now eight existing houses, adding an average of four more people to each family. Everyone's food allotments were cut in half to accommodate the new arrivals, "one as well as another, which began to be hard, but they bore it patiently under hope of supply [from England]."[60]

※※※※

Plymouth was a different place twenty-three years later, when the little Clarke family had their own house and farm. The colony had grown, food was plentiful, and their diets were more varied. But what didn't change was that they still had to work hard for every mouthful. They were barely getting by. Theirs was a subsistence economy; if they didn't grow it, they didn't eat. Under these circumstances, the colonists' faith in God's blessings and the comfort they took in their familiar routines was probably what saved and sustained them.

Chapter Ten

The Clarke Family in Plymouth
Plymouth Colony, 1644

By 1644, two years after Abigail's birth and right on Pilgrim schedule, baby Martha joined the family. In many ways, the Clarkes were very typical of the households in Plymouth Colony. They were a nuclear family consisting of an adult couple and their children. Though Alice had her own areas of competency and authority, George was the undisputed head of the household. Plymouth's patriarchal families were the foundation of social order and control in the colony. It was within the family unit that the laws of God and government and the expectations of this culture were taught and enforced.

Both husband and wife were expected to be industrious, but as with virtually everything else in the colony, farming and homemaking activities were endowed with larger importance, with divine implications. The husbandman, for example, was believed to be the "master of the earth, turning sterility and barrenness into fruitfulness and increase." God has especially blessed him, "for his labors of all others are most excellent."[1]

Perhaps predictably, George continued to have his differences with the combative Edward Doty. On February 1, 1642, Doty had prevailed in a lawsuit against George Clarke, and Clarke was ordered to pay four bushels of his Indian corn to Doty "upon the difference now depending betwixt them." Whatever the issue was, the two must have set aside their disagreement for the good of the community. In February of 1643, by court order they worked together to set wolf traps, along with Mr. Coombs, Mr. Lee, Francis Billington, and John Shaw.[2,3]

Separatist Attitudes Toward Children

Other than in exceptional cases of abuse or neglect, there is little direct information in the Plymouth Colony records about what it was like to be a child there. Children could not record their own experiences, and evidently neither did their mothers. Nonetheless, certain attitudes about children prevailed in Plymouth. William Bradford had in his personal library a copy of *Domesticall Duties* by William Gouge, as well as John Robinson's writings. Without doubt, given how influential the governor was, their ideas on parenting would have influenced the colony's culture.

Gouge describes childhood as that time "from his birth to 14 years." The primary duties of the parents were to supply their children with food, clothing, recreation, and care when they were sick. They also needed to "feed [them] in discipline." The Separatists were very good at teaching their children self-control. They believed that if parents, especially mothers, were too lenient with their children, God might take the child to punish them.[4]

The first year of a Pilgrim child's life was probably spent in relative comfort and peace. They were, of course, most influenced by their mothers, "not only because they suck their milk," Robinson frankly wrote, "but in a sort, their manners also, by being continually with them and receiving their first impressions from them." Since childhood illnesses were quite common and often fatal, babies were carefully cared for, kept warm, and protected; however, it was determined that somewhere between one and two years of age, the "mother's indulgence" needed to be eased off and the child's indoctrination into "proper Christian walking" begun.[5]

Robinson advised that at birth there is in all children "a stubbornness and stoutness of mind arising from natural pride, which must, in the first place be broken and beaten down." A child's natural instinct to exert his will, he continues, which is "the fruit of natural corruption and [the] root of actual rebellion both against God and man, must be destroyed." The foundation of a child's education must be laid in "humility and tractableness," so that "other virtues may in their time, be built thereon."[6]

For the "beating and keeping down of this stubbornness," Robinson advised that a child's will must be "restrained and repressed." It is best, in fact, if children "not know, if it could be kept from them, that they have a will in their own, but in their parents' keeping." Children must be trained that they may say the words, "'I will' or 'I will not,'" only in consent to a command.[7]

Corporal punishment in child rearing was instilled in the Pilgrim culture. To make children "tractable," Robinson insisted, to make them controllable, "children need the severe discipline of the rod." "Foolishness is bound up in the heart of a child," John Robinson advised, "which the rod of correction must drive out." Plymouth Colony respected and supported the authority of parents over their children and tended to accept a level of physical discipline that today would be considered abusive. The most common form of punishment was hitting the child with a "rod," often just a tied bundle of birch twigs.[8]

Children must be raised, Robinson recommended, to follow a "course in life" at the "same rather under than above their estate." All desires for "commodities" and any aspirations towards individual achievements must be suppressed by parents. Instead, children should be raised with a "meanness in all things," in a simple, common lifestyle, as with "a plain and homely diet."[9]

Parents were warned not to coddle their children, not to be too prideful in them, and not to favor one child over the others, for "sometimes the Lord takes away such before the rest, to punish the father's fondness." The problem, Robinson warned, is that parents who are too "partial" to their own children, think they're "better than they are. …This partiality in many is so gross as they not only deem small good things in them, great, and great evils small."[10]

The entire community was expected to watch over each other's parenting practices. Children who misbehaved were assumed to be the products of poor parenting. Robinson cautioned that, "as we judge of the plant or graft, by the stock whence it was taken,…so do we of children by their parents, till coming to years of discretion they choose their own way." Parents who rejected community standards risked the wrath of God and endangered their children's lives. The Lord "promises and affords long life to such as honor father and mother," Robinson wrote. "On the other side, he cuts off from the earth stubborn and disobedient children suddenly and in sundry ways."[11]

Even Robinson had to admit that the parental responsibilities he described were enormous. Children have no idea of the "careful thoughts, sorrows and fears, and sore pains withal of their parents," he wrote, and appreciate them only when they become parents themselves.[12]

Displays of Anger

As an essential part of their upbringing, Pilgrim children were taught very early to control any impulses towards anger. Any effort a child made to assert his own will would have been immediately and harshly met with physical discipline. Self-assertion was not tolerated because it led to anger, and the emotion of anger was disapproved of in Plymouth for both children and adults. "Anger," wrote Robinson, "hath always evil in it.... If a wrathful man saw himself in a glass, when his fit is upon [him]; his eyes burning, his lips fumbling, his face pale, his teeth gnashing, his mouth foaming, and other parts of his body trembling, and shaking...he would and worthily loathe himself." He would be "terrified at the sight of so hideous a monster." "Be like Caesar," he added, who did "not speak anything in anger till he had said over the Greek alphabet." Do not take "liberty to be a little angry at trifles,...and avoid occasions of provocation whether persons or things."[13]

Generally speaking, children were expected to act like miniature adults from a very early age, probably by six or seven years old, their desires, aspirations, and emotions firmly under control. After infancy, they were even dressed like their parents. Abigail and Martha would have worn caps over their hair, and their clothing would have been layers of shifts, petticoats, and skirts, just like their mother's. Shifts were undergarments worn next to the skin. They were made of a coarse linen, flax or hemp, and were part of the Pilgrims' regime of body care. Bathing in water had declined in the seventeenth century and cleanliness was achieved with wiping or rubbing the skin. It was believed that a shift would buff the skin and remove dirt and perspiration. Shifts were periodically laundered.[14]

No special allowance was made for children to act "childish." When they attended church services with their parents, they were expected to sit quietly through long hours of preaching without fidgeting. Like their parents, children were expected to be productive and contribute to the work of the household. Boys would go out into the fields with their fathers, and girls would help their mothers with cooking and household chores. There were no formal schools at Plymouth during its early years, and any education they received was conducted at home. They were expected to listen quietly as their fathers read from the Scriptures.

The main responsibility for raising children who lived up to the Pilgrim ideal would have been the mother's, since the children were in her care for most of the day. And everyone was watching to see if she was doing it right. This must have been stressful enough, but for Alice Clarke things were to become even more difficult.

The Death of George Clarke

Sometime between August of 1643, when George Clarke was listed in the militia as one of the "males that are able to bear arms from sixteen years old to sixty years, within the several townships," and December of 1644, when Alice remarried, Alice Clarke's husband died. A single line drawn through his name is the only record we have of George Clarke's death. It is not even clear if he lived to see the birth of his second daughter, Martha, who was born sometime in 1644.[15]

It is also not known how he died. There was no investigation into his death, so it probably did not occur under suspicious circumstances. He may have succumbed to a quick illness or may have been injured in an accident. George Clarke left no will, which indicates that his death may have been sudden, since it was the custom in Plymouth for a man foreseeing his death to write a will providing for his wife and children. It was also the law that an inventory of his belongings be made with values attached and presented to the governor. Curiously, there is no such record of an inventory for George Clarke.

George Clarke's burial would have been very simple. His body would have been wrapped in a shroud, and he may or may not have been placed in a wooden coffin. There may have been a marker, but no original Plymouth Colony grave markers have survived. Alice may have gone to stay with family or friends during her mourning period. As part of their caretaker role, Pilgrim wives were expected to tend to others in need, but that was only a temporary solution. Alice Clarke was left with a toddler and a newborn to care for, farm crops and animals that required daily attention, and financial obligations and responsibilities to met. She would have little time to mourn.

Widows in Plymouth Colony

A woman's accepted role in Plymouth was that of wife and mother. Through no fault of their own, widows, therefore, posed a problem for the community. Pilgrim widows had the responsibilities, and some of the freedoms, of both husband and wife, but were no longer subject to the daily control of a male. A widow could, in fact, assume a position of control herself as she took over the management of her deceased husband's estate, his money, his land, and other resources.

When a woman in England was widowed, by law she was entitled to a third of her husband's estate during her lifetime, but everything else would go to her eldest son, and she would be left dependent upon his generosity. English women could not own land, houses, or goods in their own names. However, inheritance laws in Plymouth Colony were more favorable to women. Separatist women had experienced the same ordeals as their husbands and fathers during their journey to the New World. The Pilgrims apparently believed it was appropriate that they should enjoy

Alone and in mourning.

some of the rights and benefits they had helped make this all possible. As a result, it was decided that Pilgrim women could own land and belongings in their own names.

According to Plymouth Colony's laws and customs, Alice would have inherited one third of George Clarke's property in her own name, as well as one third of George's goods. The law permitted her to sell any of those moveable goods if it became necessary for her support. The remaining two-thirds of George's property and possessions were left to Abigail and Martha Clarke equally. Alice's lifetime interest in any housing and land would pass to her deceased husband's children, the two girls, upon her death. Since the children were very young, an overseer was probably named to protect their interests, but there is no record to prove this was the case.

Widows made the leadership of Plymouth Colony uneasy in general, in that those women took part in both the public and private spheres of the colony. They had community responsibilities that were usually fulfilled by men, as well as private responsibilities to their families and homes. In a culture that was so driven by gender differences, a widow's position was awkward at best.

In her new role as a landowner, a widow was required to pay taxes. In fact, the first mention of women in the Plymouth Colony Court Records refers to landowning widows in the tax assessments. On the tax list of March 25, 1633, the taxes of the widows Warren, Blossom, and Harding "were rated for public use." Tax levies were assessed in corn at a rate of six shillings a bushel, to be paid by November. Widow Warren owed twelve shillings or two bushels of corn; Widows Blossom and Harding both owed nine shillings or one-and-one-half bushels each.[16]

To be sure, some widows embraced the independence their status afforded them. Several of Plymouth's female residents had extensive land holdings through inheritance and bought and sold property and livestock alongside their male neighbors. Plymouth women, married or widowed, could also enter into contracts, and could hire their own servants if they needed help.

All that considered, it would have been expected that Alice Clarke remarry, as most widows did, often within a year of losing their spouses. It should not be presumed that a quick remarriage meant there was any problems within the previous relationship; rather, in this culture it was believed that a traditional nuclear family was required to maintain an efficient household. Yet, it is another of Plymouth's curious contradictions that, while it was encouraged and even expected for a widow to remarry, the laws of inheritance made it difficult. The law stated that "her lifetime interest in any housing and land went to her and her deceased husband's children." What this meant to a prospective suitor was that while he could work the estate, he could never personally own or profit from it. If Alice died before him, the property would pass to her daughters, and any children the new couple might have would not inherit any of the property of the previous spouse.[17]

The Plymouth laws and customs of inheritance cut both ways. They were designed to ensure that a man's estate passed to his children and not to someone else's through remarriage. They also made remarriage problematic for widows. Whoever married Alice Clarke would have been expected to assume the role and responsibility of husband, father, and breadwinner, but he would never own the property he worked, and neither would his children.

◈◆◈◆◈◆◈

Alice Clarke was, of course, not the first colonist to bury her husband. Burial Hill was full of men and women who had given their all to carve out a colony in the wilderness. After more than twenty years of hard work, the community was well established. Its most obvious physical feature was a tall, strong wall, built to signify ownership and settlement .

Chapter Eleven

Growth and Change
Plymouth Colony, 1623

As they had promised their investors, the Pilgrims were hard workers. Despite all they had been through, the little settlement of Plymouth soon began to look like a real community. By 1622, a formidable palisade of pointed tree trunks enclosed the colony, which was situated on a windswept slope overlooking the harbor. The wall served as protection from attack from the American Indians and clearly defined the parameters of the Separatist domain.

Inside the enclave, the "streete," as Bradford called it, ran eastward from the fort at the top of the hill down towards the seashore, where there was a gate in the wall. Another road, which he called the "highway," crossed the main street midway and had gates at either end, providing easy access to the grazing ground. Eight private dwellings lined that main street, seven of which were on the south side. Starting at the bottom of the hill, the first house belonged to Peter Brown, who was twenty years old and had travelled on the *Mayflower* alone. Next door was John Goodman's house. Elder William Brewster's house was next, and adjacent to his was the house of John Billington and his family. His neighbor was Isaac Allerton, whose wife and newborn child had died on the *Mayflower*. Francis Cooke, who had left his wife in Leiden, had a house next door. At the top of the hill, next to the meeting house, lived Edward Winslow. His wife, Elizabeth, had died on the *Mayflower* and he had remarried to widow Susanna White. At the crossroad, directly across from Billington's and diagonally across from William Brewster's, sat widowed Governor William Bradford's home. It was probably no accident that the infamous Billingtons would be assigned a house close enough to the governor's so he could keep a watchful eye on them.[1]

At the top of the slope was the fort, which served as their religious meeting place and seat of government. At the bottom was the common storehouse, where provisions were kept. Each family house was surrounded by carefully fenced garden plots and animal pens. Open space was devoted to farming.

Six of the eight households were headed by Leiden Separatists, namely Isaac Allerton, William Bradford, William Brewster, Francis Cooke, John Goodman, and Edward Winslow. Billington and Brown were Strangers. The Separatists had successfully established complete religious control of the colony. Unattached women and children and single men had been assigned to one of the eight families, their behavior the responsibility of the man in charge of the house, who would report directly to the governor. It was a very tidy system and after two years the small colony was, if not thriving, at least self-sustaining.

Visitors began to travel to Plymouth to see for themselves what had been accomplished. Fortunately, these men made written reports of their visits, and since they were neither residents nor Separatists, their records provide a fairly objective view of the state of the colony.

John Pory – January 1623

The first of these visitors was John Pory, former secretary to the governor and council of Virginia. He was returning to England and the record of his stopover in Plymouth leaves us a vivid description of the colony as he saw it during that visit. The town, he wrote, was a wholesome place. Governor Bradford informed Pory that in the year after their first terrible one, "died not one man, woman or child."[2]

The fishing, Pory reported, was superb, along with the supply of fowl. "I know of no place in the world that can match it." The people, he continued, were "free from wickedness and vice." He especially admired the wall they had built, "a substantial palisado about their [town] of 2,700 foot in compass,[3] stronger than I have seen any in Virginia." They had also built a "blockhouse which they have erected in the highest place of the town to mount their ordnance upon, [and] from whence they may command all the harbor."[4]

Relations with the Wampanoag were peaceful, he reported: "They are in good terms with [the Native Americans] of Plymouth, because…they never did wrong to any Indians." The Pilgrims, wrote Pory, "quietly and justly sat down [at Plymouth] without either dispossessing any of the natives, or being resisted by them, and without shedding so much as one drop of blood."[5]

Despite being on "good terms" with the Wampanoag, in February of 1622 the Pilgrims received a threat from the Narragansett, the tribe who lived to the west. As Bradford described it, a messenger from the tribe delivered "unto them a bundle of arrows tied about with a great snakeskin, which their interpreters told them was a threatening and a challenge." The package was returned, the snakeskin shot through with bullet holes, accompanied by a note that said that if the Narragansett would "rather have war than peace, they might begin when they would."[6]

William Bradford does not write about it, but apparently there was a significant fire in the little settlement in 1622, a fire, "which did considerable damage." Several of the inhabitants, wrote John Josselyn, "through discontent and casualties removed to Virginia." Perhaps while he was observing Plymouth Colony, John Pory was also sharing the advantages in the Virginia Colony, and unwittingly encouraged some colonists to relocate.[7]

Emmanuel Altham – September 1623

The next snapshot of Plymouth Colony was written nine months later by Emmanuel Altham, one of the investors in New Plymouth. Altham was a firm believer in colonization of the New World. He

Plymouth in 1623.

captained the *Little James*, a ship that arrived in the summer of 1623, and later made a second expedition to Plymouth in 1625.

Altham wrote that by 1623 the colony had grown to about twenty houses, of which "four or five are very pleasant, and the rest (as time will serve) shall be made better." The town owned "six goats, about fifty hogs and pigs, also diverse hens." It was surrounded by a "pale," about eight feet tall, with three gates. High on the hill, at the top of the "great street…there is a strong fort, both by nature and art, with six pieces of reasonable good artillery mounted thereon." The fort was manned day and night, "so no Indian can come near there abouts but he is presently seen."[8]

As an investor, Altham was interested in the colony's potential for profit. The fishing, he reported, "it is beyond belief..... I can assure you thus much, that if a man be well provided with all things necessary for to make a fishing voyage, he may easily make his voyage two for one." There was also an abundance of beaver, otter, martin, fox and raccoon, whose furs and skins "will yield money good store in England." The timber was "good…as ever I saw," Altham continued, "including cedar, beech, pine, oak, and divers other sorts." Sarsaparilla and sassafras, salt, "armeniac [bole armeniac, a fine red clay] and diverse other metals" were available. Although the Indians "are very strong and are men of very able bodies," Altham said they did not present an insurmountable problem. "We mean to go well armed among them," he wrote, "to trade for their store of skins."[9]

This was a good place to live, Altham continued, but, anyone who planned to settle here, he warned, must come well prepared: "For men must provide for the worst, that they may have provision for themselves a twelvemonth if these things fail—and then they must take pains to build them houses and the like." He concluded, "If I were well provided with all things necessary, as servants and the like, I could live here contentedly with great pleasure."[10]

Altham was in Plymouth during a very important social event, the marriage of William Bradford to Alice Carpenter Southworth on August 14, 1623. Bradford most likely first met Alice in Leiden. Alexander Carpenter, Alice's father, was one of the early Separatists who left England for Holland. She was born around 1590, close in age to William Bradford. Alice had married Edward Southworth in 1613, six months before Bradford had married the now deceased Dorothy May. Edward, like so many of the other transplanted Separatists, had worked in the fabric industry as a manufacturer of silk. Two sons had been born to the Southworths before 1620, Constant and Thomas. Shortly thereafter, Edward Southworth died.

It is likely that William Bradford learned of Edward Southworth's death when the *Fortune* arrived at Plymouth on November 9, 1621. Assumedly, he wrote a letter to Alice, which was transported back to England along with the lumber and furs the colony was sending to help pay off their debts. Then all he could do was wait.

Eighteen months later, in June or July of 1623, two ships arrived in Plymouth, the *Little James* and the *Anne*. Alice Southworth was aboard the Anne, but she had left her sons in Leiden. When she disembarked, she must have been sadly disappointed by what she saw. Bradford wrote, "These passengers, when they saw [the colonists] low and poor condition ashore, were much daunted and dismayed, and according to their divers humors were diversely affected. Some wished themselves in England again; others fell a-weeping, fancying their own misery in what they saw now in others; other some pitying the distress they saw their friends had been long in, and still were under. In a word, all were full of sadness."[11]

However, "daunted and dismayed" the new arrivals were, William Bradford somehow convinced Alice Southworth that she had a future in Plymouth, and she said yes to his proposal of marriage. Alice was not the child bride that Dorothy had been. Bradford had first met Alice as a mature Separatist woman with children, a woman who may have reminded him of Mary Brewster, Elder William Brewster's wife. He probably saw in Alice the same sturdy stock that would be necessary for survival in the wilderness, and as it turned out, he was correct. As the colony grew, she would become respected and revered as the First Lady of Plymouth.

The wedding was a major social event and must have included all the citizens of Plymouth, who at this point numbered about 180. Capt. Emmanuel Altham of the *Little James* wrote a full account. Massasoit, "the king of the country, who is a great emperor among his people," he wrote, was invited. He brought his first wife, "the queen,...four other kings and about six score men." There was great pageantry and ceremony and musket salutes upon his arrival. The Wampanoag came armed with bows and arrows but left all their weapons in the governor's house. They also brought "three or four bucks and a turkey." For the governor to invite the tribe was more than a polite social move, it was also a wise and calculated political decision that honored Massasoit and strengthened the relationships among them all.[12]

Altham's recollection of the wedding included "great cheer" and delicious and abundant food. The wedding ceremony itself would likely have been simple and short. As there was no official Separatist marriage script, the couple likely composed their own vows. Afterward there was a feast, apparently a very memorable one. Recounting the meal, Altham wrote, "We had about twelve pasty venisons, besides others, pieces of roasted venison and other such good cheer in such quantity that I wish you some of our share." Fruit accompanied the meats, "the best grapes that you ever saw—and the biggest and divers sorts of plums and nuts...." The Wampanoag performed dances to honor the newlyweds, "in such [a] manner, with such a noise that you would wonder."[13]

The magnitude of the event goes beyond the respect afforded William Bradford in his role as governor; it speaks of real affection for the man himself. The wedding celebration also affirmed that the colonists had not lost their sense of civility. When the Pilgrims saw themselves reflected in the eyes of the shocked newcomers who arrived on the *Anne* and the *Little James*, they may have realized how devoid of creature comforts the little village really was. The celebration of the governor's wedding might convince everyone, themselves included, that they were still capable of practicing and appreciating civil and social conventions.

Still, there were problems. A surprising dispute in 1623 would change Plymouth's economy, and arguably influence how future colonies in New England would be structured.

Emmanuel Altham – March 1624

Emmanuel Altham returned to Plymouth six months later and reported that "I was never better nor better contented in my life." He added that for the fishing to be profitable, the colony needed to improve their ability to produce salt, which was necessary to preserve the fish for transport. Nonetheless, even Altham admits that it would be difficult to get more funding from the investors: "I think the Company will not disburse more without seeing more hopes of profit."[14]

Altham remained confident that Plymouth could be a profitable investment. In May, 1624, he wrote to an investor, "I make no question now but that New Plymouth will quickly return your money again. For the most part they are honest and careful men. However, they have had many crosses; yet now they will flourish, God blessing them, which God grant." Seeing the situation for what it was, Altham recorded that unless the Pilgrims became more successful at fishing, "you cannot have your monies again."[15]

The Pilgrims' debt to the Adventurers was never far from their minds. At this point in the colony's history, they were able to sustain themselves through farming and fishing and trade with the

Wampanoag. Their first efforts to repay their debt had not been very successful, though not for lack of trying. When the *Fortune* returned to England in 1621, the Pilgrims loaded her with lumber and furs, "laden with good clapboard as full as she could stow, and two hogsheads of beaver and otter skins. ...The freight was estimated to be worth £500." Unfortunately, the ship was "robbed on the way by the Frenchmen" before it reached England, and the whole cargo was stolen.[16,17]

In 1623, the Pilgrims filled the *Anne*, the same ship that had brought William Bradford a wife, with "clapboard by the help of many hands. Also, they sent in her all the beaver and other furs they had...." All of that clapboard had been cut by hand with axes and saws. Nothing came easy at Plymouth.[18]

Every Man for His Own Particular

As much as he tried, William Bradford could not restrain change and growth in Plymouth. Already the colonists were being molded and transformed in subtle ways by their new surroundings. In Bradford's own words, they relocated here because they "thought it better to dislodge betimes to some place of better advantage and less danger." This move was to better their lives, and while there was still suffering aplenty, many of the colonists felt that it was time to pursue some of the advantages. The insurrection began with some complaints about who was not doing their share of the work and eventually led to major changes in the colony's economy.[19]

In the first years of the settlement, the economy was a communal one. The first recorded sermon preached at Plymouth, given by Robert Cushman in 1621, was titled "The Sin and Danger of Self Love," in which he exhorted the Pilgrims to work for the success of all, not just their own personal gain. Nothing, he preached, "more resembles hellish horror, than for every man to shift for himself." With memories of all they had sacrificed in pursuit of forming a religious colony still painfully fresh in his mind, Cushman reminded the Pilgrims that, "God and natural necessity requireth, if your difficulties be great, you had need to cleave the faster together, and comfort and cheer up one another, laboring to make each other's burden lighter." He scolded the colonists that "There is no grief so tedious as a churlish companion, and nothing makes sorrows easy more than cheerful associates."[20,21]

While each Pilgrim family had their individual house and small kitchen garden plot, the entire company was required to work the common fields. The corn that was communally grown was apportioned to each household according to a formula devised by the colony's leadership. This meant that this most important food supply was controlled by the governor and his assistants. This system rankled some of the colonists, whose past experiences linked the control of food with status and tyranny. This "common course and condition," Bradford had to admit, "was found to breed much confusion and discontent and retard much employment that would have been to their benefit and comfort."[22]

Adding to their frustration, the Pilgrims missed the familiarity of their former English diet. Even though there was an abundance of food available around Plymouth, it was not the food preferred by the colonists. They longed for good bread and meat and a flagon of beer. Alas, William Bradford wrote, "The best dish they could present their friends with was a lobster or a piece of fish without bread or anything else but a cup of fair spring water."[23]

Since wheat was not available, corn was often substituted in breads and puddings. Thanks to Squanto, the Pilgrims learned to grow, harvest, grind and cook with corn. Cornmeal mush was made by cooking ground corn and salt in boiling water. Cooked over a fire in a kettle, it could be served hot or cold, with sugar or syrup or with meat and gravy. Leftover corn mush could be fried and served for another meal; this may have been the origin of the now classic New England johnnycakes. Hence, corn was an important element in the daily life of Plymouth Colony. As Bradford commented, "when they had maize (that is, Indian corn) they thought it as good as a feast…." Really, there were few other choices.[24]

What brought everything to a head was the arrival of more colonists. With the arrival of the *Fortune* in November of 1621, thirty-five new colonists were added to the population of fifty. The *Charity* and the *Swan* then brought about ninety more new settlers in July of 1623, but they only stayed for two months. In the same year, the *Anne* and the *Little James* brought another ninety-some new colonists. The Adventurers sent more and more people to Plymouth, but they did not send supplies to support those new immigrants, which placed more demand on the existing food resources. Tension and hunger created resentment among the Pilgrims. Although everyone received an equal share of the food, there were complaints that not everyone was doing an equal share of the work.

According to Bradford, the younger men began to grumble that they were doing the brunt of the work, having to "work for other men's wives and children without any recompense." It was an injustice, they protested, that "the strong, or man of parts, had no more in division of victuals and clothes than he that was weak and not able to do a quarter the other could." But it was the women who brought things to a head. The wives complained and "deemed it a kind of slavery...being commanded to do service for other men, as dressing their meat, washing their clothes, etc." That got the governor's attention.[25]

With demand for food growing, resentment brewing, and no provisions coming from England, something had to be done. Bradford wrote, "all this while no supply was heard of, neither knew they when they might expect any. So they began to think how they might raise as much corn as they could, and obtain a better crop than they had done, that they might not languish in misery." In 1623 "the governor (with the advice of the chiefest amongst them)" decided that they should assign each family its own field. The corn would be planted by "every man for his own particular." Property was then assigned to each family "according to the proportion of their number." Each colonist—man, woman, and child—was entitled to one acre. They would not own the land but would be permitted to use it for their own purposes.[26]

Bradford reported that this new plan was a great success, "for it made all hands very industrious, so as much more corn was planted than otherwise would have been by any means the governor or any

A typical Pilgrim house.

other could use, and saved him a great deal of trouble, and gave far better content." Under the new plan of land assignment, even the wives and children "now went willingly into the field, and took their little ones with them to set corn."[27]

With this development came the colonists' first understandings that there could be more to Plymouth than just a Separatist compound. While the challenges were still daunting, many elements of colony life had settled into somewhat predictable routines, and thoughts began to turn to individual needs and wants. The colonists could see for themselves that there was plenty of land beyond the palisade of Plymouth, land that could be transformed into better lives for anyone who was willin to work hard and work efficiently.

This change was significant in another way. It was the first challenge to William Bradford's authority and to the original plan to make Plymouth a compact Separatist enclave. At least some of the Pilgrims, including the women, were beginning to think of themselves as individuals. The challenge for the colony's leaders was to keep everyone together and committed to the original plan. It would not be easy for Bradford, because as much as the Pilgrims had changed this little place in the wilderness, Plymouth had also changed them. Once again, whether consciously or otherwise, his reaction would be to tighten control. Not everything, however, nor everyone, was controllable at Plymouth. Before long, one of their own would cause them much grief, and much shame.

A Massacre at Wessagussett

Thomas Weston, who had gathered together the investors for the *Mayflower* voyage, decided he wanted to start his own settlement in Plymouth. In 1622 he gathered a company and selected a site in Wessagussett, now known as Weymouth, a site "found in their judgment a place fit for plantation." They were woefully unprepared, short on supplies and unable to grow enough to feed themselves. Within a few months, the colonists were starving. Their solution was to take corn "by violence" from the Native Americans, "promising to make restitution afterward." The local Indians complained to Bradford, who warned Weston, but relations between the new settlement and the tribes worsened. Massasoit secretly told the Pilgrims that there was a plot against Mr. Weston's colony, a conspiracy among "the people of Nauset, Paomet, Succonet, Mattachiest, Manomet, Agowaywam, and the isle of Capawack," to attack and kill Weston and his men.[28]

On March 23, 1623, Governor Bradford and his advisors met to discuss whether or not to strike first and quash the Natives' plan before they could attack Wessagussett. The fear was that if "their countrymen" at Wessagussett were killed, then Plymouth would be next. It was decided "that Captain Standish should take so many men, as he thought sufficient to make his party good against all the Indians in the Massachusetts bay." He as ordered to bring back the head of Wituwamat, a Neponset considered the leader of the conspiracy, "that bloody and bold villain…that he might be a warning and terror to all of that disposition."[29]

Standish had met Wituwamat before, "a notable insulting villain," who taunted that the English "died crying, making sour faces, more like children than men." Standish had also met Pecksuot,

Wituwamat's eighteen-year-old brother, another member of the avenging party, and their meeting had not gone well. Pecksuot had taunted the shorter Standish, boasting that although he was a great captain, he was "but a little man," and that Pecksuot himself, although not a sachem, was a man of great strength and courage. Standish, sensitive about his height, was obviously stung, but held his temper, at least for the moment.[30]

On March 25, eager to finally act, Capt. Standish and eight hand-chosen men visited Wituwamat's camp, pretending to come to trade. He was able to get Wituwamat, Pecksuot, and a third unnamed man together in a small building, pretending to have items to barter. When everyone was in place, Standish gave the word, and his men slammed the door shut. Standish started with Pecksuot, and "snatching his own knife from his neck, through much struggling, killed him therewith." The others murdered Wituwamat and the third man. The Native Americans had admittedly fought bravely, "not making any fearful noise, but catching at their weapons and striving to the last."[31]

Hobomak, a friend to the Pilgrims, "stood by all this time as a spectator, and meddled not, observing how our men demeaned themselves in this action." Three more American Indians, believed to be members of the conspiracy, were murdered. Standish returned to Plymouth with Wituwamat's head in a bag and was "received with joy." Standish jammed the head onto a spike and mounted it at the battlements near the fort at the top of the hill, where it would remain for years to come, a grisly, decomposing warning to all who might do them harm.[32]

After the disastrous raid, Thomas Weston's failed colonists abandoned their settlement. They left for Maine, hoping to get passage home on a fishing ship. Local tribes were so terrified by Standish's "sudden and unexpected execution," that they abandoned their homes and ran into the swamps, "and so brought manifold diseases amongst themselves, whereof very many are dead." Trade with the Indians was now ruined, endangering the Pilgrims' ability to repay their investors. Bradford admitted that due to the attack, "we have been much endamaged in our trade, for there where we had most skins the Indians are run away from their habitations, and set no corn, so as we can by no means as yet come to speak with them."[33,34]

When Pastor John Robinson back in Leiden heard of the event, he wrote to Governor Bradford regarding "the killing of those poor Indians." "Necessity of this, especially of killing so many...I see not. Methinks [killing] one or two principals should have been full enough, according to that rule, 'the punishment to a few, and the fear to many.'"[35]

As for Captain Standish, Robinson had this to say: "Upon this occasion let me be bold to exhort you seriously to consider of the disposition of your Captain." He could be surprisingly brutal, he wrote, "a man humble and meek among you, and towards all in ordinary course. But...there is cause to fear that by occasion, especially of provocation, there may be wanting that tenderness of the life of man (made after God's image) which is meet. It is also a thing more glorious in men's eyes, than pleasing in God's...to be a terror to poor barbarous people." Robinson couldn't help but add, "Oh, how happy a thing had it been, if you had converted some before you had killed any!"[36]

No doubt William Bradford and the other leaders of Plymouth welcomed any advice from their beloved pastor. It was, therefore, with "much sorrow and sadness" that they learned of John Robinson's death in 1625 in a letter written from Leiden by Roger White. Robinson had been awake until the end, White wrote, and his family and friends "came freely to him." He added, "If either prayers, tears or means would have saved his life, he had not gone hence." This news dashed the Pilgrims' fond hope that their much-loved pastor could join them and see what had been accomplished in Plymouth.[37]

Other letters from Leiden were "full of sad laments for their heavy loss." Now those who had remained behind held little hope of joining the Pilgrims in Plymouth, "though their wills were good to come to them...saw no probability of means how it might be effected, but concluded as it were that all their hopes were cut off." Even sadder, "many, being aged, began to drop away by death."[38]

This news was distressing to Bradford and the others in Plymouth;

"being stripped in a manner of all human helps and hopes,...they were at their lowest." Their wise and loving pastor and many of their family and friends had been lost, and now they were truly alone.[39]

܀܀܀܀܀܀܀

Alice Clarke would have understood their despair. After George Clarke's death, she was also alone, a mother of two, and probably at her lowest. Perhaps she prayed for help. If so, her prayers were soon answered.

Chapter Twelve

Richard Bishop
Plymouth Colony, 1638

Hard work had built Plymouth Colony, and indentured servants filled the need for labor from the start. Of the original 102 *Mayflower* passengers, twenty were indentured servants. But, as Plymouth Colony focused on raising cattle and supplying beef to Boston, its needs for laborers increased. Not only were there more animals to attend, there were also more fields to till, plant, manage, and harvest, and many landowners turned to servants for help.

Keeping indentured servants was a daunting endeavor. At the end of the indenture period they would become free citizens, so it was the responsibility of the masters from the outset to see that their servants would become responsible residents of the colony who obeyed the laws, attended church, and understood the community's expectations. The master or mistress was something of a surrogate parent, responsible not only for housing, feeding, and clothing a servant, but also for educating and providing for his or her spiritual development.

Indentured servants, who were often children, were bound by contract to the head of a household. Two copies of the agreement were written on the same piece of paper, which was cut apart with a jagged edge, or an "indenture." When the two pieces were laid together they made a perfect fit and the document was considered genuine. The indenture contract typically included the following elements: The names of the servant and the master, the term of service, the nature of service (for example, if the servant was to be an apprentice and learn a trade), the beginning date of the term, and what the servant would be paid at the end of service. For example, in 1633, "John Smith hath covenanted to serve John Jenny the full term of seven years, after the manner of an apprentice, beginning the 24 of June, this present year; at the expiration whereof, the said John Jenny to give him twelve bushels of Indian corn, [and] twenty-five acres of land." John Smith would be in service to John Jenny for seven years, plenty of time to learn how to be a responsible citizen of Plymouth. At the end of his service, Smith would have earned twenty-five acres of land for himself and would be on his way toward becoming a full member of the community.[1]

Working for Wages

There was another category of laborer in Plymouth, one with subtle yet important distinctions. Members of this category were known as "hired men," and there were only a handful of them. One of these was Richard Bishop.

A hired man was not indentured, not bound, to a master. The hired man was an adult who entered into a contract on his own volition to work for a family for a specified period of time, usually only a year or so. Hired men worked for wages; they assisted their employers, but they did not serve them, a subtle but important distinction. They did not wait upon, attend, or minister to the comfort of a master. The master was not under any obligation to educate or enculturate the hired man. He sold his labor, and worked under contracts that were strictly observed and monitored by the courts.

Besides Myles Standish, hired by the Pilgrims to be their military officer, there were five hired men among the *Mayflower* passengers. John Alden, "tall, blond, and very powerful in physique, one of the strongest men at Plymouth," was a cooper who tended the barrels of beer, plain water, and "strong water." John Allerton was a master mariner, who had been hired to help build the colony, then return to Leiden and bring over the others left behind. Thomas English was also a master mariner; he was to be the captain of the shallop which the Pilgrims brought with them on the *Mayflower*. There were two hired seamen, William Trevor and a Mr. Ellis. All, except Standish, were under contract to stay one year at Plymouth, but not as members of the colony, and hence they were not entitled to any land grants.[2]

Of the five hired men who sailed on the *Mayflower*, John Allerton and Thomas English died in the great sickness of 1621. Mr. Ellis and William Trevor returned to England. Only John Alden stayed at Plymouth, married Priscilla Mullins and moved to Duxbury.[3]

The hired men were expected to work hard, obey local laws, and live up to the standards of the Pilgrims. They had formal employment agreements that listed both their name and their employer's name, the length of service, and the amount to be paid at the end of the service. Compensation would include room and board but was otherwise strictly financial. For example, "Richard Bishop hath hired himself with Love Brewster, for the term of one whole year from the 26th of November last [1638], [and] is to have for his year's service three pounds sterling in money, twenty bushels of Indian corn." A hired worker's employer did not have the same legal responsibilities toward him as he did to an indentured servant. The hired worker was not parented as a servant was, and his employer was not required to educate or train him.[4]

A hired employee was in a temporary situation; a long-term commitment to the community was not required. Instead of committing himself to seven years of indenture, which would have included cultural indoctrination, the hired man considered his labor to be a commodity, separate from himself and his to sell. Consequently, he enjoyed a certain level of independence comparable to no one else in the colony. He was not subject to a master; he was in a way his own man, and this made the colonial leadership more than a little uneasy.

There was even a biblical warning about the position of hired man, with which the Pilgrims surely would have been familiar. In John 10:13, the hired hand abandons the herd of sheep when the wolf approaches. The shepherd, however, stays and protects them because he is the "good shepherd" and can be counted on, unlike the undependable hired man.

Not surprisingly, "hired man" was not a common status at Plymouth. Just a few examples have been identified, and they occurred only during the years 1638 and 1639. The first hired man appeared in the colony's records on July 7, 1638. "Stephen Tracy hath hired John Price for four months; his time was to begin the first week in June." Next was John Long, who was hired by "Mr. [John] Atwood" on October 24, 1638, "to serve him from the first of September last past, to March following, for three pounds sterling, or commodities worth so much." There is no further mention of Price or Long in the colony records, so both men apparently left Plymouth.[5]

On December 3, 1638, "Edward Shaw is hired with Robert Bartlett for a year from the first of December, 1638, for eight pounds ten shillings sterling, to be paid in money." Shaw had a history of short-term work—and thievery—in the colony. In 1633, he had worked for William Bennett for a period of one month, "in sawing of boards." At the General Court held on January 2, 1638, Shaw was found guilty of "the felonious taking of xv^s [fifteen shillings] from the person of William Corvanel," and sentenced to be "severely whipped and burnt in the shoulder with a hot iron." After working for Robert Bartlett, Edward Shaw disappears from Plymouth records.[6]

On March 4, 1639, James Leighorne was "hired to serve Francis Sprague for a year for six pounds, ten pence sterling, and two pounds of tobacco. His time began of February last past." He is not mentioned again in the records, though there is mention of a Roland Leyhorne, who married and owned property in Plymouth and who may have been a relative of James.[7,8]

The general assumption was that hired men were not dedicated to the colony but were only planning to earn some money and move on. Given the examples above, it appeared true that they did not exhibit the necessary commitment to the community that was essential in the eyes of the government. Typically, the hired man worked his contracted time, collected his earnings, and left Plymouth. Richard Bishop was a different case. He left a mark on the colony that would be a lasting one.

Who Was Richard Bishop?

Richard Bishop's name first appears in the Plymouth Colony records on December 3, 1638, as noted earlier, when he entered into an employment contract with Love Brewster for a period of one year. No primary source record has yet been found that links Richard with other Bishops in the area, although he might have been related to a Bishop family that first appeared in Taunton (or Cohanett as it was then know), just east of Plymouth and west of Rehoboth. He may have been the son of John Bishop, whose name appeared on June 1, 1641, on the list of men who "propounded this Court to be admitted Freemen the next Court." James Bishop, an indentured servant to Thomas Farwell, was living in Taunton at the same time, and may also have been a son of John Bishop and, potentially, Richard's brother. What is certain is that Richard Bishop was with the Brewster family in Duxbury, the satellite community north of Plymouth, in December of 1638, about the same time that George Clarke was putting the final touches on his honeymoon cottage in Playne Dealing.[9]

For at least a year, from 1638 to 1639, Richard Bishop made Duxbury his home as he lived and worked with the Brewsters. Love was a son of William Brewster, founder of the original Separatist congregation back in England and William Bradford's mentor. Although both William and Love Brewster had been *Mayflower* passengers and builders of the new colony from its inception, they later abandoned the original settlement in favor of the opportunities to be had in Duxbury. In 1634, Love Brewster had married Sarah Collier, and they had moved in with his father.

How long Richard Bishop worked for Love Brewster is not certain, but his next appearance in the colony's records is on January 5, 1641, when he once again hired himself out, this time to Nathaniel Sowther. The record stated that "Richard Bishop hired to dwell with Nathaniel Sowther for seven pounds sterling per annum [about $1000 today], and came the 20th of January."[10]

Again, Bishop had affiliated himself with a man who was well respected in Plymouth Colony. Nathaniel Sowther was a freeman, listed in 1635 among the "Names of the Freemen of the Incorporation of Plymouth in New England." On January 3, 1637, Sowther was named "Clarke of the Court," and it became his job to maintain the colony's official records and serve as notary.[11]

Nathaniel Sowther lived within Plymouth town proper, near the meeting house, in the area now known as Burial Hill. On December 26, 1638, he purchased a "house and garden place," from William Holmes on the north side of "High street between the lands of Mr. John Alden and the fort," for the sum of sixteen pounds sterling. This was likely his primary residence, close to the enclosed town of Plymouth and the meeting house where all official transactions took place. His name appears often in the records as a witness to official acts, and he would have been well known within Plymouth Colony.[12]

Sowther had many other land holdings throughout the colony, and he may have hired Richard Bishop to manage his properties. Bishop's 1641 employment agreement with Nathaniel Sowther was open-ended in that no closing date was recorded. The only stipulation was that he would be paid seven pounds per year. Bishop may still have been in Sowther's employ in August of 1643, when he was listed among "those able to bear arms in the colony of New Plymouth," and in 1644 when he took a bride.[13]

Alice Clarke Becomes Alice Bishop

We don't know how Richard Bishop met Alice Clarke. Perhaps he was hired to care for the farm after George Clarke's death, although no record of an employment agreement exists. What is recorded is that Richard and Alice married on the fifth of December in 1644.[14]

Even though George Clarke had apparently died intestate, Plymouth law and custom dictated the distribution of his estate. As discussed earlier, Alice Clarke legally inherited a third of his lands and goods in her own name. The other two thirds of his estate would be held in the names of George and Alice's daughters, Abigail and Martha, to be awarded when they reached maturity.

When he married Alice Clarke, Richard Bishop assumed the

duties of head of the family and took over management of the farm. The house that George Clarke had built for Alice would become known as the "house of Richard Bishop," but Richard Bishop would never have any real legal claim to the property. Land was everything in Plymouth Colony, so why would a man marry a woman, take on the responsibility of another man's land, property that neither he nor his children could never have any hope of owning?[15]

Bishop's status in the colony had been as a hired man, presumably with limited financial assets, and perhaps he had little hope of acquiring his own property other than to marry into it. Or, perhaps it was simply that the two were in love. He may have been so attracted to Alice Clarke that the legal entanglements of land ownership simply didn't matter to him. Whatever the reasons, the marriage of Richard and Alice Bishop appears to have been a happy one, given that there is no record of marital discord. In fact, another daughter joined the family within two years. When Damaris Bishop was born in 1646, there was no indication of what was to come.

❧❦❧❦❧❦

Twenty years earlier, the colony was still very much contained within a tall wall. Everyone lived within its confines and ventured outside the palisado only to work in the fields. There were no suburbs yet, no Playne Dealing, no private farms, and Governor Bradford wanted to keep it that way.

Chapter Thirteen

Dispersion and Disappointment
Plymouth Colony, 1626

Perhaps it was the death of John Robinson, the loss of their anchor back in Leiden, and the realization that their pastor would never see what had been accomplished at New Plymouth, that caused the Pilgrims to reassess their situation. In some ways, things were going well. One of the early visitors, Isaack de Rasieres, a representative of the Dutch West India Company in New Netherland, remarked that the colonial town was compact and carefully designed, laid out in an elongated diamond shape, "about a cannon shot of 800 [yards] long." The town was enclosed "with a stockade, against sudden attack," and the colonists were living inside the wall in comfortable homes "constructed of clapboards," well protected from the elements. Each home had its own garden, surrounded by a fence of "hewn planks, so that their houses and courtyards are arranged in very good order."[1]

At the top of the slope inside the palisade, "they have a large square house, with a flat roof, made of thick sawn planks, stayed with oak beams, upon the top of which they have six cannons, which shoot iron balls of four and five pounds, and command the surrounding country. The lower part they use for their church, where they preach on Sundays and the usual holidays."[2]

On meeting days "they assemble by beat of drum, each with his musket or firelock, in front of the captain's door; they have their cloaks on, and place themselves in order, three abreast, and are led by a sergeant without beat of drum. Behind comes the governor, in a

Pilgrims walking to Sabbath meeting with the men armed.

long robe; beside him on the right hand, comes the preacher with his cloak on, and on the left hand, the captain with his side-arms and cloak on, and with a small cane in his hand; and so they march [to the meeting house] in good order, and each sets his arms down near him."[3]

Things may have been in good order and under careful control, but there was still the looming problem of the huge debt owed to the London Adventurers. Progress to repay it had not gone well. What was needed now was some creative thinking regarding the finances of Plymouth Colony.

The Economy of Plymouth Colony

By 1626, the colonists had settled into a tolerable subsistence economy. The residents of Plymouth worked the soil outside the wall and successfully grew corn. Using a series of traps and dams, they were able to catch enough fish both to feed themselves and to use as fertilizer for the corn, just as Squanto had taught them. The corn, a visitor remarked effusively, grew "luxuriantly." Those efforts were so successful that a market had developed between the Pilgrims and the Native Americans, with the Pilgrims trading their corn for beaver pelts. However, it could not be denied that, "their farms are not so good…because they are more stony, and consequently not so suitable for the plow."[4]

This was not the original plan for Plymouth. By 1627 the original plan must have seemed woefully naïve even to the Pilgrims, even in hindsight. With the *Speedwell*, they planned to fish the coastal waters, salt their catch and ship it back to England. Fish was richly abundant in Cape Cod Bay, as promised by its very name. "The bay is very full of fish, of cod," de Rasieres reported, and "three or four hours of fishing brings in enough to feed the whole community for a day." But the Pilgrims had not mastered the industry of fishing on a scale large enough to repay their debt. A new plan was devised. a plan that combined efficiency and organization and was to some extent fair to everyone. It would also establish an entirely different economic system in Plymouth, and that system would change everything.[5]

The Undertakers

The idea was first presented to the London investors in 1626, in the colony's name, by Isaac Allerton. The proposal was that a small group of Plymouth's leaders would "undertake" the debt; that is, they would buy out the investors for £2,400, which included the original £1,800 investment and "all the rest of the debts that lay upon the Plantation," about £600 more. That amount would cover all the "stocks, shares, lands, merchandise and chattels whatsoever" of Plymouth Colony.[6,7]

Eight men agreed to be the "Undertakers," as they called themselves: William Bradford, Myles Standish, Isaac Allerton, Edward Winslow, William Brewster, John Howland, John Alden, and Thomas Prence. (All except Thomas Prence were *Mayflower* passengers and signers of the Mayflower Compact. Prence arrived at Plymouth in 1621 on the *Fortune* and soon became a leader in the colony.) There were also four London investors who joined the Undertakers: James Sherley, John Beauchamp, Richard Andrews, and Timothy Hatherly. The Undertakers agreed to pay off the debt in six years.[8,9,10]

The plan was to apportion the land in Plymouth Colony among a select group of colonists who would be called "Purchasers." Those

Purchasers would then work the land assigned to them and make annual payments to the Undertakers, "three bushels of corn or six pounds of tobacco at the Undertakers' choice," for a term of six years. The Undertakers would have the monopoly on trade with the Natives, so they could trade the corn and tobacco for furs, which they would send to London in order to repay the loan.[11]

The first step was to determine who among the colonists would participate in the bargain. It was not easy: "[T]he governor and council with other of their chief friends had serious consideration how to settle things in regard of this new bargain or purchase made, in respect to the distribution of things both for the present and future." Bradford admits "they had some untoward persons mixed amongst them from the first," but their principal concern was to preserve peace among the colonists. "So they called the company together and conferred with them, and came to this conclusion": Those who were determined to be "either heads of families, or single young men, that were of ability and free (and able to govern themselves with meet discretion, and their affairs, so as to be helpful in the commonwealth)" would be taken into "this partnership or purchase."[12]

Fifty-two men, one woman (the widow Elizabeth Warren), and five London investors were identified as Purchasers. In the order listed in the court records they were: William Bradford, Thomas Prence, William Brewster, Edward Winslow, John Alden, John Jenney, Isaac Allerton, Myles Standish, William Collier, John Howland, Manasseh Kempton, Francis Cooke, Jonathan Brewster, Edward Bangs, Nicholas Snow, Stephen Hopkins, Thomas Clarke, Ralph Wallen, William Wright, Elizabeth Warren, widow, Edward Doty, Cutbert Cutbertson, John Winslow, John Shaw, Joshua Pratt, John Adams, John Billington, Phineas Pratt, Samuel Fuller, Clement Briggs, Abraham Pearse, Stephen Tracy, Joseph Rogers, John Faunce, Stephen Deane, Thomas Cushman, Robert Hicks, Thomas Morton, Anthony Annable, Samuel Fuller, Francis Eaton, William Basset, Francis Sprague, John Crackstone's heirs, Edward Bumpas, William Palmer, Peter Brown, Henry Sampson, Experience Michell, Phillip Delanoy, Moses Simonson, and George Soule.[13]

The next step was to assign a fair number of shares to each Purchaser, each share to eventually translate into twenty acres of land, known as the "Great Lots." It was decided that single free men should have a single share; each father of a family would have "so many shares as he had persons in his family." Servants would have no shares, except "what either their masters should give them out of theirs or their deservings should obtain from the company afterwards."[14]

"This agreement was very well liked of and approved by all the Plantation, and consented unto," Bradford commented. "Thus all were to be cast into single shares according to the order above said; and so every one was to pay his part according to his proportion towards the purchase and all other debts." Payments to the Undertakers would be made annually. The cattle and goats were also divided up, "a cow to six persons or shares, and two goats to the same."[15]

The homes of the colonists were to remain inside the walls of Plymouth. These new allocations of land would be outside, but not too far away. "Seeking to keep the people together as much as might be," was tantamount. Bradford wanted to "enable everyone to attend divine service, to maintain a vigorous community, and to keep a strict watch over sinners."[16]

It took two years to get everything agreed upon and in place. The agreement was formalized with the London investors in November 1628, and a deed on parchment with signatures and wax seals was delivered to Governor Bradford by Isaac Allerton.

Results Unforeseen

The formation of the Undertakers was an effort by the leaders of the colony to pay off the debt efficiently, and an attempt was made to treat all fairly, even those of questionable repute. However, whether intentionally or not, eight men had granted to themselves a great deal of power along with a lot of financial responsibility and risk. For instance, they had a monopoly on trade, since only the Undertakers could trade the corn and tobacco outside the colony.

If a Purchaser and his (or her) family worked hard, a colonist might be able to produce more than his debt of corn, and then sell his remaining corn to the governor. As de Rasieres explained, "at three guilders the bushel, [Governor Bradford] sends [corn] in sloops to the north for the trade in skins among the savages; they reckon one bushel of maize against one pound of beaver's skins; the profits are divided according to what each has contributed, and they are credited for the amount in the account of what each has to contribute yearly towards the reduction of his obligation. Then with the remainder they purchase what next they require, and which the governor takes care to provide every year."[17]

The Purchasers soon realized they could increase production and profit if they only had more land. What was obvious to them was that the real potential for success in Plymouth was all that fertile, open land stretching as far as the eye could see. Some—even a few of those in leadership positions—felt a growing desire for more than their allotments. It would take some time, but the day was coming when not even William Bradford and the Undertakers could control that yearning.

Isaack de Rasieres and Native American Relations

Trade with the Natives was an important part of Plymouth Colony's economy; indeed, it was the basis of the Undertakers' agreement. Around 1627 the Pilgrims established a trading outpost at Aptucxet, Manomet, about twenty miles south of Plymouth. Today it is known as Bourne, but historically it had been used by the American Indians as a convenient "carrying place" to transport goods between Buzzard's Bay and Cape Cod Harbor. A few Pilgrim servants were stationed at Aptucxet, and they made the place quite homey; according to Governor Bradford, "they planted corn and reared some swine and were always ready to go out with the bark when there was occasion.. all which took good effect and turned to their profit."[18]

Visitor Isaack de Rasieres had a suggestion for Governor Bradford. The Dutch had been very successful using sewan, or wampum, in trading with the Natives for their furs. Made out of cockle shells found on the beach, wampum was their form of currency. They would painstakingly carve the white and purple clamshells into cylindrical shapes, drill and polish them, and string them into necklaces, bracelets, headbands and belts, which they also wore as decoration. The American Indians, according to de Rasieres, considered wampum "as valuable as we do money here, since one can buy with it everything they have."[19]

De Rasieres convinced the Pilgrims that trade with the Indians, especially at their remote trading post on the Kennebec River in Maine, could be greatly improved with the use of wampum. The Pilgrims bought fifty six-foot lengths of the beads from de Rasieres for fifty pounds, but at first it was slow to catch on. Once the inland tribes got word of it, the colonists "could scarce get enough for them. As the use of wampum in trade grew, Bradford marveled that "it may prove a drug in time."[20]

Having a form of currency that was highly prized by the Native Americans facilitated trade and helped the Pilgrims pay off their debt to the London investors. Another effect, surely unforeseen, was that by providing the local Indians with wampum, they could in turn use it to trade with other tribes to the north. The problem was that they had been trading with "sundry unworthy persons, both English, Dutch, and French," and were in possession of firearms, "pieces, powder, and shot." Bradford remarked that "hitherto the Indians of these parts had no pieces nor other arms but their bows and arrows, nor of many years after; neither durst they scarce handle a gun, so much were they afraid of them. And the very sight of one (though out of kilter) was a terror unto them." All that had now changed. Prophetically, Bradford lamented that the arming of the Native Americans, "may turn to the ruin of many."[21]

A Patent of Sorts

In 1629 the Pilgrims kept a promise that was nearly ten years old. They brought the remaining Separatists from Leiden, Holland, to

New Plymouth. Without telling the other colonists, the Undertakers had planned to pay for the passage and supplies of members from the Leiden congregation who wanted to emigrate. The cost of the project would be paid from the three bushels of corn the Purchasers paid to the Undertakers each year, which the colonists understood would be used to pay off the colony's debt. Bradford wrote, "Performing their promises and covenants," and financing the passage of those who were largely strangers, proved to be very unpopular with the colonists, "especially at the paying of the three bushels of corn a year." It would cost the Pilgrims more than £500 to cover the expense, and most of the newcomers would be people who were unknown to the Pilgrims, "the most of them never saw their faces to this day."[22]

Not only that, but since they came without food, and it would be "16 or 18 months" before the new settlers could bring in their own crops of corn, and it would be up to the existing colonists to support them in the meantime. The colonists, "the generality," balked, "seeing how great the charge was to be." The Undertakers were forced to relent, and they alone bore the cost of bringing the Leiden Separatists over. They "never demanded, much less had, any repayment of all these great sums thus disbursed," wrote Bradford.[23]

Isaac Allerton was aboard the *Lyon* with the last of the Leiden Separatists in 1629, and he brought with him a very important document, a new patent from the Council for New England, signed by the Earl of Warwick. The so-called Warwick Charter officially established the borders of Plymouth Colony and granted unto William Bradford, "his heirs, associates, and assignees," all that part of New England in America designated as Plymouth Colony, which included parts of Maine. But there was a dispute over the paying of customs back to England, and the charter never "passed the King's hand." Without the king's signature and necessary seals, the document probably wasn't the official charter the colonists had wanted, but it was the best they could get to justify their existence as an English colony. Because it was issued to William Bradford directly, the patent had in effect given him complete and full authority over Plymouth Colony. In a sense, he owned the colony. To his credit, Bradford chose to stick with the original plan for a religious settlement, with colonists voluntarily united by holy covenants, and governed under a somewhat democratic government.[24]

By 1630, at the time of the Warwick Patent, Plymouth Colony had tripled in population. "By special providence of God, and their extraordinary care and industry they have increased their plantation to near three hundred people," wrote the Earl of Warwick. Things were not perfect, but they were going very well, and the colony was still independent and self-governed. It was not the church state that the Separatists had first envisioned, but at least the non-Separatists were under control and in compliance with Separatists principles. There was some semblance of equality among the colonists. Land grants and sales were carefully administered and monitored to prevent the accumulation of large tracts into baronial estates. For a few years, Plymouth Colony was probably the closest it would ever be to what Robinson, Brewster, and Bradford had dreamed of back in Leiden.[25]

※※※※

There were others in England with dreams, too, and those dreams—combined with a more favorable location—would culminate in a much larger, wealthier, and more historically significant colony to the north. The growth of the Massachusetts Bay Colony would challenge Plymouth in ways that Governor Bradford had not anticipated. Once again, the Separatist ideal would be threatened.

Chapter Fourteen

The Great Migration Begins
Massachusetts Bay Colony, 1629

In 1629, the Massachusetts Bay Company was chartered by the crown and financed by London merchants. Leadership of the company was in the hands of Puritan laymen, and in 1630, under John Winthrop's guidance, some 700 settlers sailed across the Atlantic in a fleet of eleven ships. This was a Puritan endeavor, and while motivated somewhat by economic ambitions, it was first and foremost a religious mission. They believed that they had entered into an agreement with the Almighty, and they also believed that if they succeeded, he would reward them. For Winthrop the purpose of the venture was clear: "The end is to improve our lives to do more service to the Lord, [to] increase of the body of Christ whereof we are members that ourselves, and [that] our posterity may be the better preserved from the common corruptions of this evil world to serve the Lord and work out our salvation under the power and purity of his holy ordinances."[1]

But there was something else in their purpose, something that set them apart from the Separatists. The Puritans believed that they were sent by God to set an example for all others, to demonstrate what a colony devoted to God would look like, to be "a city upon a hill," according to Winthrop, that all would look upward towards. They assumed that "the eyes of all people are upon us," and that their success or failure would reflect upon the Almighty. They believed that if they failed, they would cause God "to withdraw his present help from us," and that they would become a disgrace to God.[2]

Winthrop's Fleet.

In contrast, the Separatists goals were more modest. Their main motivation for leaving Holland was that they "thought it better to dislodge betimes to some place of better advantage and less danger, if any such could be found." The Pilgrims, wrote William Bradford, had "a great hope and inward zeal…of laying some good foundation, or at least to make some way thereunto, for the propagating and advancing the gospel of the kingdom of Christ in those remote parts of the world; yea, though they should be but even as stepping-stones unto others for the performing of so great a work." Building a "city on a hill" is a very different objective from laying "stepping-stones."[3]

While "their ends were good and honorable," as Bradford wrote, "their calling lawful and urgent," and they had God's blessing, they mainly wanted to be left alone to pursue their own beliefs. The Puritans were looking outward from themselves, aiming to influence others; the Separatists were mainly looking inward, keeping themselves separate from others. Nevertheless, the Separatists knew a good opportunity when they saw one.[4]

During the Puritans' first year in Massachusetts, seven towns were founded, including Boston, which would grow at the rate of 1,000 to 3,000 immigrants per year. The new colonists were arriving so fast that record-keeping fell by the wayside. Some who planned to settle in the Bay Colony found it not to their liking and instead settled in Plymouth. For others, it was the other way around. As became evident later, some of Plymouth's residents appeared in the colony's records years after their arrival with no way to trace their origins or ancestry. For many of those who appeared in Plymouth after 1627, it is difficult if not impossible to determine how or when they arrived.

The Great Migration, as it was called, of Englishmen to New England created a ready market, and by the early 1630s the Pilgrims had developed a successful trading relationship with the Puritan settlers to the north. The men of Plymouth carried agricultural goods, especially corn and cattle, to Boston and traded them for necessary household items, and no doubt a few luxuries. Certainly, the demand was there in the north, but producing cattle and corn required vast amounts of land.

Cattle in the Colony

Among the most important of immigrants to Plymouth were the cattle. Except for two hunting dogs, there had been no animals onboard the *Mayflower*, since cattle would have been too expensive to buy and transport. By 1623, perhaps through trade, chickens, goats, and pigs were thriving in the colony. In 1624, Edward Winslow arrived in Plymouth on the *Charity*, bringing with him from England "three heifers and a bull, the first beginning of any cattle of that kind in the land." By 1627, when the cattle were divided among the colonists, there were sixteen head of cattle and twenty-two goats, many of which were offspring of the original animals.[5]

Farm animals were probably part of the Separatists' original plan for Plymouth. As yeomen in Scrooby, they would have seen livestock as a necessary element of any successful farm. In their collective memories were the familiar emblems of the civilized country life, including herds grazing peacefully in green pastures. They knew that farm animals provided labor, food and profit for a family. Furthermore, there was plenty of grazing land around Plymouth, so much so that William Bradford remarked that "the cattle find grass, for they are as fat as need be." He added that "there is enough grass to feed one hundred times the cattle we now have."[6]

In the colony's early years, all cattle were held together in a common herd and grazed in the meadows just outside the walled town. The division of cattle to the "family" groups was the colony's way to made sure that all families shared in the care and profit of the animals. However, the Allertons, Brewsters, Standishes, and Winslows took actual physical possession of the animals, "buying out the single men who were attached to [a] family for the purposes of the division." It was probably the boys of the colony who were assigned to watch over the grazing herds in the daytime and drive them into walled Plymouth at night for care and milking.[7]

At first the livestock served only the needs of the Pilgrims. They provided milk and beef, as well as muscle to pull plows and carts. But as the Massachusetts Bay Colony grew, the opportunity to sell and trade presented itself. "By reason of the flowing of many people into the country, especially into the Bay of the Massachusetts, the people of the Plantation began to grow in their outward estates," Bradford wrote. "Corn and cattle rose to a great price," he explained, "by which many were much enriched, and commodities grew plentiful." Bradford was not entirely comfortable with this improvement in the standard of living at Plymouth. He remarked, "This benefit turned to their hurt, and this accession of strength to their weakness."[8]

To reap the full potential of trade with the north, they needed access to more grazing land. The answer came in the form of the Great Lots, the twenty-acre plots the colonists had been granted by the Undertakers. Bradford had to admit that "they could not otherwise keep their cattle, and having oxen grown they must have land for plowing and tillage. ...They must of necessity go to their great lots."[9]

There was no stopping this rush for profit, and "no man thought he could live except he had cattle and a great deal of ground to keep them, all striving to increase their stocks." Try as he might, Bradford was losing control of the colonists: "For now as their stocks increased and the increase vendible, there was no longer any holding them together." It must have seemed to William Bradford that he was the only Pilgrim who was still committed to the original plan for Plymouth as a Separatist colony where everyone lived in close proximity so they could watch over and care for one other. In truth, he was not wrong.[10]

Bonds Untwisted

At first the families remained inside the palisado of Plymouth in their original homes, sending a servant or two with the dry cattle (those not producing milk) to the Great Lots. But eventually "many of those families which had sent dry cattle away tended themselves to leave the village...." As a result, between 1632 and 1639 seven new towns were founded within Plymouth Colony. The first was Green's Harbor, which would eventually merge into Marshfield. Duxbury was established in 1633, Scituate in 1633/4, Taunton in 1636/7, Sandwich in 1637, Yarmouth in 1638, and in 1638/9 Barnstable was founded. Of them all, the founding of Duxbury was the one that probably hurt and disappointed Bradford the most. One of Duxbury's first settlers was William Brewster, the man Bradford looked up to not only as a father figure, but also as a model for all that Separatism and Plymouth Colony represented. Along with Brewster, John Alden and Myles Standish also moved out of the original settlement and norh to Duxbury.[11]

Myles Standish's house in Duxbury.

William Bradford never forgave them for their desertion, and later he would even blame them for what he saw as the eventual failure of the colony. While the bond among them was preserved, he wrote in his old age, when they still lived within the walls of Plymouth together, "how sweet and precious were the fruits that flowed from the same!" But, "when this fidelity decayed, then their ruin approached." With great sorrow Bradford wrote, "That subtle serpent hath slyly wound in himself under fair pretenses of necessity and the like, to untwist these sacred bonds and ties, and as it were insensibly by degrees to dissolve, or in a great measure to weaken, the same."[12]

As much as it hurt Bradford that Plymouth's original founders had abandoned the walled community, it was the breaking up of the church that most pained him. Those who had relocated to the north and created the village of Duxbury began to complain that it was "a burthen" to bring their wives and children to public worship in Plymouth. Consequently "they sued to be dismissed and become a body of themselves." Their request was granted, "though very unwillingly," Bradford recorded. This "scattering" of the colonists, he commented, "I fear will be the ruin of New England, at least of the churches of God there, and will provoke the Lord's displeasure against them."[13]

The fact that some of the Pilgrims were moving out of the Town of Plymouth didn't mean that they would no longer be subject to the colony's authority. As he had before, Bradford responded to this threat to the continued existence of Plymouth by working on ways to tighten power and control.

Walls and Laws

In 1633, after serving for eleven years, William Bradford was not re-elected to the office of governor. Edward Winslow succeeded him, but not without some debate. At the council meeting on January 1, probably at the insistence of William Bradford himself, there was a lengthy discussion of how a governor was to be elected. It was finally decided that, for any person elected to be governor for a second term, "it should be lawful for him to refuse...." It appears that Bradford wanted a break, perhaps because he was so disappointed that those he trusted and loved were abandoning Plymouth, or maybe he wanted to refocus his efforts. If Plymouth were to be preserved, a lot of work still needed to be done.[14]

The first act was to refortify the Town of Plymouth by rebuilding the palisade. The wall around the original settlement "by continuance of time is decayed," and it was agreed that it should be rebuilt "by the whole strength of men able to labor in the colony." The new wall was to be a formidable barrier. The wall, the court record stated, would be "nine feet high" and the posts "are to be cut sharp at ye top."[15]

The rebuilding of the wall was significant in many ways. The obvious and original purpose was to protect the colonists from attack by the local Native Americans. But symbolically the wall also served to maintain Plymouth as an exclusive colony. The thousands of Puritan immigrants living in the Bay Colony presented both opportunities and threats to Plymouth. While business dealings with the Puritans to the north were welcome, the permanent presence of them in Plymouth was not. The nine-foot wall reminded everyone that permission was needed before you could join the colony.

The palisade may also have represented the leaders'—especially William Bradford's—attempts to keep everyone together and focused on what was now called the Town of Plymouth. In October of 1633, at the General Court, it was agreed "by full consent...that the chief government be tied to the town of Plymouth, and that the governor for the time being be tied there to keep his residence and dwelling, and there also to hold such Court as concern the whole." To prevent Plymouth from being "dispeopled," it was agreed that those who had moved out of the town but still owned property inside the walls, surrender "their right to the said acres," so that others could live there.[16]

Those living outside the palisade needed to protect themselves, and that required that "every freeman or other inhabitant of this colony provide for himself, and each under him able to bear arms, a sufficient musket, and other serviceable piece for war." Furthermore, it was agreed that "all and every person within the colony be subject to such military order for training and exercise of arms as shall be thought meet."[17]

It was not enough to fortify the colony against threats, real or imagined, from outside forces. The community must be strengthened from within, too. It was the dangers that lurked unseen, "the malice of Satan and man's corruption," that these Separatists feared the most. They also believed they had a responsibility to be watchful over each other's behavior. With the colony growing and spreading out, it was decided that it was necessary to review and restate the standards of acceptable behavior.[18]

The first code of law for Plymouth Colony had been written and "ordained" on December 17, 1623, when Plymouth was a small community made up of people who knew each other well and who generally agreed on personal and public conduct. The laws were simple and straightforward and addressed land grants and practical matters. A formal code of behavior had not been necessary because everyone knew everyone else and kept an eye on each other. Governor Bradford and his assistants made decisions informally, as issues or problems arose. By 1636 two things changed: Colonists were scattering to the outer edges of the colony away from daily contact with each other, and the growing Bay Colony to the north was beginning to exert an influence over Plymouth in many different ways. To preserve the colony's original goals, new and revised rules had to be agreed upon and recorded.

A committee was appointed in October of 1636 to review the code of laws, the "ordnances of the colony and corporation," and to "rectify and prepare" the code and present it to the next General Court. The committee members, besides Governor Edward Winslow, Assistants William Bradford, Thomas Prence, John Alden, William Collier, Stephen Hopkins, Timothy Hatherly, and John Brown, were William Brewster, Ralph Smith, John Done, and John Jenney, representing the town of Plymouth, Jonathan Brewster and Christopher Wadsworth, for Duxbury, and James Cudworth and Anthony Annable from Scituate. All the existing "laws, orders, and constitutions of the Plantation within their Government," were to be reviewed. All that were "still fitting," would be codified, those that "time hath made unnecessary" would be discarded, and any new laws that were needed "might be prepared" and presented to the Court.[19]

These new laws needed to be custom made for Plymouth. Edward Winslow, governor and presumed chairman of that lawmaking committee, wrote about how laws were established in Plymouth in his essay, "New England's Salamander Discovered." Regarding the influence of English law in the colony, he stated: "As for the law of England, I honor it and ever did, and yet know well that it was never intended for New England. …But all that is required of us in making of our laws and ordinances, offices and officers, is to go as near the laws of England as may be." However, he continues, there were some elements in English law that, "we came from thence to avoid, as the hierarchy, the cross in baptism, the holy days, the Book of Common Prayer, etc."[20]

Besides their own personal experiences as Englishmen, the members of this committee had some guidelines as they reviewed and prepared laws. Of course, they would have consulted their Geneva Bibles first, but in the inventory of Love Brewster's estate there was a copy of William Lambarde's *The Duties of Constables, Householders, Tythingmen, and Such Other Low and Lay Ministers of the Peace*, first published in 1582, presumably inherited from his father, William Brewster, who served on the committee.[21]

There may also have been a copy of Lambarde's *Eirenarcha: or Of the Office of the Justices of Peace at Plymouth* as well (perhaps the 1592 edition), given its popularity at the time.[22] This may be what Edward Winslow was referring to when he wrote, "I have brought my own book of the statutes of England into our court, that so when we have wanted a law or ordinance we might see what the statutes provided in that kind…."[23] If Winslow was referring to the *Eirenarcha*, the book was not listed in any Plymouth inventories. He may also have referred to *Institutions, or Principall Grounds of the Lawes and Statutes of England*, which was also widely available.[22, 23, 24,25,26]

The revised code of laws was put into effect November 15, 1636, and it vastly expanded the simple code of 1623. The structure and powers of the government were clearly stated, and duties of officers described. Laws relating to land ownership, inheritance, fees, and other issues that might come up from time to time were also included. Eight capital offenses (including adultery) and three criminal crimes were listed. Personal behavior was strictly regulated. Marriages had to be approved by parents or, in the absence of parents, by the governor or one of his assistants. Liquor was regulated, and drunkenness would result in punishment.

Many of these laws served to "maintain and protect the Church." Any outsider, that is anyone not of a Separatist frame of mind, who wanted to settle in Plymouth, "to build any cottages or dwelling houses," had to receive the approval of the governor or his assistants first. This meant that all leadership would be kept in the hands of the Separatists. The leaders had authority over all the colonists already living in Plymouth, and they alone could decide who would be admitted to the Colony. They could—and did—exclude any who were not likely to follow Separatist principles and join the church.[27,28]

No doubt William Bradford was at the center of this rededication of Plymouth colony, but because of his uncompromising commitment to the original plan for a Separatist colony, he had fashioned his own destiny. His was to be a lifelong struggle against the inevitable forces of change and ambition, and laws and walls would not be enough. He returned to the office of governor in 1635.

※ ※ ※

In 1639, when Alice Martin first appears in the colony's records, Plymouth was poor, but functioning much as the founders had envisioned. The church was firmly established, and the investors paid off. Relations with the Massachusetts Bay Colony and the Indians were friendly and profitable. Laws had been established and a strong government was in place. Governor Bradford had a family of his own now. His son with his first wife, Dorothy May Bradford, left Leiden and arrived in Plymouth in 1625. With his additional children: William born in 1624, Mercy, born before 1627, and Joseph, born in 1630.

Plymouth's success was real but modest, especially when compared to the costs involved. The Plymouth Separatists had suffered blow after blow since their days in Scrooby, culminating in the demise of half of their party that first horrible winter. This was Plymouth Colony's history and its legacy. Perhaps its leaders—especially Governor Bradford—felt that the best way to honor the sacrifices of the early inhabitants was to make Plymouth the success that the Separatists originally envisioned, to make all that had happened before serve a godly, noble purpose. As the original founders died, as memories faded and other colonists' commitments waned, as many moved on to pursue their own interests, Bradford remained dedicated to the original plan.

Plymouth Colony was an established settlement, but one with a sorrowful history that informed its present and also its future.

Chapter Fifteen

A Murder in Playne Dealing
Plymouth Colony, 1648

July 22, 1648, was a day like any other, except it was a Saturday, and Alice Bishop needed to prepare meals that would feed her family for two days since cooking was not allowed on the Sabbath. She had been married to Richard Bishop for four years and was the mother of three daughters. Abigail and Martha were her children with her first husband, George Clarke, and were six and four years old; Damaris, Richard's daughter, was about two.

Alice had a visitor that day, Rachel Ramsden. Nothing appeared to be amiss and   presumably the two women enjoyed a chat after which Alice asked Rachel to run an errand for her. She needed some buttermilk from "Goodwife Winslow." What happened afterward is detailed in the court record of August 1, 1648.[1,2]

> At a Court of Assistants held in New Plymouth, the first of August, 1648, before Mr. William Bradford, Governor, Capt. Myles Standish, and Mr. William Collier, [and] Mr. William Thomas, Gentlemen, Assistants,
> These show that on July 22nd, 1648, we, whose names are underwritten, were sworn by Mr. Bradford, Governor, to make inquiry of the death of the child of Alice Bishop, the wife of Richard Bishop.
> We declare, that coming into the house of the said Richard Bishop, we saw at the foot of a ladder which leads into an upper chamber, much blood; and

going up, all of us, into the chamber, we found a woman child of about four years of age lying in her shift upon her left cheek with her throat cut with diverse gashes cross ways, the wind pipe cut and stuck into the throat downward, and a bloody knife lying by the side of the child, with which knife all of us adjudged, and the said Alice confessed to five of us at one time, that she murdered the child with the said knife.

The statement was signed by John Howland, James Cole, James Hurst, Giles Rickard, Robert Lee, Richard Sparrow, John Shaw, Thomas Pope, Francis Cooke, Francis Billington, John Cooke and William Nelson.

The Court Record continues:

Rachel, the wife of Joseph Ramsden, aged about 23 years, being examined, said that coming to the house of Richard Bishop upon an errand, the wife of said Richard Bishop requested her to go fetch her some buttermilk at Goodwife Winslow, and gave her a kettle for that purpose, and she went and did it; and before she went, she saw the child lying abed asleep, to the best of her discerning, and the woman was as well as she had known her at any time, but when she came [back] she found her [Alice Bishop] sad and dumpish; she asked her what blood was that she saw at the ladder's foot; she [Alice] pointed into the chamber, and bid her look, but she [Rachel Ramsden] perceived she [Alice] had killed her child, and being afraid, she refused, but ran and told her father and mother. Moreover, she [Rachel] said that the reason that moved her to think she [Alice] had killed her child was that when she saw the blood, she looked on the bed, and the child was not there.

Taken upon oath by me, William Bradford, the day and year above written.

After presenting the evidence, the record for August 1, 1648, concludes:

> At a Court of Assistants held at New Plymouth, the first of August, 1648, before Mr. Bradford, Governor, Mr. Collier, Capt. Myles Standish, and Mr. William Thomas, Gentlemen Assistants, the said Alice, being examined, confessed she did commit the aforesaid murder, and is sorry for it.

The evidence had been considered and Alice had confessed. Two months later, on October 4, the case went first before the grand jury:

> At the General Court of our Sovereign Lord the King, held at Plymouth aforesaid, the 4th of October, 1648, before Mr. Bradford, Governor, Mr. Thomas Prence, Capt. Myles Standish, Mr. Timothy Hatherly, and Mr. William Thomas, Gentlemen, Assistants.
> At this Court, Alice Bishop, the wife of Richard Bishop, of New Plymouth, was indicted for felonious murder by her committed upon Martha Clarke, her own child, the fruit of her own body. The names of the grand inquest that went on trial of the aforesaid bill of indictment, were these: John Dunham, Sr., John Barker, Isaac Wells, Joseph Colman, Mr. Thomas Burne, John Allen, Robert Finney, Thomas Boardman, Henry Wood, James Bursell, Ephraim Hicks, Joseph Tory, James Walker, Michael Blackwell, James Wyatt, Daniel Cole, and Love Brewster. These found the bill a true bill.

Alice was indicted, charged with murder, and the case went before a petty jury next. The record reads:

> The petty jury's names that went upon her trial were these: Josiah Winslow, Sr., Giles Rickard, Thomas

Shillingsworth, John Shaw, Sr., Anthony Snow, Stephen Wood, Richard Sparrow, William Merrick, Gabriel Fallowell, William Brett, Joshua Pratt and John Willis.

These found the said Alice Bishop guilty of the said felonious murdering of Martha Clarke aforesaid; and so she had the sentence of death pronounced against her, that is, to be taken from the place where she was to the place from whence she came, and thence to the place of execution, and there to be hanged by the neck until her body is dead, which accordingly was executed.

Alice Bishop was hanged.

Chapter Sixteen

Behind the Court Records
Plymouth Colony, 1648

The official court record of the crime lists only the pertinent facts, enough to describe the murder and to support the formulation of a viable charge, but putting the written records into the context of the culture of the colony provides a fuller understanding of what happened that morning. When Rachel Ramsden reported the crime to her stepparents, Francis and Christian Billington, and someone in turn alerted the governor, the murder of Martha Clarke moved from the private space of the Bishop home into the public sphere of the government and the courts. The crime migrated from what was primarily the province of women into an arena controlled completely by men. Alice Bishop and her actions would then be judged by male magistrates and three all-male juries.

Someone was sent to the gated town of Plymouth to summon the authorities. Given the distance involved, it was probably a couple of hours before Bradford arrived at the scene and began the investigation.

Governor Bradford Takes Charge

Once Rachel Ramsden reached her parents' home and shared her terrible story, such dreadful news would have travelled quickly. What the governor found when he arrived, we can only guess. Curious neighbors may already have gathered outside the house, and perhaps a few were inside with Alice. If her surviving daughters were there, a sympathetic neighbor may have taken charge of them, offering the children comfort and care. Perhaps Richard Bishop had been located and had returned from the fields to tend to his family. Surely everyone was stunned to learn that such a horrific thing had happened in the colony.

Since this was a major crime, Governor Bradford headed up the investigation himself. While it may have been intimidating for Alice Bishop and Rachel Ramsden to be questioned by the most powerful man in the colony, it was entirely within Plymouth Colony law for Governor Bradford to lead the inquiry into Martha Clarke's murder. The law said that the governor should "arrest and commit to ward any offenders" and "with all convenient speed bring the cause to hearing either of the assistants or General Court according to the nature of the offence." Furthermore, Governor Bradford had sworn to govern with "wisdom, understanding, and discerning," to "faithfully, equally, and indifferently without respect of persons to administer justice in all cases…as the governor of New Plymouth."[1]

All of Plymouth trusted that the governor would be wise and fair in such cases, but a bigger concern to the governor was how this crime affected the colony's relationship with God. In the Pilgrim point of view, God was now disappointed with them. To restore his blessing, justice must be carefully and fairly administered. This crime, a violent attack not only on an innocent child but on the ideals of the colony itself, gave the governor an opportunity and a responsibility to demonstrate to everyone—especially newcomers—how a saintly community dealt with aberrant behavior. Between 1630 and 1643 the population of Plymouth had grown from about 400 persons to about 2,000, and most of the new arrivals were servants brought over from England to work the land. Their indoctrination to Plymouth was still in process.

This was not the first time Governor Bradford had dealt with capital crimes in Plymouth. There had been three previous cases in the colony. The first had been committed in 1630 by John Billington (who was Rachel Ramsden's step grandfather). Billington had "waylaid a young man, one John Newcomen, about a former

The hanging of John Billington.

quarrel and shot him with a gun, whereof he died." Billington was hanged, but Bradford noted that "it [was] a matter of great sadness unto them."[2]

The next capital case was in 1638. Four men—Arthur Peach, Thomas Jackson, Richard Stinnings, and Daniel Cross—were indicted for murder and robbery by the highway. They killed and robbed Penowanyanquis, a Nipmuc boy, at Misquamsqueece, and stole five fathoms of wampum [about 30 feet] and three coats of woolen cloth from him. "This Arthur Peach," William Bradford wrote, was "the ringleader of all the rest. He was a lusty and desperate young man." Peach was a soldier in the Pequot War, "one of the forwardest in any attempt," but he had run out of money and fallen into "idle courses and company." He had planned to go to New Amsterdam and had convinced the others to go with him. It was later discovered that he had another reason to flee Plymouth: "he had got a maid with child…a man's servant in the town, and fear of punishment made him get away."[3,4]

While fleeing, the party stopped to camp for the night, and Penowanyanquis happened by. He was on his way to Plymouth after, "a-trading and had both cloth and beads about him." Peach and company "took a rapier and ran him through the body once or twice" and stole the wampum and coats, "leaving him for dead." The mortally wounded boy was found by three Narragansett men, who heard his story. These men sent word to Reverend Roger Williams, who came and interviewed the boy. Two physicians, Thomas James and John Green, attended him, but "found his wounds mortal and that he could not live." As predicted, he died within a few days.[5,6]

Daniel Cross escaped the colony, but the three other men were held and questioned, "being often examined and the evidence produced, they all in the end freely confessed in effect all that the Indian accused them of, and that they had done it in the manner aforesaid." The three men were put on trial, found guilty, and condemned to be hanged. "Some of the Narragansett Indians and of the party's friends were present when it was done, which gave them and all the country good satisfaction." Bradford noted of the hanging of the three men, "It was a matter of much sadness to them here, and was the second execution which they had since they came; being both for willful murder."[7]

The next capital crime in Plymouth occurred in 1642 and was not a murder but a case of bestiality. The court record is brief and reads: "Thomas Granger, late servant to Love Brewster, of Duxbury, was this court indicted for buggery with a mare, a cow, two goats, diverse sheep, two calves, and a turkey, and was found guilty, and received sentence of death by hanging until he was dead." As with the previous case, Bradford elaborates at some length about this case in his history, *Of Plymoth Plantation*.[8]

Granger, we learn, was "about 16 or 17 years old" and was observed committing the crime of buggery, or bestiality, with a mare. After first denying it, he finally gave a "free confession...not only in private to the magistrates (though at first he strived to deny it) but to sundry, both ministers and others, and afterwards, upon his indictment, to the whole court and jury; and confirmed it at his execution." His execution, wrote Bradford, on about September 9, was "a very sad spectacle." All the animals Granger violated, "the mare, a cow, two goats, five sheep, two calves and a turkey," were executed "before his face, according to the law, Leviticus 20:15; and then he himself was executed."[9]

By 1648, five men (and an assortment of farm animals) had been executed for capital crimes. While the court records are relatively succinct, William Bradford wrote of these crimes and executions at length in his history of Plymouth, revealing how strongly they affected him. However, Bradford never wrote about the murder of Martha Clarke in his history of the colony.

All that we have learned about Alice Bishop's crime was gleaned from the court record, much of which was penned by the governor. He alone chose what to include in the official report and what to leave out. Bradford's interview with Rachel Ramsden provides the few and only details of the murder, even though she was not a witness to the crime. Alice Bishop's statements, if there were any other than her confession and apologies, were not recorded. The collection of evidence that morning was mainly in two parts, Bradford's interview of the only "witness," Rachel Ramsden, and the investigation of the crime scene by a jury of inquiry. The governor probably climbed the ladder and viewed the child's body for himself and he probably asked Alice Bishop what had happened. He would have then sent some of those present out to summon the men he needed for a jury of inquiry. Then he sat down with Rachel Ramsden.

No doubt both Governor Bradford and Rachel Ramsden had personal interests in mind as they reviewed what had happened that morning. Rachel would undoubtedly wish to present herself in the best light possible. Bradford, looking ahead to a trial and most likely an execution, needed to be sure the evidence was solid and complete, so he had followed Plymouth law to the letter.

Who Was Rachel Ramsden?

Governor Bradford had known Rachel Ramsden since her birth. Rachel was the daughter of *Mayflower* passenger Francis Eaton, a non-Separatist carpenter hired by the Merchant Adventurers. He had arrived in Plymouth in 1620 with his wife, Sarah, and son, Samuel, and was a signer of the Mayflower Compact. According to the governor, Sarah had died in the first "general sickness." Francis Eaton then married a woman identified only as Dorothy. She was also a *Mayflower* passenger and had been a maidservant to John Carver. Dorothy died soon after the marriage.[10,11,12,13]

Eaton was married a third time, this time to Christian Penn, who came to Plymouth on the *Anne* in 1623. They started a family of their own and had three children: Rachel, who was born in 1625, Benjamin, born in 1628, and another unnamed and unfortunate child whom Bradford curtly labeled "an idiot." The Eatons did not do well financially. In 1633 Francis Eaton was taxed only nine shillings, the lowest tax rate, reflecting his impoverished condition.[14,15]

Francis Eaton died in 1633, leaving his widow with four children and many outstanding debts, "far more than the estate of the said Francis would make good." The court ordered Mr. Thomas Prence and Mr. John Done to review the estate inventory and settle the debts as best they could, so that "the widow be freed and acquitted from any claim or demands of all or any his creditors whatsoever." One of Eaton's creditors was Francis Billington.[16,17]

Christian Eaton and Francis Billington settled the debt and became more than friends. In July 1634 they were married. Rachel would have been about nine years old at the time. Christian brought her four children to live in Francis's home near High Cliff in Playne Dealing. The family was so closely identified with the area that for some time afterward the rocks offshore were known as Billington's Rocks.[18]

As poor as the Eatons had been, they still enjoyed some status in the colony because Francis Eaton had a useful trade. The Billingtons were quite another story. Christian had married down, not only financially, if that were possible, but also socially. Bradford called the Billingtons "one of the profanest families amongst them." They were considered to be lazy and contentious, troublemakers from the start.[19]

However unmanageable they were, the Billingtons were *Mayflower* passengers, and all were entitled to land grants. Eleanor owned two twenty-acre plots in Playne Dealing; she sold one to Thomas Armitage in 1637, and she transferred ownership of the other to her son Francis that same year. In the agreement with Francis, she stipulated that part of the parcel would "be hers to use during her natural life." Eleanor then married Gregory Armstrong in 1638. Francis, Gregory and Eleanor were living on the property adjacent to George Clarke's acreage when Christian and her brood joined the family.[20,21]

Francis and Christian Billington had nine children of their own. They were very poor and many of their children were put out into service or apprenticeships. While that was not unusual, in the Billington case some of these arrangements were court ordered because the children were not well cared for. Seven months after marrying Francis Billington, Christian put her son Benjamin Eaton into service with the widow Bridget Fuller for a term of fourteen years. Christian's daughter Elizabeth was seven years old on April 18, 1642, when she was put into an apprenticeship of thirteen years with John and Mary Barnes. In January 1643, son Joseph was six or seven and daughters Martha and Mary were about five years old when they were bound out.[22,23,24]

Not surprisingly, Francis Billington was not at this time a freeman. He was occasionally called into court over the years—for instance, on June 4, 1645, he was fined twenty shillings "or corporal punishment" for an unnamed infraction—but later in life earned a small measure of good standing in the colony. He served on various committees, and while his son Joseph was constantly in trouble, Francis was finally made a freeman in 1657.[25]

There is no record of Rachel going into service. She may have been kept at home to help care for her younger step-siblings. At the time of Martha Clarke's murder in 1648, however, Rachel was twenty-three years old and had been married for more than two years to Joseph Ramsden, who worked a pine tar kiln deep in the woods. They had no children, or at least no surviving children.[26]

Francis and Christian Billington's land abutted the Clarke/Bishop property, and Rachel was likely visiting her parents in Playne Dealing on the day of the murder. Rachel was Governor Bradford's best source of information about the crime, and perhaps she saw this as an opportunity to rescue the family's reputation from disrepute. Perhaps she enjoyed the attention, unaccustomed to a role of some importance. Whatever the case may have been, she would have made the best of the opportunity. However, her need for approval may have been exercised at Alice Bishop's expense. While there is no evidence that Rachel Ramsden lied in her testimony of the murder of Martha Clarke, it is possible that she may not have been entirely forthcoming.

The Morning of the Murder

According to Rachel Ramsden's testimony, on July 22, 1648, she visited her neighbor, Alice Bishop, "upon an errand." Perhaps she came to borrow some household item, or to return one. When she entered the house, what she observed seems to have been a very ordinary Plymouth household scene. It may have been a warm day in late July, but there would probably have been a fire in the fireplace, since there was nearly always a fire crackling in every hearth in the colony. A kettle of stew or a pudding would have been set to simmer, along with a quietly bubbling kettle of plain water for boiling vegetables or washing up. Alice was most likely preparing food and using a sharp knife when Rachel arrived.[27]

Rachel's testimony does not mention Richard Bishop being at home, so he was most likely at work in the fields. During July and August, he would have been cutting hay with a long-handled scythe, leaving it to dry in the sun before carting it to the barnyard, stacking and covering it for later use. Besides this seasonal work, Richard also had the animals to tend. There was George Clarke's goat herd to manage, and the Bishops probably had several chickens and a pig or two, as did most Pilgrim families.

According to Rachel, four-year-old Martha was in the house, apparently asleep in her bed, probably a mattress and blankets on the floor. Rachel did not mention the two other children who made up the household, although female children would normally have been at home with their mother, helping with household tasks. Richard may have taken six-year old Abigail with him, as it was common enough for girls to help feed the animals, and she was not mentioned in the court record of the crime. The baby Damaris would have been kept close to her mother and was most likely present.

From Rachel's report, the two women apparently had a friendly enough visit, Rachel finding Alice to be "as well as she hath known her at any time." The Billingtons had been neighbors of the Clarkes and then the Bishops for about ten years, so Rachel would have known Alice for a long time. They may have shared neighborhood news and gossip and talked of homely things. Then Alice asked Rachel to run an errand for her. Rachel testified that "the wife of... Richard Bishop requested her to go fetch her some buttermilk at Goodwife Winslow's, and gave her a kettle for that purpose, and she went and did it."[28]

Who Was Goodwife Winslow?

Mary Chilton Winslow was the wife of John Winslow. The couple were respected members of the community who had a large family of ten children. John Winslow was not a first-comer, having arrived in Plymouth in 1621 as a passenger on the *Fortune*. He was, however, one of the younger brothers of Edward Winslow, who was a Leiden Separatist, a *Mayflower* passenger, Plymouth's main mediator with the Indians, and later in the colony's history, one of its governors.

John Winslow was highly esteemed in the colony in his own right. He was a Purchaser and was on the 1633 Freemen list. Plymouth Colony records show that on May 7, 1638, John Winslow was granted land to enlarge his holdings "at Playne Dealing, as far as the lesser swamp, where they used to saw spruce trees." He served on many committees, and in 1642 was one of the men appointed to a committee that decided who would receive land grants, no small responsibility. They were a relatively wealthy family, as alluded to by the fact that Mary Winslow's will mentions several pieces of silver and large pieces of furniture.[29,30]

John's wife, Mary, had arrived on the *Mayflower* and was the daughter of James Chilton, a Leiden Separatist. Though there is a persistent legend that, as a young girl, Mary Chilton was the first of the Pilgrims to set foot on Plymouth Rock, a careful reading of the evidence reveals that the landing party was all male, and that even the authenticity of Plymouth Rock remains questionable. Both of her parents died during the first winter when she was about thirteen. When Rachel Ramsden visited Mary Winslow with Alice Bishop's kettle to collect buttermilk, Mary would have been about forty-one years old.

Mary Winslow may have provided milk and butter for her neighbors on a regular basis from her own cows. In its early years, there were communal herds in Plymouth tended by the town herdsman from spring to fall, grazing during the day and brought into the walled town in the evening for milking. By the mid-1640s, however, draft animals and milk cows were kept closer to home and pastured on the lands of individual owners.

Early land records are not clear, and it is impossible today to know the exact location of the Winslow farm. We do know that the lots were long and narrow, and most likely all houses were built in a row at the same narrow end of the property, creating a neat little village. A standard English acre was 66 feet by 660 feet (one chain by one furlong), and if George Clarke's original purchase was two English acres wide, the distance between next-door neighbors could have been less two hundred feet. However, the Winslow property was not immediately adjacent to Clarke's. Rachel did not recount how long it may have taken her to fetch the buttermilk and how long she was away from the home of Richard Bishop, but when she returned, it was to a shocking scene.

A Follow-Up Question

The first thing Rachel noticed when she reappeared at the Bishops' home with the buttermilk was that Alice was "sad and dumpish." Rachel also noticed a pool of blood at the foot of the ladder that led to the second floor. Alice may have appeared dazed and in shock, but she was able to speak or at least to gesture. When Rachel asked about the blood, Alice pointed up to the upper chamber and "bid her look" for herself. Instead Rachel ran to get her parents.[31]

The first part of the interview with Rachel Ramsden is a fairly straightforward relating of the events, but it appears that after considering her testimony, Bradford had a follow-up question. His record of her statement says, "Moreover, [Rachel] said the reason that moved her to think [Alice] had killed her child was that when she saw the blood she looked on the bed, and the child was not there."[32]

The word "moreover" indicates an addition to Rachel's statement, perhaps in response to a question from the governor. From her answer he may have asked her to explain why, when she saw the blood, she first thought that Alice had harmed her own child.

Rachel Ramsden had a ready answer, that the child was no longer in the bed, so Alice must have killed her. If Bradford was not satisfied with that answer, he made no note of it. If Ramsden offered any further information, he did not record it, but the subtle wording of his report invites speculation as to whether he felt he was hearing the whole story.

Chapter Seventeen

Investigation of the Crime Scene
Plymouth Colony, 1648

The collection of evidence in the investigation of Martha Clarke's murder was twofold: recording the sworn testimony from Rachel Ramsden, and the inspection of the crime scene by the jury of inquiry, whose job it was to establish the cause of death.

The report of the investigation jury, probably penned by Governor Bradford himself, stated that each man entered the Bishop home, and the first thing they saw was "much blood" at the foot of the ladder, "which leads into an upper chamber." Then each man climbed the ladder and entered the attic, where they found Martha's body. Near the body they found a bloody knife, "which knife all of us judged" was the murder weapon. The men must have questioned Alice, because they testified that she confessed "to five of us at one time, that she murdered the child with the said knife."[1]

When Alice confessed, she admitted in effect that she had committed a capital crime, that is, a crime punishable by death. Usually two witnesses were required in cases of capital crimes, but a confession, when "a man witness against himself, his own testimony is sufficient" for imposing the death penalty. Her confession also meant that the jury of inquiry would not have to prove that she committed the crime; they would only need to report what they saw at the scene.[2]

Nowhere in the court record is there a reference to Alice's motive for murdering her child. She may have offered a reason; but if so, it was not recorded. She admitted that she deliberately cut Martha's throat and in the Pilgrim mind, the crime was so heinous that no explanation could mitigate the act. In the context of all that was Plymouth Colony, once she had confessed, according to law, she must hang.

The Men on the Jury of Inquiry

It was probably in the yard in front of Bishop's house when Governor Bradford swore in each man selected for the jury of inquest to "make inquiry of the death of the child of Alice Bishop, the wife of Richard Bishop." All twelve were residents of Plymouth Township, since all are recorded on the 1643 "Able to Bear Arms" list. They were likely either neighbors who had already gathered at Richard Bishop's house when they heard of the murder, or men who lived close enough to be conveniently summoned at short notice.[3]

But not every man chosen for the inquest jury fully met the colony's laws regarding such panels. It was the law that juries should be made up of freemen, "if thought convenient," because it was assumed that no one could "do service to his majesty as well as such as have taken up their freedom." Men who were considered "freemen" had been chosen as deserving of the privilege of voting and were elected by the General Court. But three of the men who conducted the investigation were not freemen: Francis Billington, Thomas Pope, and William Nelson. (All three would later be awarded their freedom in 1657.) Perhaps Bradford judged these to be "honest men" and thus able to serve under the spirit of the law, or maybe they were already on the scene or could be easily convened, thus expediting the investigation. After all, since Alice Bishop had already confessed, the responsibility bestowed on each man was only to observe and report, not to build a case that would eventually be used to identify the guilty party.[4,5]

Of course, the inquest jury was all male. Of the nine whose ages are known, the average age was forty-seven. The oldest was probably Francis Cooke, who was sixty-five in 1648; the youngest may have been Thomas Pope, who was thirty-six. All of the men were married, and nearly all were fathers. In fact, John Howland had a four-year child of his own at the time, the same age as the murdered Martha.

Some of the men were leaders in the community. Giles Rickard had once been Plymouth Township's constable, and James Hurst was a deacon of the Plymouth Church. Some had trades: James Cole was a shoemaker, and Thomas Pope was a cooper. Some were neighbors of George Clarke and later of Richard Bishop in Playne Dealing, including Robert Lee, Francis Billington, John Shaw, and John Cooke. In 1643, Lee, Billington, and Shaw had set wolf traps with George Clarke. Some of the men had less than stellar reputations among the Pilgrims. Francis Billington's father, John, had been hanged for murder.

Nonetheless, the jury of inquiry represented a cross section of the males of Plymouth Colony. Considering how few people lived in the colony in 1648, and that all of them gathered on Sundays for religious services, it can be assumed that all the members knew George Clarke, Richard Bishop, and Alice Clarke Bishop personally.

Governor Bradford apparently did not make any attempt to screen the members of the jury for bias against the Bishop family. However, it is curious to note that Edward Doty, although a neighbor of the Bishops, was not called to serve on the jury of inquiry; neither did he later serve on the grand jury or the petty jury in this case. Considering that he was an adversary of George Clarke's in their property dispute, it may be that Governor Bradford excluded him deliberately, or perhaps Doty, who was well known for his dubious dealings, was considered unfit for jury duty. Or is also entirely possible that he was not present on that particular day and simply missed the opportunity.

Unlike our contemporary justice system wherein prospective jurors are carefully screened for bias, Plymouth Colony juries were made up of men who had likely known a defendant and his or her family for decades. A defendant on trial for a specific offense would have been judged not only on his or her culpability for that crime but, even if unconsciously, on the behavior of a lifetime. This is one of the reasons why an individual's reputation was so important in Plymouth. Some colonists were considered godly, and others were not. How Alice Bishop was regarded is unknown, but having confessed to murder, her previous reputation was irrelevant.

Analyzing the Report of the Jury of Inquiry

The jury of inquiry's report does not contain any conflicts with Rachel Ramsden's testimony. Looking at the evidence in the interview and the report, at least a few aspects of the crme seem certain.

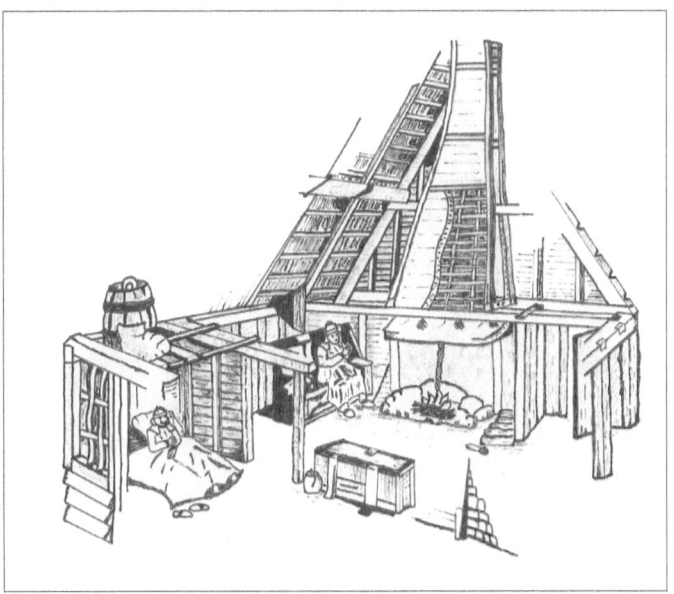

Cut-away view of house similar to George Clarke's.

When each of the jury members entered the house, the first thing they saw was "much blood" at the food of the ladder, "which leadeth into an upper chamber." Viewing George Clarke's original plans, it is apparent that a full-length second floor was built into the house. A simple wooden ladder led up to that space, which was probably used for storage. Perhaps the children played up there.[6]

While the jury of inquest's report states that the body was found in the upper chamber, it does not say where the murder took place.

The evidence suggests that the murder took place in the upper floor of the house, probably near the top of the ladder where the knife was found, but according to Rachel Ramsden's testimony, she last saw the child downstairs in bed when she left the house to get buttermilk. There is no evidence in the indictment that Alice moved the body of Martha Clarke, and there is no mention of blood on Alice's clothes or on her person. Furthermore, the only obvious reason for her to move the body would have been to hide it, and Alice seems to have made no efforts to conceal the crime. She directed Rachel to the murdered child, and the murder weapon, the knife, was in plain view. It seems unlikely, therefore, that she would have carried the child's bloody body up the ladder.

Ladder leading to upper chamber as viewed from doorway.

Also, both Rachel Ramsden's statement and the report of the jury of inquiry tell of a quantity of blood at the foot of the ladder. That blood at the bottom of the ladder probably indicated that the child died in the upper chamber, and her blood flowed down one of the ladder's legs and collected into a pool on the main floor of the home. It is probable, therefore, that the murder was committed either in the upper chamber or on the ladder at some point. How Alice and Martha got up there is a question not answered in the report.

The commentary then addressed the wounds. The injuries to the child were severe and had been administered with great violence. There were several long, deep cuts across the child's throat. The cuts were so brutal that the child's windpipe, a tough organ protected with cartilage rings and muscle fibers, was cut and forcibly folded downward into her throat. Martha's carotid artery and jugular veins were undoubtedly cut, resulting in the large amount of blood loss.

The injury to the windpipe is significant. Forensic experts today say that a simple knife cut differs from a chopping wound in that the first is a straight wound with sharp edges, but the second produces a crushing effect that results when blow after blow after blow hits bony body parts. Martha's throat was not simply cut; it was chopped or hacked. Martha was killed with several chopping wounds across her throat, "diverse gashes cross ways, the windpipe cut and stuck in the throat downward."[7]

All we know about the knife is that it was bloody and lying near the body. It was probably a knife Alice Bishop had been using to prepare food. The knife was a weapon of convenience, a common, readily available household implement. Seventeenth-century knives served not only as cutting implements but also as forks do today. They had long, thin blades and pointed ends that were used to pierce food and convey it to the mouth. Meals were mostly made up of mixed dishes, soups, stews, or pottages. Large pieces of meat were roasted and then boiled into a stew with other ingredients. The Pilgrims ate with knives, spoons, and their fingers.

The way Alice murdered her child, chopping at her throat with a knife, mimics the act of slaughtering a farm animal. As a farmer's wife, Alice would have had some experience in slaughtering animals, holding them down with one hand while cutting their throats with the other. The child was found lying on her left cheek and was apparently not moved by the jurymen, so it is most likely that the cuts were to the right side of her throat. It may be that Alice held her daughter down with her left hand, pinning the child's arms still, and attacked Martha with the knife in her right hand, as she would have when she chopped off the head of a chicken or turkey. There is no mention of defense wounds to Alice's person, such as fingernail scratches to show that Martha resisted the attack. But, by pinning Martha's arms against her body, Alice had prevented her from fighting back.

Martha's wounds and external bleeding were the obvious causes of death, but her death was not immediate. The child's heart apparently beat long enough after the injury to pump out the large amount of blood that flowed down the leg of the ladder and pooled on the floor.

Alice's Confession

One of the most important pieces of evidence in Alice Bishop's case was her confession. The jury of inquiry's report states: "Alice hath confessed to five of us at one time that she murdered the child with the said knife." It was almost certain she gave her confession freely, since she had already, to some extent, confessed to Rachel Ramsden when she gestured to the upper floor. However, there were no legal rights in place to protect her from a making a spontaneous statement and later regretting it, no rules or warnings against self-incrimination.[8]

Another reason the confession was so important was in its religious significance to Plymouth. The Pilgrims believed that God's forgiveness could come only after confession and repentance. Alice clearly regretted her crime and expressed remorse. When she appeared before the Court of Assistants on August 1, 1648, she again "confessed she did commit the aforesaid murder" and added that she was "sorry for it." Within this culture, Alice Bishop's soul could thence be saved and—even more important—the community be restored to God's favor. Obtaining a full confession also reassured the magistrates that they were doing the right thing.[9]

The governor took Alice at her word when she said she committed the crime, and there is no evidence to suggest that someone else did it. However, given the quick and full confession, the question must be raised if only to dismiss it—was Alice innocent and in fact protecting the real murderer? The only other possible suspect would have been her six-year-old daughter, Abigail. Could an argument between sisters have escalated into violence? Was Abigail strong enough to wield the knife? If so, was Alice faced with the choice to assume responsibility herself, or surrender her young daughter to Plymouth justice? If that was the situation, it is easy to imagine a mother choosing her child's life over her own and taking the secret to her grave. It is intriguing to consider this possible explanation of the crime and the aftermath; however, once Alice made a confession, all efforts to prosecute the crime would have focused on her alone.

Alice Bishop's Arrest

Once the investigation was completed, Alice Bishop must have been taken into custody, and Richard Bishop was likely left at home to clean up his house, comfort the couple's remaining daughters, Damaris and Abigail, and prepare his stepchild Martha's body for burial, perhaps with the help of neighbors.

Ephraim Morton was the Plymouth Township constable, newly elected on June 7, 1648, at the same General Court that had admitted him as a freeman. It was part of the constable's duties to "bind over persons for matters of crime to answer at the next ensuing court of his Majesties after the fact committed or the person apprehended." Morton would have taken Alice Bishop to the Plymouth Colony jail, the two-story building located "upon the waste land near betwixt Mistress Fuller and Mr. Hicks."[10]

During Alice's incarceration, Richard Bishop would have to pay for her care and food. On October 28, 1645, the court voted "that the colonies shall allow [two pence] per day to maintain a prisoner for felony or misdemeanor." A provision was made that if the prisoner's family was "not able to maintain themselves," that the funds would come out of the colony's treasury. With no record of any charges against the treasury, it can be assumed that Richard Bishop paid for Alice's care.[11]

Alice Bishop's First Appearance in Court

On August 1, 1648, the case of the murder of Martha Clarke was brought before the Court of Assistants in Plymouth Town. On that day the court was made up of Governor William Bradford, Mr. William Collier, Capt. Myles Standish, and Mr. William Thomas. Courts usually met on Tuesdays. In the summertime they met at seven in the morning, taking a dinner break at eleven, and returning to finish their business "until a convenient hour in the evening."[12,13]

Alice's crime wasn't the only matter before the court that day. Debts were settled. Bills were paid. Bridges and highways were discussed. One Richard Burton was "censured by the court," fined, and ordered to "be publicly whipped," for stealing a calf.[14]

After the mundane matters of the colony were addressed, Alice was presented to the court, along with evidence of the crime, the report of the jury of inquiry, and Governor Bradford's interview with Rachel Ramsden. The governor and his assistants questioned Alice Bishop about the murder of her daughter. Again, she confessed, this time adding she was "sorry for it." No further action was taken that day.[15]

Alice was set to return to court on October 4 to appear before the grand jury and then before the petty jury for trial.

Pleading Pregnancy

Being allowed two months between her first appearance in court and her trial would seem to be arbitrary, but if so, it was a fortuitous coincidence. Two months would give Plymouth matrons time enough to determine whether Alice Bishop was pregnant. The English honored an old Roman law that said no woman who was carrying a child would be hanged until the birth of the child. The law was often used by women prisoners in London's Old Bailey in "the hanging days" as a ploy to save their necks when any felonious offense could result in execution. The accused could have "pleaded her belly"; that is, she could have claimed to be pregnant and thereby avoided execution—at least temporarily.

At that time pregnancy was the province of women, and it might have been relatively easy to convince an all-male court that a child was on the way. The prisoner would then have been examined by a "jury of matrons," who would verify the pregnancy. Perhaps the female panel could be persuaded or bribed to be merciful and "confirm" the pregnancy to allow the prisoner time to gain a reprieve or to actually become pregnant.

In 1633 in Virginia, Margaret Hatch was indicted for murdering her child. A petty jury found her guilty and she was sentenced to hang, but Margaret told the court that she was pregnant in an effort to forestall her fate. However, she was examined by a "jury of Matrons," who found that she was not pregnant, and she was executed.[16]

Alice would probably have been aware of this practice, but there is no record of her pleading pregnancy to save her neck or delay punishment. While in custody, she would have been ministered to by her pastor, visited by friends and family, and watched carefully by women tending to her personal needs. Someone would have noticed if she menstruated, negating any claim of pregnancy.

Alice Bishop was headed to trial—and most assuredly to the gallows.

Chapter Eighteen

The Trial and the Verdict
Plymouth Colony, 1648

The air would certainly have been cool and crisp in Duxbury that October in 1648, with autumn leaves turning shades of yellow, gold, and brown. It was time for the semiannual Plymouth Colony Fair, held every October in Duxbury, and the mood of the colonists would have been as bright as the leaves.

By law the Duxbury Fair began on the first Wednesday in October every year —October 4 in 1648—and continued for two days, for the trading of "cattle and commodities." The colony practiced a barter economy and, following English tradition, did most of its trading at markets or fairs. Each township had a weekly market for the trade of local produce, dairy products, and live poultry, but the fairs had all this and more. In addition to all the local vendors, sellers ventured south from the Bay Colony to market their wares either manufactured there or imported from England. They set up stalls offering such things as iron pots and kettles and skillets; ladles and spoons and knives; mortars and pestles for grinding corn and herbs; axe heads, chisels, and saws; bowls, beakers, and cups; ceramic jars, pitchers, and crocks for storing cheese; trivets and table linens; fishing gear; woolen cloth, canvas, and leather; shoes and boots; and much more. They might bring a few luxury items, too, such as casks of wine or lengths of colorful silk ribbon.[1]

Bostonians came to buy products, too, especially the Plymouth Colony cattle. Even the local tribes took part, offering baskets and brooms woven by the women. The air smelled of outdoor fires and simmering stews and frying meats. There was beer, too, big, foamy mugs of it, and sweet apple cider poured from wooden barrels.

Fairs were social gatherings as well, the farmers discussed the weather, and haggled over the price of a pig or a pair of geese or a flock of chickens, the women shared local news, recipes, and gossip. Children ran free, devising games of tag or hide-and-seek. Young men and women sought out friends and flirted with potential mates. All the hustle and bustle and gaiety took place under the watchful eye of the constable. Order need be maintained, especially in the midst of Pilgrim pleasure. Public drunkenness was a crime, as was selling guns to the Indians.

Besides all the commerce and socializing, there was another purpose to the Duxbury Fair. The first day of the fair was set aside as the meeting day of the General Court. All the colony's freemen were members of the General Court and were expected to attend. So it was that on October 4, 1648, at the General Court meeting in Duxbury, nearly every Plymouth Colony freeman would be there, most likely with their families. Many of the men would take part in Alice Bishop's trial, but by then everyone would have known she had confessed to the crime, so it was a foregone conclusion that she was guilty.

The Pilgrims preferred their punishments to be carried out in public where they would have the most psychological effect. Public whippings and executions were designed to impress and shock the entire community into a fear so intense that it would ensure future compliance with community standards.

Sometime between her first appearance before the courts and her second, Alice was moved from her place of confinement in Plymouth Town to Duxbury.

Effects of a Public Trial

Not only did the Pilgrims prefer to administer punishments in public, they also held trials in public. They wanted a broader engagement in the case beyond just those individuals who would participate in the formal judicial proceedings.

Word of Alice Bishop's crime would have traveled quickly in this small community. Shock would have led to curiosity; rumor and gossip would soon have followed. This case was not only a matter of law; it was a matter of morality. Hearing about evil in a church sermon is one thing; knowing someone who succumbed to it is entirely another. The case would give the colony's leaders an opportunity to emphasize community beliefs and standards in a very effective way.

In this community, religion and government were tightly intertwined, and trying the case of Martha Clarke's murder, bringing out in public all the bloody details, would underscore that Plymouth Colony was committed to God's law. As John Robinson had written, "Punishments in all societies, family, church, and commonwealth, which they that exercise, bear the image of God's justice, and holiness."[2]

At the same time, this case would remind the community of the Devil's power—and presence—in Plymouth. Robinson had also said, "when therefore, we thus suffer any heinous injuries of any kind by any, we must pray the Lord both to deliver us out of their hands, and them out of the Devil's, whose instruments they are, in so doing."[3]

Certainly the colony's leaders would see the trial and execution of Alice Bishop as a deterrent to crime. "It is by rewards and punishments societies are preserved," wrote Robinson. "And of these two, though occasion of rewards be more to be desired, yet the execution of punishments is more diligently to be looked unto, for the preserving of human socieites. ....Vice and villany...can be restrained in the most, and worst, only by the fear of punishment." The punishment, he added, may reach the guilty one, but "the fear and warning [reach] many."[4]

Another effect of a public trial would be to remind the community of their shared responsibility for Martha's murder. In the minds of the Pilgrims, the entire community was culpable in this crime. Robinson wrote: "He that says expressly 'Thou shalt not kill,' means also, as well, thou shalt preserve thy neighbor's life."[5]

From their days in Holland the Pilgrims described themselves as "knit together as a body in a more strict and sacred bond and covenant of the Lord...and by virtue whereof we do hold ourselves straightly tied to all care of each other's good, and of the whole by every, and so mutual." That Alice could entertain a state of mind that would lead her to murder her child and that no one would have noticed would have bothered the community's leaders greatly. They had been neglectful in watching over each other and needed to be reminded of their sacred responsibility to pay close attention to their neighbors.[6]

Furthermore, the community would have been concerned for Alice Bishop's eternal soul, and a public trial would make it possible for the convicted person to repent in public and thereby seek redemption from a merciful God. We know from other cases of child murder in New England that ministers visited the accused in prison, giving comfort and preaching repentance. That Alice might be restored to God's love would have comforted this community greatly.

Wednesday, October 4, 1648 – The Grand Jury Gathers at Duxbury Meeting House

Today it is known as the Myles Standish Burial Ground and it sits on the north side of Chestnut Street, just beyond Hall's corner, in Duxbury. It is famous not only for Capt. Standish's presumed grave, but also as the oldest maintained cemetery in the United States. The "Old Burying Ground" covers one and a half acres and is near the former locations of the first and second Meeting Houses. To the right of the entrance is a granite marker showing the site of Duxbury's first Meeting House, which was built in 1637.[7]

This small building was the political, religious, and social center of the community. Sabbath services were held here every week. The township's court met here. Marriage notices were nailed on the walls, and so were animal heads, brought in as proof to collect bounty rewards. Capt. Standish trained the militia in a field nearby, and stray animals were collected into a pound and held for claiming. It was in this meeting house that Alice Bishop's case would be heard.

Early in the day Governor William Bradford and his assistants,

This illustration depicts the trial of John Billington in Plymouth in 1630. Alice Bishop's trial may have been similarly held.

Timothy Hatherly, Thomas Prence, William Thomas, and Capt. Myles Standish, convened the General Court. They would be seated behind a plain table at the front of the room, the juries and spectators woud sit on plain wooden benches.

The first order of business that day was Alice Bishop's case: "At this court," the record reads, "Alice Bishop, the wife of Richard Bishop, of New Plymouth, was indicted for felonious murder by her committed, upon Martha Clarke, her own child, the fruit of her own body."[8]

After two months in custody we can only guess at Alice's appearance. The two pence Richard Bishop was paying for her care may have covered food and simple sanitation, but whether laundry was included is open to question. Perhaps her husband Richard or a kindhearted neighbor would have made sure her clothes were presentable. Surely, she was terrified .

The bill of indictment, or formal charge of felony murder, was presented to the grand jury to determine if the charges seemed reasonable and if the case should proceed to trial. The members, listed above, had been selected at the June Court of Elections to serve an entire year. Their job was to investigate crimes and misdemeanors, "enquiring into the abuses and breaches of such wholesome laws and ordinances as tend to the preservation of the peace and the good of the subject." All had sworn the Oath of Grandjury man: "You shall true presentment make of all things given you in charge, you shall present Nothing of Malice or ill will, your own council and your fellows in reference to this oath you shall well and truly keep so help you God."[9,10]

It is interesting to note that Love Brewster was permitted to sit in judgment of Alice Bishop even though her husband, Richard Bishop, was once in Love's employ. The concept of an impartial jury was not acknowledged in Plymouth Colony. Each juror had sworn not to employ "malice or ill will," and that was apparently considered enough to insure a fair decision.

The charge presented to the grand jury included the jury of inquiry's report, Governor Bradford's interview with Rachel Ramsden, and probably some informal statements by the governor. There may have been some questions asked and some discussion held among jury members, but any deliberations were not recorded.

The grand jury found the indictment "a true bill," meaning that the charges seemed reasonable and that the case could proceed to trial. At this point Alice Bishop was not determined to be innocent or guilty, only charged, and the case now went before the petty jury.

Wednesday, October 4, 1648 – The Petty Jury Meets

Justice moved fast on October 4. In the tiny courthouse the grand jury stood and changed seats with the members of the petty jury, and the actual trial commenced immediately. The members of Alice Bishop's petty jury, listed above, were selected especially for this trial. Their average age was about forty-eight. Unlike the jury of inquiry, which was made up of local residents of Plymouth Township and especially of Playne Dealing, a petty jury such as the one that would decide Alice Bishop's case could have been made up of representatives from several Plymouth townships, including Duxbury, Barnstable, Sandwich, Yarmouth, Taunton, and Scituate, whose freemen made up the General Assembly. This practice assured a wider participation of colonists in the decision.

Even though Alice Bishop had confessed that she murdered her child with a knife, she was still given the full benefits of public Pilgrim justice and brought to trial before a jury to determine her guilt or innocence. The governor and his assistants wanted to make absolutely sure she was guilty and deserved to hang. As John Robinson advised, "He that punishes another, whether as judge or executioner either, must know legally, that he hath done evil, and deserved it.... Otherwise," he continued, "the authority of the whole world cannot bear him out, from being a murderer before God. The law which says, 'Thou shall not murder,' forbids especially violence in judgment."[11]

There is no evidence that Alice Bishop spoke at her trial. No lawyer defended her, as it was not the custom at the time. We can assume, however, that her case was thoroughly deliberated, at least among the governor and his assistants. The Pilgrims, as practiced as they were in debate, would have discussed and reflected on her case since the crime was committed. Bradford's written history asserts that he carefully considered each capital offense, pondering over the circumstances. For example, he asked Thomas Granger, accused of bestiality in 1642, how he first came to "the knowledge and practice of such wickedness," demonstrating a desire for a deeper understanding of the crime. He and the other men may have brought similar compassion to Alice Bishop's offense, but there is no record to support that, just as there is no record of any discussion or deliberation among the jurors.[12]

It was the custom that trial juries eliminate all doubt about a case and determine their verdicts by a unanimous vote. After reviewing the facts of the case, and perhaps asking questions, the petty jury unanimously "found the said Alice Bishop guilty of the said felonious murdering of Martha Clarke aforesaid."[13]

Wednesday, October 4, 1648 – The Sentence

The guilty verdict came as no surprise to anyone. Now it was up to the governor and his assistants to determine Alice's punishment, although this too may have been a foregone conclusion. There may have been private discussions among them, since they had some discretion as to how any criminal in Plymouth was punished, but the law was very clear in cases of capital crime.

Immediately following the guilty verdict, Governor William Bradford and his assistants all agreed, and Alice Bishop "had the sentence of death pronounced against her, [that is] to be taken from the place where she was to the place from whence she came, and thence to the place of execution, and there to be hanged by the neck until her body is dead...."[14]

Capital Punishment in Plymouth

To a twenty-first century sensibility, that sentence may seem harsh, but in the minds of the Pilgrims it was necessary. All their legal and social institutions served the purpose of controlling man's sinful and passionate nature so that God would find favor in their endeavors. To punish wrongdoers would be rational and just and would also provide the guilty a way to achieve redemption in God's mercy. John Robinson called punishment a "merciful cruelty, when men save, by severity, the persons themselves that are punished." "Vice and Villainy," he added, "can be restrained in the most, and worst, only by the fear of punishment."[15]

First and foremost, this was a community committed to living the biblical ideal, and the Bible is clear on the subject of murder: "He that smites a man so that he die, shall be surely put to death" reads Exodus 21;12; "he that kills any man shall surely be put to death" says Leviticus 24:17; and Numbers 35:21 reads that anyone "in enmity [anger] [who] smite him with his hand that he shall die; he that smote him shall surely be put to death; for he is a murderer."

Beyond those injunctions, the Pilgrims followed another of

God's commands—balance must be restored to regain God's favor. The Bible states that "blood it defiles the land, and the land cannot be cleansed of the blood that is shed therein, but by the blood of him that shed it."[16]

A mixture of English law, Mosaic law, common sense, Separatism, and a splash of Dutch law made Plymouth Colony justice different, not only from England but from all the other colonies. The founders of Plymouth Colony made a conscious decision to maintain the death penalty but tempered its severity somewhat, compared to the way it was applied in England. First, the Pilgrims greatly reduced the number of capital crimes punishable by death. In England capital crimes included "treason, murder, manslaughter, rape, robbery, burglary, arson, counterfeiting, theft," and more. Conversely there was no death penalty in Plymouth for crimes against property, and no death penalty for theft. Plymouth determined that capital crimes would include treason, murder, witchcraft, adultery, rape, sodomy, and arson. However, there were other settlers in New England who disputed having a prescribed set of punishments for each class of crime.[17]

In Massachusetts, Governor Winthrop argued against the death penalty with the legislature, citing that the Bible is full of examples where murderers were not punished by death. He felt that judges should not be bound by a rigid code but should rather have flexibility to temper justice with wisdom and mercy. The legislature won out, and by March 1648, the Bay Colony committed itself to a code of law that included punishing "murther" with death. (They also prescribed death for "blasphemy, idolatry, witchcraft, false worship, Sabbath breaking…adultery, incest, sodomy, bestiality, man stealing [kidnapping], false witness, reviling the magistrates, cursing or smiting of parents").[18]

Both colonies, however, gave their magistrates discretionary judgment. Plymouth's governor and his assistants had the power to set aside the law and impose any punishment they saw appropriate after reviewing the circumstances of each crime. For Alice Bishop, however, there would be no special allowances. Her guilt was so obvious, based not only on evidence, but also on her confession, that

Bradford and his assistants doubtless had no choice but to impose the death sentence. They knew all of John Robinson's teachings, and were no doubt reflecting on his warning that "to favor wicked and lewd persons, is really to invite and persuade men to evil...."[19]

Death was necessary for several reasons, and they must have pondered them all, given as they were to discussion and analysis. In the end they all decided that Alice Bishop would forfeit her life to atone for murdering little Martha Clarke. "And so she had the sentence of death pronounced against her, that is, to be taken from the place where she was to the place from whence she came, and thence to the place of execution, and there to be hanged by the neck until her body is dead, which accordingly was executed."[20]

Chapter Nineteen

Moving On

Alice Bishop was hanged. The biblical commandments and customs had been honored, the colony's laws adhered to, the crime investigated, judged, and the accused executed, and still there remained a lingering unease in the community. Whether motivated by honor or by revenge the governor and his assistants turned their attention to the loose ends left untied even after the execution. There was no moving on for Plymouth, not just yet.

Richard Bishop

Under their practice of "watchfulness," the entire Plymouth community held themselves responsible for the murder of Martha Clarke. They believed they should have foreseen problems brewing in that family. Nonetheless, the person ultimately responsible for what went on in a household was the head of that household. Before Plymouth could purge itself of its collective guilt, Richard Bishop had to be dealt with, and he provided the perfect opportunity.

Bishop had never been a troublemaker in the colony and, in fact, had appeared to be an honest and hardworking resident. Before the murder he had appeared in the court records only in employment contracts with Love Brewster in 1638 and Nathaniel Sowther in 1641, and in the notice of his marriage to Alice Clarke in 1644. The only element of his colonial life that had set him apart was that he was a hired man, not an indentured servant. As such, he was not completely under the control of a master; he held a level of autonomy and independence that would make this community very apprehensive.[1,2,3]

Shortly after the execution of his wife, Richard Bishop was brought before the court for theft. In March of 1649, he was charged with stealing a spade from Andrew Ring, who also lived in Playne Dealing. The theft of a farm tool was not a trivial matter. Most of the implements the Pilgrims used for their survival, especially in the early years, were handmade and were very valuable to their owners. Punishment was tough for this first-offender: "He was sentenced to sit in the stocks, and to pay a new spade to Andrew Ring before the next June court, or otherwise to be publicly whipped."[4,5]

Andrew Ring was the son of William and Mary Ring. William was on board the *Speedwell* when it was forced to abandon the voyage to New Plymouth. He died shortly after the ship returned to Leiden. Mary Ring and her three children, Elizabeth, Susanna, and Andrew, arrived at Plymouth around 1629. Before Mary died in 1631, she named Samuel Fuller and Thomas Blossom (members of the original Leiden congregation) as caretakers of the minor Andrew. Andrew married Deborah Hopkins, daughter of *Mayflower* passenger Stephen Hopkins, and after her death, Lettice Morton, widow of John Morton, another Leiden family. In 1650 he was appointed to the grand inquest and as such took part in the persecution of the Quakers. In other words, Andrew Ring was well-connected in Plymouth Colony.[6]

Apparently, Richard Bishop was still living in Playne Dealing after Alice Bishop's execution, probably in the same house where the murder took place, but that is not known for certain. It is also unknown whether Abigail and Damaris were living with him at the time.

In May 1649, the court reviewed the theft of the spade once again and for the last time. Apparently, Richard settled with Andrew Ring outside of court. But, the court jumped on the opportunity to settle the issue of George Clarke's property once and for all, perhaps using the charge against Richard Bishop as the opening they needed. As has already been discussed, Richard Bishop may have been responsible for the household, but he never did own the house or the property.[7] While in the court record of the murder, the property was referred to as "the house of Richard Bishop," after the murder and execution, it was called "George Clarke's property." Bishop had been erased. Almost.

Abigail Clarke

When Martha was murdered and Alice was executed, all of George Clarke's land and moveable property were inherited by Abigail Clarke, George's remaining heir. As she was only six or seven years old at the time, a guardian had to be appointed to oversee her upbringing and manage her land holdings. The court ordered that "John Churchill, of Plymouth, shall have the disposing of the house and land that was George Clarke's for the use and good of Abigail Clarke, daughter unto the said George Clarke, either to let or sell the said house and land with the court's consent."[8]

Who was John Churchill that he should be given this responsibility? In a later record, Abigail Clarke is referred to as Churchill's "kinswoman," but how they were related has not yet been proven. Churchill was a landowner but was not yet a freeman in 1649. He had been married in 1644 to Hannah Pontus, daughter of William Pontus and Wybra Hanson. When Abigail joined the household, the couple had a two-year-old son, and Hannah was expecting a second child. That infant, also named Hannah, was born on November 12, 1649. Abigail Clarke would have been expected to help with the new baby and do her part of the work of the household even though she was a child herself.

From what little can be discovered, both Abigail and her property holdings were well cared for by the Churchills. In 1653, when she was about ten years old, the official cattle mark or brand signifying her ownership was registered, "a half moon on the right ear." John Churchill also trusted Abigail with his oral last will and testament when he was on his deathbed in 1662. In March, 1663, she was called into court to testify about that exchange and said "that on December 24th last her kinsman John Churchill being ill, had expressed as his will that his sons Joseph and Eleazer should have his lands at Plymouth except fifty acres which he left to his son John." The estate was worth about seventy-four pounds. There was no mention of Abigail Clarke among the heirs, but this is probably because she had holdings in her own name that were inherited from her father.[9,10]

There were four more children born to John and Hannah Churchill during the time Abigail lived with them, and she was surely involved in their care. When John died in 1662, the oldest child of the six was fifteen, and the youngest only five. Abigail was about twenty years old. She stayed on with the family for at least four more years.

In 1666 Abigail Clarke, a "spinster of Plymouth" who was then about twenty-four years old, sold some property to Richard Wright, a tailor. "Matron" Hannah Churchill witnessed the documents. The property Abigail sold was described as "my parcel of upland ground lying and being at or near a place commonly called and known by the name of Rocky Nook in the township of Plymouth aforesaid being by estimation six acres be it more or less and is bounded with the land of John Cooke on the north, and the land of Francis Billington on the south, and the common highway to the east; and extending itself up into the woods westerly."[11]

This parcel of land appears to be the same land George Clarke first bought in 1637, bordering John Cooke's, in the Playne Dealing area. Or at least it may have been a part of the same land. The parcel George bought from James Skiff was a ten-acre plot with a house already started on it. In 1639 George added to his holdings, buying an adjoining eight-acre plot from William Hoskins. George Clarke owned eighteen adjacent acres, yet Abigail sold only six.

This is the last mention of Abigail Clarke in the Plymouth public record. It appears that she still owned land in the colony, but it is not known whether she lived on in Plymouth. There is no record of her marrying, but it is quite possible that she did. With names as common as "Abigail" and "Clarke," it has been impossible to single this Abigail Clarke out from all the others with the same name in New England in the same time period with an acceptable level of certainty.[12]

Hannah Churchill, however, did remarry. On June 25, 1669, she married Giles Rickard Sr., the same Rickard who had served on Alice Bishop's jury of inquiry in 1648.[13,14]

Richard and Damaris Bishop

Richard Bishop's whereabouts during the six years after Alice Bishop's execution in 1648 are unknown. He may have stayed on Clarke's property as a caretaker, but there is no record of him being hired for that job. It is also unknown whether Damaris was with him or in someone else's care. What is known is that he was in Eastham on Cape Cod peninsula in 1654. Eastham, also called Poncha by the indigenous peoples, was about fifty miles directly east of Plymouth, and was made a township in 1646.[15]

Whatever Plymouth Colony may have thought of him in terms of any culpability in Martha Clarke's murder, Richard Bishop did well in Eastham. In 1654, he was granted parcels of land and then made his living as a farmer. Specifically, Bishop's land grant was located near Tonset, in the area now known as East Orleans.[16]

By 1655 Richard Bishop was a freeman and shared in the communal ownership of a bull, along with Richard Knowles, Joseph Rogers, George Crispe, and Thomas Roberts. In 1670 Crispe would bring Richard Bishop into court for stealing a "parcel of sheep's wool." Bishop was ordered to pay Crispe thirty shillings, "on receipt whereof [Crispe] is to rest satisfied concerning the matter, and the said Bishop cleared." Most likely this was a case of a sale or trade gone wrong rather than an actual theft, since no corporal punishment was meted out.[17,18,19]

In 1673, the court ordered that "all such persons as have right unto the said grant as old servants" appear in court to make their claims, "or otherwise lose their right." Richard Bishop was entitled to these land grants because he was considered an "old servant" to the original colonists, recalling his work as a hired man for Love Brewster.[20]

Benjamin Church represented Richard Bishop in his claim, and Bishop was awarded grants, but it is not clear where those land grants were located. Later evidence suggests he may have received land in Duxbury which was later sold or traded. In any case, it appears that he and most likely Damaris continued to maintain their homestead in Eastham.[21,22]

There is no record of Richard Bishop marrying again, however, in 1666, Damaris did marry. She was about twenty years old when she married William Sutton, "who hailed from Scituate, Mass." Sutton was a curious choice of a partner for a Pilgrim since he was a Quaker.[23]

Plymouth and the Quakers

Many of Richard Bishop's neighbors on Cape Cod Bay were Quakers. The Plymouth government's official position was that Quakers would not be tolerated in the colony. Even so, a large group of them had settled in Sandwich, located about halfway between the Town of Plymouth and Eastham.

The Quakers were one of the many dissenting Christian groups that arose after the English Civil War (1642-1651). This group believed in a personal experience with Christ, as informed by the New Testament in the Bible. They thought of themselves as restoring the original true church. Quakers refused to take oaths of allegiance, refused to bear arms or pay taxes. In Bradford's little book of verse, it was written about the Quakers that "scarce of them can make good sense," and rhymed that "well they do deserve the whip, even at a cart's axel to skip."[24,25]

Everyone in Plymouth Colony was required to attend Pilgrim services, which gave the vocal Quakers an opportunity to speak out, argue with the ministers, and generally disrupt the services. For example, in 1657 Jane Launder and Sarah Kerby from Sandwich were charged by the Plymouth court for speaking out during services, "opposing and abusing the speaker amongst them." Disturbing the peace was a misdemeanor, and Sarah Kerby was publicly whipped; Jane Launder got off with a warning.[26]

A series of laws were passed in Plymouth to control the Quakers. Residents were forbidden from bringing outsiders into the colony, "to inveigh against ministers and magistrates, to the dishonor of God and contempt of government." Those who disobeyed were apprehended and whipped. Anyone who conducted Quaker meetings in his home could be brought before the court. John Newland of Sandwich owned a house that was the scene of Quaker meetings and was ordered by the court to cease these meetings, "either on the Lords day or at other times," or the court warned, "you will answer the contrary at your peril."[27]

Quakers were punished and fined for not swearing loyalty to the colony. In June of 1658 the Sandwich Quakers were before the court, ordered to "give a reason for their refusing to take the oath of fidelity to this government and unto the State of England." The Quakers answered that "they held it unlawful to take any oath at all." As a consequence, fines were levied against them.[28]

In 1658 the Plymouth court took extraordinary measures against the Quakers. October 21 was designated as a "general day of humiliation." There had been "signs of God's displeasure" with the colony, the court decreed, "manifested…by his visitation [on] many families and persons with sickness and weakness…by the unseasonableness of the weather…and also by letting loose as a scourge upon us those [preaching] gangrene-like doctrines and persons commonly called Quakers." The "infection and disturbance" caused by the Quakers had led to "a spirit of division and disunion both in church and civil affairs."[29]

All the prayers notwithstanding, Quakers continued to visit and mettle in Plymouth. Several were now making their way to Sandwich by sailing into Manomet, a seaside village which was part of Plymouth Colony. The court ordered that such boats be arrested, "taking their sails from their masts...and likewise that you apprehend the bodies of all such Quakers you shall there and then find, and to proceed with them as effectually as if you found them within the bounds of Sandwich or any town within your liberties."[30]

On June 10, 1660, a new set of laws were passed by the General Court stating that Quaker "doctrine and practices manifestly tends to the Subversion of the fundamentals of Christian Religion Church order and the Civil peace of this government." Anyone who would entertain a Quaker in his home was subject to a fine of five pounds or a whipping. The court went so far as to order that cages be built in Sandwich, Duxbury, Marshfield, and Scituate to house Quakers who attended meetings in private homes.[31]

Quakers were almost universally despised and persecuted in Plymouth Colony; their presence blamed for a variety of calamities from diseases to bad weather. If a young Pilgrim woman wanted to reject and disengage herself from the community that had hanged her mother, one of the best ways to do it was to marry a Quaker.

William and Damaris Sutton

Damaris Bishop married William Sutton on July 11, 1666. Damaris was about twenty years old, and William was in his midtwenties. Many sources cite George Sutton and Sarah Tilden as his parents, but recent DNA testing has disproved that claim. His parents are unknown, although it is believed he was born in Scituate about 1641.

William first appears in the Plymouth Colony records on June 5, 1666, as a resident of Barnstable, where his family had resettled. William was called before the courts "for taking away a Bible out of the meeting house at Barnstable, and keeping it, and saying he bought it and would have sold it." He was fined twenty shillings for the theft and an extra ten shillings, "for telling of a lie about it." Apparently, Damaris believed that William had indeed paid for the Bible even if the court did not and they were married about a month later.[32]

In 1668 their first child was born, a girl they named Alice, presumably in honor of her late grandmother. In November 1669, they welcomed a son they named Thomas, and in 1671 they had a second daughter, named Marah but called Mary. This name may have been a version of the name Martha, meaning that Damaris honored the memories of her half-sister as well as her mother.[33]

The persecution of Quakers made life uncomfortable in Eastham. One group of Quaker men and their families had already left for a new colony to the southwest. Located about three hundred miles away, "between the great North [Hudson] and South [Delaware] Rivers," it was known as "the Jerseys." Founded in 1666, it was promoted as a place where the soil was fertile, the weather excellent, where newcomers were welcome and religious freedom guaranteed.[34]

The Suttons made the move in 1672. They likely sailed most of the way and then followed Native American trails into the forest wilderness. They joined their former Eastham Quaker neighbors in Piscataway, New Jersey, where they settled in to enjoy freedom to worship without government interference. Quaker meetings were held there in the home of Nathaniel Fitz-Randolph, who had sailed to Boston with the Winthrop Fleet in 1630.[35]

In 1673 Richard Bishop sold his property at Tonset in Eastham to his neighbor, Thomas Cole. He also sold Capt. Church some property he presumably had been most recently granted, which was probably located near Duxbury. In the records he is then described as residing in Piscataway in New Jersey, having joined his Quaker daughter and her family.[36,37]

On January 30, 1677, William Sutton is listed as the grantee (purchaser) of 120 acres of land in Piscataway. In the subsequent years, William and Damaris' family continued to grow, and by 1682 Damaris had given birth to ten children. In addition to the three who were born in Eastham, Massachusetts, seven joined them in Piscataway, including Damaris, born in 1673, John, born April

20, 1674, Judah, born January 24, 1675, Richard (his grandfather's namesake), born July 18, 1676, Joseph, born June 27, 1678, Benjamin, born February 24, 1680, and the last child, Daniel, born February 25, 1682. Today Suttons Lane, the site of the "old Sutton farm," still exists in Piscataway, not far from the intersection of Highways 95 and 287.[38,39,40]

Life as a Quaker in New Jersey was simple—quite literally. Members of the group were encouraged to keep to "plainness of apparel," to avoid fabrics "striped or flowered," to lay aside "superfluous furniture in house, as double-curtains and valances, great fringes, etc." and to refrain from speaking "the corrupt and unscriptural language of *you* to a single person."[41]

The family would lose four-year old Joseph and two-year old Benjamin in 1682, within just a few days of each other. Perhaps a disease ravaged the family, or maybe it was heartache or too many childbirths in a row, but two months later, on February 6, 1683, at thirty-seven years old, Damaris Sutton also died, leaving William with nine living children. They ranged in age from one-year-old Daniel to fifteen-year-old Alice. Within two years, on January 3, 1684, William Sutton married Jane Barnes and they had a child that same year.[42,43]

Sutton remained an active Friend for his entire life. At a quarterly meeting on August 24, 1704, William Sutton is listed among those proposing that a "Preparative-meeting" be held in Woodbridge once a month. When it came time to move the congregation out of Fitz-Randolph's living room, William Sutton donated a "year-old steer" towards building a new meeting house. The building was completed in 1713, and "William Sutton and his wife, an aged couple, [were offered] the privilege of living up-stairs." The couple apparently lived in the meeting house until William Sutton's death on June 28, 1718. He had fathered a dozen children whose descendants today are too numerous to count.[44,45]

The last mention of Richard Bishop in the historical record was in February of 1677, when he was granted sixty acres of land in Piscataway. It appears that he settled in the area and once again enjoyed the quiet life of a farmer. There is no record that he remarried and no record of his death. One researcher claims he died in 1683/4, but no primary source for that assertion has been found. However, Richard Bishop was still remembered in Eastham on Cape Cod as late as 1690. A land record referred to a feature of the property he once owned at Poncha as "a place called Bishop's Butter Hole," a colloquial reference to a depression in the ground reminiscent of a hollowed-out potato or some other food waiting for a spoonful of butter.[46,47,48,49]

Rachel Ramsden

When Rachel Ramsden gave her testimony to Governor Bradford on the day of Martha Clarke's murder in 1648, she had been married to Joseph Ramsden for about three years. As far as records indicate, they as yet had no children. Sadly, it appears that she had not married well.

Not one of the "old comers," Joseph Ramsden was first documented in Plymouth in 1641 "when he planted a piece of land." On May 3, 1642, he appeared in court requesting the settlement of differences between himself, John Jenney, and Samuel Sturtevant, that appear to have resulted from one of Edward Doty's complicated trading transactions involving a corn partnership. One year later, on June 6, 1643, John Jenney sued both Sturtevant and Ramsden, and the case was settled by the courts. In August of 1643, Joseph Ramsden was included in the list of those able to bear arms in Plymouth, and in March of 1645 he married Rachel Eaton.[50,51]

In addition to farming, Joseph Ramsden produced pine tar. The Ramsdens lived "remotely" in the forest, where there was ready access to pine trees. He had a kiln of sorts to heat the split pine heartwood and then collect the hot, seeping sap. John Josselyn described the process as follows:

> First a place must be paved with stone or the like, a little higher in the middle, about which there must be made gutters, into which the liquor falls, then out

from them other gutters are to be drawn, by which it may be received, then it is put into barrels. The place thus prepared, the cloven wood must be set upright, then must it be covered with a great number of fir and pitch boughs; and on every part all about with much loam and sod of earth, and great heed must be taken, lest there be any cleft or chink remaining, only a hole left in the top of the furnace, through which the fire may be put in, and the flame and smoke to pass out: when the fire burns, the pitch or tar runneth forth first thin and then thicker, of which when it is boiled is made pitch.[52]

Pine tar was then in high demand both in the colony and back in England. It was used for waterproofing in ship building, but also had medicinal applications as an anti-bacterial agent. Dried pitch was ground into a powder that was used to treat open wounds and sores. Pine tree knots were used in place of candles, which were long-burning, however, "it makes the people pale," according to Josselyn, and may have been an unhealthy yet cheap alternative. Although there were plenty of trees available Joseph Ramsden apparently had difficulties making his business a success, and he and Rachel were living in poverty.[53]

In 1649 Rachel Ramsden had a son, whom the couple named Daniel. Two years later, however, she was brought before the court for lewd behavior. On October 7, 1651, Rachel was charged with "lascivious going in the company of young men." After being counseled and told to watch her step—"further admonished to labor to walk inoffensively"—she was cleared of the offense. Perhaps Rachel's behavior was a symptom of something awry in the Ramsden household.[54]

On May 4, 1652, the court stepped in again: "Whereas Joseph Ramsden hath for some time lived with his family remotely in the woods from neighbors, whereby his wife has been exposed to great hardship and peril of losing her life, and other inconveniences have followed thereupon, the court has ordered that the said Joseph Ramsden be warmed by the constable of Plymouth, to bring his wife and family, with all convenient speed, near unto some neighborhood that so she may be in a way of help as necessity shall require [or] he will answer the neglect thereof at his peril." That Rachel might need help "as necessity shall require," may refer to her lack of female aid during childbirth. She may even have lost a child, prompting the court to step in.[55,56]

The Ramsdens continued to be of concern to the community. On June 3, 1656, the court again intervened in the marriage: "Whereas Joseph Ramsden hath lived long in the woods, in an uncivil way. . .with his wife alone, whereby great inconveniences have followed, the court has ordered, that he repair down to some neighborhood between this and October next, or that then his house be pulled down." Perhaps Rachel again suffered a difficult childbirth, or perhaps there was concern over the possibility of domestic violence.[57]

Sometime between that year and 1661, Rachel Ramsden died, leaving behind her only known child, Daniel. Her cause of death remains unknown. Joseph Ramsden then married Mary Savory in 1661, and he died in 1674.[58,59]

Chapter Twenty

William Bradford and the Decline of Plymouth

Historians are in general agreement that by the end of the 1640s William Bradford was a sad and despondent man. He had stopped writing his history of the colony, most likely disappointed over the dispersal of both the community and the church. He was probably discouraged because Plymouth Town was shrinking, and he may have believed that the sacred enterprise had, after all, come to nothing. Bradford returned to his unfinished history, *Of Plimoth Plantation*, around 1651, updating it to the year 1646. At that point, he stopped writing, perhaps because he felt there was no longer a need to keep a record of its failure.

Yet, he was able to take some pride in his accomplishments. In his *Of Plymouth Plantation* he made a list of *Mayflower* passengers, "these being about a hundred souls, came over in this first ship and began this work, which God of his goodness hath hitherto blessed." He added, "and seeing it hath pleased him to give me to see thirty years completed since these beginnings, and that the great works of his providence are to be observed, I have thought it not unworthy my pains to take a view of the decreasings and increasings of these persons and such changes as hath passed over them and theirs in this thirty years." Bradford obviously had some moments when he felt optimistic about Pilgrim successes.[1,2]

There are several logical reasons that may account for Bradford's depression. During that time the founding fathers of Plymouth were dying off, and a new generation was steering the colony in a different direction from Bradford's vision. Boston, now with over 15,000 residents, was growing and becoming the center of industry, trade,

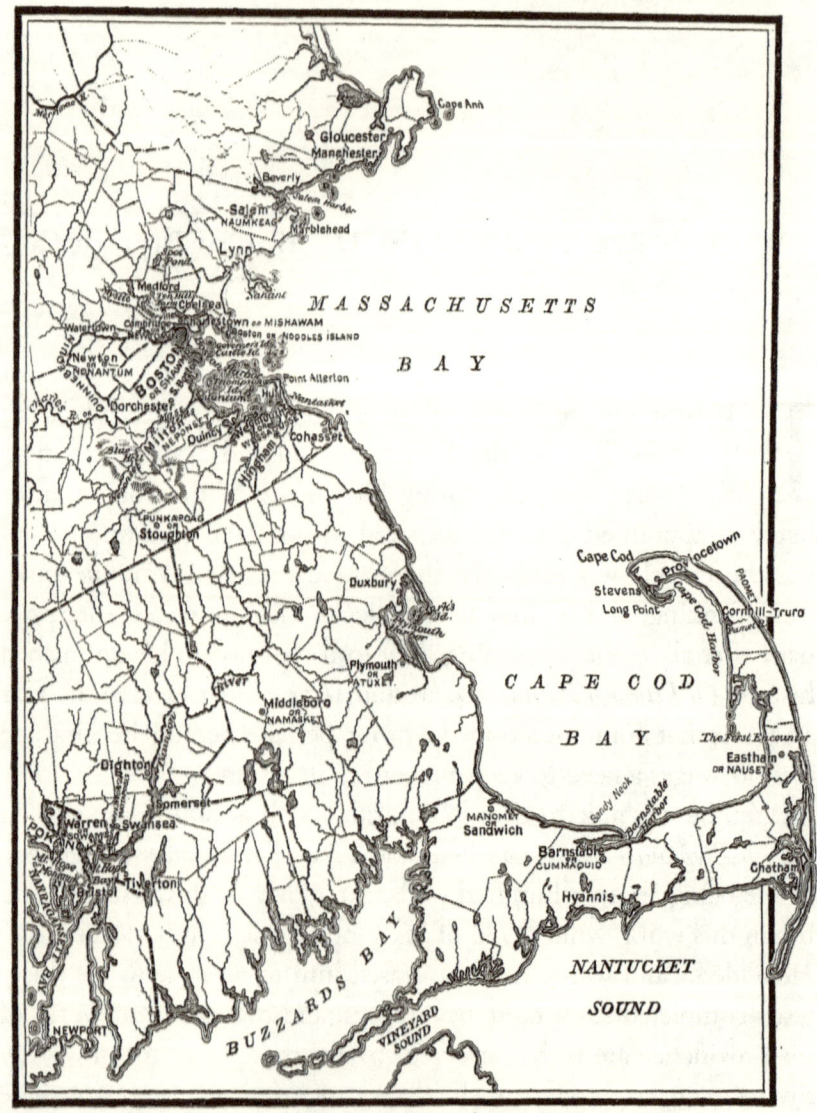

A map of the Massachusetts coast.

and culture, thus diminishing Plymouth's importance. Furthermore, Bradford was still obsessed with what he saw as the betrayal by "those ancient members" who had abandoned the walled settlement of Plymouth, its church, and Bradford himself.

When William Brewster died in 1643, Bradford was the only one left of the original Separatists. Not only did he lose the only father figure he had ever known, a man he loved and deeply respected, he also lost his purpose in life. The original plan for Plymouth had curdled into something entirely different. No longer were the lofty goals of the founders in the forefront of men's minds. They were more interested in building their personal estates. It must have seemed to him as if no one else was still committed to the original dream.

In 1648 William Bradford was in Boston, helping to negotiate a dispute between the Colony of New Haven and the Dutch. Bradford asked to be excused from attending a meeting in Hartford because of "bodily infirmities and some other reasons." This was the first sign of his physical decline. He was a man whose distress and disappointments often resulted in physical ailments, as we have seen. However, in the litany of frustrations and failures and illness, expressed then or later, no one seems to have thought that the murder of Martha Clarke (who was the same age at her death as Bradford's son John was when the child was left in Leiden), and the execution of Alice Bishop that same year may have contributed to William Bradford's despair. Perhaps one of the "other reasons" Bradford could not attend the meeting was that he was dealing with a capital crime in the colony.[3]

Everything Changes Again

By 1648 Plymouth Colony was twenty-eight years old. A new generation was poised to take over, a generation that was born and grew up in the New World. They did not experience the struggles in England and Holland, the terrifying *Mayflower* voyage, nor that cruel first winter. Their attitudes were very different, and Bradford must have felt that he faced them alone.

There were problems on every side. Quakers were challenging religious control. Even the natural environment was against them. By 1651 wolves had become such a problem that a bounty of fifteen shillings was established for anyone who killed one, since the vicious carnivores were brutally attacking livestock. For example, John Josselyn wrote an account of a encounter with a wolf in 1638: "About the tenth of August, I happened to walk into the woods, not far from the seaside...near half a mile from the house; of a sudden I heard a hollow thumping noise upon the rocks approaching toward me, which made me presently to recover my piece, which I had no sooner cocked, than a great and grim over-grown she wolf appears, whom I shot, and finding her Gor-belly [large belly] stuffed with flesh newly taken in. I began presently to suspect that she had fallen foul upon our goats."[4,5]

Investigating the area, Josselyn later found a wolf actively "feeding upon the remainder of the goat, which was only the fore shoulders, head and horns, the rest being devoured by the she-wolf, even to the very hair of the goat; and it is very observable that when the wolves have killed a beast or a hog, not a dog-wolf amongst them offers to eat any of it, till the she-wolves have filled their paunches." A related and rather chilling order from the Plymouth court directed that "all graves especially for grown persons be digged five foot deep...."[6,7]

Relations with the local tribes were strained. As the colonists expanded into the wilderness, even if the land was purchased, wandering English livestock had ravaged Natives' crops, causing resentment and ill feelings.

But it was changes back in England that created the most frustrating dilemma for Bradford. The 1640s saw a rise of popular challenges to the sovereignty of the Crown and its relationship with Parliament. Also, the authority of the king's church was challenged by the Puritans and their like. In 1642 civil war broke out, and in 1649 the Puritans, under Oliver Cromwell, took control of the government. King Charles I was beheaded. The Church of England, the national church, was on the losing side; its bishops were abolished, and its prayer book was banned.

Diminishing the influence of the Church of England was a tangential aim of the Separatist movement, but now that it had actually happened, it posed a conundrum for William Bradford. The Separatists had always measured themselves against other religions, especially the Church of England. The Plymouth Separatists now had no counterweight to their position. Bradford was left with the problem of keeping the Separatist movement, and the original plan for Plymouth, alive.

"Full little did I think," he wrote, "that the downfall of the bishops, with their courts, cannons and ceremonies, etc., had been so near, when I first began these scribbled writings (which was about the year 1630, and so pieced up at times of leisure afterward)." Ironically, the downfall of the bishops made Separatism, and by extension Bradford, irrelevant.[8]

Bradford's Complaints

Aging, losing influence and support, Bradford turned—as he had as a young man—to scholarly study. He found challenge and delight in studying the ancient languages, especially Hebrew:

> Though I am grown aged, yet I have had a longing desire, to see with my own eyes, something of that most ancient language, and holy tongue, in which the Law, and oracles of God were write; and in which God, and angels, spake to the holy Patriarchs of old time; and what names were given to things, from the creation. And though I cannot attain to much herein, yet I am refreshed, to have some glimpse hereof; as Moses saw the Land of Canan afar off. My aim and desire is, to see how the words, and phrases lie in the holy text; and to discern somewhat of the same, for my own content.[9]

Realizing that the future of Plymouth as a Separatist colony was in jeopardy, he also began to write long poems as a way to present, preserve, and defend his arguments. Adhering to his Separatist position, Bradford's later writings argued unapologetically for the validity of the Pilgrims' beliefs and the existence of Plymouth as a Separatist community. In 1648, the year of Alice Bishop's hanging, Bradford began a series of three *Dialogues,* works of a didactic style written for the younger generation. Bradford pits "some young men" against "sundry ancient men" in a conversation meant to convince the younger men of the Separatist position. He also wrote poems, which he considered "sundry useful verses," but which, along with the *Dialogues,* reveal some of what was occupying his thoughts as he aged and reflected on the past.[10,11]

Overall, Bradford's later writings ponder the loss of what should have been. To him the past had meaning, the deaths of fully half of the first comers that winter in 1621 still spoke to him as explanation enough for the continued existence of Plymouth as a Separatist colony. Some of Bradford's reflections on the past seem romantic. In 1654 he wrote "Some Observations of God's Merciful Dealing with Us in This Wilderness," in which he said that things were going very well in New Plymouth, at least in the beginning:

> Whilst things thus did flourish and were in their prime,
> Men thought it happy and a blessed time,
> To see how sweetly all things did agree.
> Both in the Church and State, there was true amity.[12]

But not all of his writings were quite so positive. Sitting at his desk, alone with his thoughts, a lot of anger also flowed through his pen. In his third *Dialogue* he blasted other expressions of faith. For example, he described the Catholic Church as a "scarlet-colored whore, that great Babylon, that mother of whoredoms and abominations of the earth."[13]

These writings again reveal his rage and disappointment with the early Plymouth founders who abandoned the colony and moved to Duxbury. He never forgave them, and in fact blamed them for much of the failure of the colony. For example, in his poem "Epitaphium Meum," he wrote:

> Oft left of them whom I did trust;
> How vain it is to rest on dust!
> A man of sorrows I have been,
> And many changes I have seen.[14]

And in his poem entitled "A Word to New Plymouth," he addresses the colony as if a person:

Some thou has had, it is well known,
That sought thy good before their own,
But times are changed; those days are gone,
And therefore thou art left alone.

To make others rich thyself art poor,
They are increased out of thy store,
But growing rich they thee forsake
And leave thee poor and desolate.[15]

Bradford was especially proud of his poems. In his will he wrote, "I commend unto your wisdom and discretion some small books written by my own hand to be improved as you shall see meet. In special I commend to you a little book with a black cover, wherein there is A Word to Plymouth, A Word to Boston, and A Word to New England, with sundry useful verses."[16]

Today, William Bradford's later writings are not widely read. Taken as a whole, these pieces are the sad and angry reflections of a tired and bitter Bradford.

The Death of William Bradford

On February 3, 1657, William Bradford spent his last day presiding over the Plymouth Court. As much as things had changed over the thirty years or so he had served the colony as governor, some had remained very familiar. Edward Doty was represented by his widow in a "controversy betwixt Thomas Lucas and the widow Doty." Lucas was ordered to pay Faith Doty three shillings. Francis Billington was in court suing over the ownership of two iron wedges; the court found the wedges to be Billington's and ordered them returned. Billington further sued William Brown over wages due Joseph Billington. Brown was ordered to pay Billington four shillings.[17]

A case of adultery came before the court concerning "a certain Scot, a single man, and an Irish woman named Katherine Aines." The case was held over until witnesses could be heard. Complaint was made against Quakers Jane Launder and Sarah Kerby—yet again—"for disturbance by them made in the public worship of God on the Lord's day at Sandwich, by opposing and abusing the speaker amongst them." In a related case Nicholas Upshall, a visiting Quaker, had overstayed his welcome and was "warned to depart the government by the first of March next."[18]

At the next court session, on March 5, 1657, the notation was made that "the governor was sick at this court." William Collier served in his place. The record later notes that on May 9, in the year 1657, "it pleased God to put a period to the life of his precious servant Mr. William Bradford." He died at sixty-nine years of age as the richest man in the colony, leaving an estate valued at £900.[19,20]

It can be certain that his was a simple farewell, yet one of great sadness and solemnity; Bradford was respected and loved as the colony's leader and its conscience. He was buried on Burial Hill overlooking his beloved Plymouth. Today there is a tall obelisk marking his grave with the Latin inscription, "*Qua patres difficillime adepti sunt nolite turpiter relinquere.*" Still protecting his beloved colony, he reminds us that "what our forefathers with so much difficulty secured, do not basely relinquish."[21]

One of his poems, "Epitaphium Meum," foretold his passing and spelled out his faith in a heavenly reward:

> My days are spent, old age is come,
> My strength it fails, my glass near run:
> Now I will wait when work is done,
> Until my happy change shall come,
> When from my labors I shall rest
> With Christ above for to be blest.[22]

There can be no doubt as to Bradford's place in history, considered by many to be one of the greatest of New England founders. Cotton Mather called him a Moses, and a person "of a well-tempered spirit, or else it had been scarce possible for him to have kept the affairs of Plymouth in so good a temper for thirty-seven years together."

Mather suggested that of all Bradford's acts of generosity, "let this one piece of self-denial be told for a memorial of him," that he surrendered the patent for the colony into the hands of the residents, "reserving no more for himself than was his proportion."[23]

Bradford was a man for study, Mather continued, as well as action. He was proficient in several languages, including Hebrew. He was also "well skilled in History, Antiquity, and in Philosophy.... But the crown of all was his holy, prayerful, watchful, and fruitful walk with God, wherein he was very exemplary."[24,25]

Bradford had kept the Plymouth ideal alive and had devoted himself throughout his adult life to the cause of the Separatist movement, but he was the last of the original founders, and life in the New World had changed the inheriting generations. Everything would be different after his death.

The Demise of Plymouth Colony

After William Bradford's death, Plymouth Colony survived another thirty-four years as an independent colony, and they were not easy years. Internally, there was an edgy tension between the Separatists and the Quakers. Thomas Prence, who became governor after Bradford's death, was especially hard on the Quakers. His view of them, for example, was that they all "deserved…to be destroyed, both they, their wives and their children, without pity or mercy."[26,27]

Those years would also see relations with the Native Americans sour. Immigration into the region meant deeper incursion into tribal lands and sporadic skirmishes finally erupted into the bloody King Philip's War between 1675 and 1678, and the colony suffered greatly.

While the colonists were surviving, they were not thriving. In 1664, King Charles II sent a commission to New England to review the general problem of Quakers in New England. What they found in Plymouth is sad to recount. Plymouth Town, Samuel Maverick reported, "is a small poor town now, the people being removed into farms in the country." In 1665 Governor Prence concurred with that description. In a letter to the general court in Massachusetts, he wrote: "The truth is, we are the meanest [poorest] and weakest, least able to stand of ourselves, and little able to contribute any helpfulness to others and we know it, though none should tell us of it." However, he added, "through God's goodness we have not hitherto given you much trouble."[28,29,30]

Even though Plymouth Colony did not cause much trouble for King Charles II, there was little else to cite in their favor. In 1666, the King's Commission reported that in Plymouth Colony there are "about twelve small towns, one saw-mill for boards, one bloomery for iron, neither good river, nor good harbor, nor any place of strength; they [are] so poor they [are] not able to maintain scholars for their ministers, but [are] necessitated to make use of a gifted brother in some places."[31]

In 1691 England made the decision to merge the Plymouth and Maine Colonies into the Massachusetts Bay Colony, under their authority. The last meeting of the Plymouth Court was held on June 8, 1692.

The Separatist dream of a religious utopia was finished. The independent Plymouth Colony itself was gone, but not its influence. Bradford foresaw this as he wrote, "Thus out of small beginnings greater things have been produced by his hand that made all things of nothing, and gives being to all things that are; and, as one small candle might light a thousand, so the light here kindled hath shone unto many, yea in some sort to our whole nation; let the glorious name of Jehovah have all the praise."[32]

Writing nearly 300 years later, George Willison, author of *Saints and Strangers*, wrote of Plymouth Colony, "In time she would wield greater influence and enjoy a wider fame than ever she had in the heyday of her temporal power. She would shape the ideas, manners, customs, ways of life, and moral values of millions of Americans."[33] It can be argued that the same could be said of William Bradford.

Chapter Twenty-One

Why Did Alice Do It?

Governor Bradford completely controlled the historical report of the murder of Martha Clarke, and his record left many questions unanswered, the most obvious of which is this: Why did Alice Bishop murder her daughter? To be fair, at the time the courts both in England and the colonies did not concern themselves with motives. Although, in his history of the colony, Bradford did recount his questioning young Thomas Granger, who was charged with bestiality, curious to know, "how they came first to the knowledge and practice of such wickedness."[1]

It may be that Bradford never asked Alice why she did such a thing, or if he did, was not convinced of the answer he received. Yet, Bradford himself did wonder how such an act could be committed in Plymouth. In his history, Bradford wrote after the Granger incident, "Marvelous it may be to see and consider how such kind of wickedness did grow and break forth here, in a land where the same was so much witnessed against and so narrowly looked unto, and severely punished when it was known, as in no place more, or so much, that I have known or heard of."[2]

Bradford, after consideration, offered three possibilities for immorality in the colony, one religious, one social, and one surprisingly modern. First, he wrote, the Devil works harder in Plymouth. It may be that "the Devil may carry a greater spite against the churches of Christ and the gospel here, by how much the more they endeavor to preserve holiness and purity amongst them and strictly punish the contrary when it arises either in church or commonwealth." Second, perhaps there really weren't more evils in Plymouth than anywhere else, but the residents worked harder to identify wickedness "by due search, inquisition, and…punishment." The church and its members keep watch over all, Bradford wrote, "more strictly than in other places," and evils are "brought into the light and set in the plain field, or rather on a hill, made conspicuous to the view of all."[3]

The third possibility Bradford offered for wickedness in Plymouth is one that most resonates with modern psychological thought. "Another reason may be that…as it is with waters when their streams are stopped or dammed up. When they get passage they flow with more violence and make more noise and disturbance than when they are suffered to run quietly in their own channels; so wickedness being here more stopped by strict laws, and the same more nearly looked unto so as it cannot run in a common road of liberty as it would and is inclined, it searches everywhere and at last breaks out where it gets vent."[4]

Could he have been thinking of Alice Bishop when he wrote those lines? They were written between 1648 to 1650, after she was tried and hanged. Was it possible that a lifetime of "stopped or dammed up" passion and frustration finally broke forth into a murderous fury? Twentieth century criminologists have confirmed what Bradford posited, that "the extremely assaultive criminals appeared to be more repressed and more overcontrolled than those who were convicted of crimes in which they were only moderately aggressive." Sudden murder, that is murder without any previous aggressive or antisocial acts, seems directly related to the degree of control in the environment.[5]

Over the past four centuries many theories about Martha Clarke's murder have been posited, some more credible than others. The difficulty is that Alice Bishop lived a long time ago, within a culture that was unique to a particular time and place. What made sense to the Pilgrims often bewilders us today. But those caught up in Alice Bishop's story want to understand why she would commit such a horrible crime, and several speculations have been offered. Most of the speculations acknowledge the role of stress in the crime, just as Bradford did when he wrote about "waters when their streams are stopped or dammed up."[6]

Stress in the Pilgrim Family

Was there stress between family members in the Bishop household? In their book *The Times of Their Lives: Life, Love and Death in Plymouth Colony,* James and Patricia Deetz cite the case of Alice Bishop and state that "while children in second-marriage situations were generally integrated into a stable new family unit, as was certainly the case among remarriages in the early years of the colony, there were also instances where there were considerable stresses between spouses and stepchildren that ended in violence."[7]

If Richard Bishop had any quarrels with his stepdaughters, there is no record of it. Considering that Abigail was only around two years old and Martha was an infant at the time of his marriage to Alice, Richard was probably the only father they really knew. Did he favor Damaris, his biological child, over Abigail and Martha? Was Alice caught in the middle? It was rare, but not unknown, that there were problems in some of the Pilgrim families, but as soon as neighbors became aware of discord, if they heard arguing, they would have immediately informed the colony's leaders and those cases most likely addressed in court. Pilgrims, after all, prided themselves in keeping an eye on each other.

Was the family stressed due to overcrowding? In his book *A Little Commonwealth: Family Life in Plymouth Colony,* John Demos asks about Plymouth residences, "How, in particular, did these cramped little households avoid an atmosphere of constant bickering and recrimination?" Demos hypothesizes that the residents of Plymouth learned to handle their anger and aggression within their homes, restraining themselves within their own families and redirecting their frustrations in "the field of neighborly relations." Court records, he writes, "contain a relatively modest number of cases reflecting conflict within a particular family...however, an enormous quantity of actions between neighbors." In other words, they controlled their emotions at home at the expense of their relationships with their neighbors. Firm discipline, he offers, "was a touchstone of household organization in this culture," and "domestic peace, in short, was achieved only with an element of real struggle."[8]

Was there stress in the family because Martha may have had special needs? In her genealogical study of the Chambers family, Queen Perry wrote that "the tragedy of Alice Martin must be considered as the mercy killing of a child mentally or physically defective who was destroying the happiness of all members of the family." This speculation offers an opportunity to discuss how careful we must be about imposing our contemporary cultural environment upon the past.[9]

Perry's study was submitted to the The Church of Jesus Christ of Latter-day Saints' Family History Library in 1983, an era when mercy killing was being debated around the globe. For example, in 1972 the United States Senate Special Commission on Aging held its first national hearings on euthanasia, "Death with Dignity: An Inquiry into Related Public Issues." In 1976 the Supreme Court ruled that Karen Ann Quinlan could be removed from a life-sustaining respirator in a case that became "a legal landmark, drawing national and international attention to end-of-life issues." In 1980 the Catholic Church issued a declaration stating its position on euthanasia. In 1984 the American Medical Association supported withholding or withdrawing life-prolonging medical treatment in certain circumstances. With the topic of euthanasia, or "mercy killing," so much in the news of the day, it is understandable that Queen Perry would have projected the contemporary debate back in time on the case of the murder of Martha Clarke. But the Pilgrims living in the seventeenth century were never in on that discussion. To them, murder was murder.[10,11,12]

Moreover, there was nothing "merciful" about this killing. This was a vicious attack. Alice was apparently in a rage when she attacked her daughter, as the evidence clearly shows. There were, after all, "diverse gashes cross ways, the windpipe cut," and blood spilled so abundantly that it ran down the ladder and pooled on the floor below. If Alice had ever given any thought to doing away with her child for "merciful" reasons—and there is no evidence of this—she would certainly have devised a less painful way to do it. Furthermore, there is nothing in the record to indicate that "mercy killings" were a common or even less-than-common practice at Plymouth.[13]

Was Alice Bishop Mentally Ill?

In his book *The Pilgrim Republic: An Historical Review of the Colony of New Plymouth,* published in 1888, John Goodwin wrote that "the case of Mrs. Bishop is especially sad. It is evident that she was insane, but the medical skill of that day was not sufficient to perceive it." Goodwin compares Alice Bishop with Dorothy Talby, who was hanged in Boston in 1638 for murdering her child "while, as now is clearly seen, she was insane from religious excitement." Governor Winthrop of the Massachusetts Bay Colony wrote that Dorothy Talby suffered from "melancholy or spiritual delusions." Furthermore, she was "so possessed with Satan that he persuaded her (by his delusions, which she listened to as revelations from God) to break the neck of her own child, that she might free it from future misery."[14,15,16]

It appears from the records that the Pilgrims not only recognized physical and mental disabilities but dealt with them compassionately. For instance, any soldier who returned from battle "maimed and hurt" would be "maintained competently by the colony during his life." Another example is that of a young man named Edward Bumpas, who was brought before the court in 1679. He was charged with "striking and abusing his parents." As punishment he was sentenced to be whipped at the post. This was an "alleviated," or lessened punishment, because Edward was considered "crazy brained;" else he would have "been put to death or otherwise sharply punished." Despite these considerations, there is nothing in the record indicating that Alice Bishop was physically or mentally defective.[17,18]

Was Alice Bishop possessed by the Devil? As William Bradford noted, the Devil was perceived as a real presence in Plymouth Colony, as in all of New England, and it was a common practice to blame Satan for evil behavior or for what today would be considered mental illness. As expressed by the Deetzes, this was a culture that was "deeply rooted [in] folk tradition of superstition and belief in the super-natural, which existed alongside their religious faith." If the courts had suspected demonic possession, they certainly would have said so during Alice's trial. Nothing in the record supports that notion.[19]

Unlike Puritan New England, Plymouth Colony never

experienced witchcraft hysteria. One of the capital crimes cited in the 1636 code of laws was the practice of witchcraft, but only two cases were brought before the courts. In 1661 Dinah Sylvester accused the wife of William Holmes of witchcraft. Dinah was charged in court with making a false accusation. On March 6, 1677, Mary Ingham was indicted for witchcraft, tried, and the jury found her not guilty.[20]

Was it ergot poisoning that led Alice to kill her daughter? Ergot is a fungus that grows in rye, wheat, and other cereal grains. When eaten, the contaminated grain can cause bizarre behavior, including delusions and hallucinations. Some historians have cited ergot poisoning as a possible cause of the behavior of those accused of witchcraft in Salem, and one contemporary explanation offered that Alice may have suffered from ergot poisoning. But there is no record of ergot poisoning occurring in Plymouth.[21,22]

Could postpartum psychosis have caused Alice Bishop to have a psychotic breakdown? This is the most frequent speculation offered today, but again it is important not to project modern thinking back four hundred years. Contemporary culture has different viewpoints and expectations.

Many professionals today agree that the main cause of postpartum depression is the hormonal fluctuations occurring during pregnancy. These are physical causes that would be common to all women regardless of the time or culture in which they lived. However, other contemporary American professionals often cite causes that are culturally based, such as a low sense of self-esteem due to appearance, feeling isolated or inadequate, having financial problems, or moving and starting a new job, factors not common among women living in other times and societies.

Still, postpartum difficulties have been recognized as far back as Hippocrates, who described postpartum psychosis as "a kind of madness," explaining that it was caused by excessive blood flow to the brain. The eleventh-century Italian gynecologist Trotula of Salerno posited the unique view that postpartum problems were caused by too much water in the womb, which caused too much water in the brain, which was then shed as tears. A form of postpartum psychosis may have been known in New England in the 1600s. John Josselyn wrote that seal oil, "being cast upon the coals, will bring women out of their Mother Fits." "Mother fits," also known as "mother passion" or "hysterical passion," referred to a medical condition, a type of mental illness that was believed to be caused by "the woman's seed and the menstrual blood being retained and corrupted." Treatments included sneezing powders, "drawing poultices" applied to the feet, or laxatives to stimulate menstruation. To expel the "woman's seed" from her womb, "carnal conjunction," or sexual intercourse was recommended. If the woman was not married, the midwife was instructed that "the patient may be rubbed and tickled in the neck of her womb, into which the midwife must put her fingers anointed with oil of spices so that the offensive female sperm may be voided." By the 1800s, as medicine advanced, physicians began to seriously consider a connection between physical events, such as childbirth, and the mind.[23,24,25,26]

Appearing within ninety days after giving birth, the symptoms of postpartum psychosis may include hallucinations and delusions, which can impair a woman's rationality and could lead to violent acts. The condition may be caused by the new mother's fluctuating hormones. Some women feel that they are being ordered by God to do things they would normally never do. They may have trouble sleeping and refuse to eat. Some have extreme feelings of anxiety or periods of delirium or mania. Some have suicidal or homicidal thoughts and may be agitated, prone to angry outbursts, or feel irrational guilt. Women suffering from postpartum psychosis often hide their thoughts and feelings from others, and everything may appear fine to an outsider.

If Alice had postpartum psychosis at the time she murdered her daughter, it would suggest that she gave birth to another child after Damaris, who was about two at the time. There is no record of a newborn child in the Bishop household in 1648; however, Plymouth records do not cite the deaths of infants or of miscarriages, so it is possible that Alice had another child who had not survived. Church records do show that there was a Day of Humiliation, a day of prayer, set aside on July 22, 1647, imploring God to lift an epidemic of "sickness [that has affected] upon every family, in a manner of every one in every family." Perhaps this disease had visited the Bishop family and left a dead infant behind.[27]

If Alice were suffering from postpartum psychosis or depression, she must have hidden her symptoms well, because Rachel Ramsden testified that Alice was "as well as she hath known her at any time."[28]

Were There Troublemakers in the Community?

Perhaps it was the newcomers who were to blame. William Bradford lamented that over time the very nature of the colony had changed. Over time it had become infiltrated with undesirables who may have had an influence on others. Writing about the year 1642, Bradford asked "how came it to pass that so many wicked persons and profane people should so quickly come over into this land and mix themselves amongst [us]?" One of the answers he offered was that the need for labor was so great in the early years that "many untoward servants," were brought over. When they finished their seven years of service, they "became families of themselves." "By this means," he adds, "the country became pestered with many unworthy persons…." Their behavior may have added stress to the community as they influenced others by their very presence.[29]

Was the Culture Itself to Blame?

Another possibility is that the source of tension in the community was the community itself—that the very nature of Plymouth Colony caused stress for its residents—and especially for Pilgrim women. While most women coped with the environment and its demands, some did not.

The real answer to the question of why Alice Bishop murdered her daughter can never be known, given the lack of reliable proof. However, looking at the context within which the killing took place, there is another possibility to consider. Admittedly, we are looking at the past through the lens of the twenty-first century experience, but this version of events is based on what we know about how women navigated their way through the Plymouth Colony experience and the unique and hidden culture practiced among them.

And this brings us to Rachel Ramsden and her role in events that morning. When Rachel arrived at the Bishop house, she found Alice to be as well as she had ever seen her. After Rachel left on the errand, a murderous rage overtook Alice and she viciously attacked her child. What had happened during that visit?

When Rachel called on Alice on July 22, 1668, she noticed that Martha was still in bed, not up and dressed like everyone else. If Rachel made an offhand critical remark about the child's behavior, it could have been perceived by Alice as an unfavorable assessment of her mothering skills. What if, after Rachel left on her errand, Martha then woke up and was cross with her mother, misbehaving and defying her mother's authority? Perhaps Alice, her anger already sparked by Rachel's comments, then disciplined the child. Maybe things escalated and Alice, who was preparing a meal and may have already had a knife in her hand, began to chase after the child, who ran up the ladder.

In this scenario, as Alice chased her daughter up the ladder, her anger might have grown into a blind rage. Perhaps in her fury she grabbed the child, pinned her to the floor, and—all reason now having abandoned her—began hacking at the child's throat with the knife in her other hand. It may only have been Martha's gasps and gurgles or the appearance of so much blood that finally shocked Alice and restored some of her sanity so that she stopped her wild attack.

This theory, and it is only a theory, of how the crime may have occurred can be supported by what is known about the culture of Plymouth Colony. Not only were Pilgrims ever watchful over each other and critical of each other's behavior, but corporal punishment was the expected way to control children. Martha was at a difficult age, and it was Alice's responsibility to break her spirit, in a sense. At the same time, the culture demanded that all emotions be held under firm control. It is not hard to imagine Alice letting anger and frustration get the better of her. It would have taken only a moment for suppressed rage and murderous anger to replace reason and judgement.

This theory of the motives behind the crime is strengthened by a hint in Governor Bradford's interview of Rachel Ramsden.

A Curious Question

A careful reading of the court record reveals that Governor Bradford may have had some suspicions about Rachel Ramsden's story. The clue is in one word—"moreover."

At the end of the interview, after Rachel testified that she returned from the errand and "found [Alice Bishop] sad and dumpish," she says that she saw the blood at the foot of the ladder, and "perceived [that Alice] had killed her child." "Moreover," the governor wrote, "the reason that moved [Rachel] to think [that Alice Bishop] had killed her child was that when [Rachel] saw the blood she looked on the bed, and the child was not there."[30]

The word *moreover*, which indicates that something had been added to the statement and suggests two possibilities. Perhaps the governor had reviewed the initial statement and had one more question. He may have wondered what made Rachel think that it was Martha who had been killed. Why not one of the other children? Or couldn't there have been a more reasonable explanation for the blood on the floor? Perhaps some meat had been prepared for dinner, and the bloody floor had not yet been cleaned. Or perhaps a wounded animal had come inside looking for shelter, and had left the pool of blood. The other possibility is that Rachel spontaneously offered further information. Perhaps given some time to think about what had happened, she suddenly had more to offer.

Either way, Rachel's reply—that the child's bed was empty—is weak at best. By her own words, Rachel found Alice in a good mood that morning, and yet after Rachel left, Alice had exploded in a rage. What had happened that morning between the two women? If Rachel had made some critical remark, what could she have said that would provoke such anger? Where was Alice most vulnerable to the community's judgement?

Watching and Judging

As already discussed, culturally sanctioned snooping was part of the fabric of Plymouth Colony. The governor and his assistants ruled overall, based on law and Separatist religious tenets. The grand jury panel appointed by the court was entrusted to watch over the community "for the preventing of idleness and other evils." Within their jurisdictions the grand jurymen had the power "to take a special view and notice of all manner of persons married or single dwelling within. . .and are suspected to live idly and loosely and to require an account of them how they live." Anyone could bring a matter to the attention of his local juryman, who would investigate, and those "they find delinquent" could be brought before the court.[31]

Control was officially mandated from many authoritative sources at Plymouth, such as the government and the church, but it was also enforced from within by the community itself. Someone was always watching and judging, and women, along with children and servants, were at the bottom of the heap with few if any defenses. As William Gouge wrote, "Though in the kind and extent of many duties, the same things are required of wives which are required of children and servants, because God hath made them all inferiors, and exacted subjection of all."[32]

While Plymouth women could be a welcome source of support for each other, they could also turn competitive in order to achieve a hierarchical foothold further up the community ladder. Who better to judge how a woman fulfilled her cultural responsibilities than another woman? A husband's judgment might be clouded by love and loyalty, but a neighbor could be more unbiased and critical when evaluating a woman's housekeeping, parenting, or even her piousness and feminine demeanor.

Petty jealousies could also be at work. In her apology to the courts for accusing the wife of William Holmes of being a witch in 1660, Dinah Sylvester admitted to having "hard thoughts against the woman," which she should have "declared to a magistrate" instead of gossiping among her neighbors.[33]

Rachel Ramsden might have harbored her own "hard thoughts" against Alice. After all, Rachel had not married well, had no living children at that time, and was linked to the infamous Billingtons, long regarded as Plymouth's troublemakers. It is not hard to imagine Rachel Ramsden watching and judging Alice Bishop's behavior that summer day, looking for any lapse in her mothering skills. Martha was still probably in bed asleep while the women of the colony were up, dressed, and already working at their chores. Rachel may have wondered about that and made a comment to Alice, suggesting that Alice was coddling the child by letting her sleep in.

Pilgrim Parenting

As previously noted, Separatist views on children were that they needed to be "restrained and repressed," their wills "broken and beaten down," and they must be taught "humility and tractableness." How a child behaved reflected on her parents. Robinson wrote, "As we judge of the plant or graft, by the stock when it was taken…so do we of children by their parents…." To discipline their children, parents were expected to use corporal punishment. "Foolishness is bound up in the heart of a child," John Robinson advised, "which the rod of correction must drive out." In addition, children must be taught to control their anger. "Anger hath always evil in it," wrote Robinson. Backtalk from children was not to be tolerated. In fact, displays of anger in anyone, child or adult, were strongly warned against. It was thought a form of insanity, "differing from plain madness in nothing, but time."[34,35]

The pressure on Pilgrim mothers, having been warned by Robinson against a "mother's indulgence," was tremendous. Mothers were charged with the task of forcing their children into submission, using physical punishment if necessary, but keeping their own frustrations under full control, all the while under the watchful and judging eyes of the community. A near impossible situation to contemplate today, especially if the child is four years old.[36]

Martha – a Typical Four-Year-Old

Why did Alice Bishop in her anger single out Martha when she had two other daughters who were most likely in the house at the time, one older and one younger? By age six Abigail would have been "broken," expected to take on a full female role in the household and have chores and responsibilities of her own. Damaris was the baby of the family and was still enjoying her "mother's indulgence." Martha, however, was a work in progress at the age of four, still in the process of being indoctrinated into Separatist society. That course of action may not have been going well.

John Robinson warned that children are naturally rebellious, "stubbornness and stoutness of mind arising from natural pride." Martha was at an age when she was discovering her own will. Early childhood professionals cite the four-year-old as temperamental, sufficiently physically developed to perform more tasks independently, and resistant to help from adults. Martha may have been moody, rude and obstinate. A child of this age uses more language than younger children and may talk back and argue with parents. In general, this is an age when children are developing more capabilities and are eager to exercise their independence. This would have been an especially difficult age for molding a child into the Separatist ideal.[37]

John Robinson's advice on dealing with a headstrong child was that the child must be "restrained and repressed." It would be best "if it could be kept from them that they have a will in their own, but [are] in their parents' keeping." He adds that a child should not even be allowed to say, "I will or I will not." But how did Separatists control their children?[38]

In his essay advising parents on child-rearing, Robinson acknowledges that using corporal punishment on children is controversial: "It is much controverted, whether it be better, in the general, to bring up children under the severity of discipline, and the rod, or no. And the wisdom of the flesh out of love to its own, alleges many reasons to the contrary." However, he is clear where he stands in the debate: "But say men what they will, or can, the wisdom of God is best; and that saith, that 'foolishness is bound up in the heart of a child, which the rod of correction must drive out:' and that 'he, who spared his rod, hurts his son,' Prov. [22:15, 13:24]...."[39]

Disciplinary violence against children was common in Plymouth; in fact, it was an accepted and recommended form of child-rearing. The courts recognized the parents' rights and responsibilities to discipline their children and were reluctant to step in, except in the most egregious of situations.

Discipline began at an early age in Plymouth. Infants may have been rapped with thimbles on their foreheads. Toddlers were probably smacked on their hands with small bundles of twigs. Older children were usually whipped with a birch rod, or a bundle of twigs. With violence against children commonplace among the Pilgrims, it is easy to imagine how a simple act of discipline could escalate into child abuse and even murder.

Controlling Emotions at All Costs

Amidst all this aggression in the atmosphere, Pilgrims were expected to check their emotions, especially anger, which Robinson said was a blind thing; "There is nothing so sacred and precious which it will spare; but without difference it flieth, where the wings are not clipped, upon friends as well as foes; and upon unreasonable creatures, as well as upon men."[40]

Control your anger, he wrote, with "a little delay and forbearance, either for the inward working or outward uttering of anger, whilst we gather our wits about us." Do not be angry with little things, with "trifles, for he that useth himself to that, will not keep from extremity in great matters" Avoid people or things that anger you, he advised, lest you "make way for the Devil's temptations, unto which they give way afterwards." Replace anger with another emotion, he wrote; try sorrow or fear, for example. But if your anger "happen to run so strong, as that we cannot well turn it another way; it is wisdom to get it upon such some object in the same way, as wherein it may freely take its scope...." Chop some wood, for example.[41]

But anger is not an easy emotion to control, even with the distractions that Robinson suggests, and especially within the repressive confines of Pilgrim culture. Perhaps Alice Bishop was angry with Rachel Ramsden that day but took it out on Martha. Perhaps the constant stress imposed by the community, combined with Alice Bishop's own personality and her unique reactions to those stresses, had finally and tragically resulted in one woman's complete disconnect with reality. Perhaps her final rational act was to chase Martha up the ladder to discipline her. However, if Alice had been chopping vegetables and alre ady had a knife in her hand when she ran after her daughter, and if little Martha had one more insubordinate word to say, it may have been enough for a blind and murderous rage to overtake her mother.

Chapter Twenty-Two

Plymouth's Legacy and Its Secrets

The history of the Plymouth Colony largely faded away after it was merged into the Massachusetts Bay Colony in 1691. As the first generation died, the Pilgrims were nearly forgotten, except in the pages of works by a few historians. For example, Cotton Mather had written about them when he included a biography of William Bradford in his *Magnalia Christi Americana*, published in London in 1702. Thomas Hutchinson told their story, much of which was based on Bradford's *Of Plymouth Plantation*, in his *History of the Colony of Massachusetts Bay*, first printed in Boston in 1764. Among the locals of Plymouth, tales were handed down through generations, but outside the region, Plymouth Colony and the Pilgrims were basically historical footnotes, considered to have had little influence in the building of the nation.

All that changed when the colony's simple "day of thanksgiving" became Thanksgiving Day and the Pilgrims were transformed into cultural icons. Their story grew to be the story of America, the myth we teach to our children because we believe it explains and describes best who we are as Americans.

It started in 1769. A small group of men who were descended from the Pilgrims formed The Old Colony Club in Plymouth. It was mainly a social club, but they did introduce the first public event dedicated to their ancestors—Forefather's Day—which was commemorated on December 22 in celebration of the arrival of the *Mayflower*. This was the period leading up to the Revolutionary War, and Forefather's Day gave the little group an opportunity to recall and celebrate the Pilgrims' independent spirit and their escape from the oppression they experienced in England.[1]

The Old Colony Club eventually faded into history, but in 1819 John Watson organized the Pilgrim Society, "for the purpose of procuring in the town of Plymouth a suitable lot or piece of ground for the erection of a monument to perpetuate the memory of the virtues, the enterprise and unparalleled sufferings of their ancestors who first settled in that ancient town, and for the erection of a suitable building for the accommodation of the meetings of said association."[2]

In this spirit, the Pilgrim Society raised money and built the Pilgrim Hall in 1824. Years later, in 1867, they would erect a large granite structure over Plymouth Rock, the presumed steppingstone of the first Pilgrims to arrive at Plymouth. They would also erect the National Monument to the Forefathers, completed in 1889. Previously known as the Pilgrim Monument, this structure stands over eighty feet tall, and is topped with a heroic figure representing the Pilgrims' faith, and four seated figures, one on each side representing their devotion to morality, law, education, and liberty.[3]

In 1855, Nathaniel Shurtleff, who later served on the building committee for the Pilgrim Society's National Monument, transcribed and published the *Records of the Colony of New Plymouth in New England*, whose twelve volumes would tell the stories of the Pilgrims' daily struggles as reflected in court records. That same year, William Bradford's lost history of the colony, *Of Plymouth Plantation*, was discovered in Fulham Palace, the home of the Bishop of London. Although its existence was known, the manuscript had been missing since the Revolutionary War when it had disappeared from Boston. The bishop allowed a copy to be made, which was published by the Massachusetts Historical Society in 1856, but the original remained in England. Publication of the history was an occasion for patriotism and celebration and ignited a desire to have the manuscript returned. After many complications, which eventually involved Queen Victoria, the manuscript was returned to America in 1897 and, with much ceremony, displayed in the Massachusetts State House.[4,5]

These publications and monuments created tremendous interest in the Pilgrims because, "for the first time in their posthumous lives the Pilgrims stood out strong and clear, in three dimensions.... They began to breathe once more—and love, and hate, and fight, as only they could." The old records were searched and researched, and books and articles were written about the Pilgrim experience. Artists painted scenes of Pilgrims stepping onto Plymouth Rock. Longfellow's poem, *The Courtship of Miles Standish* was published in 1858. Everyone wanted to be descended from a Pilgrim, and many genealogical studies were undertaken by people hoping to be related to them.[6]

On October 3, 1863, in the midst of the Civil War, President Abraham Lincoln proclaimed a day of thanksgiving because "harmony has prevailed everywhere except in the theatre of military conflict," and there was a lot to be thankful for. "Peace has been preserved with all nations," the proclamation read, "order has been maintained, the laws have been respected and obeyed…" Let us all give thanks, he urged, and while he did not mention it, he and Secretary of State William Seward, who actually wrote the proclamation, may have been thinking of the recent Union victories in Gettysburg and Vicksburg. But this proclamation did not establish the regularly recurring national holiday we now know as Thanksgiving Day, as many have come to believe. Instead, it was a call for a national "day of thanksgiving," which was not only an old English custom, but also a local New England custom of an autumn "thanksgiving day."[7]

The Pilgrims did not celebrate holidays like Christmas or Easter, since the celebration of annual designated holidays, or holy days, reminded them of Catholicism. However, more than once in its history, in response to an event which indicated God's displeasure, Plymouth Colony participated in the ancient custom of setting aside special days of prayer called by church or community leaders. These were called "days of humiliation" and everyone was expected to spend the day, twenty-four hours, in fasting and prayer in order to regain God's favor. William Bradford wrote about a day of humiliation held in Plymouth in 1623, when a "great drought" from mid-May until the middle of July withered their crops and threatened starvation. All that fasting and praying worked. Even though the day was clear and hot, by evening "it began to overcast, and shortly after to rain with such sweet and gentle showers as gave them cause of rejoicing and blessing God."[8]

Likewise, there were also "days of thanksgiving," occasionally declared to celebrate God's blessings. In Plymouth in 1621, a day of thanksgiving was called to celebrate a successful harvest. As a part of the festivities, dinner was served, and it was this dinner that became the source event of the First Thanksgiving narrative.

When President Lincoln declared a "day of thanksgiving" in 1863, he was honoring this old tradition; there was no mention of Plymouth Colony or the Pilgrims. That story would come later.

In 1889, Jane G. Austin published a novel entitled *Standish of Standish*, which became immensely popular. In her book, which went through nearly thirty printings, she wrote a romantic account of the "First Thanksgiving," an outdoor feast with Pilgrims and American Indians that caught the national imagination. In 1897, W. L. Taylor published an illustration, *The First Thanksgiving Dinner, with Portraits of the Pilgrim Fathers*, in the November issue of Ladies Home Journal, based on Austin's description. The depiction was reproduced and sold as a Plymouth souvenir.[9,10,11]

The Pilgrim story was becoming more familiar, but, as James Baker writes, "It was in the classroom that Thanksgiving had its greatest impact at the turn of the twentieth century. Anyone who grew up in the United States after 1890 was exposed to an annual sequence of classroom holiday activities through which civic education and American patriotism were inculcated."[12]

During World War II, when home and family were especially important, the military went to great effort to celebrate the Thanksgiving holiday. The Pilgrim story was told, reinforcing American values, and traditional holiday dinners were served. For some servicemen it was their first Thanksgiving dinner, and they brought the custom home with them at war's end. By 1950, the story of Plymouth and the Thanksgiving feast were being observed coast-to-coast.

Thanksgiving Day, celebrated every fourth Thursday of November since 1941 throughout America, with turkey and stuffing, potatoes and gravy, cranberries and pumpkin pie, recalls the Pilgrim story, or rather the myth it has become. The Pilgrims and Plymouth Colony became America's origin story—they came to escape religious persecution, through hard work and sacrifice, they established a colony, instituted democracy, and gave God the glory for all their achievements with a day of thanksgiving. So pervasive is this myth in American culture that no amount of debunking by historians has put even a dent in the November celebration of Pilgrims depicted in their buckled hats, sitting outdoors at picnic tables with their invited Native American guests.

In the Plymouth myth, the Pilgrims became revered as America's founding fathers, hard workers who pursued noble purposes. The colonists were credited with infusing the New World with democracy, religious freedom, and unlimited economic opportunity. But Alice Bishop did not murder her daughter in mythical Plymouth; Martha Clark's throat was cut in the real, historical Plymouth.

Historical Plymouth was not a democracy in practice. The authorities used the concept of a democracy, of equality, when it served their purposes. In reality, the governor and his assistants carefully controlled who was permitted to participate in important decisions.

Plymouth did not support religious freedom for everyone. From the very beginning the Separatists were motivated towards freedom of religion only for themselves. Practitioners of other religions in the colony were vigorously persecuted. The Pilgrims apparently had no awareness of the irony when they tormented the Quakers.

Economic ambition was a problem for the Pilgrims. Beginning in childhood, they were taught to expect a "meanness in all things," to appreciate a "plain [and] homely diet, and apparel," to seek a station at "the same rather under than above their estate," and to avoid competition. Bradford understood the desire for larger farms and greater financial opportunities, but believed that it was best for everyone to stay close together and watch over each other. His was a losing battle.[13]

Historical Plymouth had a culture of control. Strict laws and religious precepts governed the Pilgrims' behavior, but the genius of the system lay in the concept of watchfulness, especially among women who were vulnerable in their isolation and dependent on their neighbors.

Most colonists were able to function within this culture and managed to devise their own ways to navigate through it satisfactorily. The best example is Edward Doty, who unapologetically conducted almost-illegal business transactions, time after time, for nearly three decades, and achieved financial success in the process. Some were not able to manage the pressure. Alice Bishop was one who probably cracked under the stress. Surprisingly, William Bradford may have been the only person who understood how that could happen. He made the analogy of the blocked stream, that once allowed to flow freely, runs with violence and noise and disorder. All the frustration, fear, and restraint that had apparently been building up in Alice Bishop's mind finally broke through with more violence than even Bradford could have imagined when she picked up the knife and hacked at her daughter's throat.[14]

Questions Unanswered

Aside from the Alice's motives behind the murder, several questions remain. Who were Alice Martin Clarke Bishop, George Clarke, and Richard Bishop? Where did they come from? Who were they related to? What happened to Abigail Clarke? Did she marry and leave Plymouth? Information available at this writing does not answer those questions, but perhaps there are records still to be uncovered, with more to be learned.

Another mystery remains. Given that he wrote extensively of other capital crimes in Plymouth, why didn't William Bradford write about what was arguably the most disturbing crime in the colony's history? The last chapter in his history, *Of Plymouth Plantation*, was devoted to the year 1646, though it was written in about 1650, two years after Alice Bishop was hanged. No narrative of the event written by anyone else from the period has surfaced. Furthermore, there was apparently never a probate performed for George Clarke's estate, even though it was the law to do so.[15]

Is it possible that Governor William Bradford was closer to the case than previously assumed? Could he and Alice Bishop have been related in some way by blood or through marriage? Reliable evidence does not support this speculation at this time, yet it is an intriguing point to consider.

From the court record we know that Abigail Clarke, Alice's daughter with George Clarke, was related to John Churchill, who became her guardian. The record states that John Churchill died on January 1, 1663, and Abigail was called into court to testify as to final wishes. In her statement, Churchill is referred to as "her kinsman." How was Alice related to John Churchill?[16,17,18]

One source claims that the Churchills were related to the Martins of Plymouth. The argument cites that John Churchill had a cousin named Beaton Churchill and she married Robert Martin, "who was in Plymouth Colony in 1643." This claim assumes that Robert Martin and Alice Martin were related, but there is currently no reliable proof.[19, 20]

Could Alice have been related to John Churchill through his wife, Hannah, either through her mother or her father? If so, there is potential there for a Bradford connection.

Hannah Pontus Churchill was the daughter of William Pontus and Wybra Hanson, and was born in Austerfield in 1590, the same place and year Bradford was born. Wybra has been widely referred to as "a relative of future Plymouth Colony leader William Bradford," a claim that has not been supported with citations from primary sources. Yet, it is possible that Wybra Hanson was related to Alice Hanson (b. 1562), who was William Bradford's mother. Perhaps she was Alice's niece and, therefore, William Bradford's cousin.[21,22,23]

If William Bradford were related to Abigail Clarke, even very remotely, that might explain why Bradford did not write about the murder and execution of Alice Bishop. It may have been too painful for him. That could also explain why no one else wrote about it. Bradford was a very powerful man, both loved and feared in the community, and there may have been an unspoken agreement to suppress the whole incident afterwards out of respect for the governor. Furthermore, as mentioned earlier, Bradford's melancholy began to manifest itself in 1648. Many causes for his unhappiness have been proffered, but no one has noted that this was the year he sentenced Alice Bishop to hang.

Undeniably, further research is needed to confirm these speculations.

Alice Bishop's Legacy

Admittedly, Alice Bishop's life and death in Plymouth Colony have left a very small footprint on history's sands. Yet, her story may have saved a life.

More than twenty years after her hanging, a case came before the Plymouth court. A complaint had been filed against Mary Morey for "turbulent carriages" against her son Jonathan. So violent was their relationship that "several of the neighbors feared murder would be in the issue of it."[24]

Perhaps those neighbors remembered the murder of Martha Clarke and wanted to prevent another crime. But this time they promptly reported the violence in the household to the authorities. On March 2, 1669, the court addressed the complaint, interviewed both mother and son, and admonished them both. After tears and promises, the court decided to let Jonathan remain with his mother until the next June court.[25]

Fortunately, there is no further mention of the issue in the extant records. Jonathan Morey grew up, married Mary Bartlett, had three children, and lived to be seventy-five years old.[26]

Afterword

"To Come to a Conclusion"

It was the custom in seventeenth-century London to write pamphlets recounting notorious crimes and executions and to hawk them to the curious on the streets of the city. Called "gallows literature," these essays may have contained the criminal's last words, his remorse, and no doubt, the promise of God's redemption to the villain. They were wildly popular bestsellers.

One such pamphlet, entitled "A Pittilesse Mother," published in London in 1616, recounts the case of Margaret Vincent, who was hanged for the murder of two of her children. It calls to mind Alice Bishop's own offense because Margaret had also confessed, and the murders were also "begot by a strange occasion." This pamphlet provides a fitting closure to this book with these sad words:

> And now to come to a conclusion, as well of this discourse as of her life: she deserved death, and both Law and Justice hath awarded her the same, for her examination and free confession needed no Jury. Her own tongue proved a sufficient evidence and her conscience a witness that condemned her; her judgment and execution she received with a patient mind.
>
> Forgive and forget her, good Gentlewomen; she is not the first that hath been blemished with blood, nor the last that will make a husband wifeless. Her offense was begot by strange occasion but buried, I hope with true repentance.[1]

Appendix

Plymouth Colony Court Records

The following pages display two versions of the Plymouth Colony Court Records for August 1 and October 4, 1648, both pertaining to the murder of Martha Clarke by her mother Alice Bishop. They include a copy of the original hand-written Plymouth Colony court records, most likely penned by Nathaniel Morton, who was clerk of the court from 1645 to 1685, and modern transcriptions by the author opposite.

1648 175 Mr Bradford &c &c   1a

These Showeth that on July the 22cond 1648 wee whose names are vnderwritten weare sumond by mr Bradford Corouner to make Inquiry of the death of the child of Allis Bishop the wife of Richard Bishop: Wee declare that in cominge into the house of the said Richard Bishope, wee saw at the foote of a ladder that leadeth into an vpper chamber much blood: and goinge vp all of vs into the chamber wee found a woman child of about foure yeares of age lyinge in her shift vppon her left cheeke with her throate cutt with divers gashes crose wayes with a knife runn into the throate forward: and a bloody knife lyinge by the side of the child: with the knife all of vs: viz Truly and the said Allis hath confessed to five of vs at one time that shee murdered the child with the said knife

John Howland   James Cole
James Hurst   Anthony Sinard
Robert Lee   Richard Sparrow
John Shawe   Thomas Pope
Francis Cooke   Francis Billington
John Cooke   William Nelson

Rachell the wife of Robert Ramsden aged about 23 yeares beinge examined saith that cominge to the house of Richard Bishope vppon an errant the wife of the said Richard Bishope requested her if you left her and it; and before that went thence saw the child lyinge about to goe to her left doe tinny and the woman went and tott and shee hath knowne her at any time but when shee came shee found her sad and humpish shee asked her what blood was that shee saw at the ladder foot shee poincted vpp to the chamber and bid her goe vpp there: goeinge vpp shee saw that shee had kild her child and lyinge of said that brother and San and bid her father and mother mournd That saith the Coroner of moneth her to thinke shee had kild her child was of when shee saw the blood that looked on the bed: and the child was not there

Taken vppon Oath by mee William Bradford
The day and yeare above written

At a Court of Assistants holden at newplymouth the first of August 1648 before mr Bradford Gouvr mr Colier Captain Miles Standish and mr William Thomas your assistants this said Allis being examined confesed shee did comit the aforsaid murther and is Sorry for it

	Mr. Bradford Govr
1648	

These show that on July 22nd, 1648, we, whose names are underwritten, were sworn by Mr. Bradford, Governor, to make inquiry of the death of the child of Alice Bishop, the wife of Richard Bishop.

We declare, that coming into the house of the said Richard Bishop, we saw at the foot of a ladder which leads into an upper chamber, much blood; and going up, all of us, into the chamber, we found a woman child of about four years of age lying in her shift upon her left cheek with her throat cut with diverse gashes cross ways, the wind pipe cut and stuck into the throat downward, and a bloody knife lying by the side of the child, with which knife all of us judged, and the said Alice confessed to five of us at one time, that she murdered the child with the said knife.

John Howland	James Cole
James Hurst	Giles Rickard
Robert Lee	Richard Sparrow
John Shaw	Thomas Pope
Francis Cooke	Francis Billington
John Cooke	William Nelson

Rachel, the wife of Joseph Ramsden, aged about 23 years, being examined, said that coming to the house of Richard Bishop upon an errand, the wife of said Richard Bishop requested her to go fetch her some buttermilk at Goodwife Winslows, and gave her a kettle for that purpose, and she went and did it; and before she went, she saw the child lying abed asleep, to the best of her discerning, and the woman was as well as she had known her at any time; but when she came [back] she found her [Alice Bishop] sad and dumpish; she asked her what blood was that she saw at the ladder's foot; she [Alice] pointed into the chamber, and bid her look, but she [Rachel Ramsden] perceived she [Alice] had killed her child, and being afraid, she refused, and ran and told her father and mother. Moreover, she [Rachel] said the reason that moved her to think she [Alice] had killed her child was that when she saw the blood she looked on the bed, and the child was not there.

Taken upon oath by me, William Bradford,
the day and year above written.

At a Court of Assistants held at New Plymouth, the first of August, 1648, before Mr. Bradford, Governor, Mr. Collier, Capt. Myles Standish, and Mr. William Thomas, Gentlemen, Assistants, the said Alice, being examined, confessed she did commit the aforesaid murder, and is sorry for it.

New plymouth ### Mr Bradford Governor

1648)

At the generall Court of our Soueraine lord the King holden at plymouth aforsaid the 4th of October 1648) before Mr Bradford Gouernor Mr Thomas prence Captaine Miles Standish Mr Timothy Hatherly and Mr William Thomas gent; Assistants

At this court Alice Bishope the wife of Richard Bishope of newplymouth was Indited for felonius murther by her comited vppon Martha Clark her owne Child the frute of her owne body

The names of the grand Jnquest that went on triall of the aforsaid bill of Jndictment were these:

John Dunham sen. John Barker
Isaak Wells   Joseph Colman
Mr Thomas Burne   John Allin
Robert Hicks   Thomas Bordman
Henry Wood   James Bursoll
Ephraim Hickes   Joseph Cory
James Walker   Mirable Blackwell
James Weat   Samuell Cole
Paule Brewster

These found the bill a trew bill

The petty Jury names that went vppon her tryall were these:

Josias Winslow   Thyrells Richard
Thomas Shillingworth John Shaw sen.
Anthony Snow   Steuen Wood   sworne
Richard Sparrow from William Merrick
Gabriell Fallowell William Crocker
Joshua Prat   John Willis

These found the said Alice Bishope guilty of the said felonius murthering of Martha Clarke aforsaid and so shee had the sentence of death pronounced against her viz: to bee taken from the place where shee was to the place from whence shee came and thence to the place of execution and there to bee hanged by the necke vntill her body is dead which accordingly was executed

Appendix

New Plymouth   Mr. Bradford Governor

1648   At the General Court of our Sovereign Lord the Kind, holden at Plymouth aforesaid, the 4th of October, 1648 *before* Mr. Bradford, Governor Mr. Thomas Prence Captaine Miles Standish Mr. Timothy Hatherly, and Mr. William Thomas
Gentlemen, Assistants.

At this Court, Alice Bishop, the wife of Richard Bishop, of New Plymouth, was indicted for felonious murder by her committed upon Martha Clarke, her own child, the fruit of her own body

The names of the grand inquest that went on trial of the aforesaid bill of indictment, were these:

John Dunham, Sr.	John Barker
Isaac Weels (Wheels?)	Joseph Colman
Mr. Thomas Burne	John Allen
Robert Finney	Thomas Boardman
Henry Wood	James Bursell
Ephraim Hickes	Joseph Tory
James Walker	Michael Blackwell
James Wyatt	Daniel Cole
Love Brewster	

These found the bill a true bill.

The petty jury's names that went upon her trial were these:

Josiah Winslow, Sr.	Gyles Rickard
Thomas Shillingsworth	John Shaw, Sr.
Anthony Snow	Stephen Wood
Richard Sparrow	William Merrick
Gabriel Fallowell	William Brett
Joshua Pratt	John Willis

These found the said Alice Bishop guilty of the said felonious murdering of Martha Clarke aforesaid; and so she had the sentence of death pronounced against her, that is, to be taken from the place where she was to the place from whence she came, and thence to the place of execution, and there to be hanged by the neck until her body is dead, which accordingly was executed.

Acknowledgments

I first encountered Alice Bishop around 1990 when I was doing family history research and came across the account of her hanging. Over the past thirty years my interest grew from simple curiosity to a deep need to understand my ancestor. The question, "Why would she murder her child?" haunted me and eventually led me to write this book.

Educating myself about Plymouth Colony led to serious research and I am indebted to those historians and scholars who have transcribed handwritten seventh-century documents, making those primary sources accessible today, especially Nathaniel B. Shurtleff, who transcribed the Plymouth Court Records in 1855. Jeremy Bangs tackled the seventeenth century Dutch records, revealing usable data that had been hidden for centuries. When clarity required it, however, I did consult the original handwritten Plymouth records myself. I am further indebted to those who authored the many secondary sources I consulted. Their insights and interpretations were helpful to my understanding of events; however, all conclusions are my own.

The unsung heroes of historical research are those who compile bibliographies. Early in my project I was fortunate to find George Langdon's bibliographic essay in his book *Pilgrim Colony: A History of New Plymouth, 1620-1691*, which led me to important and rare sources. For finding those sources, I am indebted to the modern magicians who have made many of them available online. Thanks to the magic of a Google search, I was able to virtually visit distant archives and libraries to track down obscure details.

Two online sites were especially useful to me. Patricia Scott Deetz, Christopher Fennell, and J. Eric Deetz manage the award winning "Plymouth Colony Archive Project" (http://www.histarch.illinois.edu/plymouth/). This comprehensive resource is an essential site for anyone interested in the Plymouth Pilgrims. Both Trish Deetz and Christopher Fennel have also been most generous in their encouragement for my project and I referred to their supportive emails more than once to bolster my confidence. I also used author and historian Caleb Johnson's excellent "Mayflower History" (www.mayflowerhistory.com). This site provides biographies, historic materials, and links to primary documents online. Dennis Sutton has compiled an impressive Sutton Family history, "Homegrown in the Garden State" (njsuttonfamily.org), that not only includes extensisve research, but updates the information with 21st century DNA technology.

I am not the only descendant of Alice Bishop who was drawn to her story and I am very grateful to the long line of genealogists—professional and amateur—who painstakingly followed the trail that led from the twenty-first century all the way back to the seventeenth. Special thanks to Virginia Smith and Queen Perry, whose research was done before records were digitized.

I am grateful also for the extensive and professional work done on my behalf by the research staff at the New England Historic Genealogical Society, especially Suzanne M. Steward and Sheilagh Doerfler. D. Brenton Simons, president and CEO of the NEHGS, encouraged me at an early point in my research; his enthusiasm and encouragement filled my sails for several years. Renowned genealogist Gary Boyd Roberts, retired Senior Research Scholar of the NEHGS, kindly met with me and helped guide my search.

I spent many happy hours roaming the shelves and viewing microfilm and microfiche at several public libraries. Among the list are the Family History Library in Salt Lake City, Utah; Allen County Public Library, in Fort Wayne, Indiana; Carlsbad City Library; the Southern California Genealogical Society Library, Burbank, and the Los Angeles Public Library, all in California. University libraries at University of California at Irvine and California State University Fullerton were welcoming and very helpful. Especially memorable were the stormy afternoons I spent in the warm and cozy local history rooms of the Plymouth, Duxbury, Eastham, and Piscataway Public Libraries.

My visits to Plimoth Plantation, the living-history recreation of

Plymouth Colony in Plymouth, were especially enlightening. This simulacrum of the seventeenth century, with its sounds, sights, and smells, gave me a better idea of Alice Bishop's world. While in Plymouth, I received friendly help and warm encouragement from Eliana M. Kimball, Librarian at the General Society of Mayflower Descendants, and Peggy M. Baker, Director of the Pilgrim Hall Museum, both since retired. In Taunton, Old Colony Historical Society Archivist and Library Manager Andrew D. Boisvert was very helpful early in my research.

Clerks at the Plymouth County Commissioner's Office Kelly Perez and Tammy Correa, who have since moved on to other positions, enabled me to get photocopies of the original handwritten court records. When I needed help with Plymouth records, professional genealogist Christine Cook was at the ready. Rebecca Griffith of the Pilgrim Hall Museum provided copies of valuable documents that helped me understand the intricacies of Plymouth law.

I am thankful for the many individuals who have offered encouragement and enthusiasm for my project. My gratitude to Pamela Steinle, Ph.D., and Terri Snyder, Ph.D., Department of American Studies, California State University Fullerton, who helped me shape my goals for this book as I completed my master's degree. Early in my research Paula Manning, professor of law at Western States College of Law, patiently explained English law, Plymouth's court system and the legal aspects of the Alice Bishop's case. David Lupher, Ph.D., Professor Emeritus of Classics, University of Puget Sound, and author of *Greeks, Romans, and Pilgrims: Classical Receptions in Early New England,* has been most helpful and patient answering questions and offering insights. His scholarly influence lifted my work to a higher level and always challenged me to do better.

My first editor, Deanna Brady, took my earliest completed draft, smoothed it out, cleaned it up, and made it much, much better. I am most grateful to American History Press for seeing some potential in my project. Franci Ferguson has taken on the case of Alice Bishop and Martha Clarke as enthusiastically as I have. Her encouragement and good cheer have boosted my commitment when I felt unsure about the manuscript. Many thanks also to David Kane at AHP for his expert and creative editing, which challenged me to dig deeper into my research. I looked forward to each of David's edits as his corrections and suggestions always made the story better. Lori Kremer, proof-reader extraordinaire, flushed out the little mistakes that all of us had missed.

Regarding the illustrations, I am indebted to Henry Glassie for permitting me to use the drawings he originally made for the design of Plimoth Plantation way back in the 1970s. The drawing of the Billington House is especially appreciated as it approximates the scene of the murder. Mary K.B. Carter helped prepare and create several of the illustrations for this book. Her interest in this project and her talent and creativity have made this book better.

Anyone who knew me during writing this book, knew about Alice, too. I have received encouragement and enthusiasm for my project from many dear friends whose interest never faded, some of whom were kind enough to read my very rough first drafts. Special thanks to Joyce, Larry, and Dawn Brock, to the Chillingtons, Alice and Jesse, Diane and John Sr., Kristy and John, Jr., Tom and Laura Elling, Carol Fernandez, John Heubner, George and Sue Phaneuf, John Schwenk, Nvart Stepanian, and Donna and Al Wallace. Bishop/Sutton cousins Harry Frye and Michal Marshall, and my aunt, the late Rozella Weber, shared my interest in family history research and offered many helpful leads.

My family, those who lived most intimately with me and Alice as I was writing this book, have been most patient and encouraging during this long project, cheering me on when I needed reassurance. Thank you, David Watkins and Brian Clark, for your unwavering encouragement and professional advice. Thank you to the Korchas, Karen (Watkins), Michael, and Anica for believing in me. Thank you to my brother, Bill Jennings, for always offering his support.

Special appreciation to my husband, Dennis Watkins, whose loving enthusiasm never wavered, who completely believed in me, read over the endless "finished" drafts, assisted in research, scanned illustrations, kept me in printer ink and paper, and who gave me time and space to work when my Pilgrims were yelling at me.

Source Notes

Abbreviations Used

CCL *The Compact with the Charter and Laws of the Colony of New Plymouth.*
DD *Domesticall Duties* by William Gouge
LCA *Little Commonwealth* by John Demos
MCA *Magnalia Christi Americana; or the Ecclesiastical History of New England* by Cotton Mather.
MR *A Relation or Journall of the beginning and proceedings of the English Plantation settled at Plimoth in New England by certaine English Adventurers both Merchants and others.* ("Mourt's Relation"), by Edward Winslow, William Bradford, and others.
NEM *New England's Memorial* by Nathaniel Morton.
ODM *Observations Divine and Moral in Works of John Robinson*, by John Robinson
OPP *Of Plymouth Plantation* by William Bradford, edited by Samuel Eliot Morison.
PCHP *Plymouth Colony, Its History and People*, by Eugene Stratton
PCR *Plymouth Colony Records*
RCA *Registers of the Chapel of Austerfield, in the Parish of Blyth and in the County of York.*
RTP *Records of the Town of Plymouth.*
SS *Saints and Strangers* by George Willison
TVEP *Three Visitors to Early Plymouth* by John Pory, Emmanuel Altham, and Isaac De Rasieres.
WJ *Winthrop's Journal: History of New England, 1630-1649,* by John Winthrop.

Chapter One [pages 1-7]

1. John Robinson, *Works of John Robinson, Pastor of the Pilgrim Fathers, with a Memoir and Annotations by Robert Ashton*, 3 vols. Vol. 1 *Observations Divine and Moral*, (London: John Snow, 1851), Ch. 53, "Of Rewards and Punishments by Men," 216. Hereinafter referred to as *ODM*.
2. *ODM*. Ch. 3, "Of God's Promises," 10.
3. *Records of the Colony of New Plymouth in New England*, Edited by Nathaniel B. Shurtleff, M.D. 12 vols. (Boston: The Press of William White, 1855), 2:123. Hereinafter referred to as *PCR*.
4. *PCR*, 11:19.
5. John Winthrop, *Winthrop's Journal: History of New England, 1630-1649* (New York: Charles Scribner's Sons, 1908), 317-318. Hereinafter referred to as *WJ*.
6. *WJ*, 318.
7. George Willison, *Saints and Strangers* (New York: Reynal & Hitchcock, 1945), 481. Hereinafter referred to as *SS*.
8. E.J.V. Huiginn, *The Graves of Myles Standish and Other Pilgrims*. Revised and Enlarged. (Massachusetts: Published by the Author, 1914), 25-26.

Chapter Two [pages 8-25]

1. The Registers of the Chapel of Austerfield, in the Parish of Blyth and in the County of York, 1559-1812. George Denison Lumb, Ed., (Privately printed for the Yorkshire Parish Register Society, 1910), 3, 4, 13. Hereinafter referred to as *RCA*. All dates are changed into New Style.
2. *Book of Common Prayer 1559*. "The Ministration of Baptism," http://justus.anglican.org/resources/bcp/1559/BCP1559.pdf (accessed on November 14, 2017).
3. Ibid.
4. Ibid.
5. Anne Hollingsworth, *English Ancestral Home of Noted Americans* (Philadelphia and London: J.B. Lippincott Co., 1915), 43.
6. *RCA*, 4, 5, 11, 13.
7. *RCA*, 14 and Cotton Mather, *Magnalia Christi Americana; or the Ecclesiastical History of New England* (Hartford: Silas Andrus and Son, 1855), 110. Hereinafter referred to as *MCA*.
8. "Did George Morton of Leiden come from Bawtry?" Pilgrim Fathers Origins, http://www.pilgrimfathersorigins.org/bawtry-chapel-and-george-morton-research.html (accessed on January 21, 2019).

9. *RCA,* 11.
10. *MCA,* 110.
11. *RCA,* 11.
12. *RCA,* 11.
13. Sue Allen has suggested to the author that William Brewster may have been William Bradford's tutor based on the similarities in their signatures and handwriting.
14. *MCA,* 110.
15. William Bradford, *Of Plymouth Plantation, 1620-1647.* Edited by Samuel Eliot Morison. (New York: Alfred A. Knopf, 2004, first published in 1952), Book 1, Ch. 1, 5. Hereinafter referred to as *OPP.*
16. "The Act Against Puritans (1593) 35 Elizabeth, Cap. 1." Henry Gee and William John Hardy, ed., D*ocuments Illustrative of English Church History,* (New York: Macmillan, 1896), 492-498.
17. *MCA,* 110.
18. Ibid.
19. I James I, King of England, *Basilikon Doron.* 1599. Reprinted in Fortier, Mark and Daniel Fischlin (eds.). *James I, The True Law of Free Monarchies and the Basilikon Doron* (Toronto, Ont.: Centre for Reformation and Renaissance Studies, 1996), 95.
20. *OPP,* Book 1, Ch. 1, 10.
21. Sue Allen, *In Search of Mayflower Pilgrim Susanna White-Winslow,* (UK: DPS Partnership, 2018), 47.
22. John Ogilby, *Brittannia.* 1675. Cited by Nottinghamshire History, "Scrooby," http://www.nottshistory.org.uk/articles/mellorsarticles/scrooby1.htm (accessed on November 14, 2017).
23. Sue Allen, *In Search of Mayflower Pilgrim Susanna White-Winslow,* (UK: DPS Partnership, 2018), 47.
24. John Leland, "Leland the Antiquary to Lord Cromwell Gives a Character of John Bale and Solicits the Release of Him from Imprisonment." Cited in *Original Letters, Illustrative of English History; Including Numerous Royal Letters: from Autographs in the British Museum, the State Paper Office, and One or Two Other Collections.* (London: Richard Bentley, 1846), 15.
25. *ODM,* Ch. 9, "Of Authority and Reason," 54, "Parting Advice," xliv.
26. Robinson, *A Defense of the Doctrine Propounded by the Synod at Dort,* Ch. 1, "Of Predestination," 271.
27. Nathaniel Morton, *New England's Memorial, 1669,* edited by Howard J. Hall, facsimile of the first edition. (New York: Scholars Facsimiles & Reprints, 1937), 1-2. Hereinafter referred to as *NEM.*
28. William Barlow, "Summe and Substance of the conference which it

pleased his Excellent Majesty to have with the Lords, Bishops, and other of his Clergy (at which most of the Lords of the Council were present) in his majesty's privy-chamber, at Hampton Court, January 14, 1603[4], contracted of William Barlow, Doctor of Divinity and Dean of Chester. In *A History of Conferences and Other Proceedings Connected with the Revision of the Book of Common Prayer; from the Year 1558 to the year 1690.* (Oxford University Press, 1840), 203.
29. Jeremy Dupertuis Bangs, *The Pilgrims, Leiden, and the Early Years of Plymouth Plantation.* "Disordered and Unlawful Conventicles," 2006. www.sail1620.org/Articles/the-pilgrims-leiden-and-the-early-years-of-plymouth-plantation-chapter-1 (accessed on November 14, 2017).
30. *ODM,* xx.
31. *OPP,* Book 1, Ch. 1, 10, fn.
32. *OPP,* Book 1, Ch. 1, 10.
33. John Waddington, *Congregational History, 1567-1700, in Relation to Contemporaneous Events, and the Conflict for Freedom, Purity, and Independence.* (London: Longmans, Green, and Co., 1874), 163.
34. *OPP,* Book 1, Ch. 1, 10.
35. *ODM,* Ch. 59, "Of Marriage," 240.
36. Thomas Brooks, *The Legacy of a Dying Mother to Her Mourning Children Being the Experiences of Mrs. Susanna Bell, Who Died March 13, 1672* (London: John Hancock, 1673), 45.
37. Ibid.
38. Ibid.

Chapter Three [pages 26-36]

1. *PCR,* 1:108.
2. *OPP,* 445.
3. Sheilagh Doerfler, "Churchill, Martin, and Bradford family research case number M040714C." New England Historic Genealogical Society. July 25, 2014.
4. *ODM,* Ch. 59, "Of Marriage," 240.
5. Jeremy Dupertuis Bangs, *Plymouth Colony's Private Libraries as recorded in wills and inventories, 1633-1692.* (Leiden: Leiden American Pilgrim Museum, 2016), 219.
6. William Gouge, *Of Domesticall Duties, Eight Treatises* (London: John Haviland for William Bladen, 1622), 272-273. Hereinafter referred to as *DD.*
7. *DD,* "Of Wife-like Mildness," 278-279.
8. *ODM,* Ch. 59, "Of Marriage," 240.
9. Ibid.

10. *DD*, "Of a Wife's Laboring to Bring her Judgment to the Bent of her Husband's," 337.
11. *ODM*, Ch. 59, "Of Marriage," 239-240.
12. John Robinson, *The Works of John Robinson, Pastor of the Pilgrim Fathers*, Vol. 3, (London: John Snow. 1851). "An Appendix to Mr. Perkins' Six Principles of Christian Religion."
13. William Bradford, "A Dialogue or the sum of a conference between some young men born in New England and sundery Ancient men that came out of Holland and old England, 1648." (The First Dialogue.) *Plymouth Church Records 1620-1859,* Part 1. (Boston: Colonial Society of Massachusetts, 1920), 139-140.
14. John Robinson, "A Just and Necessarie Apologie of Certain Christians, no lesse contumeliously than commonly called Brownists or Barrowists." In *The Works of John Robinson, Pastor of the Pilgrim Fathers* Vol. 3, Ch. 8, "Of the Exercise of Prophecy."
15. William Bradford, "Letter of William Bradford and Isaac Allerton." Reprinted in *The American Historical Review*, Vol. 8, No. 2 (Jan. 1903) 294-301.
16. *PCR*, 5:262.
17. *ODM,* Ch. 26, "Of Labor and Idleness," 113, 114.
18. *The Compact with the Charter and Laws of the Colony of New Plymouth: Together with the Charter of the Council at Plymouth and an Appendix Containing the Articles of Confederation of the United Colonies of New England and Other Valuable Documents.* (Boston: Dutton and Wentworth, 1836), 64. Hereinafter referred to as *CCL*.
19. *Records of the Town of Plymouth, Published by Order of the Town, Vol. 1, 1636-1705.* (Plymouth: Avery & Doten, 1889), 1:115. Hereinafter referred to as *RTP.*
20. "Last Will & Testament of Mary (Chilton) Winslow, 1676," *Plymouth Colony Archive Project.* http://www.histarch.illinois.edu/plymouth/winslowwill.html (accessed on November 14, 2017).
21. *PCR,* 12:29.
22. "Last Will & Testament of Elizabeth (Tilley) Howland, 1686," *Plymouth Colony Archive Project.* http://www.histarch.illinois.edu/plymouth/howlandwill.html (accessed on November 14, 2017)
23. *PCR*, 1:20.
24. *PCR*, 1:36-37.
25. John Pory, Emmanuel Altham, and Isaack de Rasieres, *Three Visitors to Early Plymouth: Letters About the Pilgrim Settlement in New England During Its First Seven Years.* (Bedford, MA: Applewood Boks, 1997), 77. Hereinafter referred to as *TVEP.*

26. *PCR*, 11:12.
27. *PCR*, 5:32.
28. *PCR*, 1:12.
29. John Robinson, *Works of John Robinson,* Vol. 1, *A Defence of the Doctrine Propounded by the Synode at Dort Against John Murton and His Associates* ... "Of Baptism," Printed in the year 1624, 461.
30. Thomas Prince, *A Chronological History of New England: In the Form of Annals* ... (Cummings, Hilliard and Company, 1826), 177.
31. *PCR,* 2:75, 85-86.
32. *ODM,* Ch. 59, "Of Marriage," 239.
33. *ODM,* Ch. 58, "Of Modesty," 233.
34. *ODM,* Ch. 59, "Of Marriage," 238.
35. John Robinson, "Mr. Bernard's Counsels Debated." *The Works of John Robinson,* Vol. 2, 12.

Chapter Four [pages 37-50]

1. *OPP,* Book 1, Ch. 1, 10.
2. John Smith is generally regarded as the founder of the modern Baptist churches.
3. *OPP,* Book 1, Ch. 1, 10.
4. *OPP,* Book 1, Ch. 2, 11.
5. "Boston, Lincolnshire: The Pilgrims and a Thread to America." My Boston UK, https://www.myboston.com/boston-lincolnshire-the-pilgrims-and-a-thread-to-america/ (accessed on October 4, 2019)
6. *OPP*, Book 1, Ch. 2, 12.
7. Ibid.
8. Ibid.
9. *PRA*
10. G.M. Fessenden, "A Genealogy of the Bradford Family." *The New England Historical and Genealogical Register*, Vols. 3 and 4, (January 1850), 39.
11. *OPP,* Book 1, Ch. 2, 12.
12. Ibid.
13. Ibid.
14. *OPP,* Book 1, Ch. 2, 13.
15. Ibid.
16. *OPP,* Book 1, Ch. 2, 14.
17. Ibid.
18. Ibid.
19. Ibid.
20. *OPP,* Book 1, Ch. 2, 13.

21. *OPP*, Book 1, Ch. 2, 13, 14.
22. *OPP*, Book 1, Ch. 2, 15.
23. Keith Thomas, "Women and the Civil War Sects." *Crisis in Europe, 1560-1660, Essays from Past and Present*. Edited by Trevor Aston. (London, Routledge & Kegan Paul, 1965), 318.
24. "Presentment Bill relating to William Brewster, Scrooby parish, 1598." University of Nottingham. http://www.nottingham.ac.uk/manuscriptsandspecialcollections/exhibitions/online/thebawdycourt/beliefandpersecution.aspx (accessed on November 14, 2017).
25. William Whittingham, et al., trans. *The Bible and Holy Scriptures, Conteyned in the olde and newe Testament ...* ("Geneva Bible."). "Fifth Book of Moses Called Deuteronomy" 21:18. http://www.genevabible.org/files/Geneva_Bible/Old_Testament/Deuteronomy_F.pdf (accessed on November 14, 2017).
26. Bangs, *The Pilgrims, Leiden, and the Early Years of Plymouth*, 20.
27. *OPP*, Book 1, Ch. 2, 10.
28. *OPP*, Book 1, Ch. 2, 14.
29. *OPP*, Book 1, Ch. 2, 11.
30. *OPP*, Book 1, Ch. 3, 16.
31. Ibid.
32. *OPP*, Book 1, Ch. 2, 9.
33. *OPP*, Book 1, Ch. 3, 17.
34. *OPP*, Book 1, Ch. 3, 19.
35. Eugene Aubrey Stratton, *Plymouth Colony, Its History & People, 1620-1691*. (Salt Lake City, Utah: Ancestry Publishing, 1986), 249. (*PCHP*)
36. *OPP*, Book 1, Ch. 3, 17, Ch. 4, 24-25.
37. *NEM*, 2.
38. *OPP*, Book 1, Ch. 4, 23.
39. *NEM*, 3.
40. *OPP*, Book 1, Ch. 4, 26.
41. Ibid.
42. *NEM*, 4.
43. *OPP*, Book 1, Ch. 4, 25, 26.
44. *OPP*, Book 1, Ch. 4, 27.
45. *NEM*, 2, 4.
46. *OPP*, Book 1, Ch. 4, 24.

Chapter Five [pages 51-71]

1. "Petition of the Directors of the New Netherland Company," February 12, 1620. *Documents Relative to the Colonial History of the State of New York*

Procured in England, Holland, and France, Vol. I. Albany, (New York: Weed Parsons and Company, Printers, 1856), 22-23.
2. Stephen Vincent Benét, *Western Star* (New York: Farrar & Rinehart, Inc., 1943) 120.
3. *OPP,* Book 1, Ch. 9, 61, etc.
4. John Smith, *A Description of New England (1616),* (London: Humfrey Lownes, 1616), 21.
5. Ibid., 24, 29.
6. Ibid., 25, 32, 41, 47.
7. Ibid., 42, 53.
8. Ibid., 48.
9. Peggy Baker, "The Plymouth Colony Patent: Setting the Stage," Plymouth Hall Museum, 2007.
10. *OPP*, 39n.
11. *OPP,* Book 1, Ch. 6, 40.
12. *OPP,* 356-358.
13. *OPP*, 357.
14. *OPP,* Book 1, Ch. 4, 26.
15. *OPP*, Book 1, Ch. 6, 36.
16. Ibid.
17. *OPP,* Book 1, Ch. 2, 14.
18. *OPP,* Book 1, Ch. 6, 41.
19. *OPP*, Book 1, Ch. 6, 40.
20. *OPP,* Book 1, Ch. 6, 43.
21. John Josselyn, *An Account of Two Voyages ...*, 19-20.
22. *OPP*, Book 1, Ch. 7, 47.
23. Ibid.
24. Edward Winslow, *Hypocrisie Unmasked, a True Relation of the Proceedings of the Governor and Company of the Massachusetts Against Samuel Gorton of Rhode Island.* (Providence, Rhode Island: The Club for Colonial Reprints, 1916. Originally published in 1646), 90.
25. Jeremy Bangs, *Strangers and Pilgrims, Travellers and Sojourners: Leiden and the Foundations of Plymouth Plantation* (Plymouth, MA: General Society of *Mayflower* Descendants, 2009), 179.
26. Winslow, *Hypocrisie Unmasked,* 91.
27. *OPP,* Book 1, Ch. 7, 47.
28. *OPP*, Book 1, Ch. 7, 48.
29. Ibid.
30. Robinson, *The Works of John Robinson,* Vol. 1, xlvii-li.
31. *OPP*, Book 1, Ch. 7, 51.
32. *OPP*, Book 1, Ch. 8, 53.

33. *OPP,* Book 1, Ch. 8, 54-56.
34. *PCHP,* 259.
35. Audrey Drummond and Nancy J. Springer, *Mayflower Passengers: 1620,* 2nd ed. (Massachusetts: Massachusetts Society of *Mayflower* Descendants, 1996).
36. Patricia Scott Deetz and James F. Deetz, "Passengers on the *Mayflower*: Ages & Occupations, Origins and Connections," *The Plymouth Colony Archive Project.* www.histarch.uiuc.edu/plymouth/Maysource.html (accessed on November 14, 2017).
37. David Lindsay, *Mayflower Bastard, a Stranger Among the Pilgrims.* (New York: Thomas Dunne Books, an imprint of St. Martin's Press, 2002), 25.
38. Audrey Drummond and Nancy J. Springer, *Mayflower Passengers: 1620,* 2nd ed. (Massachusetts: Massachusetts Society of *Mayflower* Descendants, 1996).
39. Deetz, "Passengers on the *Mayflower* ..."
40. *OPP,* Book 1, Ch. 8, 55.
41. *OPP,* Book 1, Ch. 9, 58.
42. Letter of Edward Winslow, 11 December 1621, Caleb Johnson's *Mayflower* History.com. http://mayflowerhistory.com/letter-winslow-1621/ (accessed on November 14, 2017).
43. Ibid.
44. George F. Willison, *The Pilgrim Reader: The Story of the Pilgrims as Told by Themselves and Their Contemporaries Friendly and Unfriendly* (Garden City, NY: Doubleday and Co., Inc., 1953), 170.
45. John Josselyn, *An Account of Two Voyages to New England: Made During the Years 1638, 1663.* (Boston: William Weazie, 1865), 9.
46. Ibid., 7.
47. Benet, 134.
48. *OPP,* Book 1, Ch. 9, 58.
49. There is speculation that the "great iron screw" may have been a remnant of Brewster's printing press. See Bangs, *Strangers and Pilgrims,* 607-608.
50. *OPP,* Book 1, Ch. 9, 58-59.
51. Ibid., 59.
52. John Josselyn, *An Account of Two Voyages to New England...*, 9.

Chapter Six [pages 72-87]

1. *PCR,* 11:26, 43.
2. *PCR,* 7:5.
3. Samuel Eliot Morison, *The Ropemakers of Plymouth: A History of the Plymouth Cordage Company, 1824-1949.* (Boston: Houghton Mifflin Co., 1950), 2-3.

4. *PCR*, 12:26.
5. James Savage, *A Genealogical Dictionary of the First Settlers of New England,* Vol. 1. (Baltimore: Genealogical Publishing Co., 1969), 403.
6. *PCR*, 1:32, 46.
7. *PCR*, 1:23. John Smith successfully petitioned the court to free him from his indenture to Edward Doty because Doty "had disbursed but little for him."
8. *PCHP,* 283.
9. *PCR*, 1:3, 6-7, 43.
10. *PCR*, 7:5.
11. *PCR*, 1:43, 47.
12. *PCR*, 1:43
13. *PCR*, 1:75.
14. *PCR*, 12:26.
15. Ibid.
16. Ibid.
17. Ibid.
18. *PCR*, 11:4.
19. *PCR*, 12:26.
20. *PCR*, 12:26.
21. *ODM,* Ch. 59, "Of Marriage," 236, 241.
22. *DD,* "Of the Ends of Marriage." 210.
23. *ODM,* Ch. 59. "Of Marriage." 240.
24. *ODM,* Ch. 59 "Of Marriage,"237, 238, 240.
25. *DD,* "Of impotent persons that ought not to seek after marriage," 181-183.
26. *ODM,* Ch. 59 "Of Marriage," 239.
27. *PCHP,* 50.
28. *PCHP,* 70.
29. *PCR*, 11:13.
30. *PCR*, 11:13, 29.
31. *CCL,* 79-80.
32. *PCR*, 11:13, 18-19.
33. *PCR*, 11:46.
34. Craig Chartier, Plymouth Archaeological Rediscovery Project. "Livestock in Plymouth Colony," http://plymoutharch.tripod.com/id133.html (accessed on November 14, 2017). 4, 8 of 11.
35. *PCR*, 12:26.
36. *OPP,* Book 2, Ch. 29, 1638, 302.
37. Craig Chartier, Plymouth Archaeological Rediscovery Project. "Livestock in Plymouth Colony," http://plymoutharch.tripod.com/id133.html (accessed on November 14, 2017). 4, 8 of 11.

Source Notes

38. Darrett B. Rutman, *Husbandmen of Plymouth: Farms and Villages in the Old Colony, 1620-1692.* (Boston: Beacon Press, 1967), 33.
39. *PCR,* 11:14.
40. *CCL,* 61.
41. John Demos, *A Little Commonwealth,* 2nd ed. (Oxford University Press, 2000), 160-161. Hereinafter referred to as *LC.*
42. *OPP,* Book 2, Ch. 12, 1621, 86.
43. *DD,* "Of ill or well ordering marriage feasts," 208.
44. *ODM,* Ch. 36, "Of Peace," 154.
45. *ODM,* Ch. 56, "Of Anger," 226.
46. *ODM,* Ch. 59, "Of Marriage," 239, 241.
47. *PCR,* 2:28.
48. *ODM,* Ch. 59, "Of Marriage," 242.
49. Jane Sharp, *The Midwives Book, or the Whole Art of Midwifry Discovered, 1671,* Ed. Elaine Hobby, (New York: Oxford University Press, 1999), 41, 58.

Chapter Seven [pages 88-105]

1. Bradford, *OPP,* Book 1, Ch. 9, 59-60.
2. *OPP,* Book 1, Ch. 9, 60.
3. *OPP,* Book 2, Ch. 11, 1620, 75.
4. Edward Winslow, William Bradford, and others. A *Relation or Journall of the beginning and proceedings of the English Plantation settled at Plimoth in New England by certaine English Adventurers both Merchants and others.* ("*Mourt's Relation*") 1622. Ed. Dwight B. Heath. (Bedford, Massachusetts: Applewood Books, 1963), 17.
4. *OPP,* Book 1, Ch. 9, 61.
5. Benet, *Western Star,* 136.
6. *OPP,* Book 1, Ch. 9, 61, 62.
7. *OPP,* Book 1, Ch. 9, 60.
8. Bradford Smith, *Bradford of Plymouth,* 108-109.
9. Ibid.
10. *OPP,* Book 1, Ch. 4, 25.
11. *OPP,* Book 2, Ch. 11, 75-76.
12. George Ernest Bowman, "Why did only 41 passengers sign The Compact?" *Pilgrim Notes and Queries,* Vol.1 (1913), 18.
13. *NEM,* 15-16.
14. George Ernest Bowman, *The Mayflower Compact and Its Signers.* (Massachusetts Society of *Mayflower* Descendants: Boston, 1920), 17-18.
15. *OPP,* Book 2, Ch. 11, 1620, 76.

16. Ibid.
17. *MR*, 18.
18. Ibid.
19. Prince, *A Chronological History of New England*, 162.
20. *MR*, 19.
21. Prince, *A Chronological History of New England*, 162-3.
22. *OPP*, Book 1, Ch. 10, 64.
23. *MR*, 20-21, 23.
24. *MR*, 22.
25. *OPP*, Book 1, Ch. 10, 65, 66.
26. *MR*, 23.
27. Ibid., 23, 24.
28. Ibid., 26.
29. Ibid., 26, 28.
30. Ibid.
31. Ibid.
32. Ibid., 30.
33. *OPP*, Book 1, Ch. 10, 70.
34. *MR*, 32.
35. *OPP*, Book 1, Ch. 10, 69, 70.
36. *MR*, 35, 37.
37. *OPP*, Book 1, Ch. 10, 72.
38. Megan Gambino, "John Smith Coined the Term New England on This 1616 Map." Smithsonian.com. https://www.smithsonianmag.com/history/john-smith-coined-the-term-new-england-on-this-1616-map-180953383/ (accessed on November 8, 2017).
39. John Smith, "A Description of New England (1616): An Online Electronic Text Edition," Electronic Texts in American Studies, https://digitalcommons.unl.edu/etas/ (accessed on January 21, 2019).
40. *MR*, 38.
41. Drummond, *Mayflower Passengers, 1620*, 7.
42. *MCA*, 111.
43. *OPP*, Book 1, Ch. 9, 59.
44. *MCA*, 111.
45. George D. Langdon, Jr., *Pilgrim Colony: A History of New Plymouth, 1620-1691*. (New Haven and London: Yale University Press, 1966), 12.
46. Samuel Eliot Morison, *The Story of the "Old Colony" of New Plymouth* (New York: Alfred A. Knopf, 1956), 56.
47. *OPP*, xxiv.

48. Nathaniel Philbrick, *Mayflower, a Story of Courage, Community, and War* (New York: Viking, 2006), 76.
49. *OPP*, Book 1, Ch. 9, 61-62.
50. *OPP*, Book 2, Ch. 11, 1620, 77.
51. Josselyn, *New England's Rarities Discovered* (London: G. Widdowes, 1672), 14.
52. Richard Henry Dana, *Two Years Before the Mast*. (Boston: Fields, Osgood, & Co., 1869), 411.
53. *OPP*, Book 1, Ch. 2, 14.
54. *MR*, 39.
55. Ibid.
56. Sarah Y. Bailey, *The Story of the Jones River in Pilgrim Plymouth, 1620-1726* (Kingston Branch of the Alliance of Unitarian Women, 1920), 4,7.
57. *MR*, 39-40.
58. Ibid., 40.
59. Ibid., 41.

Chapter Eight [pages 106-118]

1. Josselyn, *New England's Rarities Discovered*, 89.
2. Ibid., 91.
3. *PCR*, 11:32.
4. *PCR*, 11:26.
5. A bushel is 36 quarts, and a pottle is 2 quarts.
6. *PCR*, 11:32.
7. Ibid.
8. Robinson, "A Just and Necessary Apologie of Certain Christians, no lesse contumeliously than commonly called Brownists or Barrowists." In *The Works of John Robinson,* Vol. 3, Ch. 3, "Of Written Liturgies," 26.
9. Martha L. Finch, *Dissenting Bodies: Corporealities in Early New England* (New York: Columbia University Press, 2010) 153.
10. Ibid., 157.
11. Winifred Cockshott, *The Pilgrim Fathers: Their Church and Colony* (New York: G.P. Putman's, 1909), 329.
12. *PCR*, 11:86-87,92, 225.
13. *PCR*, 12:55.
14. *PCR*, 1:76.
15. *PCR*, 1:82.
16. *PCR*, 1:119.

17. William Bradford, "Letter of William Bradford and Isaac Allerton, September 8, 1623," http://mayflowerhistory.com/letter-bradford-and-allerton (accessed on November 14, 2017).
18. *ODM*, Ch. 60, "Of Children and their Education," 242.
19. Sharp, *The Midwives Book,* 82.
20. Ibid., 135-136.
21. *DD,* "Of mother's care over her child while it is in her womb," 505.
22. Sharp, 139, 140.
23. *LC,* 66, 131,132.
24. Quoted in Wertz, Richard W. and Dorothy C. Wertz. *Lying-in: A History of Childbirth in America* (Yale University Press, 1989), 21.
25. *ODM*, Ch. 60, "Of Children and their Education," 244.
26. Anne Bradstreet, *To My Husband and Other Poems.* "Before the Birth of One of Her Children," (Mineola, NY: Dover Publications, Inc., 2000), 5.
27. Sharp, 145.
28. Ibid., 153,158-159.
29. Thomas Reynald, *The Birth of Man-kinde; Otherwise Named The Woman's Booke* (London: James Boler, 1626), Bk. 2, Ch. 3. 101.
30. It was noted in a court record that Abigail was twenty years old in March of 1663. See record of John Churchill's will in DeForest, L. Effingham, and Anne Lawrence DeForest, *Moore and Allied Families, the Ancestry of William Henry Moore.* New York: DeForest Publishing, 1938.
31. Thurston Clarke had a child named Abigail, who stayed in England when he emigrated to America. She died in Ipswich in January 1637. See NEHGS, Vol LXIX, 1915, 253.
32. *ODM*, Ch. 60, "Of Children and their Education," 244.
33. Sharp, 272.
34. *DD,* "Of mothers giving suck to their own children," 512.
35. *DD,* "Of parents joint care about their children's Baptism," 519.
36. Sharp, 163.
37. Josselyn, *An Account of Two Voyages...*, 86.

Chapter Nine [pages 119-135]

1. *OPP,* Book 2, Ch. 11, 1620, 84.
2. Deetz, "Passengers on the *Mayflower*: Ages & Occupations, Origins and Connections,"
3. *OPP*, Book 2, Ch. 11, 1620, 77.
4. Patricia Scott Deetz and James F. Deetz, "*Mayflower* Passenger Deaths, 1620-1621." *The Plymouth Colony Archive Project.* www.histarch.uiuc.edu/plymouth/Maydeaths.html (accessed on November 14, 2017).

5. Deetz, "Passengers on the *Mayflower*: Ages & Occupations, Origins and Connections."
6. Drummond, *Mayflower Passengers, 1620*, 4
7. *MR*, 42.
8. *OPP*, 445.
9. *MR*, 42.
10. Ibid.
11. *OPP*, Book 2, Ch. 11, 1620, 72.
12. *MR*, 42.
13. *MR*, 43.
14. *MR*, 44.
15. Prince, 169.
16. *PCHP*, 342.
17. *MR*, 43-44.
18. *PCHP*, 323.
19. *MR*, 44, 45.
20. *MR*, 47.
21. *MR*, 48.
22. Ibid.
23. *MR*, 49.
24. Deetz. "*Mayflower* Passenger Deaths."
25. *MR*, 50.
26. Ibid.
27. *MCA*, 55.
28. *OPP*, Book 2, Ch. 11, 79-80.
29. Ibid., 79.
30. *MR*, 52.
31. *OPP*, Book 2, Ch. 11, 1620, 80.
32. Ibid.
33. *NEM*, 291-292.
34. *OPP*, Book 2, Ch. 11, 1620, 77, 78.
35. Ibid.
36. *OPP*, Book 2, Ch. 11, 1620, 84.
37. Prince, 189.
38. *OPP*, Book 2, Ch. 11, 1620, 85.
39. *OPP*, Book 2, Ch. 21, 1630, 234.
40. *OPP*, Book 2, Ch. 12, 1621, 85.
41. Ibid., 86.
42. Prince, 190.
43. *OPP*, Book 2, Ch. 12, 1621, 86.
44. Prince, 190.

45. *OPP*, Book 2, Ch. 12, 1621, 90.
46. Ibid., 87.
47. Ibid.
48. *MCA,* 55.
49. *OPP*, Book 2, Ch. 12, 1621, 87-88.
50. Ibid., 88.
51. Ibid., 90.
52. *MR,* 82.
53. Ibid.
54. Ibid.
55. *DD,* "Of husbands and wives mutuall helpe in hospitality," 262.
56. *MR,* 82.
57. *OPP*, Book 2, Ch. 12, 1621, 92.
58. Caleb Johnson, "Peter Browne," Caleb Johnson's *Mayflower* History. http://mayflowerhistory.com/browne/ (accessed on November 14, 2017).
59. *OPP*, Book 2, Ch. 12, 1621, 93, 95-96.
60. Ibid., 96.

Chapter Ten [pages 136-144]

1. Gervase Markham, *The English Husbandman,* (London: John Browne, 1613), 5. http://www.gutenberg.org/files/22973/22973-h/22973-h.htm (accessed on November 14, 2017).
2. *PCR,* 2:33.
3. *RTP,* 1:16.
4. *DD,* "Of parents providing things needful for the life and health of their children," 526.
5. *ODM,* Ch. 60, "Of Children and Their Education," 244.
6. Ibid., 244, 246.
7. Ibid., 247.
8. Ibid., 246.
9. Ibid., 247.
10. Ibid., 248, 249.
11. Ibid., 243, 250.
12. Ibid., 245.
13. *ODM,* Ch. 56, "Of Anger," 225.
14. Kathleen M. Brown, *Foul Bodies: Cleanliness in Early America* (New Haven: Yale University Press, 2009), 26.
15. *PCR,* 8:187.
16. *PCR,* 1:9,10-11.

17. James Deetz and Patricia Deetz. *The Times of Their Lives: Life, Love, and Death in Plymouth Colony.* (New York: W.H. Freeman and Co., 2000), 104.

Chapter Eleven [pages 145-159]

1. Deetz, *Time of Their Lives,* 66.
2. *TVEP,* 3.
3. Slightly larger than two football fields.
4. *TVEP,* 7, 11.
5. Ibid., 7, 11-12.
6. *OPP,* Book 2, Ch. 12, 1621, 96.
7. Edward Winslow, *Good Newes from New England: a True Relation of Things Very Remarkable at the Plantation of Plimoth in New England.* (Bedford, Massachusetts: Applewood Books. Nd. Originally published in 1624), 10.
8. Josselyn, *An Account of Two Voyages,* 188.
9. *TVEP,* 24.
10. Ibid., 25, 26, 27.
11. Ibid., 28.
12. *OPP,* Book 2, Ch. 14, 1623, 130.
13. *TVEP,* 29
14. Ibid., 29, 30.
15. Ibid., 39, 40.
16. Ibid., 49, 51.
17. Letter of Weston to Bradford, quoted in *OPP,* Book 2, Ch. 13, 1622, 103.
18. *OPP,* Book 1, Ch. 12, 1621, 94.
19. *OPP,* Book 2, Ch. 14, 1623, 132.
20. *OPP,* Book 1, Ch. 4, 24
21. Robert Cushman, *The First Sermon Ever Preached in New England: The First Printed and the Oldest American Discourse Extant. 1621* (New York: J.E.D. Comstock, 1859), 42. 44.
22. The main purpose of Cushman's visit to Plymouth in 1621, was to get the leaders to sign the revised contract. See Lupher, David. *Greeks, Romans, and Pilgrims: Classical Receptions in Early New England.* Leiden: Brill, 2017, 289-304.
23. *OPP,* Book 2, Ch. 14, 1623, 120.
24. Ibid.
25. *OPP,* Book 2, Ch. 14, 1623, 122.
26. Ibid., 121.
27. Ibid.
28. Ibid.

29. Winslow, *Good Newes from New England,* 19, 40-41.
30. Ibid., 40-41, 43.
31. Ibid., 28, 47.
32. Ibid., 48.
33. Ibid., 48, 50.
34. Ibid., 52.
35. William Bradford. "Letter of William Bradford and Isaac Allerton," Reprinted in The American Historical Review, Vol. 8, No. 2, (Jan. 1903), 294-301.
36. *OPP,* 375.
37. Ibid., 374-375.
38. *OPP,* Book 2, Ch. 17, 1626, 179.
39. Ibid., 180.
40. Ibid., 181.

Chapter Twelve [pages 160-166]

1. *PCR,* 1:16.
2. *SS,* 131, 133.
3. Ibid., 442.
4. *PCR,* 1:92 (John Price), 1:100 (John Long), 1:103 (Richard Bishop), 1:103, 115 (James Leighhorne), 1:122 (Robert Eldred).
5. *PCR,* 1:92, 100.
6. *PCR,* 1:7, 74, 104.
7. *PCR,* 1:115.
8. *PCR,* 1:36 - Roland Laherne, 1:50 - Roland Leyhorne, 1:51 - Rowland Leyhorne.
9. *PCR,* 1:128, 2:17.
10. *PCR,* 2:6
11. *PCR,* 1:4, 48.
12. *PCR,* 12:40-41.
13. Nathaniel Shurtleff, "List of Those Able to Bear Arms in the Colony of New Plymouth in 1643", *New England Historical Genealogical Society Register* (July 1850), 255.
14. *PCR,* 2:79.
15. *PCR,* 2:132.

Chapter Thirteen [pages 167-175]

1. *TVEP,* 76.
2. Ibid.
3. Ibid., 77.

4. Ibid., 76, 77.
5. Ibid., 76.
6. Ibid., 77, fn.
7. *OPP,* Book 2, Ch. 18, 1627, 184.
8. Harry M. Ward, *Statism in Plymouth Colony* (Port Washington, New York: Kennikat Press, 1973), 38.
9. Ruth A. McIntyre, *Debts Hopeful and Desperate.* (Plimoth Plantation, 1963), 47-52.
10. Ward, *Statism in Plymouth Colony,* 39.
11. *OPP,* Book 2, Ch. 18, 1627, 195.
12. *OPP,* Book 2, Ch. 18, 1627, 186-187.
13. *PCR,* 2:177.
14. *OPP,* Book 2, Ch. 18, 1627, 187.
15. *OPP,* Book 2, Ch. 18, 1627, 186, 187.
16. Ibid., 188. Fn.
17. *TVEP,* 77.
18. *OPP,* Book 2, Ch. 18, 1627, 193.
19. *TVEP,* 70.
20. *OPP,* Book 2, Ch. 19, 1628, 203.
21. Ibid., 204.
22. *OPP,* Book 2, Ch. 20, 1629, 214-215.
23. Ibid., 214.
24. Ibid., 216.
25. *Compact with the Charter ...,* Earl of Warwick, "Charter of the Colony of New Plymouth Granted to William Bradford and His Associates, 1629," 21.

Chapter Fourteen [pages 176-186]

1. John Winthrop, *The Winthrop Papers,* Vol. 2, "A Modell of Christian Charity," (Boston: MHS, 1931), 293.
2. Ibid.
3. *OPP,* Book 1, Ch. 4, 24, 25.
4. Ibid., 27.
5. *OPP,* Book 2, Ch. 15, 1624, 141.
6. Ibid., 143.
7. Rutman, *Husbandmen of Plymouth,* 12.
8. *OPP,* Book 2, Ch. 23, 1632, 253.
9. Ibid.
10. By 1642, the price of cattle would drop suddenly from twenty-two pounds each cow to about seven, causing great financial losses. See Josselyn, *An Account of Two Voyages,* 197.

11. Rutman, *Husbandmen of Plymouth,* 18.
12. *OPP,* Book 1, Ch. 5, 33, fn
13. *OPP,* Book 2, Ch. 23, 1632, 253-254.
14. *PCR,* 1:5.
15. *PCR,* 1:6, 34.
16. *PCR,* 1:16, 17.
17. *PCR,* 1:6, 22.
18. Robinson, *Works of John Robinson,* Vol. 1, "Farewell Letter," xlviii.
19. *PCR,* 11:6.
20. Edward Winslow, *New England's Salamander Discovered* (London: Printed by Ric. Cotes, for John Bellamie, 1647), 23-24.
21. "Love Brewster's Will and Inventory." *Mayflower Descendant,* Vol. 2, 1900, p. 205.
22. Bangs, *Plymouth Colony's Private Libraries,* p. 185. This reference in Bangs is unclear. The actual title in Love Brewster's inventory was *Duties of Constable and householder* by William Lambarde, yet that book in Bangs is described as *Eirenarcha,* which is a different book.
23. D.C. Parnes, *Plymouth and the Common Law, 1620-1775* (Kingston, MA: Pilgrim Publishers, 1971), 22-23.
24. Winslow, Edward. *New England's Salamander Discovered,* 24.
25. George Crabb, *A History of English Law...* (London: Baldwin and Cradock, 1829), 471.
26. Roland Usher, *The Pilgrims and Their History,* (Williamstown, Massachusetts: Corner House Publishers, 1984, Originally published in 1918), 202.
27. *PCR,* 11:17.

Chapter Fifteen [pages 187-190]

1. PCR, 2:132-134.
2. The spelling has been modernized and the names of individuals made consistent with current usage.

Chapter Sixteen [pages 191-201]

1 *PCR,* 11:7, 8.
2. *OPP*, Book 2, Ch. 21, 1630, 234.
3. *PCR,* 1:96-97.
4. *OPP*, Book 2, Ch. 29, 1638, 299-301.
5. Ibid.

6. Nathan Dorn, "The Murder of Penowanyanquis and the Trial of Arthur Peach," Law Librarians of Congress, https://blogs.loc.gov/law/2018/09/the-murder-of-penowanyanquis-and-the-trial-of-arthur-peach-plymouth-1638/, accessed on 9/18/2019.
7. Ibid.
8. *PCR*, 2:44.
9. *OPP*, Book 2, Ch. 32, 1642, 320.
10. Caleb Johnson, *The Mayflower and Her Passengers*, Xlibris Corp. 2006, 138.
11. *PCHP*, 286.
12. Johnson, *The Mayflower and Her Passengers*, 138.
13. *OPP*, 446.
14. Johnson, *Mayflower and Her Passengers*, 139.
15. *PCR*, 1:10.
16. *PCR*, 1:19-20.
17. Johnson, *Mayflower and Her Passengers*, 140.
18. *PCR*, 1:31.
19. *OPP*, Book 2, Ch. 21, 1630, 234.
20. *PCR*, 12:22, 29.
21. Susan E. Roser, *Mayflower Increasings*, 2nd ed. (Baltimore, MD: Genealogical Publishing Co., Inc., 1996), 6.
22. Roser. *Mayflower Increasings*, 16-17.
23. *PCR*, 1:36-37. 2:38.
24. *RTP*, 1:12.
25. *PCR*, 2:87, 8:173-174.
26. *PCR*, 3:102, 8:7.
27. *PCR*, 2:132.
28. Ibid.
29. *PCR*, 1:84.
30. "Last Will and Testament of Mary Chilton Winslow." Pilgrim Hall Museum. http://www.pilgrimhallmuseum.org/pdf/Mary_Chilton_Winslow_Will_Inventory.pdf (accessed on November 11, 2017).
31. *PCR*, 2:132-133.
32. Ibid.

Chapter Seventeen [pages 202-211]

1. *PCR*, 2:132.
2. Charles Chauncy, "The Answer of Mr. Charles Chauncy." *OPP*, 413.
3. *PCR*, 2:132.
4. *PCR*, 11:11.

5. *PCR,* 8:173-174.
6. *PCR,* 2:132.
7. Ibid.
8. Ibid.
9. *PCR,* 2:133.
10. *PCR,* 2:133, 1:115, 11:9.
11. *PCR,* 2:93.
12. *PCR,* 2:132.
13. *PCR,* 11:49.
14. *PCR,* 2:127.
15. *PCR,* 2:132.
16. William Waller Henning, *The Statutes at Large, a Collection of All the Laws of Virginia from the First Session of the Legislature in the Year 1619,* Vol. 1. (New York: R. & W. & G. Bartow, 1823), 209.

Chapter Eighteen [pages 212-221]

1. *PCR,* 11:32.
2. *ODM,* Ch. 53, "Of Rewards and Punishments by Men," 216.
3. *ODM,* Ch. 34, "Of Injuries." 147.
4. *ODM,* Ch. 53, "Of Rewards and Punishments by Men," 215.
5. *ODM,* Ch. 8, "Of the Holy Scriptures," 51.
6. Robinson, *Works of John Robinson,* Vol. 1, "To Sir Edwin Sandys." xl.
7. In 1712 the first meeting house was considered too small for the growing population and a second meeting house was build. The newer building measured 40x33 feet and was 17 feet tall, so we can assume the older meeting house was considerably smaller.
8. *PCR,* 2:134.
9. *PCHP,* 149.
10. *PCR,* 11:85.
11. *ODM,* Ch. 53, "Of Rewards and Punishments by Men." 216.
12. *OPP,* Book 2, Ch. 32, 1642, 321.
13. *PCR,* 2:134.
14. Ibid.
15. Ibid.
16. Numbers 35:33.
17. Cited in Stuart Banner, *The Death Penalty, an American History.* (Cambridge, MA: Harvard University Press, 2002), 5.
18. Thorsten Sellin, *The Penalty of Death.* (Sage Publications, 1980), 29.
19. *ODM,* Ch. 53, "Of Rewards and Punishments of Men." 215.
20. *PCR,* 2:134.

Chapter Nineteen [pages 222-234]

1. *PCR,* 1:103.
2. *PCR,* 2:6.
3. *PCR,* 2:79
4. *PCR,* 2:137.
5. "Sketches of the Early History of the Town of Middleborough, in the County of Plymouth," *The New England Historical & Genealogical Register,* 1849, 335.
6. *PCR,* 2:162.
7. *PCR,* 2:138.
8. Ibid.
9. *RTP,* 1:2.
10. Louis Effingham DeForest, *Moore and Allied Families* (New York: DeForest Publishing, 1938), 179.
11. Land Record dated December 5, 1666, recorded July 1, 1672, Abigail Clark to Richard Wright. Plymouth Colony Registry of Deeds in Plymouth, MA, Record No. DPL III(2):228[a].
12. There were at least two other Abigail Clarkes living in Plymouth at about this same time and a researcher must be careful not to confuse them. One was the daughter of Thomas Clarke and Susanna Ring and was born in 1639. (Susanna Ring was the sister of Andrew Ring, who accused Richard Bishop of stealing his spade.) This Abigail Clarke would go on to marry John Sutton of Plymouth. The other Abigail Clarke was Abigail Lothrop (daughter of John Lothrop and Anne Dimmock) who married James Clarke. They also had a daughter named Abigail Clarke born about 1667.
13. *PCR,* 8:32.
14. *PCR,* 2:132.
15. Frederick Freeman, *The History of Cape Cod: The Annals of the Thirteen Towns of Barnstable County*, Vol. II, (Boston: Geo. C. Rand & Avery, 3 Cornhill, 1862), 350.
16. Joshua Paine, *Founders' Day Edition, August 26, 1916, of the Early Settlers of Eastham: Containing sketches of all early settlers of Eastham.* (Library of Cape Cod History & Genealogy, 1916), 472.
17. Freeman, *The History of Cape Cod,* 359.
18. Charles Libby, "The Knowles Family of Eastman, MA," *New England Historic Genealogical Society Register*, (July 1925), 289-290.
19. *PCR,* 5:30-31.
20. *PCR,* 5:126.
21. Richard LeBaron Bowen, *Early Rehoboth, Documented Historical Studies of Families and Events in This Plymouth Colony Township*, 3 Vol. (Rehoboth, MA: privately printed, 1948), 1:8.

22. Justin Winsor, *History of the Town of Duxbury, Massachusetts* (Boston: Crosby & Nichols, 1849), 228.
23. "Eastham and Orleans, Mass., Vital Records," *Mayflower Descendant*, Vol. VIII, (January 1906), No. 1, published by the Massachusetts Society of *Mayflower* Descendants, Boston.
24. William Bradford, "On the Various Heresies in Old and New England, With an Appeal to the Presbyterians." Reprinted at https://www.poemhunter.com/poem/on-the-various-heresies-in-old-and-new-england-with-an-appeal-to-the-presbyterians/ (accessed on November 14, 2017).
25. There has been some question that this poem was authored by Bradford, even though it was copied into his "little book with black covers." See Lupher, 338, fn. 168.
26. *PCR*, 3:111, 112.
27. *PCR*, 3:111-113, 127, 129, 130.
28. *PCR*, 3:138.
29. *PCR*, 5:30-31.
30. *PCR*, 3:154.
31. *PCR*, 11:125.
32. *PCR*, 4:129.
33. *Vital Records of the Towns of Eastham and Orleans: an authorized facsimile reproduction of records published serially 1901-1935 in The Mayflower Descendant. With an added index of persons,* (Baltimore, Clearfield Co., Inc., by Genealogical Publishing Co., Inc., 1976, 1980), 16.
34. Doris Ellen Bland, *Sutton, Sutton, and More Suttons. A Study of the Ancestors and Descendants of Jonathan Sutton Who Came to Wayne County, Illinois, in the year 1853* (Fairfield, Illinois: Bland Books, 1992), 12.
35. Rev. Joseph W. Dally, *Woodbridge and Vicinity, The Story of a New Jersey Township* (Madison, NJ: Hunterdon House, 1967), 62.
36. Paine, *Founders Day Edition*, 472.
37. Winsor, *History of the Town of Duxbury*, 228.
38. Twila Birnie Shafer and Francis Beasley Odell. *Descendants of the Sutton-Beasley family of Brown County, Ohio* (Topeka, KS: Myers & Co., Pictorial Press, 1946), 7.
39. Olive Barrick Rowland, *An Ancestral Chart and Handbook: Genealogical Notes of the Sutton and Rittenhouse Families of Hunterdon County*, New Jersey. (Richmond, 1935), Chart I.
40. Isaac Sutton, *Notes of Family History: the Anderson, Schofield, Pennypacker, Yocum, Crawford, Sutton ... Families.* (Philadelphia: Stephenson Brothers, Nd.), 102-113.
41. Dally, *Woodbridge and Vicinity*, 65-66.

42. Rowland, *An Ancestral Chart,* 4.
43. Piscataway, New Jersey Marriage and Death Records. Births, 1671-179. *New Jersey Historical Society Proceedings,* Third Series, Vol. 2-3, 40.
44. Dally, *Woodbridge and Vicinity,* 62, 66, 70.
45. Charles Carroll Gardner, "Death Records of the Rahway and Plainfield Monthly Meeting of Friends." *The Genealogical Magazine of New Jersey,* Vol. 27, No. 1 (Jan. 1952), 1-3.
46. Orra Eugene Monette, *First Settlers of Ye Plantations of Piscataway and Woodbridge, Old East New Jersey, 1664-1714, a Period of Fifty Years, Part One.* (Los Angeles: The Leroy Carman Press, 1930), 105.
47. Queen Perry, "The History of the Chambers Family of Niagara Falls, Canada: A *Mayflower* Family." Unpublished manuscript. 1983. Film No. 1035547, Family History Library, Church of Jesus Christ of the Latter Day Saints, Salt Lake City, Utah.
48. Katherine Chapin Higgins, *Richard Higgins, a Resident and Pioneer Settler at Plymouth and Eastham, Massachusetts, and Piscataway, New Jersey, and His Descendants* (Worcester, Massachusetts: printed by the author, 1918), 52.
49. Paine, *Founders Day Edition,* 472.
50. *Mayflower Families Through Five Generations: Descendants of the Pilgrims Who Landed at Plymouth, Mass. December 1620,* Vol. 1. Edited by Lucy Kellogg. (General Society of *Mayflower* Descendants, 1975).
51. *PCR,* 2:38-39, 57, 94, 8:187.
52. Josselyn, *An Account of Two Voyages ...,* 54.
53. Ibid.
54. *PCR,* 2:174, 8:7.
55. *PCR,* 3:6-7
56. Mary Beth Norton, *Founding Mothers & Fathers: Gendered Power and the Forming of American Society* (New York: Vintage Books, 1997), 244.
57. *PCR,* 3:102.
58. *PCR,* 8:22.
59. Susan Roser, *Mayflower Births & Deaths, Vol. 1.* (Genealogical Publishing Co., Inc. 1992), 446.

Chapter Twenty [pages 235-244]

1. *OPP,* 443.bid.
2. Lupher, *Greeks, Romans, and Pilgrims,* 312-313.
3. *WJ,* 347.
4. *RTP,* 31.
5. Josselyn, *An Account of Two Voyages...,* 20-21.

6. Ibid.
7. *RTP,* 32.
8. *OPP*, 351.
9. William Bradford, *Of Plymouth Plantation; Along with the full text of the Pilgrims' journals for their first year at Plymouth,* Edited by Caleb H. Johnson. (Xlibris, 2006), 28.
10. Bernard Bailyn, *The Barbarous Years: The Conflict of Civilizations, 1600-1675* (New York: Alfred A. Knopf, 2012), 160.
11. William Bradford, *A Dialogue or Third Conference Between Some Young Men Born in New England, and Some Ancient Men Which Came Out of Holland and Old England Concerning the Church and the Government Thereof, 1652,* Reprint. (Boston: John William, 1870), xii.
12. Ibid., 68.
13. Ibid., 21.
14. Bradford, "Epitaphium Meum." Reprinted at https://www.poemhunter.com/poem/epitaphium-meum-certain-verses-left-by-the-honoured-william-bradford-esq-governour-of-the-jurisdic/ (accessed on November 14, 2017).
15. Bradford. *A Dialogue or Third Conference*, 74.
16. Ibid., 59.
17. *PCR,* 3:110.
18. *PCR,* 3:110, 111.
19. Ibid.
20. *NEM,* 44.
21. James Shepard, *Governor William Bradford and His Son, Major William Bradford.* (New Britain, Conn.: Herald Print, 1900), 62.
22. Bradford, "Epitaphium Meum."
23. *MCA*, 113.
24. Mather may have exaggerated about how many languages Bradford could speak. See Lupher, 316-334, 346-59.
25. *MCA*, 113-114
26. Cited in *SS,* 373.
27. Prence would have a Quaker son-in-law when his daughter Elizabeth married Arthur Howland, Jr., much to the governor's chagrin. See *PCR,* 4:140-142, 158-159.
28. Samuel Maverick, *A Briefe Discription of New England and the Severall Townes Therein ... from a Manuscript written in 1660 by Samuel Maverick,* Reprinted (Boston: Press of David Clapp & Son, 1885), np
29. Quoted in *SS,* 383.
30. Francis Baylies, *An Historical Memoir of the Colony of New Plymouth.* (Boston: Milliard, Gray, Little, and Wilkins, 1830), 178.

31. *Lectures on the Growth and Development of the United States.* Ed. By Edwin Wiley. (New York: American Educational Alliance, 1916), 348.
32. *OPP,* Book 2, Ch. 21, 1630, p. 236.
33. *SS,* 409.

Chapter Twenty-One [pages 245-259]

1. *OPP,* Book 2, Ch. 32, 1642, 321.
2. Ibid., 316.
3. Ibid, 317.
4. *OPP,* Book 2, Ch. 32, 1642, 316-317.
5. David Lester, *Crime of Passion: Murder and the Murderer.* (Chicago: Nelson Hall, 1975), 213-214.
6. *OPP,* Book 2, Ch. 32, 1642, 316-317.
7. Deetz, *The Times of Their Lives,* 159-160.
8. *LC,* 49, 50.
9. Perry, *The History of the Chambers Family....,* 250
10. "Historical Timeline: History of Euthanasia and Physician-Assisted Suicide." *ProCon.org.* https://euthanasia.procon.org/view.timeline.php?timelineID=000022 (accessed on November 14, 2017).
11. "Declaration Issued by the Sacred Congregation for the Doctrine of the Faith, Declaration on Euthanasia, May 5, 1980." http://www.vatican.va/roman_curia/congregations/cfaith/documents/rc_con_cfaith_doc_19800505_euthanasia_en.html (accessed on November 14, 2017).
12. "Historical Timeline: History of Euthanasia and Physician-Assisted Suicide."
13. *PCR,* 2:132.
14. John A. Goodwin, *The Pilgrim Republic, an Historical Review of the Colony of New Plymouth* (Boston: Ticknor and Co., 1888), 601.
15. Peter C. Hoffer and N.E.H. Hull. *Murdering Mothers: Infanticide in England and New England, 1558-1803.* (New York: New York University Press, 1984), 40.
16. *WJ,* 282-283.
17. *CCL,* 44.
18. *PCR,* 6:20.
19. Deetz, 86.
20. *PCR,* 5:223.
21. "The Witches Curse" Secrets of the Dead, *Public Broadcasting System,* http://www.pbs.org/wnet/secrets/witches-curse/1498/ (accessed on November 14, 2017).
22. "Alice Martin Bishop" http://alicemartinbishop.com/ (accessed on November 14, 2017).

23. Lazare Riviere, *Six Hundred Miseries, the Seventeenth Womb, Book 15 of the 23. Practice of Physick.* Translated by Nicholas Culpeper. (London, 1678) 68, 73-75.
24. Cheryl L. Meyer, Ph.D., J.D., "Medical and Legal dilemmas of Postpartum Psychiatric Disorders" in *Infanticide: Psychosocial and Legal Perspectives on Mothers Who Kill.* Ed. By Margaret G. Spinelli, M.D. (Washington, D.C. American Psychiatric Publishing, Inc., 2003), 168.
25. Josselyn, *New England's Rarities Discovered*, 35.
26. Lazare 68, 73-75.
27. *"Scituate and Barnstable Church Records."* New England Historical and Genealogical Register, Vol. 10, 1856, 38.
28. *PCR,* 2:132.
29. *OPP,* Book 2, Ch. 32, 1642, 321.
30. *PCR,* 2:132-134.
31. *PCR,* 11:32.
32. *DD,* "Of Wife-like Courtesie and Obeysance," 279.
33. *PCR,* 3:211.
34. *ODM,* Ch. 60, "Of Children and Their Education." 243, 246, 247.
35. *ODM,* Ch. 56, "Of Anger," 226.
36. *ODM,* Ch. 60, "Of Children and Their Education." 244.
37. Ibid., 246.
38. Ibid., 247.
39. Ibid., 246.
40. *ODM,* Ch. 66, "Of Anger," 226.
41. Ibid., 221, 228.

Chapter Twenty-Two [pages 260-267]

1. James W. Baker, *Thanksgiving: the Biography of an American Holiday.* (Hanover: University Press of New England, 2009), 63.
2. *The Proceedings at the Celebration by the Pilgrim Society at Plymouth, August 1st, 1889, of the Completion of the Nation Monument to the Pilgrims.* (Plymouth: Avery & Doten, 1889), 6-7.
3. Ibid., 13.
4. Ibid.
5. John Seelye, *Memory's Nation; the Place of Plymouth Rock.* (Chapel Hill: The University of North Carolina Press, 1998), 548.
6. *SS,* 430.
7. Abraham Lincoln, "Proclamation of Thanksgiving." http://www.7.abrahamlincolnonline.org/lincoln/speeches/thanks.htm (accessed on November 26, 2017).
8. *OPP*, Ch. 14, 1623, 131.
9. It may be recalled that Austin was the author of *William Bradford's Love Life* which first mentioned his wife Dorothy's death as a suicide.

10. Baker, 14-15.
11. Ibid., 15, 111.
12. Ibid., 115-116.
13. *ODM* Ch. 600, "Of Children," 247-248.
14. *OPP*, Book 2, Ch. 32, 1642, 316-317.
15. *PCHP,* 74-75. (Edward Winslow left Plymouth in 1646; Bradford wrote of Winslow being "absente this 4 years" at the end of the 1647 chapter.)
16. "Will of John Churchill," in G.A. Churchill, *Churchill Family in America* (Boston: Published by the Family of G.A. Churchill, 1904) 3.
17. *PCR,* 8:23.
18. "Will of John Churchill," in G.A. Churchill, *Churchill Family in America*(Boston: Published by the Family of G.A. Churchill, 1904) 3.
19. Churchill, Bill, "John Churchill of the Plymouth Colony," at "John Churchill," Wikitree, https://www.wikitree.com/wiki/Churchill-220 (accessed on July 31, 2018).
20. Case Subject: Churchill, Martin, and Bradford Family Research, New 19.England Historical Genealogical Society, Case Number M040714C, July 25, 2014.
21. Gardner Asaph Churchill, Nathaniel Wiley Churchill, and George Madison Bodge. *The Churchill Family in America.* (Boston, MA. "Published by the Family of George M. Churchill," 1904), 2.
22. "William Pontus," Wikipedia, https://en.wikipedia.org/wiki/William_Pontus (accessed on July 31, 2018).
23. In a private correspondence with the author, dated Sept. 9, 2019, Pilgrim historian Sue Allan reported that after "looking very closely at the Hanson family in Austerfield," found no evidence that she and William Bradford were related.
24. *PCR*, 5:16.
25. Ibid., 24.
26. Mrs. Washington Roebling, "Richard Warren of the *Mayflower*" New England Historical and Genealogical Record, Vol. 55 1901, 72.

Afterword [page 268]

1. "A pittiilesse Mother. That most unnaturally at one time murdered two of her owne children at Acton within five miles from London upon holy Thursday last 1616, the ninth of May, being a gentlewoman named Margaret Vincent, wife of Mr. Aarus [?] of the same town, with her examination, confession, and true discovery of all the proceedings in the said bloody accident." http://access.bl.uk/item/pdf/lsidyv3351198b (accessed on July 28, 2018).

Bibliography

Primary Sources

"Alice Bradford." (estate inventory) *Plymouth Colony Archive Project.* http://www.histarch.illinois.edu/plymouth/P178.htm (accessed on May 19, 2017).

Arber, Edward. *The Story of the Pilgrim Fathers, 1606-1623 A.D.; as Told by Their Friends, and Their Enemies. Edited from the Original Texts.* London: Ward and Downey Limited, 1897.

Barlow, William. "Summe and Substance of the conference which it pleased his Excellent Majesty to have with the Lords, Bishops, and other of his Clergy (at which most of the Lords of the Council were present) in his majesty's privy-chamber, at Hampton Court, January 14, 1603[4], contracted of William Barlow, Doctor of Divinity and Dean of Chester." In *A History of Conferences and Other Proceedings Connected with the Revision of the Book of Common Prayer; from the Year 1558 to the year 1690.* Oxford University Press, 1840.

Book of Common Prayer, 1559, accessed at http://justus.anglican.org/resources/bcp/1559/BCP_1559.htm (accessed on May 19, 2017).

The Book of the General Lawes and Libertyes Concerning the Inhabitants of the Massachusets, Reproduced in facsimile from the unique 1648 edition in the Huntington Library. San Marino, CA: The Huntington Library, 1975.

Bradford, William. *Bradford's History 'Of Plimoth Plantation,' From the Original Manuscript with a Report of the Proceedings Incident to the Return of the Manuscript to Massachusetts. Printed under the Direction of the Secretary of the Commonwealth by Order of the General Court.* Edited by William M. Olin. Boston: Wright and Potter, State Printers, 1898.

———. "A Dialogue or the sum of a conference between some young men born in New England and sundery Ancient men that came out of Holland and old England, 1648." *Plymouth Church Records 1620-1859*, Part 1. Boston: Colonial Society of Massachusetts, 1920. (The First Dialogue.)

———. *A Dialogue or Third Conference Between Some Young Men Born in New England, and Some Ancient Men Which Came Out of Holland and*

Old England Concerning the Church and the Government Thereof 1652. Boston: John Wilson & Son, 1870. (The Third Dialogue.) Note: This also includes some of Bradford's poems.

———. "Epitaphium Meum." In *New England's Memorial 1669*, 144-5. 1669. New York: Scholars Facsimiles & Reprints, 1937.

———. *Governor William Bradford's Letter Book*. Bedford, MA: Applewood Books, 2001.

———. "Letter of William Bradford and Isaac Allerton." *The American Historical Review*, Vol. 8, No. 2 (Jan. 1903): 294-301. Also http://mayflowerhistory.com/letter-bradford-and-allerton (accessed on November 14, 2017).

———. *Of Plymouth Plantation*. Edited by Samuel Eliot Morison. New York: Alfred A. Knopf, 2004. First published in 1952.

———. *Of Plymouth Plantation; Along with the full text of the Pilgrims' journals for their first year at Plymouth*, Edited by Caleb H. Johnson. Xlibris. 2006.

———. "On the Various Heresies in Old and New England, With an Appeal to the Presbyterians." https://www.poemhunter.com/poem/on-the-various-heresies-in-old-and-new-england-with-an-appeal-to-the-presbyterians/comments/

———. "A Word to New Plymouth." In *A Dialogue or Third Conference Between Some Young Men Born in New England, and Some Ancient Men Which Came Out of Holland and Old England Concerning the Church and the Government Thereof 1652*. Boston: John Wilson & Son, 1870.

Bradstreet, Anne. *To My Husband and Other Poems*. Mineola, NY: Dover Publications, Inc., 2000.

———. *The Works of Anne Bradstreet*. Cambridge, MA: Belknap Press of Harvard University Press, 1967.

Brooks, Thomas. *The Legacy of a Dying Mother to Her Mourning Children Being the Experiences of Mrs. Susanna Bell, Who Died March 13, 1672*. London: John Hancock, 1673.

The Colonial Laws of Massachusetts. Boston, 1887.

The Compact with the Charter and Laws of the Colony of New Plymouth: Together with the Charter of the Council at Plymouth and an Appendix Containing the Articles of Confederation of the United Colonies of New England and Other Valuable Documents. Boston: Dutton and Wentworth, 1836.

Copy of the Old Records of the Town of Duxbury, Mass., from 1642-1770. Plymouth: Avery & Doten, Book and Job Printers, 1893.

Cushman, Robert. *The First Sermon Ever Preached in New England: The First Printed and the Oldest American Discourse Extant. 1621*. Reprint. New York: J.E.D. Comstock, 1859.

Earl of Warwick. "Charter of the Colony of New Plymouth Granted to William Bradford and His Associates, 1629." In *The Federal and State Constitutions Colonial Charters, and Other Organic Laws of the States, Territories, and Colonies Now or Heretofore Forming the United States of America*. Washington DC: Government Printing Office, 1909.

"Eastham and Orleans, Mass., Vital Records," Reprinted in *Mayflower Descendant*, Vol. VIII, January, 1906, No. 1, published by the Massachusetts Society of Mayflower Descendants, Boston.

Elizabeth I. "The Act Against Puritans." (1593) In *Documents Illustrative of English Church History*, 492-498. New York: Macmillan, 1896. Hanover Historical Texts Project. http://history.hanover.edu/texts/engref/er86.html (accessed on November 14, 2017).

Geneva Bible – see Whittingham.

Gouge, William, *Of Domestical Duties: Eight Treatises*. London: John Haviland for William Bladen, 1622.

H, T. *A Looking-glasse for Women, Or, A Spie for Pride: Shewing the Unlawfulnesse of Any Outward Adorning of Any Attire of Haire, Either in Laying Forth the Haire, Or in Crisping of the Haire, Or in Broidered Haire in All Women, But Especially in Godly Women Declared Fully by the Scripture: Also Those Scriptures and Carnall Objections Answered which are Seemingly Made for it*. London: Printer for R.W., 1644.

Hening, William Waller. *The Statutes at Large, a Collection of All the Laws of Virginia from the First Session of the Legislature in the Year 1619*, Vol. 1. New York: R. & W. & G. Bartow, 1823.

Hilton, William. "Letter of William Hilton to His Family." 1621? Caleb Johnson's Mayflower History. http://www.mayflowerhistory.com/primarySources/WilliamHilton.php (accessed on May 19, 2017).

James I. *Basilikon Doron*. 1599. Reprinted in Fortier, Mark and Daniel Fischlin (eds.). *James I, The True Law of Free Monarchies and the Basilikon Doron*, Toronto, Ont.: Centre for Reformation and Renaissance Studies. 1996.

Johnson, Edward A. *A History of New England, From the English Planting in the Yeere 1628 until the Yeere 1652*. London: Printed for Nath. Brooke at the Angel in Corn-Hill. 1653.

Josselyn, John. *An Account of Two Voyages to New England: Made During the Years 1638, 1663*. Boston: William Weazie. 1865.

———. *New England's Rarities Discovered*, London: G. Widdowes. 1672.

Josselyn, John. "Provisions List from An Account of Two Voyages to New England by John Josselyn, 2nd ed., London, 1675." Pilgrim Hall Museum. http://www.pilgrimhallmuseum.org/pdf/Provisions_List_1675.pdf (accessed on May 19, 2017)

Lambarde, William. *The Duties of Constables, Borsholders [Householders], Tythingmen, and Such Other Low and Lay Ministers of the Peace.* London. 1610.

———. *Eirenarcha, Of the Office of the Justices of Peace, in Foure Bookes. First Gathered 1579, published 1581...* London: Thomas Wight. 1599.

"Land Record dated December 5, 1666, recorded July 1, 1672, Abigail Clarke to Richard Wright." Plymouth Colony Registry of Deeds in Plymouth, MA, Record No. DPL III (2):228[a].

"Last Will & Testament of Elizabeth (Tilley) Howland, 1686." Plymouth Colony Archive Project. http://www.histarch.illinois.edu/plymouth/howlandwill.html (accessed on May 20, 2017).

"Last Will & Testament of Mary (Chilton) Winslow, 1676." Plymouth Colony Archive Project. http://www.histarch.illinois.edu/plymouth/winslowwill.html (accessed on November 14, 2017).

The Laws of the Pilgrims: A Facsimile Edition of "The Book of the General Laws of the Inhabitants of the Jurisdiction of New Plimouth, 1672 & 1685. Wilmington, Delaware: Michael Glazier, Inc., 1972.

Leland, John. "Leland the Antiquary to Lord Cromwell Gives a Character of John Bale and Solicits the Release of Him from Imprisonment." In *Original Letters, Illustrative of English History; Including Numerous Royal Letters: from Autographs in the British Museum, the State Paper Office, and One or Two Other Collections.* Vol 3, p. 154. London: Richard Bentley, 1846.

Lincoln, President Abraham, "Proclamation of Thanksgiving." Abraham Lincoln Online. http://www.abrahamlincolnonline.org/lincoln/speeches/thanks.htm (accessed on November 29, 2017).

Markham, Gervase. *The English Housewife: Containing the Inward and Outward Virtues Which Ought to be in a Complete Woman.* 1615. Montreal & Kingston: Mc Gill-Queen's University Press. 1986. Originally published in 1615.

———. *The English Husbandman.* London: John Browne. 1613.

Mather, Cotton. *Magnalia Christi Americana; or the Ecclesiastical History of New England.* Hartford: Silas Andrus and Son, 1855. Originally published in 1702.

Maverick, Samuel. *A Briefe Discription of New England and the Severall Townes Therein ... from a Manuscript written in 1660 by Samuel Maveric.* Boston: Press of David Clapp & Son, 1885.

Morton, Nathaniel. *New England's Memorial*, 1669. Edited by Howard J. Hall. Facsimile of the first edition. New York: Scholars Facsimiles & Reprints, 1937.

Morton, Thomas. *The New English Canaan.* Boston: The Prince Society, 1883. Originally published in 1627.

Mourt's Relation - see Winslow.

Ogilby, John. *Brittannia.* 1675. Cited by Nottinghamshire History, "Scrooby." http://www.nottshistory.org.uk/articles/mellorsarticles/scrooby1.htm (accessed on May 22, 2017).

"Petition of the Directors of the New Netherland Company, February 12, 1620." In *Documents Relative to the Colonial History of the State of New York Procured in England, Holland, and France.* Vol. I. Albany, New York: Weed Parsons and Co., Printers, 856.

"Piscataway, New Jersey Marriage and Death Records. Births, 1671-1793." In *New Jersey Historical Society Proceedings*, Third Series, Volumes 2-3.

"A Pittilesse Mother. That most unnaturally at one time murdered two of her owne children at Acton within five miles from London upon holy Thursday last 1616, the ninth of May, being a gentlewoman named Margaret Vincent, wife of Mr. Aarus [?] of the same town, with her examination, confession, and true discovery of all the proceedings in the said bloody accident." http://access.bl.uk/item/pdf/lsidyv3351198b (accessed on July 28, 2018).

Plymouth Church Records, 1620-1859. Vol. 1, Part 1. Boston: Colonial Society of Massachusetts: 1920.

Pope, Charles Henry, ed. *The Plymouth Scrap Book: the Oldest Original Documents Extant in Plymouth Archives.* Boston, MA: C.E. Goodspeed & Co., 1918.

Pory, John, Emmanuel Altham, and Isaack de Rasieres. *Three Visitors to Early Plymouth: Letters About the Pilgrim Settlement in New England During Its First Seven Years.* Massachusetts: Applewood Books. 1997.

"Presentment Bill relating to William Brewster, Scrooby parish, 1598." University of Nottingham. http://www.nottingham.ac.uk/manuscriptsandspecialcollections/exhibitions/online/thebawdycourt/beliefandpersecution.aspx (accessed on November 14, 2017).

"Probate Inventory for Estate of Mary Ring, 1633." Plymouth Colony Archive Project. http://www.histarch.illinois.edu/plymouth/Pring.html (accessed on November 11, 2017).

The Proceedings at the Celebration by the Pilgrim Society at Plymouth, August 1st, 1889, of the Completion of the Nation Monument to the Pilgrims. Plymouth, Avery & Doten, 1889.

Records of the Colony of New Plymouth in New England. (Commonly referred to as PCR.) Edited by Nathaniel B. Shurtleff. 12 vols. Boston: William White, 1855.

Records of the Town of Plymouth, Published by Order of the Town, Vol. 1, 1636-1705. Plymouth: Avery & Doten, 1889.

Registers of the Chapel of Austerfield, in the Parish of Blyth and in the County of York. Transcribed and edited by George Denison Lumb. Privately Printed for the Yorkshire Parish Register Society. 1910.

Reynald, Thomas. *The Birth of Man-kinde; Otherwise Named The Woman's Booke*. London: James Boler. 1626.

Riviere, Lazare. *Six Hundred Miseries, the Seventeenth Womb, Book 15 of the Practice of Physick*. Translated by Nicholas Culpeper. London. 1678.

Robinson, John. "Mr. Bernard's Counsels Debated." In *The Works of John Robinson, Pastor of the Pilgrim Fathers*. Vol. 2, Chap. 1. http://oll.libertyfund.org/title/856/144599/2704419 (accessed on November 15, 2017).

———. "A Just and Necessarie Apologie of Certain Christians, no lesse contumeliously than commonly called Brownists or Barrowists." In *The Works of John Robinson, Pastor of the Pilgrim Fathers*. Vol. 3, Ch. 8, "Of the Exercise of Prophecy."

———. "A Just and Necessary Apologie of Certain Christians, no lesse contumeliously than commonly called Brownists or Barrowists." In *The Works of John Robinson, Pastor of the Pilgrim Fathers*. Vol. 3, Ch. 3, "Of Written Liturgies."

———. Observations Divine and Moral. In *The Works of John Robinson, Pastor of the Pilgrim Fathers*. Vol. 1. London: John Snow. 1851.

———. "A Defense of the Doctrine Propounded by the Synod at Dort," Ch. 1, "Of Predestination," In *The Works of John Robinson, Pastor of the Pilgrim Fathers*, Vol. 1, 271.

———. *The Works of John Robinson, Pastor of the Pilgrim Fathers, with a Memoir and Annotations by Robert Ashton*, 3 Vols. London: John Snow. 1851.

"Scituate and Barnstable Church Records." New England Historical and Genealogical Register, Vol. 10, 1856, p. 38.

Sharp, Jane. *The Midwives Book, or the Whole Art of Midwifry Discovered, 1671*. New York: Oxford University Press. 1999.

Smith, John. "A Description of New England (1616): An Online Electronic Text Edition," Electronic Texts in American Studies, https://digitalcommons.unl.edu/etas/ (accessed on January 21, 2019).

Vital Records of Duxbury, Massachusetts to the Year 1850. Boston, Mass: New England Historical Genealogical Society, 1911.

Vital Records of the Town of Plymouth; An authorized facsimile reproduction of the records published serially 1901-1935 in The Mayflower Descendant. With Added Index of Persons. Baltimore: Genealogical Publishing Co., 1992.

Vital Records of the Towns of Eastham and Orleans: an authorized facsimile reproduction of records published serially 1901-1935 in The Mayflower Descendant. With an added index of persons. Baltimore: Genealogical Publishing Co., Inc., 1976.

Whittingham, William, et al., trans. *The Bible and Holy Scriptures, Conteyned in the olde and newe Testament* .... ("Geneva Bible"). Geneva: Rowland Hall, 1560.

Winslow, Edward. *Good Newes from New England: a True Relation of Things Very Remarkable at the Plantation of Plimoth in New England.* Bedford, MA: Applewood Book. 1996. Originally published in 1624.

———. *Hypocrisie Unmasked, a True Relation of the Proceedings of the Governor and Company of the Massachusetts Against Samuel Gorton of Rhode Island.* Providence, Rhode Island: The Club for Colonial Reprints, 1916. Originally published in 1646.

———. "Letter of Edward Winslow, 11 December 1621." Caleb Johnson's Mayflower History. http://mayflowerhistory.co/letter-winslow-1621/ (accessed on November 14, 2017).

———. *New England's Salamander Discovered.* London: Printed by Ric. Cotes, for John Bellamy. 1647.

Winslow, Edward, William Bradford, and others. *A Relation or Journall of the beginning and proceedings of the English Plantation settled at Plimoth in New England by certaine English Adventurers both Merchants and others. ("Mourt's Relation") 1622.* Ed. Dwight B. Health. Bedford, Massachusetts: Applewood Books, 1963.

Winthrop, John. "A Model of Christian Charity." In *The Winthrop Papers*, Vol. 2, Boston: MHS. 1931. 293.

———. *Winthrop's Journal: History of New England, 1630-1649.* Vol II. New York: Barnes & Noble, Inc., 1908.

Secondary Sources

Abbott, Geoffrey. *Execution: The Guillotine, the Pendulum, the Thousand Cuts, the Spanish Donkey, and 66 Other Ways of Putting Someone to Death.* New York: St. Martin's Press, 2005.

Abramovitz, Mimi. *Regulating the Lives of Women.* Boston, MA: South End Press, 1988.

Addison, A. C. *The Romantic Story of the Mayflower Pilgrims and its Place in the Life of Today.* Boston: L.C. Page & Co., 1911.

Allen, Sue. *In Search of Mayflower Pilgrim Susanna White-Winslow.* UK: DPS Partnership Ltd., 2018.

———. *In Search of Scrooby Manor.* UK: DPS Partnership Ltd., 2013.

———. *Steps along the Mayflower Trail.* UK: Domtom Publishing Ltd., 2011.

Ames, Louise Bates, PhD., Frances L. Ilg, M.D. *Your Four Year Old: Wild and Wonderful.* New York: Bantam Doubleday Dell Publishing Group, 1976.

Anderson, Bert G. "The Teeth of Colonial Americans as Reported by Three Contemporary Observers." *Yale Journal of Biology and Medicine* 19, no. 6 (1947): 909-922.

Anderson, Robert Charles. *The Pilgrim Migration: Immigrants to Plymouth Colony, 1620-1633.* Boston: New England Historic Genealogical Society, 2004.

———. "Plymouth Village Families Sketch: John Coombs." American Ancestors, New England Historic Genealogical Society. http://www.americanancestors.org/pilgrim-families-john-coombs/ (accessed on May 24, 2017).

Anderson, Virginia DeJohn. *Creatures of Empire: How Domestic Animals Transformed Early America.* Oxford University Press, 2004.

———. *New England's Generation: the Great Migration and the Formation of Society and Culture in the Seventeenth Century.* Cambridge University Press, 1991.

Applebaum, Herbert. *The American Work Ethic and the Changing Work Force.* Connecticut: Greenwood Press, 1998.

———. *Colonial Americans at Work.* Lanham, Maryland: University Press of America, 1996.

Arber, Edward. *The Story of the Pilgrim Fathers, 1606-1623 A.D.; as Told by Themselves, their Friends, and their Enemies.* London: Ward and Downey Limited. 1897.

Archer, Gleason. *With Axe and Musket at Plymouth.* New York: The American Historical Society, 1936.

Atwood, W.F. *Pilgrim Plymouth Guide to Objects of Special Historic Interest.* Np. 1921.

Bailey, R.B. "Pilgrim Possessions: 1620-1640," in *They Knew They Were Pilgrims,* 33-44. New York: Poseidon Books, Inc., 1971.

Bailey, Sarah Y. *The Story of the Jones River in Pilgrim Plymouth, 1620-1726.* Kingston Branch of the Alliance of Unitarian Women, 1920.

Bailyn, Bernard. *The Barbarous Years: The Conflict of Civilizations, 1600-1675.* New York: Alfred A. Knopf, 2012.

———. *The New England Merchants in the Seventeenth Century.* Cambridge, MA: Harvard University Press, 1955.

Baker, J.W. "John Doane in Plymouth, 1630-1644." Doane Family Association of America. http://www.doanefamilyassociation.org/JWBaker2012.pdf (accessed on May 24, 2017).

Baker, James. *Thanksgiving: the Biography of an American Holiday.* University Press of New England, 2010.

Baker, Peggy. "The Plymouth Colony Patent: Setting the Stage." Pilgrim Hall Museum. http://www.pilgrimhallmuseum.org/pdf/The_Plymouth_Colony_Patent.pdf (accessed on May 25, 2017)

Bangs, Jeremy Dupertuis. "Pilgrim Country Tour, 2006." Pilgrim Fathers. www.pilgrimfathersorigins.org (accessed on May 25, 2017).

———. *The Pilgrims, Leiden, and the Early Years of Plymouth Plantation.* "Disordered and Unlawful Conventicles." 2006. www.sail1620.org/Articles/the-pilgrims-leiden-and-the-early-years-of-plymouth-plantation-chapter-1 (accessed on November 24, 2017).

———. *Plymouth Colony's Private Libraries, as recorded in wills and inventories, 1633-1692.* Leiden, the Netherlands: Leiden American Pilgrim Museum, 2016.

———. *Strangers and Pilgrims, Travellers and Sojourners: Leiden and the Foundations of Plymouth Plantation.* Plymouth, MA: General Society of Mayflower Descendants, 2009.

Banks, Charles Edward. *The English Ancestry and Homes of the Pilgrim Fathers.* Reprinted from the 1929 edition. Baltimore, Genealogical Publishing Co., Inc., 2001.

———. *The Planters of the Commonwealth: a Study of the Emigrants and Emigration in Colonial Times ....* Baltimore: Genealogical Publishing Co., originally published 1930.

Banner, Stuart. *The Death Penalty, An American History.* Cambridge, MA: Harvard University Press, 2002.

Banvard, Joseph. *Plymouth and the Pilgrims or Incidents of Adventure in the History of the First Settlers.* Boston: Gould and Lincoln, 1856.

Barck, Oscar Theodore, Jr. *Colonial America,* 2nd ed. New York: The Macmillan Co., 1968.

Baumgarten, Linda. *What Clothes Reveal: The Language of Clothing in Colonial and Federal America.* New Haven: Yale University Press, 2002.

Baxandall, Rosalyn, Linda Gordon, eds. *America's Working Women: A Documentary History 1600 to the Present.* New York: W.W. Norton & Co., 1995.

Baylies, Francis. *An Historical Memoir of the Colony of New Plymouth.* Boston: Milliard, Gilav, Little, and Wilkins, 1830.

Benet, Stephen Vincent. *Western Star.* New York: Farrar & Rinehart, Inc., 1943.

Bennett, Wayne W. *Criminal Investigation.* 4th ed. Minneapolis, MN: West Publishing Co., 1994.

Bethell, Tom. "How Private Property Saved the Pilgrims." *Hoover Digest* No 1 (1999) http://www.hoover.org/research/how-private-property-saved-pilgrims (accessed on June 4, 2017).

"Beyond the Pilgrim Story – Edward Dotey," Pilgrim Hall Museum, http://www.pilgrimhallmuseum.org/edward_dotey.htm (accessed on May 25, 2017)

Bland, Doris Ellen (Witter). *Sutton, Sutton, and More Suttons. A Study of the Ancestors and Descendants of Jonathan Sutton Who Came to Wayne County, Illinois, in the year 1853.* Fairfield, Illinois: Bland Books, 1992.

"Boston, Lincolnshire: The Pilgrims and a Thread to America." *My Boston UK*, https://www.myboston.com/boston-lincolnshire-the-pilgrims-and-a-thread-to-america/ (accessed on October 4, 2019)

Bowen, Richard LeBaron. *Early Rehoboth, Documented Historical Studies of Families and Events in This Plymouth Colony Township,* Vol. 1-3. Concord, New Hampshire: The Rumford Press, 1945.

Bowman, George Ernest. "Governor William Bradford's First Wife Dorothy (May) Did Not Commit Suicide." *The Mayflower Descendant* 29, no. 3 (1931): 97-102.

———. *The Mayflower Compact and Its Signers.* Massachusetts Society of Mayflower Descendants: Boston, 1920.

———. "Why did only 41 passengers sign The Compact?" *Pilgrim Notes and Queries,* 1913, 18.

Brachlow, Stephen. *The Communion of Saints: Radical Puritan and Separatist Ecclesiology, 1570-1625.* Oxford University Press, 1988.

Bradford, E.F. "Conscious Art in Bradford's History of Plymouth Plantation." *The New England Quarterly,* Vol. 1, No. 2. (April, 1928), p. 133-157.

Bradford, Gershom. *Historic Duxbury in Plymouth County Massachusetts. Boston, 1920.* (Pamphlet based on Laurence Bradford's *Historic Duxbury*.)

Bradford, Laurence. *Historic Duxbury in Plymouth County, Massachusetts.* Boston: The Fish Printing Co., 1900.

Bremner, Robert H., ed. *Children and Youth in America: a Documentary History, Vol 1: 1600-1865.* Harvard University Press, 1970.

Brewster, Lyman Denison. "William Brewster, His True Position in Our Colonial History." In *The Mayflower Reader, a Selection of Articles from the Mayflower Descendant.* 267-276. Genealogical Publishing Co., 1978.

"Brief History of the Village," *North Plymouth Village Center, Master Plan Update*, Adopted by Plymouth Planning Board September 12, 2011, p. 14.

Brown, Cornelius. *A History of Nottinghamshire.* London: Elliot Stock, 1891.

Brown, Kathleen M. *Foul Bodies: Cleanliness in Early America.* New Haven: Yale University Press. 2009.

———. *Good Wives, Nasty Wenches, & Anxious Patriarchs: Gender, Race, and Power in Colonial Virginia.* Chapel Hill: University of North Carolina Press, 1996.

Bunker, Nick. *Making Haste from Babylon: the Mayflower Pilgrims and Their World, a New History.* New York: Alfred A. Knopf, 2010.

Bush, Sargent, Jr. "America's Origin Myth: Remembering Plymouth Rock." *American Literary History,* Vol. 12, No. 4 (winter, 2000): 745-756.

Calhoun, Arthur W. *The American Family in the Colonial Period.* New York: Dover Publications, Inc., 2004. First published in 1917.

Callaway, Peter. "Making Tar at Tar Kiln Hollow." *Farm a Forest*. www.watersheds.org (accessed on June 3, 2017).

Canup, John. *Out of the Wilderness: The Emergence of an American Identity in Colonial New England*. Middletown, Connecticut: Wesleyan Press, 1990.

Capp, Bernard. *When Gossips Meet: Women, Family, and Neighborhood in Early Modern England*. Oxford University Press, 2003.

Caulfield, Dr. Ernest. "Some Common Diseases of Colonial Children." *The Colonial Society of Massachusetts* Vol. 35 (April, 1942): 4-65.

Chapin, Bradley. *Criminal Justice in Colonial America, 1606-1660*. Athens, GA: University of Georgia Press, 1983.

Chartier, Craig S. "Livestock in Plymouth Colony." Plymouth Archaeological Rediscovery Project (PARP). P. 4 of 11. www.plymoutharch.tripod.com/id133.html. (accessed on May 26, 2017).

Cheever, George. *The Pilgrim Fathers or the Journal of the Pilgrims at Plymouth, New England, in 1620*. New York: John W. Lovell Co., 1849.

Churchill, Gardner Asaph, Nathaniel Wiley Churchill, George Madison Bodge. *The Churchill Family in America*. Boston, MA. "Published by the Family of George M. Churchill." 1904.

Clayton, W. Woodford, ed. *History of Union and Middlesex Counties, New Jersey, with Biographical Sketches of Many of Their Pioneers and Prominent Men*. Philadelphia: Everts & Peck, 1882.

Cline, Duane A. "Clothing of the Pilgrims." *The Pilgrims and Plymouth Colony: 1620*. 1999. http://www.rootsweb.ancestry.com/~mosmd/clothing.htm (accessed on May 25, 2017).

Cockshott, Winnifred. *The Pilgrim Fathers, Their Church and Colony*. New York: G.P. Putman, 1909.

Coldham, Peter Wilson. *The Complete Book of Emigrants, 1607-1660*. Genealogical Publishing Co., Inc., 1987.

Colket, Meredith B. *Founders of Early American Families: Emigrants from Europe 1607-1657*. Cleveland, Ohio: The General Court of the Order of Founders and Patriots of America, 1985.

Collinson, Patrick. *The Religion of Protestants: The Church in English Society 1559-1625*. Oxford: Clarendon Press, 1982.

"Colonial Culture: Cuisine." *Colonial America*. http://www.smplanet.com/teaching/colonialamerica/culture/cuisine (accessed on May 27, 2017).

Crabb, George. *A History of English Law; or an Attempt to Trace the Rise, Progress, and Successive Changes, of the Common Law; From the Earliest Period to the Present Time*. London: Baldwin and Cradock. 1829.

"Crafts: The color of the cloth (The American Pilgrims used natural dyes for their clothes; craft project making dyes)." *Hopscotch* Vol. 10, No. 3, (Oct-Nov 1998): 38-41.

Crawford, Mary Caroline. *In the Days of the Pilgrim Fathers.* New York: Grossett & Dunlap, Inc., 1920.

Crawford, Patricia. "Attitudes to Menstruation in Seventh-Century England." *Past & Present* No. 19 (May, 1981): 47-73.

———. *Women and Religion in England, 1500-1720.* London and New York: Rutledge, 1993.

Cuckson, John. *A Brief History of the First Church in Plymouth, from 1606-1901.* Boston: Geo. H. Ellis Co., 1902.

Dally, Rev. Joseph W. *Woodbridge and Vicinity, the Story of a New Jersey Township.* Madison, NJ: Hunterdon House, 1967.

Dana, Richard Henry. *Two Years Before the Mast.* Boston: Fields, Osgood, & Co., 1869.

David, William T. "Who Were the Pilgrims?" *Harper's New Monthly Magazine,* Vol. 64, (Dec. 1881-May, 1882): 246-256.

Davis, William T. *Ancient Landmarks of Plymouth.* Boston: Damrell &Upham, 1882.

"Declaration Issued by the Sacred Congregation for the Doctrine of the Faith, May 5, 1980." http://www.vatican.va/roman_curia/congregations/cfaith/index.htm (accessed on May 27, 2017).

Deetz, James. *In Small Things Forgotten*, Rev. Ed. New York: Anchor Books, 1996.

Deetz, Patricia Scott, and James F. Deetz. "*Mayflower* Passenger Deaths." Plymouth Colony Archive Project. http://www.histarch.illinois.edu/plymouth/Maydeaths.html (accessed on May 27, 2017).

———. "Passengers on the *Mayflower*: Ages & Occupations, Origins & Connections." Plymouth Colony Archive Project. http://www.histarch.illinois.edu/plymouth/Maysource.html (accessed on November 14, 2017).

———. "Population of Plymouth Town, Colony & County, 1620-1690." Plymouth Colony Archive Project. http://www.histarch.illinois.edu/plymouth/townpop.html (accessed on May 27, 2017).

———. *The Times of Their Lives: Life, Love and Death in Plymouth Colony.* New York: W.H. Freeman and Co., 2000.

DeForest, L. Effingham, Anne Lawrence DeForest. *Moore and Allied Families, the Ancestry of William Henry Moore.* New York: DeForest Publishing, 1938.

Delaney, Janice, Mary Jane Lupton, and Emily Toth. *The Curse: a Cultural History of Menstruation.* Rev. Ed. Urbana: University of Illinois Press, 1988.

DeMarly, Diana. *Dress in North America, Vol. I, The New World, 1492-1800.* New York: Holmes &Meier, 1990.

Demos, John. *Entertaining Satan: Witchcraft and the Culture of Early New England.* Oxford University Press, 2004.

———. *A Little Commonwealth: Family Life in Plymouth Colony.* Second edition. Oxford University Press, 2000.

———. "Notes on Life in Plymouth Colony." *The William and Mary Quarterly* 3rd series, Vol. 22, No. 2 (April, 1965): 264-286.

———. *Past, Present, and Personal: the Family and the Life Course in American History.* Oxford University Press, 1986.

"Desperate Crossing: the Untold Story of the Mayflower." Lone Wolf Documentary for the History Channel. DVD. 2006.

"Detailed History - An Established Church." Church of England. https://www.churchofengland.org/about-us/history/detailed-history.aspx (accessed on May 28, 2017).

Dexter, Henry Martyn, Morton Dexter. *The England and Holland of the Pilgrims.* New York: Houghton, Mifflin & Co., 1906. Facsimile printed by Kessinger Publishing's Rare Reprints. Nd.

Dillon, Francis. *The Pilgrims.* New York: Doubleday & Co., Inc., 1975.

Doerfler, Sheilagh. "Case Subject: Churchill, Martin, and Bradford Family Research, Case Number M040714C." Unpublished Manuscript. July 25, 2014. New England Historic Genealogical Society.

———. "Case Subject: Martin/Clarke/Churchill Family Research, Case Number M040714C-2." Unpublished Manuscript. 12/15/2014. New England Historic Genealogical Society.

Doherty, Kieran. *William Bradford, Rock of Plymouth.* Brookfield, CT: Twenty-First Century Books, 1999.

Donegan, Kathleen. *Seasons of Misery: Catastrophe and Colonial Settlement in Early America.* Philadelphia: University of Pennsylvania Press, 2014.

Dorn, Nathan, "The Murder of Penowanyanquis and the Trial of Arthur Peach," Law Librarians of Congress, https://blogs.loc.gov/law/2018/09/the-murder-of-penowanyanquis-and-the-trial-of-arthur-peach-plymouth-1638/, accessed on 9/18/2019.

Dow, George Francis. *Every Day Life in the Massachusetts Bay Colony.* New York: Dover Publications, Inc., 1988.

Drummond, Audrey, Nancy J. Springer, ed., *Mayflower Passengers.* 2nd edition. Massachusetts: Massachusetts Society of Mayflower Descendants, 1996.

Duff, Charles. *A Handbook on Hanging: Being a Short Introduction to the Fine Art of Execution ....* New York: New York Review Books, 1928.

"Dumpish." Oxford English Dictionary Online. http://dictionary.oed.com.lib-proxy.fullerton.edu

Eales, Jacqueline. *Women in Early Modern England, 1500-1700.* London and New York: Routledge. 1998.

Earle, Alice Morse. *Child Life in Colonial Days.* Stockbridge, MA: Berkshire House Publishers, 1993. First published in 1899.

———. *Curious Punishments of Bygone Days.* Chicago: Herbert S. Stone & Co., 1896.

"Edmund Bonner, Afterwards Bishop of London, to Cromwell, to Borrow Some Italian Books." (Written in the summer of 1530.) In *Original Letters Illustrative of English History; Including Numerous Royal Letters* .... Third Series, Vol. 2, 177-178. London: Richard Bentley, 1846.

Ellis, Albert, John M. Gullo. *Murder and Assassination.* New York: Lyle Stuart, Inc., 1971.

"English Clothing in the 1620s: Not what you think." Plimoth Plantation. http://www.plimoth.org/learn/just-kids/homework-help/what-wear (accessed on May 28, 2017).

Erickson, Paul. *Daily Life in the Pilgrim Colony, 1636.* New York: Clarion Books, 2001.

Erikson, Kai T. *Wayward Puritans: a Study in the Sociology of Deviance.* Boston: Pearson, 2005.

Ewing, Elizabeth. *Everyday Dress, 1650-1900.* London: B.T. Batsford Ltd., 1984.

Fenn, William Wallace. "John Robinson's Farewell Address." *The Harvard Theological Review*, Vol. 13, No. 3 (July, 1920): 236-251.

Ferrer, Millie and Sara McCrea. "The Fantastic Four-Year-Old." University of Florida IFAS Extension. www.edis.ifas.ufl.edu/he360 (accessed on May 28, 2017).

Fessenden, G.M. "A Genealogy of the Bradford Family." *The New England Historical and Genealogical Register* 3, 4 (1850): 39.

Finch, Martha A. *Dissenting Bodies: Corporealities in Early New England.* New York: Columbia University Press, 2010.

———. "Fashions of Worldly Dames: Separatist Discourses of Dress in Early Modern London, Amsterdam, and Plymouth Colony." *Church History* 74, no.3 (2005): 494-533.

Fischer, David Hackett. *Albion's Seed: Four British Folkways in America.* Oxford: Oxford University Press, 1989.

Fish, Henry A. *Duxbury, Massachusetts, Ancient and Modern: A Sketch with Map and Key.* Binghamton, New York: no pub., 1924.

Fisher, Barry. *The Techniques of Crime Scene Investigation.* Boca Raton, FL: CRC Press, 2004.

Foster, Thomas A. "New Type of Sex Scandal." *Los Angeles Times* August 22, 2012: A15.

Fox, James Alan, Jack Levin and Kenna Quinet. *The Will to Kill: Making Sense of Senseless Murder*, 2nd ed. Boston: Pearson Education Group, Inc., 2001.

Fred A. Leuchter Assoc., Inc. *Execution by Hanging: Operation and Instruction Manual.* Department of Correction, State of Delaware, Delaware Correctional Center, May 1, 1990.

Freeman, Frederick. *The History of Cape Cod: The Annals of the Thirteen Towns of Barnstable County.* Vol. 2. Boston: Geo. C. Rand & Avery, 1858-62.

French, Howard Dakin, "Sutton Family" *New England Historical and Genealogical Register* 91, (1937): 65-67.

Galle, Jillian. "Servants and Masters in the Plymouth Colony." The Plymouth Colony Archive Project. http://www.histarch.illinois.edu/plymouth/Galle1.html (accessed on May 25, 2017).

Gambino, Megan. "John Smith Coined the Term New England on This 1616 Map." Smithsonian.com. https://www.smithsonianmag.com/history/john-smith-coined-the-term-new-england-on-this-1616-map-180953383/ (accessed on November 15, 2017).

Gardner, Charles Carroll. "Death Records of the Rahway and Plainfield Monthly Meeting of Friends." *The Genealogical Magazine of New Jersey* 27, no. 1 (1952).

"A Genealogical Profile of William Pontus," Plymouth Ancestors. https://www.plimoth.org/sites/default/files/media/pdf/pontus_william.pdf (accessed on May 28, 2017).

George, Timothy. *John Robinson and the English Separatist Tradition.* Georgia: Mercer University Press, 1982.

———. "Predestination in a Separatist Context: The Case of John Robinson." *Sixteenth Century Journal*, Vol. 15, No. 1 (Spring, 1984): 73-85.

Goldberg, Jonathan. *Sodometries: Renaissance Texts, Modern Sexualities.* Stanford University Press, 1992.

Goodwin, John A. *The Pilgrim Republic: An Historical Review of the Colony of New Plymouth.* Boston: Ticknor and Co., 1888.

Greaves, Richard L. "The Role of Women in English Nonconformity." *Church History* 52, no. 3 (1983).

Griffis, William Elliot. *The Pilgrims in their Three Homes: England, Holland, America.* Boston: Houghton, Mifflin and Co., The Riverside Press, Cambridge, 1898.

Hall, M. Clement. *A Calendar of Miseries: Mothers Who Killed Children.* Lulu, 2010.

Hamblin, David. "The First Settlers of Eastham, Mass." *The New England Historical and Genealogical Register* Vol. 6 (1852): 41.

"Hanged by the Neck Until You Are Dead! (USA)." http://www.capitalpunishmentuk.org/hanging.html (accessed on June 2, 2017).

Hawke, David Freeman. *Everyday Life in Early America.* New York: Harper & Row, 1988.

Haxton, Annie Arnoux. *Signers of the Mayflower Compact.* New York, 1897-99.

Hearn, Daniel Allen. *Legal Executions in New England: A Comprehensive Reference, 1623-1960.* Jefferson, North Carolina: McFarland & Co., Inc., 1999.

Henderson, Katherine Usher, Barbara F. McManus. *Half Humankind: Contexts and Texts of the Controversy about Women in England, 1540-1640.* University of Illinois Press, 1985.

Higgins, Katharine Chapin. *Richard Higgins, a Resident and Pioneer Settler at Plymouth and Eastham, Massachusetts, and at Piscataway, New Jersey, and His Descendants.* Worcester, MA: printed for the author, 1918.

Hills, Leon Clark. *Cape Cod Series, Vol. 1, History and Genealogy of the Mayflower Planters and First Comers to Ye Olde Colonie.* Washington, D.C.: Hills Publishing Co., 1941.

Hirschmann, J.V., Gregory J. Raugi. "Adult Scurvy." Puget Sound Veterans Affairs Medical Center and the University of Washington School of Medicine. No. 16/2/101091.

"Historical Timeline: History of Euthanasia and Physician-Assisted Suicide." http://euthanasia.procon.org/view.resource.php?resourceID=000130 (accessed on May 29, 2017).

"A History of Our Four Municipal Cemeteries & Tombs," http://duxburyma.virtualtownhall.net/Public_Documents/DuxburyMA_Cemetery/standish/history.pdf (accessed on May 29, 2017).

Hoffer, Peter C., N.E.H. Hull. *Murdering Mothers: Infanticide in England and New England, 1558-1803.* New York: New York University Press, 1984.

Holifield, E. Brooks. *Era of Persuasion: American Thought and Culture, 1521-1680.* Boston: Twayne Pub., 1989.

Holliday, Carl. *Woman's Life in Colonial Days.* Mineola, New York: Dover Publications, Inc., 1922.

Horn, James. *A Land as God Made It: Jamestown and the Birth of America.* New York: Basic Books, 2005.

Howe, Daniel Wait. *The Puritan Republic of The Massachusetts Bay in New England.* Indianapolis: The Bowen-Merrill Co., Pub., 1899.

Hubbard, Rev. William. *A General History of New England, from the Discovery to 1680.* 2nd ed. Boston: Charles C. Little and James Brown, 1848.

Huiginn, Rev. E.J.V. *The Graves of Myles Standish and Other Pilgrims,* Revised and Enlarged. Massachusetts: Published by the Author. 1914.

Hull, N.E.H. *Female Felons, Women and Serious Crime in Colonial Massachusetts.* Urbana, IL: University of Illinois Press, 1987.

Hume, Ivor Noel. *A Guide to Artifacts of Colonial America.* New York: Alfred A. Knopf, 1972.

Hunter, Joseph. *Collections Concerning the Church or Congregation of Protestant Separatists Formed at Scrooby in North Nottinghamshire, in the Time of James I: the Founders of New-Plymouth, the Parent-Colony of New-England.* London: John Russell Smith, 1854.

Hurd, D. Hamilton. *History of Plymouth County, Massachusetts, with*

Biographical Sketches of Many of Its Pioneers and Prominent Men. Philadelphia: J.W. Lewis & Co., 1884.
"I Cannot Tell a Lie – Colonial Dentistry." Dr. Samuel Harris National Museum of Dentistry. www.dentalmuseum.org (accessed on June 4, 2017).
Jagger, Andrew. "Austerfield." Doncaster and District Family History Society. 2001. www.doncasterfhs.co.uk/austerfield (accessed on May 31, 2017).
Jensen, Vickie. *Why Women Kill: Homicide and Gender Equality.* Boulder, CO: Lynne Reinner Publishers, Inc., 2001.
Johnson, Caleb H. "Animals and Livestock." Caleb Johnson's Mayflower History. http://mayflowerhistory.com/livestock (accessed on May 31, 2017).
———. "Clothing." Caleb Johnson's Mayflower History. http://mayflowerhistory.com/clothing (accessed on May 31, 2017).
———. "Crime and Punishment in Plymouth Colony. *Caleb Johnson's Mayflower History.* http://mayflowerhistory.com/crime (accessed on May 31, 2017).
———. *The Mayflower and Her Passengers.* Xlibris Corp., 2006.
———. "Peter Browne," Caleb Johnson's Mayflower History. http://mayflowerhistory.com/browne/ (accessed on May 31, 2017).
———. "Plymouth Colony Division of Land." Plymouth Colony Archive Project. http://www.histarch.illinois.edu/plymouth/landdiv.html (accessed on November 14, 2017).
Jones, Emma C. Brewster. *The Brewster Genealogy, 1566-1907.* New York: The Grafton Press, 1908.
Jones, Ann. *Women Who Kill, a Vivid History of America's Female Murderers from Colonial Times to the Present.* New York: Fawcett Columbine, 1981.
Jordan, Jason. "Domestic Violence in Plymouth Colony," Plymouth Colony Archive Project, http://www.histarch.illinois.edu/plymouth/Domestic.html (accessed on May 26, 2017).
Kamensky, Jane. *Governing the Tongue: the Politics of Speech in Early New England.* New York: Oxford University Press, 1997.
Karasik, Gary, Anna M. Aschkenes. *Middlesex County, Crossroads of History.* Sun Valley, CA: American Historical Press, 1999.
Kellogg, Lucy, ed. *Mayflower Families Through Five Generations: Descendants of the Pilgrims Who Landed at Plymouth, Mass. December 1620.* Vol. 1. General Society of Mayflower Descendants. 1975.
King, H. Roger. *Cape Cod and Plymouth Colony in the Seventeenth Century.* Lanham: University Press of America, 1994.
Knox, Robert. "Scan Discovers Possible Site of Meeting House." *The Boston Globe.* 2/2/2013. http://www.boston.com/news/local/massachusetts/2013/02/03/archeology-project-may-have-found-site-first-

meeting-house-duxbury/eomGZeZvHvxmplFoQ3siNI/story.html Accessed on 2/11/2014 (accessed on June 3, 2017).

Krusell, Cynthia Hagar, Betty Magoun Bates. *Marshfield, a Town of Villages, 1640-1990.* Marshfield Hills, MA: Historical Research Associates, 1990.

LaCombe, Michael A. *Political Gastronomy: Food and Authority in the English Atlantic World.* Philadelphia: University of Pennsylvania Press, 2012.

Langdon, George D., Jr. *Pilgrim Colony: A History of New Plymouth, 1620-1691.* New Haven and London: Yale University Press, 1966.

Lester, David, Gene Lester. *Crime of Passion: Murder and the Murderer.* Chicago: Nelson Hall, 1975.

Levy, Barry. *Town Born: The Political Economy of New England from Its Founding to the Revolution.* University of Pennsylvania Press, 2009.

Libby, Charles. "The Knowles Family of Eastham." *New England Ancestors* (July, 1925): 289-290.

———. *The Knowles Family of Eastham, MA.* Portland, Maine: C.T. Libby, 1920-?

Lindsay, David. *Mayflower Bastard: A Stranger Among the Pilgrims.* New York: Thomas Dunne Books, an imprint of St. Martin's Press, 2002.

"A List of Mayflower Passengers, 1620." Plymouth Colony Archive Project. http://www.histarch.illinois.edu/plymouth/Maylist.html (accessed on May 25, 2017).

Long, E. Waldo. *The Story of Duxbury, 1637-1937.* Duxbury: The Duxbury Tercentenary Committee, 1937.

Love, W. DeLoss. *The Fast and Thanksgiving Days of New England.* Boston: Houghton, Mifflin, and Co., 1895.

Lovejoy, David S. "Plain Englishmen at Plymouth." *The New England Quarterly,* Vol. 63, No. 2. (June, 1990): 232-248.

———. *Religious Enthusiasm in the New World: Heresy to Revolution.* Cambridge: Harvard University Press, 1985.

Lowe, Alice. *Nauset on Cape Cod: A History of Eastham.* Falmouth, Mass.: Kendall Print Co., 1968.

Lupher, David. *Greeks, Romans, and Pilgrims: Classical Receptions in Early New England.* Leiden: Brill, 2017.

Mackennal, Alexander. *Homes and Haunts of the Pilgrim Fathers.* London: The Religious Tract Society, 1899.

Maddox, Nonda Lee. "Early Plymouth Government." *The Mayflower Quarterly* Vol. 66, No. 3 (Sept, 2000): 251-260.

"Map of Early Pilgrim and Indian Trails of Old Plymouth Colony." Plymouth-Provincetown Celebration Commission, 1971.

Marks, Rev. Gary L. "The Faith and Theology of the Pilgrims." *The Pilgrim Journal* Vol. 1, No. 1, (Dec., 1985): 3-11.

Marsh, Margaret, Wanda Ronner. *The Empty Cradle: Infertility in America from Colonial Times to the Present*. Baltimore: The Johns Hopkins University Press, 1996.

Martin, Henry J. *Notices, Genealogical and Historical, of the Martin Family of New England who Settled at Weymouth and Hingham in 1635 ....* Boston: Lee and Shepard, 1879.

Matthews, Albert. "The Terms Hired Man and Help." *The Colonial Society of Massachusetts* 5 (1897-98): 225-257.

Mays, Dorothy A. *Women in Early America: Struggle, Survival, and Freedom in a New World*. Santa Barbara CA: ABC-CLIO, 2004.

McIntyre, Ruth A. *Debts Hopeful and Desperate: Financing the Plymouth Colony*. Plymouth Plantation, Inc., 1963.

McKee, E.S. "Jury of Matrons," *The Lancet-Clinic, a Weekly Journal of Medicine and Surgery* 57 (Oct. 13, 1906): 372.

McMahon, Vanessa. *Murder in Shakespeare's England*. London: Hambledon and London, 2004.

"Medical Definition of Postpartum Psychosis" Medicine Net. http://www.medicinenet.com/script/main/art.asp?articlekey=26212 (accessed on June 1, 2017).

Meuly, Walter C. Meuly, *History of Piscataway Township, 1666-1676*. Somerville, NJ: Somerset Press Inc., 1976), http://familytreemaker.genealogy.com/users/w/o/l/Glenn-A-Wolfson/FILE/0002text.txt (accessed on June 1, 2017).

Meyer, Cheryl L., Ph.D., J.D., Margaret G. Spinelli, M.D. "Medical and Legal dilemmas of Postpartum Psychiatric Disorders." In *Infanticide: Psychosocial and Legal Perspectives on Mothers Who Kill,* 167-185. Washington, D.C.: American Psychiatric Publishing, Inc., 2003.

Meyer, Cheryl L., Michelle Oberman. *Mothers Who Kill Their Children*. New York: New York University Press, 2001.

Meyer, Isidore S. *The Hebrew Exercises of Governor William Bradford*. Plymouth, MA: Pilgrim Society, 1973.

Miller, Perry. *Errand into the Wilderness.* Cambridge, MA: The Belknap Press of Harvard University Press, 1956.

Mofford, Juliet Haines. *The Devil Made Me Do It! Crime and Punishment in Early New England.* Guilford, CT: Globe Pequot Press, 2012.

Molloy, Anne Stearns Baker. *The Years Before the Mayflower: The Pilgrims in Holland.* New York: Hastings House, 1972.

Monnette, Orra Eugene. *First Settlers of Ye Plantations of Piscataway and Woodbridge, Old East New Jersey, 1664-1714, a Period of Fifty Years, (A Series of Eight or More Parts).* Los Angeles: The Leroy Carman Press, 1930.

Moody, Joanna, ed. *The Private Life of an Elizabethan Lady: The Diary of Lady Margaret Hoby, 1599-1605*. University of Michigan: Sutton Publishing, 1998.

Moore, Jacob Bailey. *Governors of New Plymouth and Massachusetts Bay*. New York: Gates and Stedman, 1848.

Moore, Susan Hardman. *Pilgrims: New World Settlers and the Call of Home.* Yale University Press, 2007.

Morgan, Edmund S. *The Puritan Family: Religion and Domestic Relations in Seventeenth-Century New England.* New York: Harper & Row, 1966.

Morison, Samuel Eliot. *The Ropemakers of Plymouth: A History of the Plymouth Cordage Company, 1824-1949.* Boston: Houghton Mifflin Co., 1950.

———. *The Story of the "Old Colony" of New Plymouth.* New York: Alfred A. Knopf, 1956.

Murphy, Barbara. *Scituate: The Coming of Age of a Plymouth Colony Town.* Np. 1985.

Nelson, William E. *The Common Law in Colonial America.* Vol. 1, *The Chesapeake and New England, 1607-1660.* Oxford University Press, 2008.

———. "Court Records as Sources for Historical Writing." In *Law in Colonial Massachusetts, 1630-1800,* 499-518.

Neuzil, Anna. "Women in Plymouth Colony, 1633-1668" Plymouth Colony Archive Project. http://www.histarch.illinois.edu/plymouth/PCR.htm (accessed on May 25, 2017).

Nickerson, W. Sears. *Land Ho! 1620: a Seaman's Story of the Mayflower, Her Construction, Her Navigation, and Her First Landfall.* East Lansing: Michigan State University Press, 1977.

Norton, Mary Beth. *Founding Mothers & Fathers: Gendered Power and the Forming of American Society.* New York: Vintage Books, 1997.

Noyes, Ethel J.R.C. *The Women of the Mayflower and Women of Plymouth Colony.* Plymouth, MA: Memorial Press, 1921.

Pafford, John M. *How Firm a Foundation: William Bradford and Plymouth.* Bowie, MD: Heritage Books, Inc., 2002.

Paige, Lucius R. *List of Freemen of Massachusetts, 1630-1691.* Baltimore: Genealogical Publishing Co., Inc., 1980.

Paine, Josiah. "Founders' Day Edition, August 26, 1916, of the Early Settlers of Eastham, Containing Sketches of All Early Settlers of Eastham." In *Facsimile Edition of 108 Pamphlets Published in the Early 20th Century,* 457-488. Baltimore: Genealogical Publishing Co., Inc., 1992.

Palfrey, John Gorham. *History of New England During the Stuart Dynasty.* Vol. 1. Boston: Little, Brown, and Co., 1858.

Parnes, D.C. *Plymouth and the Common Law, 1620-1775.* Kingston, MA: Pilgrim Publishers. 1971.

"Passengers on the Anne and the Little James." Pilgrim Hall Museum. http://www.pilgrimhallmuseum.org/pdf/Passenger_List_Anne_Little_James_1623.pdf (accessed on May 31, 2017).

Perkins, Edwin J. The Economy of Colonial America. New York: Columbia University Press, 1988.

Perry, Queen M. "The History of the Chambers Family of Niagara Falls, Canada, a Mayflower Family." Unpublished manuscript. LDS Microform #1035547, 198? (Full date not given.)

Peterson, Frederick, and Walter S. Haines. A Text-Book of Legal Medicine and Toxicology, Vol. 2. Philadelphia and London: W.B. Saunders Co., 1907.

Philbrick, Nathaniel. Mayflower, a Story of Courage, Community, and War. New York: Viking, 2006.

The Pilgrim Memorial to be erected in the Town of Plymouth, Massachusetts: The Program. Plimoth Plantation, Inc. 1948.

"The Pilgrim Number of the Journal of American History." *Journal of American History.* Vol. 15, No. 4, 1921: 330-382.

Pillsbury, Katherine H., Robert D. Hale, Jack Post. *The Duxbury Book, 1637-1987.* Duxbury, MA: The Duxbury Rural and Historical Society, 1987.

———. *Duxbury, a Guide.* Duxbury, MA: Duxbury Rural and Historical Society, 1999.

The Piscataway Town Book: Minutes of Town Meetings and Records of Elections, 1683-1933. Manuscript in Rutgers University Library Special Collections.

Pleck, Elizabeth. *Domestic Tyranny: The Making of American Social Policy against Family Violence from Colonial Times to the Present.* New York: Oxford University Press, 1987.

Plimoth Plantation: A Story of Two Cultures. Plymouth: Plimoth Plantation, 2005.

Plooij, D. *The Pilgrim Fathers from a Dutch Point of View.* New York: AMS Press, 1932.

Plymouth County Directory and Historical Register of the Old Colony .... Middleboro, Mass.: Stillman B. Pratt & Co., 1867.

Pope, Charles Henry. *The Pioneers of Massachusetts, a descriptive list drawn from Records of the Colonies, Towns and Churches, and other Contemporaneous Documents.* Baltimore: Genealogical Publishing Co., 1969.

"Postpartum Depression," Web MD. http://www.webmd.com/depression/postpartum-depression/default.htm

"Postpartum Psychosis," Pregnancy Info.net. http://www.pregnancy-info.net/postpartum_psychosis.html (accessed on June 3, 2017).

Powers, Edwin. *Crime and Punishment in Early Massachusetts, 1620-1692, a Documentary History.* Boston: Beacon Press, 1966.

Powicke, Frederick James. "John Robinson and the Beginnings of the Pilgrim Movement." *The Harvard Theological Review* Vol. 13, No. 3 (Jul., 1920): 252-289.

Pratt, Edwin A. *A History of Inland Transport and Communication in England.* New York: E.P. Dutton & Co., 1912.

Pratt, Enoch. *A Comprehensive History, Ecclesiastical and Civil, of Eastham, Wellfleet and Orleans, County of Barnstable, Mass., from 1644-1844.* Yarmouth: W.S. Fisher and Co., 1844.

"Prices of Grain and other Commodities, for the Payment of Taxes in Plymouth Colony." In *Collections of the American Statistical Association.* Vol. 1, 289. Boston: T.R. Marvin, 1847.

Prince, Thomas. *A Chronological History of New England in the Form of Annals.* Boston: Cummings, Hilliard, and Company, 1826.

Rath, Richard Cullen. *How Early America Sounded.* Ithaca: Cornell University Press, 2003.

Reis, Elizabeth. *Damned Women: Sinners and Witches in Puritan New England.* Ithaca: Cornell University Press, 1997.

Richard, Maureen. "Washing Household Linens and Linen Clothing in 1627 Plymouth." In *Women's Work in New England, 1620-1920,* 10-21. Boston: Boston University, 2001.

Richards, Lysander Salmon. *History of Marshfield.* Plymouth: The Memorial Press, 1901.

Ricord, Frederick W., ed. *Documents Relating to the Colonial History of the State of New Jersey.* Vol. XIII. Trenton: The John L. Murphy Publishing Co., 1890.

Roebling, Mrs. Washington, "Richard Warren of the Mayflower" *New England Historical and Genealogical Record* 55, (1901): 70-78, 161-179.

Roediger, David R. *The Wages of Whiteness: Race and the Making of the American Working Class,* Rev. Ed. London, New York: Verso, 1991.

Rogers, Alan. *Murder and the Death Penalty in Massachusetts.* University of Massachusetts Press, 2008.

Roser, Susan E. *Mayflower Births & Deaths*, Vol. 1. Genealogical Publishing Co., Inc., 1992.

———. *Mayflower Increasings.* Second edition. Baltimore, MD: Genealogical Publishing Co., Inc., 1996.

Roth, Randolph. "Child Murder in New England." *Social Science History* 25:1 (spring 2001): 101-147.

Rowland, Olive Barrick. "Piscataway Records of Birth, Marriage and Death." In *An Ancestral Chart and Handbook: Genealogical Notes of the Sutton and Rittenhouse Families of Hunterdon County, New Jersey: with Mattison, Bonham, Fuller, and Fox connections, and some record of the Barrick and Shepherd Families.* Richmond: Garrett & Massie, 1935.

The Royal Line of Succession: The British Monarchy from Egbert AD 802 to Queen Elizabeth II. Gloucestershire, UK: Pitkin Publishing, 2014.

Russell, William S. *Pilgrim Memorials and Guide to Plymouth* .... Boston: Crosby and Nichols, 1864.

Rutman, Darrett B. *Husbandmen of Plymouth: Farms and Villages in the Old Colony, 1620-1692.* Boston: Beacon Press, 1967.

———. *The Morning of America, 1603-1789.* Boston: Houghton Mifflin Co., 1971.

Sargent, Mark L. "The Conservative Covenant: The Rise of the Mayflower Compact in American Myth." *The New England Quarterly* Vol. 61, No., 2 (June, 1988): 233-251.

Savage, James. *A Genealogical Dictionary of the First Settlers of New England.* Vol. 1. Baltimore: Genealogical Publishing Co., 1969.

Saxton, Martha. "Bearing the Burden? Puritan Wives." *History Today* Vol. 44, No.10 (Oct. 1994) 28-33.

Schmidt, Gary D. *William Bradford, Plymouth's Faithful Pilgrim.* Grand Rapids, MI: Eerdmans Books for Young Readers, 1999.

Schwartz, Sydney, "They Found Answers in the Dirt in Duxbury," *The Patriot Ledger* October 20, 2008. http://www.patriotledger.com/x1412466246/ The-found-answers-in-the-dirt-in-Duxbury (accessed on June 4, 2017).

Seelye, John. *Memory's Nation; the Place of Plymouth Rock.* Chapel Hill: The University of North Carolina Press, 1998.

Sellin, Thorsten. *The Penalty of Death.* Beverly Hills, CA: Sage Publications, 1980.

Shafer, Twila Birnie, Francis Beasley Odell, *Descendants of the Sutton-Beasley family of Brown County, Ohio.* Topeka, KS: Myers & Co., Pictorial Press, 1946.

Shaw, Albert. "The Pilgrim Mothers." *The American Review of Reviews* (December 1920): 653.

Sherman, Ruth Wilder and Robert S. Wakefield. *Plymouth Colony Probate Guide: Where to Find Wills and Related Data for 800 People of Plymouth Colony, 1620-1691.* Warwick, RI: Plymouth Colony Research Group, 1983.

Shepard, James. *Governor William Bradford and his son, Major William Bradford.* New Britain, Conn.: Herald Print, 1900.

Shurtleff, Harold R. *The Log Cabin Myth: A Study of the Early Dwellings of the English Colonists in North America.* Cambridge, MA: Harvard University Press, 1939.

Shurtleff, Nathaniel, "List of Those Able to Bear Arms in the Colony of New Plymouth in 1643." *New England Historical Genealogical Society Register* 4 (1850): 255.

"Sketches of the Early History of the Town of Middleborough, in the County of Plymouth," *The New England Historical & Genealogical Register* 3, (1849):213-220, 330-344.

Smith, Bradford. *Bradford of Plymouth.* Philadelphia: J.B. Lippincott Co., 1951.

———. *A Dangerous Freedom.* New York: Dell Publishing Co., 1963.

Spufford, Margaret. *Small Books and Pleasant Histories: Popular Fiction and Its Readership in Seventeenth Century England.* Athens, Georgia: The University of Georgia Press, 1982

Staub, Susan C. *Nature's Cruel Stepdames: Murderous Women in the Street Literature of Seventeenth Century England.* Pittsburgh, PA: Duquesne University Press, 2005.

Stradley, Linda. "Johnnycake History." What's Cooking America. http://whatscookingamerica.net/History/Johnnycakes.htm (accessed on June 2, 2017).

Stratton, Eugene Aubrey. *Plymouth Colony: Its History and People, 1620-1691.* Salt Lake City, UT: Ancestry Publishing, 1986.

Stuart, Beth. "The weird and wonderful mind of a 4-year-old finally makes sense." http://www.sheknows.com/parenting/articles/814238/your-4-year-old-development-behavior-and-parenting-tips-1 (accessed on June 7, 2017).

Sutton, Edward F.H. *Genealogical Notes of the Sutton Family of New Jersey.* New York: T.A. Wright, 1900.

Sutton, Isaac. *Notes of Family History: the Anderson, Schofield, Pennypacker, Yocum, Crawford, Sutton ... Families.* Philadelphia: Stephenson Brothers, nd.

Taylor, Alan. *American Colonies: The Settling of North America.* New York: Penguin Books, 2001.

Teems, David. *Tyndale: the Man Who Gave God an English Voice.* Nashville: Thomas Nelson, 2012.

Teeters, Negley K. *Hang by the Neck: the Legal Use of Scaffold and Noose, Gibbet, Stake, and Firing Squad from Colonial Times to the Present.* Springfield, IL: Charles C. Thomas, 1967.

Thacher, James. *History of the Town of Plymouth; from its first settlement in 1620, to the year 1832.* Boston: Marsh, Capen & Lyon, 1832.

Thomas, Heather. "To what extent are books of advice or 'conduct books' accurate guides to the relationship between husbands and wives in the Tudor and Stuart period?" http://www.elizabethi.org/contents/essays/marriage.htm

Thomas, Keith. "Women and the Civil War Sects." *Crisis in Europe, 1560-1660, Essays from Past and Present,* 317-340. London, Routledge & Kegan Paul, 1965.

Torrey, Clarence Almon. *New England Marriages Prior to 1700.* Baltimore: Genealogical Publishing Co., Inc., 1987.

Tortora, Gerald J., Sandra Reynolds Grabowski. *Principles of Anatomy and Physiology.* 7th ed. New York: Harper Collins, 1993.

Travers, Carolyn Freeman. "College of Sobriety: Servitude in Plymouth Colony." *The Compact* 31, No. 2 (Summer 2010): 1, 4-5, 8-9.

———. "Were they all shorter back then?" Plimoth Plantation. http://www.plimoth.org/learn/history/myth/fourfttwomyth.asp (accessed on June 2, 2017).

Ulrich, Laurel Thatcher. *Good Wives: Image and Reality in the Lives of Women in Northern New England, 1650-1750.* New York: Vintage Books, 1980.

Underhill, J.W. "Observations on Pseudocyesis, and on Pregnancy in its Relation to Capital Punishment." *The American Journal of Obstetrics.* Vol. 11 (Jan., April, July, Oct., 1878): 21-36.

Usher, Roland G. *The Pilgrims and Their History.* Williamstown, MA: Corner House Publishers, 1984. Originally published in 1918.

Virkus, Frederick Adams. *Compendium of American Genealogy,* Vol. 6, Baltimore: Genealogical Pub. Co., 1987. Originally published in 1937.

Waddington, John. *Congregational History, 1567-1700, in Relation to Contemporaneous Events, and the Conflict for Freedom, Purity, and Independence.* London: Longmans, Green, and Co., 1874.

Wakefield, Robert. "The Ramsden Family of Plymouth, Mass." *Mayflower Descendant* 36, no. 2 (1986): 187.

Waldrup, Carol Chandler. *Colonial Women: 23 Europeans Who Helped Build a Nation.* Jefferson, North Carolina: McFarland & Co., 1999.

Ward, Harry M. *Statism in Plymouth Colony.* Port Washington, New York: Kennikat Press, 1973.

Warwick, Edward. *Early American Dress.* New York: Benjamin Bloom, 1965.

Wecht, Cyril H., ed. *Crime Scene Investigation, Crack the Case with Real Life Experts,* New York: Reader's Digest Books, 2004.

Welcome to All Saints' Church, Babworth. Heritage Inspired: South Yorkshire's Faith Tourism Initiative. Undated pamphlet.

Welcome to St. Helena's Church, Austerfield. Heritage Inspired: South Yorkshire's Faith Tourism Initiative. Undated pamphlet.

Wentworth, Dorothy. *Settlement and Growth of Duxbury, 1628-1870.* Massachusetts, Duxbury Rural and Historical Society, 1973.

Wertz, Richard, and Dorothy C. Wertz. *Lying-In: a History of Childbirth in America.* New York: Shocken Books, 1979.

Wharton, Anne Hollingsworth. *English Ancestral Homes of Noted Americans.* Philadelphia and London: J.P. Lippincott Co., 1915.

"What's Cooking at Plimoth Plantation." *New England Antiques Journal.* https://www.antiquesjournal.com/Pages04/Monthly_pages/nov05/cooking.html (accessed on June 3, 2017).

Whitehead, William A. "Piscataway Register of Births." Fragment from *Piscataway Town Book,* "which has since disappeared."

Wiley, Edwin, ed. *Lectures on the Growth and Development of the United States*. New York: American Educational Alliance, 1916.

"William Bradford Introduction - Essay." *Notes.com*. Accessed at http://www.enotes.com/iterary-criticism/bradford-william

Willison, George F. *The Pilgrim Reader: The Story of the Pilgrims as Told by Themselves and Their Contemporaries Friendly and Unfriendly*. Garden City, NY: Doubleday and Co., Inc., 1953.

———. *Saints and Strangers: Being the Lives of the Pilgrim Fathers & Their Families, with Their Friends & Foes; & an Account of Their Posthumous Wanderings in Limbo, Their Final Resurrection & Rise to Glory, & the Strange Pilgrimages of Plymouth Rock*. New York: Reynal & Hitchcock, 1945.

Winsor, Justin. *Elder William Brewster, of the Mayflower: His Books and Autographs, with Other Notes*. Cambridge: John Wilson and Son, 1887.

———. *History of the Town of Duxbury, Massachusetts, with Genealogical Registers*. Boston: Crosby & Nichols, Washington Street; Samuel G. Drake, Cornhill, 1849.

"The Witches Curse," Secrets of the Dead, Public Broadcasting System, http://www.pbs.org/wnet/secrets/previous_seasons/case_salem/clues.html (accessed on June 4, 2017).

Wisner, Katherine L. "Postpartum Disorders." In *Infanticide: Psychosocial and Legal Perspectives on Mothers Who Kill*, 35-60. Washington, D.C. American Psychiatric Publishing, Inc., 2003.

Wood, William. *New England's Prospect*. Amherst: University of Massachusetts Press, 1977.

Wright, Louis B. *The Cultural Life of the American Colonies, 1607-1763*. New York: Harper & Row, 1957.

Young, Alexander. *Chronicles of the First Planters of the Colony of Massachusetts Bay, from 1623-1636*. Boston: C.C. Little and J. Brown, 1846.

———. *Chronicles of the Pilgrim Fathers of the Colony of Plymouth, from 1602-1695*. Second edition. Boston: Charles Little, 1844.

Zagorin, Perez. *The Court and the Country: the Beginning of the English Revolution*. New York: Atheneum, 1971.

Websites of Interest

Note: All websites have been confirmed as of 1 February 2020.

"Alice Martin Bishop." http://www.alicemartinbishop.com/
"British History Online." http://www.british-history.ac.uk

Chartier, Craig. Plymouth Archaeological Rediscovery Project. http://www.plymoutharch.com

Cline, Duane. "The Pilgrims and Plymouth Colony: 1620." http://www.rootsweb.ancestry.com/~mosmd

Deetz, Patricia Scott and James Deetz. "The Plymouth Colony Archive Project." http://www.histarch.illinois.edu/plymouth/

Johnson, Caleb. "Caleb Johnson's Mayflower History" http://www.mayflowerhistory.com

"The Pilgrim Fathers UK Origins Association." http://www.pilgrimfathersorigins.org

"Pilgrim Hall Museum: America's Museum of Pilgrim Possessions." http://www.pilgrimhall.org

"Plimoth Plantation." http://www.plimoth.org

Sutton, Dennis. "Home Grown in the Garden State." http://www.njsuttonfamily.org

Ilustration Credits

Brown, John. *The Pilgrim Fathers of New England and their Puritan Successors*. New York: Fleming H. Revell Co., 1895. [p.11]

Bryant, William Cullen and Sydney Howard Gay. *A Popular History of the United States from the First Discovery of the Western Hemisphere by the Northmen, to the End of the First Century of the Union of the United States*. New York: Scribner, Armstrong, & Co., 1876. [pp. 9, 41, 101, 125]

Carter, Mary K. B., [drawings on p. 77, 206]

―――――. [drawings on p. 155, 205, based on drawings by Henry Glassie, used with his kind permission]

Cyr, Ellen M. *The Children's Third Reader*. Boston: Ginn & Co., 1901. [p.168]

Ellis, Edward S. *The History of Our Country from the Discovery of America to the Present Time*. Vol. 1. Philadelphia: The History Company, 1899. [pp. 193, 216]

John Hancock Mutual Life Insurance Company, *The Story of the Pilgrims*, Boston:1923. [p. 84]

Hanks, Charles Stedman. *Our Plymouth Forefathers*. Boston: Author's Publishing Assoc., 1907. [p. 68, 133, 148]

Harper, Charles G. *The Great North Road: The Old Main Road to Scotland, London to York*. London: Cecil Palmer: 1901. [p. 18]

Markham, Richard. *Colonial Days, Being Stories and Ballads for Young Patriots…* New York: Dodd, Mead & Co., 1879. [pp. 59, 142, 180]

Moore, N. *Pilgrims and Puritans; the Story of the Planting of Plymouth and Boston*. Boston: Ginn & Co., 1888. [pp. 7, 46, 177, 236]

Plymouth Colony Court Orders from 1633-1691. [pp. 270, 272]

Plymouth Colony Records, 1:108. [p. 26]

"A pittiilesse Mother. That most unnaturally at one time murdered two of her owne children at Acton within five miles from London upon holy Thursday last 1616, the ninth of May, being a gentlewoman named Margaret Vincent, wife of Mr. Aarus [?] of the same town, with her examination, confession, and true discovery of all the proceedings in the said bloody accident." http://access.bl.uk/item/pdf/lsidyv3351198b (accessed on July 28, 2018). [p. xi]

Pratt, Mara L. *Stories of Colonial Children.* Boston: Educational Publishing Co., 1925. [pp. 96, 108, 128, 223]

Pumphrey, Margaret B. *Pilgrim Stories.* Chicago: Rand McNally & Co., 1910. [pp. 31, 118, 1992, 257]

Index

A Description of New England, J. Smith, 52, 101
A Little Commonwealth: Family Life in Plymouth Colony, J. Demos, 247
A Pittilesse Mother, Anon., 268
A Word to New Plymouth, W. Bradford, 240
Able to Bear Arms, list of 1643, 203
Act Against Seditious Sectaries, 14
Adams, John, as Purchaser, 170
Adey, Webb, 111
adultery, punishment for, 86
Agowaywam (Agawam) Native American settlement, 156
Aines, Katherine, 241
alcohol, fermentation of ale or cider, 108
Alden, John, 66, 92, 161, 165
    as member of Code of Law review committee (1636), 183
    as Purchaser, 170
    as undertaker of original debt, 169
    marries Priscilla Mullins, 162
    moves from original settlement, 180
Alden, Priscilla Mullins, 162
Allen, John, 189
Allerton, Bartholomew, 64
Allerton, Isaac, 30, 32, 64, 92, 120, 124, 145-146, 171
    as assistant to Gov Bradford, 129
    as Purchaser, 170
    as undertaker of original debt, 169
    proposes to investors a buy out of debt, 169
    sails aboard the *Lyon* (ship) to Plymouth (1629), 174
    takes possession of farm animals, 179
Allerton, John, 66, 92, 161
    death of, 162
Allerton, Mary, 64, 129
    birth of stillborn son, 120
    death of, 124
Allerton, Remember, 64, 129

Altham, Emmanuel, 147-151
    recounts Bradford's wedding feast in detail, 150
    reports on Plymouth Colony, 148
    returns to Plymouth, 151
    sees Plymouth Colony as potential for profit, 148
    warns of homesteading in Plymouth Colony, 149
    writes investors of Pilgrims ability to repay loan, 151
American Civil War, 262
American Medical Association, 248
American Revolutionary War, 260-261
Amsterdam, Netherlands, 37-38, 42, 44-45, 47, 54
Ancient Brethren in Amsterdam, 44-45, 54
Andrews, Richard, as undertaker of original debt, 169
animals, farm, in Plymouth, 178
    chickens, 110, 207
    cows, 107, 200
    goats, 76, 78, 82, 107, 148, 171, 178, 194-195, 238
    slaughtering of, 207
Annable, Anthony
    as Purchaser, 170
    represents Scituate as member of Code of Laws review committee (1636), 183
Anne (ship), 69, 151, 196
    arrives in Plymouth (1623), 154
    arrives in Plymouth with Anne Southworth onboard, 149
    Pilgrims load with cargo for repayment to investors, 152
Aptucxet, Manomet (Bourne), Massachusetts, 172
Archbishop of Canterbury, 17, 23
Archbishop of York, 17
Armitage, Thomas, 197

Index

Armstrong, Eleanor Billington, 196
  marries Gregory Armstrong, 197
Armstrong, Gregory, 197
Atlantic Ocean, 67, 102, 176
Atwood, John, 163
Austerfield, England, 7-8, 10, 17, 21
Austin, Jane G., 263

Babworth, Nottinghamshire, England, 15, 19, 21-22
Baker, James, 263
Bancroft, Richard, 23
Bangs, Edward, as Purchaser, 170
baptism of newborns, 117
Barker, John, 189
Barnes, John, 197
Barnes, Mary, 197
Barnstable, Massachusetts, 180, 218, 229
Bartlett, Robert, 163
Basilikon Doron, 16
Basset, William, 170
Bawtry, Yorkshire, England, 21
Beauchamp, John, as undertaker of original debt, 169
Bell, Susanna, 23-24
Benét, Stephen Vincent, 52
Bennett, William, 163
bestiality in Plymouth, 194, 218, 220, 245
  punishment for, 194-195
Bible, Geneva, 13, 43
Bible, King James, 22
Billington, Christian Penn Eaton (wife of FB), 191, 197
  arrives in Plymouth onbard the *Anne* . (1623), 196
  marries Francis Billington, 196
  marries Francis Eaton, 196
  puts son, Benjamin Eaton, into service, 197
Billington, Eleanor, 32, 65
Billington, Elizabeth, 197
Billington, Francis, 65, 128, 131, 136,88, 191, 196-197, 204, 225, 241
  awarded freedom (1657), 203
  made a freeman (1657), 197
  marries Christian Penn Eaton, 196
  receives ownership of land from Eleanor (1637), 197
  serves on Jury of Inquiry (1648), 203
Billington, John, 3, 65, 92, 131-132, 145
  as Purchaser, 170
  murders John Newcomen, 192
  hangs for murdering John Newcomen, 193, 204
Billington, Joseph, 197, 241
Billington, Martha, 197
Billington, Mary, 197
Billington's Rocks, 196
Birth of Mankind, The (published 1545), 116
Bishop, Alice Martin Clarke, 1-6, 24, 26-. 27, 33, 71, 73, 76, 79-82, 85, 105-106, 113-114, 118, 140, 143-144, 165-166, 185, 187-188, 190-192, 195, 198, 200, 203-205, 207-210, 213-218, 220-222, 226, 237, 245-250, 252, 254, 256-257, 259, 264-268
  and murder of Martha Clarke
    arrested for murder, 209
    charge from Grand Jury, 217
    confesses to murder, 1, 188, 202, 208
    confinement moved from Plymouth to Duxbury, 213
    execution of, 223
    found guilty of murder by petty jury, 7, 218
    hanging of, 1, 3-4, 190, 222, 239, 265
    preparation for, 4-5
    indicted for murder, 189
    murder case, court record of, 195
    no motive for murder, 202
    questioned by Court of Assistants, 210
    sentenced to hang for murder, 219
  as widow, 141-142, 159
  as young woman, 72
  before marriage, 72
  burial of, 7
  delivers first child, 116
  drudgery of daily life, 106
  maiden name unknown, 27
  marries George Clarke, 26, 106
  marries Richard Bishop, 165
  pregnant with first child, 113
  preparation for future marriage, 84
  role in household, 136
Bishop, Damaris (daughter of RB), *see* Sutton, Damaris Bishop
Bishop, James, 164
Bishop, John, 164
Bishop, Richard, 6, 161-165, 187-189, 192, 198, 203-204, 209, 216-217, 222-224, 226-227, 232, 265
  and murder of Martha Clarke

Index

pays for food and care of Alice while incarcerated, 209
becomes a freeman (1655), 226
charged with theft, 223
  settles with Andrew Ring outside of Court, 224
found guilty of theft (1670), 226
hires on with Nathaniel Sowther, 164
in service to Love Brewster, 164
living in Eastham, MA, 226
  obtains land grant in Eastham, MA, 226
  sells Eastham property to neighbor, 230
living in Piscataway, NJ (1677), 231
  receives land grant, 231
marries Alice Clarke, 165
  cause for possible stress in family life, 247
  no legal claim to house George Clarke built, 166
Bishop's Butter Hole, 232
Bitteridge, Richard, 92
Blackwell, Francis, 54-55, 61
  death of, 55
Blackwell, Michael, 189
Blossom, Thomas, 223
Blossom, Widow, 143
Boardman, Thomas, 189
Book of Common Prayer, 8, 10, 14, 184
Boston, Lincolnshire, England, 38-39
Boston, Massachusetts, 4, 110, 160, 230, 237, 249, 260-261
Bowes, Lady Isobel, 43
Bradford of Plymouth, B. Smith, 90
Bradford, Robert (uncle to WB Gov), 12, 21, 39
Bradford, Alice (sister of WB Gov), 8, 39
Bradford, Alice Carpenter Southworth (second wife of WB Gov), 185
  as First Lady of Plymouth, 150
  birth of, 149
  marries Edward Southworth (1613), 149
  marries William Bradford (1623), 149
Bradford, Alice Hanson (mother of WB Gov), 8, 10, 266
  death of, 12
  marries for second time, 11
Bradford, Alice Waingate (aunt to WB Gov), 12
Bradford, Dorothy May (first wife of WB Gov), 47, 56, 149, 185
  death of, 102-103

Bradford, Elizabeth (cousin of WB Gov), 39
Bradford, John (son of WB Gov), 47, 56, 64, 102, 237
Bradford, Joseph (son of WB Gov), birth of, 185
Bradford, Margaret (cousin of WB Gov), 8, 39
Bradford, Mary (cousin of WB Gov), 39
Bradford, Mercy (daughter of WB Gov), birth of, 185
Bradford, Robert (cousin of WB Gov), 39
Bradford, Robert (uncle of WB), 12, 15-16
Bradford, William (father of WB), 8, 10
  death of, 11
  marriage to Alice Hanson, 10
Bradford, William (grandfather of WB Gov), 12
Bradford, William (son of WB Gov), birth of, 185
Bradford, William, Governor, 7-8, 26, 30, 38-40, 43, 55, 59, 64, 70, 146, 156, 158, 171, 175, 185-186, 195, 210, 232, 265-266
and *Mayflower* voyage
  alone in Plymouth, 103
  arrives in Plymouth, 103
  as signer of Mayflower Compact, 92
  writes of asking select Pilgrims to return to London, 63
  writes briefly about voyage across the Atlantic, 67
  writes of first death aboard *Mayflower* (ship), 70
  writes of sickness onboard *Mayflower* (ship), 67
and the murder of Martha Clarke
  controls reporting of Martha's murder, 245
  convenes General Court, 215
  heads murder investigation, 192
  instructs inquiry into death of Martha Clarke, 187
  possibly questions Rachel Ramsden story of murder, 254
  sentences Alice Bishop to hang for murder, 219
  swears in jurists for inquest, 203
Catholic Church, description of, 240
commits to Separatism, 21
deems marriage should not be "laid on the ministers as part of their office", 85

questions practices of Church of
England, 15
Governor of Plymouth Colony
elected Governor after John
Carver's death, 129
enforces Code of Law of 1623, 183
first capital crime he presided over, 192
named Governor by Earl of
Warwick, 112
no longer Governor (1633), 181
presides over General Court
(October 1648), 189
presides over Plymouth Court, 241
reports of second execution in
colony, 194
returns to office (1635), 185
in England
as a sickly child, 12
attends church outside of his village,
15
baptism of, 8-9
birth of, 10, 266
birthplace of, 11
early health of, 12
education of, 13
moves to grandfather's home after
father's death, 12
moves to Scrooby Manor House, 21
moves to uncle's home after
grandfather's death, 12
in Holland
applies for Leiden citzenship, 47
arrives in Amsterdam, 42
as maker of fustian, 47
enthusiastic to venture to America,
56
marries Dorothy May, 47
reflects on leaving Leiden, 60
writes of difficulties of supporting a
family in Leiden, 47
in Plymouth
and Francis Billington and family,
disdain of, 196
and John Robinson, distressed at the
passing of, 158
writes of letter from J. Robinson
(1620), 62
and Richard Clyfton, 19
arrives in Cape Cod, 89-90
as member of Code of Laws review
committee (1636), 183
as original planner of Plymouth
Colony, 175
as Purchaser, 170
as undertaker of original debt, 169
attends Court of Assistance (1648),
187
argues that God is on the
Separatist's side, 50
blames others for failure of
Plymouth Colony, 181
caught in deer trap, 97
concerned that Pilgrims are
starting to think of themselves as
individuals, 155
describes Aptuxcet, Manomet, 172
describes welcoming, 61
despairs of losing control of
Pilgrims' and Separatists' colony,
179
grants request of original members
to leave church, 181
hurt by original members leaving
church in Plymouth, 181
illness during first winter, 122
immorality in colony, possible
reasons for, 245
location of home, 146
marries Alice Carpenter Southworth,
149
proposes to Alice Southworth, 150
tries to maintain control and keep
original plan for Separatists
colony, 155
writes of concern about growing
food shortage in Plymouth, 154
writes response to Weston's scathing
letter, 134
laments arming Native Americans, 173
later years
asks to be excused from meeting in
Boston, 237
death of, 242
buried on Burial Hill, 242
melancholy begins to manifest
itself (1648), 267
misses court due to illness, 242
stops writing history of Plymouth
Colony, 235
studies ancient languages, 239
suffers from depression, 235
writes poetry, 239
Warwick Charter
given complete authority over
Plymouth Colony thru Warwick
Charter, 174

Index 339

granted Plymouth Colony in
   Warwick Charter, 174
surrenders authority granted him in
   Warwick Patent, 113
Bradstreet, Anne, 115
Bray, Thomas, 86
breastfeeding, 117-118
   as contraception, 118
Brett, William, 190
Brewster, Fear (daughter of WB), 64
Brewster, Jonathan (son of WB), 19, 47, . 64
   as Purchaser, 170
   represents Duxbury as member of
      Code of Laws review committee
      (1636), 183
Brewster, Love (son of WB), 64, 162,
   164, 184, 189, 194, 217, 222, 227
   marries Sarah Collier, 164
Brewster, Mary (wife of WB), 19, 21, 43,
   64, 150
Brewster, Patience (daughter of WB), 64
Brewster, Sarah Collier, 164
Brewster, William, 1, 17-21, 23, 39, 43,
   45, 48, 64-65, 92, 94, 129, 145-146,
   150, 164, 184
   arrives in Amsterdam, 42
   as author of Mayflower Compact, 91
   as caregiver to dying, 126
   as Colony preacher, 111
   as original planner of Plymouth
      Colony, 175
   as publisher of books and pamphlets,
      48-49
   as Purchaser, 170
   as undertaker of original debt, 169
   death of, 236
   first settlers in Duxbury, 180
   goes into hiding, 23, 49
   invited to travel to America as
      spiritual leader, 58
   loses job as Scrooby Post Master &
      Bailiff, 23
   represents Town of Plymouth as
      member of Code of Laws review
      committee (1636), 183
   takes possession of farm animals, 179
Brewster, William (father of WB), 18
Brewster, Wrestling (son of WB), 64
Briggs, Agnes, 11
Briggs, Alice, death of, 11
Briggs, Clement, as Purchaser, 170
Briggs, Robert, 11

Britteridge, Richard, 66
   death of, 120
Brown (Browne), John, as member of
   Code of Laws review committee
   (1636), 183
Brown (Browne), Peter, 66, 92, 145
   as Purchaser, 170
Browne, Robert, early leader of Separatist
   movement, 23
Browne, William, 241
Brownist, 23
buggery, *see* bestiality in Plymouth
Bumpas, Edward, Jr.
   charged with abusing parents, 249
   "crazy brained", 249
Bumpass, Edward, Sr., as Purchaser, 170
Burial Hill, 144, 165
   burial place of Gov William Bradford,
      242
burial
   first Pilgrim buried in America, 99
   practices at Plymouth, 141
   preparations for, 6
Burne, Thomas, 189
Bursell, James, 189
Burton, Richard, 210
Butten, William, 64, 71
Buzzard's Bay, Massachusetts, 172

Calderwood, David, 49
Cambridge University, 15, 18, 21
Capawack Native American settlement,
   156
Cape Cod Bay, 89-90, 100, 103, 123,
   169, 172, 227
Cape Code Harbor, 102, 117, 195
Cape Cod, Pilgrims first impressions of,
   95
Carpenter, Alexander, 149
Carter, Robert, 66
Carver, John, Governor, 64-65, 71, 92-93,
   196
   death of, 129
   elected as Governor, 63, 94, 127
   illness of, 122
   visits Christopher Martin's deathbed,
      122
Carver, Katherine (wife of JC), 63-64
   death of, 129
Catherine of Aragon, Queen of England,
   14
Catholic Church, *see* Roman Catholic
   Church

cattle in Plymouth
  brought from England, 178
  common herds, 179
  raising of, 160
  sale of, 212
  value of, 179
Charity (ship)
  arrives in Plymouth (1623), 154
  arrives in Plymouth with farm animals (1624), 178
Charles I, King of England, 238
Charles II, King of England, 243-244
Chesapeake Bay, 55
child rearing
  attitudes of Separatists, 137-138
  in Plymouth Colony, 34
childbirth
  dangers of, 114-115
  death rate of child, 115
  fear of, 115
  feeding of newborn, 117
  food during, 116
  help during, 35, 115-116
  newborn survival rate, 115
  procedure afterward, 116-117
  procedure during, 115-116
children in Plymouth
  assertiveness discouraged, 139
  behavior in church, 14
  binding of newborns, 117
  controlling behavior of, 138
  corporal punishment of, 138
  education of, 140
  expectations of, 48
  Pilgrim families desire of, 113
  punishment of, 253
  training of boys, 32
  training of girls, 31
Chilton, James, 64, 92, 200
  death of, 101
Chilton, Mary, *see* Winslow, Mary Chilton
Chilton, Susanna, 64
Christmas, Pilgrims' inobservance of, 120
Church of England, 10, 13-15, 18-19, 43, 47, 238
Church of Jesus Christ of Latter-Day Saints' Family History Library, 248
Church, Benjamin, 227, 230
Church of Plymouth Colony, 30, 74, 204
Churchill, Beaton, 266
Churchill, Hannah (daughter of JC), 224
Churchill, Hannah Pontus, *see* Rickard, Hannah Pontus Churchill
Churchill, John, 224-225, 266
  as guardian to Abigail Clarke, 224
  death of, 225
  entrusts Aligail with last will and testament, 225
Churchill, Joseph, 225
"CityUpon a Hill" (sermon), 176
Civil War, English (1642-1651), 227
Clarke, Abigail (daughter of GC), 136, 139, 142, 165, 187, 208-209, 224-226, 247, 257, 265-266
  birth of, 116
  guardianship of, 266
  inherits father's property, 224
  sells property to Richard Wright, 225
Clarke, Faith, 74
Clarke, George, 1, 71, 73-76, 79-85, 105, 113, 118, 142, 159, 164-166, 187, 197, 200, 204-205, 224-225, 265-266
  and Edward Doty, 136
    lawsuits, 75-76
    ordered to pay Edward Doty four bushels of corn, 136
  as head of household, 136
    no inventory of estate, 141
    probate of estate, 266
  as yeoman, 82
  death and burial of, 140-141
  expands property holdings, 111-112
  house, design of, 77
  in militia, 140
  in Playne Dealing, 74
  instructs on design of house, out buildings and fields, 78
  makes final payment on farm, 78
  marries Alice Martin, 26, 106
  not entitled to land grant, 73
  property of, 224
  purchases additional land from William Hoskins, 226
  sale of land is complete, 76
Clarke, John, 100
Clarke, Martha, 7, 139-140, 142, 165, 187, 189-190, 195, 197-198, 202, 206, 209, 214, 216, 218, 221-222, 226, 232, 237, 245-248, 253, 257-259, 264, 267
  birth of, 136
  murder of, 191-192
    description of death scene, 187
    description of murder, 7
    description of knife injuries, 207-208

Index 341

Clarke, Richard, 66, 92
Clarke, Thomas, as Purchaser, 170
Clarke, Thurston, 74-75, 112
Clarke's Island, 100, 104
clothing
   children, 139
   female, descriptions of, 139
Clyfton, Richard, 15, 19, 22, 39, 43
   arrives in Amsterdam, 42
   education of, 15
   excommunication of, 22
Code of Laws, revised (1636), 185
Cole, Daniel, 189
Cole, James, 188
   as shoemaker, 204
Cole, Thomas, 230
Collier, William, 210
   as member of Code of Laws review committee (1636), 183
   as Purchaser, 170
   attends Court of Assistance (1648), 187
   serves in Court for William Bradford, 242
Colman, Joseph, 189
common fields, farming and grazing of, 153
common house, description of, 120
confession, Pilgrims' belief in, 208
construction of Plymouth homes, description of, 76
Cooke, Francis, 64, 92, 145-146, 188, 203
   as Purchaser, 170
Cooke, John, 64, 188, 204, 225
Cooper, Humility, 65
Coppin, Robert, 99-100
corn in Plymouth
   as commodity, 172
   as diet staple, 153, 168
   value of, 179
corporal punishment
   drawn and quartered, 2
   hanging, 2, 110
      description of event, 5
      preparing body for burial, 6
      preparation for, 3
      procedure of, 3
   in child rearing, 138
   women, failed attempts, 3-4
Corvanel, William, 163
Council for New England, 54, 112, 174
Court of Assistants, 30, 75, 187, 208-209
   meeting (1648), 189

Court of Assizes, 39
Court of Elections, duties of, 217
court record of murder of Martha Clarke, 191
Courtship of Miles Standish, The, H.W. Longfellow, 262
courtship under eyes of community, 72-73, 80
Coventry, Warwickshire, England, 43
Crackstone, John, Sr., 64, 92
   as Purchaser, 170
Crackstone, John, Jr., 64
crime scene investigation of murder of Martha Clarke, 202, 205-206
   description of, 207
crimes punishable by death, 220
Crispe, George, sues Richard Bishop for theft, 226
Cross, Daniel, 193
   escapes colony, 194
Cudworth, James, represents Scituate
   as member of Code of Laws review committee (1636), 183
Cushman, Robert, 55, 57-58, 152
   as elected leader of group on *Speedwell* (ship), 62
   quits journey to America, 63
   writes harshly of Christopher Martin, 67
Cushman, Thomas, as Purchaser, 170
Cutbertson, Cutbert, as Purchaser, 170

days of humiliation, 50, 262
   against sickness in the colony, 251
de Rasieres, Isaack, 33, 172-173
   describes Plymouth Colony, 167
   reports on fishing at Plymouth Colony, 169
   sells wampum to Pilgrims, 173
deaconess in Separatism in Leiden, 29
disciplinary violence against children in Plymouth, 258
Deane, Stephen, as Purchaser, 170
death penalty in Plymouth, reasons for, 220
deaths in Plymouth, 119, 124
debt to investors, 168
   repayment to investors, 152
Deetz, James, 247, 249
Deetz, Patricia, 247, 249
Delanoy, Phillip, 170
Delaware River, 230
Delfshaven Canal, 60

Delfshaven, Rotterdam, Netherlands, 60, 66
Demos, John, 247
Derby's Pond, 112
desecration and robbery of graves in Plymouth, 105
Dialogues, W. Bradford, 239-240
disease in colony, first winter, 120
dissenters in Scrooby, 20
Doane (Done), John, 196
  represents Town of Plymouth as member of Code of Laws review committee (1636), 183
dogs
  aboard *Mayflower*, 64
  for hunting, 178
Domesticall Duties, W. Gouge, 28, 78, 137
Dorothy (maidservant to Carver family), 64
Doty, Edward, 66, 74-76, 92, 130, 232, 241, 265
  as Purchaser, 170
  charged with breaking the Kings peace, 76
  found guilty of making "deceitful bargain" for land, 75
  lawsuits, 75, 136
  listed as free man, 74
  makes living buying and selling, 75
  marriage to Faith Clarke, 74
  never served on a jury, 204
Doty, Faith Clarke, 74, 241
drought in Plymouth (1623), 263
drunkenness, as crime, 213
duels
  first in New England, 130
  punishment for, 130
Dunham, John Sr., 189
Dutch ship to Leiden, (bark grounds at low tide), 40
Dutch West India Company, 167
Duties of Constables, Householders, Tythingmen, and Such Other Low and Lay Ministers of the Peace, The, W. Lambarde, 184
Duxbury Fair, 1, 4, 7, 110, 212-213
Duxbury, Massachusetts, 6, 162, 164, 180-181, 194, 212-213, 215, 218, 227, 229-230, 240
East Orleans, Massachusetts, 226
Eastham, Massachusetts, 100, 226-227, 230, 232
Eaton, Benjamin, 32, 196-197

Eaton, Dorothy
  death of, 196
  marries Francis Eaton, 196
Eaton, Francis, 66, 92, 95, 196
  arrives in Plymouth (1620), 195
  as Purchaser, 170
  death of, 196
  marries Christian Penn, 196
  marries Dorothy, 196
Eaton, Samuel, 66, 196
Eaton, Sarah, 66
  death of, 196
economy of Plymouth Colony, 152, 168-169, 171
Edmund Grindal, Archbishop of Scrooby, 17
Edward VI, King of England, 14
Eirenarcha: or Of the Office of the Justices of Peace, W. Lambarde, 184
Elizabeth I, Queen of England, 8, 14-16, 18-19
  death of, 16
Ellis, Elizabeth, 34-35
Ellis, John, 34
Ely, (Mr.), 66
engagement, length of, 81
English, Thomas, 66, 92, 161
  death of, 162
Epitaphium Meum, W. Bradford, 240, 242
ergot poisoning, description of, 250
exploring party, first expedition, 96-97
  William Bradford caught in deer trap, 97
exploring party, second expedition, 97-99
exploring party, third expedition, 99-100, 102

fairs, as social gathering place, 213
Fallowell, Gabriel, 190
Farwell, Thomas, 164
Faunce, John, as Purchaser, 170
Finney, Robert, 189
fire in Plymouth Colony (1622), 147
fire, arson, dangers of, 109
firearms, laws governing, 83
fireplace, tools for, 83
First Encounter Beach, 100
First Thanksgiving Dinner, with Portraits of the Pilgrim Fathers, W.L. Taylor, 263
fish
  as fertilizer, 168
  as food, 17, 51-53, 69, 104, 107, 110, 132, 153, 168-169

Fish, Jonathan, 34
Fish, Mary, 34
Fish, Nathaniel, 34
fishing
   fishing, challenges of, 122
   industry in Plymouth Colony, 148
Fitz-Randolph, Nathaniel, 230-231
Fletcher, Moses, 64, 92
Fletcher, Sarah, 64
food in Plymouth, 153, 207
   allotments of, 134
   meals
     breakfast, 107
     dinner/lunch, 107
       preparation of, 108, 109
     supper, 107
   shortages in Plymouth Colony, 154
Ford, Widow, gives birth, 134
Forefather's Day, 260
fort
   construction of, 120
   description of location in Plymouth, 146
   Plymouth Colony, 165
Fortune (ship), 134, 169
   arrives in Plymouth (1621), 134, 149, 153, 199
   returns to England (1621), 152
   robbed of cargo by Frenchmen, 152
   transports letter from Thomas Weston, 134
Francis (ship), 74
freemen,
   as members of General Court, 213
   list (1633), 200
   privileges of, 203
Fulham Palace, 261
Fuller, Anna Hopkins, 64
Fuller, Bridget, 32, 197
Fuller, Edward, 64, 92
Fuller, Samuel, Sr., 64, 71, 92, 223
   as Purchaser, 170
furniture, description of common, 83
furs in Plymouth
   abundance of, 148
   as commodity, 172

Gainsborough, Lincolnshire, England, 19, 39
Gardiner, Richard, 66, 92
General Court, meeting of, 2, 163, 182, 183, 192, 203, 209, 213, 216, 229
   meeting of October 1648 (murder of Martha Clarke), 189
Gettysburg, battle of, 262
Goodman, John, 64, 92, 145, 146
Goodwin, John, 249
gossip, watchfulness and slander, 35
Gouge, William, 28-29, 78, 85, 133, 137, 255
government of Plymouth, structure of, 113
grand jurymen, power of, 255
Granger, Thomas, 218, 245
   confesses to bestiality, 194
   ordered death by hanging for bestiality, 194
Great Lots, 171, 179-180
Great Migration of Puritans, 72, 176, 178, 180
Great North Road, 15, 17-18
Green Close, home of John Robinson, 46
Green, John, 194
Green's Harbor, 180
Grimsby, Lincolnshire, England, 39
Grinder, Alice, 32

Hague, The, 49
Hampton Court Palace, 22
Hanson, John, 10
Hanson, Margaret Gresham, 10
Hanson, Wybra Pontus, 224, 266
Harden Hill, 6
Harding, Widow, 143
Hatch, Margaret, 211
Hatherly, Timothy, 216
   as member of Code of Laws review committee (1636), 183
   as undertaker of original debt, 169
   attends General Court meeting,
   murder of Martha Clarke (October 1648), 189
Helwys, Thomas, 37
Henry Frederick, Prince of Wales, 16
Henry VIII, King of England, 13-14, 17
Hercules (ship), arrives in Plymouth (1634), 229
herds in Plymouth, communal, 200
Herring River, 100
Hewes, Joan, 33
Hewes, John, 33
Heyward, Thomas, Sr., 2-3, 5-6
Hickes, Ephraim, 189
Hicks, Robert, 170
Hingham, Massachusetts Bay Colony, 27
Hippocrates, 250

hired men in Plymouth, contract, wages and responsibilities, 161-163
History of the Colony of Massachusetts Bay, T. Hutchinson, 260
Hobomak, Pokanoke Native American, 157
Hodgkinson (Hoskins), William, 112
Holbeck, William, 65
holidays not celebrated by Pilgrims, 262
Holly, Rose, 34
Holmes, William, 165, 250, 255
Holy See, 14
Hooke, John, 64
Hopkins, Constance, 66
Hopkins, Damaris, 66, 84
Hopkins, Elizabeth, 66, 70
Hopkins, Giles, 66
Hopkins, Lettice Morton, 223
Hopkins, Oceanus, 66, 70, 102
Hopkins, Stephen, 66, 74, 92, 130
   as member of Code of Laws review committee (1636), 183
   as Purchaser, 170
   marries Lettice Morton, 223
Hoskins, William, 112, 226
Howland, Elizabeth, 32
Howland, John, 64, 71, 92, 102, 188, 204
   as Purchaser, 170
   as undertaker of original debt, 169
Hudson River, 89-90, 230
Hull, Yorkshire, England, 39
Hurst, James, 188
   as Deacon of Plymouth Colony Church, 204
Hutchinson, Thomas, 260

indentured servants in Plymouth Colony, 32, 63, 160
   contracts of, 32, 160
   responsibility of masters, 160
Ingham, Mary, 250
inheritance laws in England, wills, 141
inheritance laws in Plymouth, 141-143, 165
Institutions, or Principall Grounds of the Lawes and Statutes of England, Anon., 184
insurrection in Plymouth Colony, 152-153
Jackson, Thomas, 193
jail, Plymouth Colony, 209
James I, King of England, 18, 48-49
James VI, King of England, 16-17, 22, 91-92
James, Thomas, 194
Jamestown, Virginia, 55
Jenney (Jenny), John, 108, 161, 232
   as Purchaser, 170
   represents Town of Plymouth as member of Code of Laws review committee (1636), 183
   sues Sturtivant and Ramsden, 232
Johnson, Francis, 45, 54
Jones River, 104
Jones, Christopher, Captain, 91, 97-98, 104, 120, 122
Josselyn, John, 69, 118, 232, 250
   writes of colonists moving to Virginia, 147
   writes of wolf encounter (1638), 237
juries in Plymouth Colony
   all male, 203
   partiality of, 217
   rules governing, 203

Kempton, Manasseh, as Purchaser, 170
Kennebec River, 173
Kerby, Richard, 34
Kerby, Sarah, 228
   court complaint against, 242
   public whipping for speaking out during church services, 228
Killingholme, Lincolnshire, England, 44
Killingholme/Immingham Creek, 39-40
King Philip's War (1675-1678), 243
Kingston, Massachusetts, 104
kitchen utensils, cutlery, 207
knife, as murder weapon of Martha Clarke, 207
Knowles, Richard, 226

laborers in Plymouth Colony, needs for, 160
Ladies Home Journal, 263
Lady Jane Grey, 14
Lambarde, William, 184
land grants in Plymouth, 54
   fairness of, 113
   procedure to acquire, 112
   questioning of, 112
land in Plymouth
   demand for land to raise cattle, 179
   patent for, 53-54
   potential for profit, 172
Langmore, John, 66
Latham, William, 64

Launder, Jane, 228
  court complaint against, 242
  receives warning for speaking out during church services, 228
laundry, process of, 109
laws
  first Code of Law (1623), 183
  Code of Laws, revised (1636), 185
  Committee to review laws (1636), 183
Lee, Robert, 136, 188, 204
Leiden Separatists, 55, 57, 64, 88, 93, 129, 146, 173-174, 199-200
Leiden Separatist Congregation, 48, 58, 64, 88, 174, 223
Leiden, Netherlands, 1, 27, 36, 45-49, 52-56, 58, 60-61, 64-65, 91, 102
Leighorne, James, 163
Leister, Edward, 66, 92, 130
Leland, John, 17
Leyhorne, James, 163
Leyhorne, Roland, 163
life in Amsterdam, adjusting to, 44-45
Linceford, Anne, 86
Lincoln, Abraham, President, 262-263
  proclaims day of thanksgiving, 262
Little James (ship), 148-151
  arrives in Plymouth (1623), 154
Long, John, 163
Longfellow, Henry Wadsworth, 262
Lord and Proprietor of Plymouth, William Bradford as, 112
Lords of the Privy Council, 39
Lucas, Thomas, 241
Lyon (ship), 174

Maas River, 60
Maggner, Captain of the *William and Thomas* (ship), 55
  death of, 55
Magnalia Christi Americana, C. Mather, 260
Manomet (Plymouth), Massachusetts, 132, 229
Manomet Native American settlement, 156
Margesson, Edmund, 66, 92
market days in Plymouth Colony, 109, 212
marriage
  arranged, 79
  ceremony, 43
  civil vs religious ceremony, 47, 85, 130
  contract of, 80
  description of ceremony, 85
  fitness for, 79
  husband's role and responsibilities, 79, 84, 86
  laws governing, 80
  notice posted in town meeting house, 81
  obligations of, 85
  parents role in, 44, 80
  permission for, 80
  purpose of, 78
  wife's role and responsibilities, 85
Marshfield, Massachusetts, 229
Marshfield, settlement in Plymouth Colony, 180
Martin, Abraham, 27
Martin, Christopher, 26-27, 58, 66-67, 92-93, 120
  as elected leader of group on *Mayflower*, 62
  as treasurer and representative of investors, 88
  death of, 122
  unpopular with passengers and crew, 63
Martin, Elizabeth, 27
Martin, Isaac, 27
Martin, Mary, 4, 66
Martin, Robert, 27, 266
Martin, Solomon, death of, 120
Mary I, Queen of England, 14
Massachusetts Bay Colony, 1, 72, 111, 175, 179, 185, 212, 220, 249
  chartered by Crown, 176
  exerts influence over Plymouth Colony, 183
  King merges Plymouth and Maine Colonies with, 244
  merges with Plymouth Colony (1691), 260
Massachusetts Historical Society, 261
Massachusetts State House, 262
Massasoit, Wampanoag Sachem, 125-126, 130-132, 150
  tells Bradford of plot against Weston's new colony, 156
Mather, Cotton, 13, 102, 115, 242-243, 260
Mattachiest Native American settlement, 156
Maverick, Samuel, 243
May, Henry, 47

Mayflower (ship), 1, 26, 49, 52, 56, 61, 63-65, 67-68, 70-71, 74, 88-91, 93, 104, 162
   accommodations onboard, 68-69
   all passengers finally disembark, 127
   arrival in Cape Cod, 87
   attempts to freshen below decks, 94
   broken beam supported with "great iron screw," 71
   childbirth onboard, 70
   Christmas onboard, 120
   company moves onshore, 119
   daily life onboard, 69
   deaths onboard, 126
      Bradford, Dorothy rumored to fall overboard, 102
      Martin, Solomon, 120
      More, Jasper, 99, 102
      second instance, 71
   description of meals onboard, 69
   dogs onboard, 178
   encounters rough seas off Cape Cod, 100
   illness of crew, 127
   illness of passengers, 123
   in danger from gale force winds, 123
   infants onboard, 102
   no farm animals onboard, 178
   passenger list - Separatists, 64
   passenger list - Strangers, 65
   puts into Dartmouth for repairs to *Speedwell* (ship), 62
   puts into Plymouth, England for repairs, 62
   sails into Plymouth Harbor, 104
   sales around northern tip of Cape Cod, 90
   sets sail for return to England, 127
   sets sail from Southampton, 62
   sickness onboard, 67, 122-123
   Weston complains of empty cargo upon return, 134
   women and children living onboard, 121
   women care for family onboard, 70
Mayflower Compact, 88, 91-94, 169, 196
   signers of, 92
Meeting House, first, Duxbury, 215
men, role as head of family, 43, 121
Merchant Adventurers, 54, 90, 196
Merrick, William, 190
metals available in Plymouth Colony, 149
Michell, Experience, 170

midwives at Plymouth, 115
military protection, training, 183
ministers, description of, 110
Minter, Desire, 64
miscarriage, rules for avoidance of, 114
Misquamsqueece (Sekonk), Massachusetts, 193
More (Moore), Ellen, 65
More (Moore), Jasper, 65
   death of, 99, 102
More (Moore), Mary Bartlett, 65, 267
More (Moore), Richard, 65
More (Moore), Samuel, 65
Morey, Jonathan, 267
Morey, Mary, 267
Morton, Ephraim, 209
Morton, George, 69
Morton, John, 32, 223
Morton, Nathaniel, 126
Morton, Thomas, 170
"mother fits," *see* postpartum psychosis/depression
Mullins, Alice, 66
Mullins, Joseph, 66
Mullins, Priscilla, 66
Mullins, William, 66, 92
murder, as crime before God, 219
Myles Standish Burial Ground, 215
Names of the Freemen of the Incorporation of Plymouth in New England (1635), 165

Narragansett tribe, 131, 147, 194
   threaten Pilgrims, 147
National Monument to the Forefathers, 261
Native Americans
   as trading partners, 110, 149, 168, 172
      wampum, 173
   attack Pilgrims, 100
   communication with, 123, 125, 131
   description of homesite, 96
   fear of, 49, 55, 83, 96, 99, 105, 122, 123, 182
   peace agreement with, 125-126
   relations deteriorate with Pilgrims, 243
   strained relationship with, 238
   terms of peace agreement with, 125
   trade with, irreputably damaged by murders at Wessagusset, 157
Nauset tribe, 131-132, 156
needlework, knitting and sewing, 47

Nelson, William, 188
  awarded freedom (1657), 203
Neponset Native American settlement, 156
New England's Salamander Discovered, E. Winslow, 184
New Netherland Colony, 53
New Netherlands Company, 53
New Plymouth, Pilgrims' naming of colony, 105
Newcomen, John, 192
North Plymouth, Massachusetts, 74
North Sea, 42, 60
Norwich, Diocese of, 21-22
Nuns Bridge, 60

Oath of Grandjury, 217
Of Plimoth Plantation, W. Bradford, see *Of Plymouth Plantation*
Of Plymouth Plantation, W. Bradford, 27, 194, 235, 260-261, 265
Old Colony Club, 260-261
Old North Road, 19, 21

Palmer, William, 170
Paomet Native American settlement, 156
parental assistance to newlyweds, 81
parenting in Plymouth
  beating with a rod, 256, 258
  discipline, 256-259
  parents should control their own anger, 259
  suppressing childs will, 256
  taught to control anger, 256
Partridge, Ralph, Reverend, 5
Peach, Arthur, 193
  execution of, 194
  murders Penowanyanquis, 193-194
Pearse, Abraham, as Purchaser, 170
Pecksuot, 156-157
  death of, 157
Peirce Patent, 89
Peirce, John, 54
Penowanyanquis, Narragansett Native American, 193-194
Pequot War, 193
Perry, Queen, 248
Perth Assembly, The, D. Calderwood, 49
Peterhouse College, 18
Pilgrim Hall, 261
Pilgrim men
  as head of family, 107
  roles in entertaining, 133

Pilgrim Monument, *see* National Monument to the Forefathers
Pilgrim Republic: An Historical Review of the Colony of New Plymouth, J. Goodwin, 249
Pilgrim Society, 261
Pilgrim women
  ability to enter contracts and hire servants, 143
  daily life, 106-108
  role in educating children, 140
  role in entertaining, 133
Pilgrims
  acceptable behavior, 183
  altered contract with Merchant Adventurers, description of, 57
  disdane for passengers of the *Fortune* (ship), 134
  goals of, 177
  original contract, description of, 57
  plant crops, 129
  take legal control of Plymouth Colony, 94
pine tar, manufacture and use of, 232-233
Piscataway, New Jersey, 230-231
Playne Dealing, 1, 74-75, 112, 164, 196-197, 200, 204, 217, 223, 225
Plymouth Colony, 1-2, 22, 26-27, 30-34, 43, 54, 71-75, 79-80, 82, 86, 88, 104, 106, 109, 112, 115, 141, 168-169, 181-182, 227
  borders of, 174
  building of, 119
  cannons carried ashore for protection, 124
  cemetery, 124
  challenged by Massachusetts Bay Colony, 175
  common house is destroyed in fire, 122
  construction of common house, 120, 122
  description of (1666), 244
  first Code of Law (1623), 183
  first homes, description of, 123
  first impressions, 104
  first Sabbath meeting held on land, 123
  last meeting of (1692), 244
  membership of, 73
  Native American, first visit of, 124
  new towns founded within, 180
  newcomers take "oath of fidelity", 73

planning of the settlement, 121
palisado, 147, 166, 180
    rebuilding of, 182
planting of gardens, 124
population of
    (1630), 175
    (1643), 192
    Quakers not tolerated inside colony, 227
    rules for membership of, 87
    wall around Plymouth, palisade, 182
Plymouth colonists trade land grants, 73
Plymouth Colony Fair, 110, 212
Plymouth Rock, 200, 261-262
Plymouth, England, 62, 64
Poncha (Eastham), Massachusetts, 226, 232
Pontus, William, 224, 266
Pope, Thomas, 188, 203
    as cooper, 204
    awarded freedom (1657), 203
Pory, John, 146, 147
    visits Plymouth Colony, 146
    writes positive report of Plymouth Colony, 146
postpartum psychosis/depression, symptoms and treatment, 250-252
property, allocated to Pilgrims by governor, 154
Pratt, Joshua, 81, 190
    as Purchaser, 170
Pratt, Phineas, 74
    as Purchaser, 170
pregnancy
    claim of as tactic to delay corporal punishment, 210
    clothing during, 114
    food and ale during, 114
    frequency of, 118
Prence, Thomas, 169, 196, 216, 243
    and murder of Martha Clarke, October 1648, 189
    as governor, 243
    as member of Code of Laws review committee (1636), 183
    as Purchaser, 170
    as undertaker of original debt, 169
Price, John, 163
Priest, Degory, 65, 92
    death of, 122
Priest, Sarah Allerton, 64
primogeniture, 21, 81
Protestants in England, burning of, 14
Provincetown Harbor, 90

Prower, Solomon, 66
punishment for crimes,
    as redemption for sins, 219
    in public, 110, 213
Purchasers, land allotted to, 170
Purchasers, list of, 170
Puritan philosophy, beliefs of, 20
Puritans
    challenge authority of Church of England, 238
    in Massachusetts Bay, goals of, 176-177

Quakers, 223, 227-229
    beliefs of, 227
    cages built to house, 229
    challenging religious control in colony, 237
    despised in Plymouth Colony, 229
    disrupting Pilgrim church services, 228
    in New Jersey, 230-231
    laws against, 228-229, 242
    persecution of, 230
    punishment of, 228-229
    refuse to take Oath, 228
    tension with Separatists, 243
    torment of, 264
Quinlan, Karen Ann, 248

Ramsden, Daniel, 234
    birth of, 233
Ramsden, Joseph, 188, 197, 233
    court orders relocation closer to town, 233-234
    marries Mary Savory, 234
    marries Rachel Eaton, 232
    produces pine tar, 232
    requests court to settle differences over a corn partnership, 232
    sued by John Jenney (Jenny), 232
Ramsden, Mary Savory, 234
Ramsden, Rachel Eaton, 188, 191-192, 195-196, 198, 200-201, 208, 210, 252, 254, 256, 259
    and murder of Martha Clarke
        describes discovering the murder, 188
        runs errand for Alice Bishop, 187
        testimony July 22, 1648, 198
        testimony of, 202, 205-207, 232
        visits with Alice Bishop, 253
    charged with lascivious behavior, 233

death of, 234
marries Joseph Ramsden, 232
Rapenburg Canal, 60
Rasmden, Joseph, death of, 234
Records of the Colony of New Plymouth in New England, N. Shurtleff, 261
Rehoboth, Massachusetts Bay Colony, 27, 164
Religion Act of 1593, *see* Act Against Seditious Sectaries
reputation, personal, value of, 204
Rickard, Giles Sr., 188-189
  as Plymouth constable, 204
  marries Hannah Pontus Churchill, 226
Rickard, Hannah Pontus Churchill, 224, .. 226
  marries Giles Rickard Sr., 226
Rigsdale, Alice, 66
Rigsdale, John, 66, 92
Ring, Andrew, 223-224
  appointed to Grand Inquest, Quakers, 223
  marries Deborah Hopkins, 223
Ring, Deborah Hopkins, death of, 223
Ring, Elizabeth, 223
Ring, Mary, death of, 223
Ring, Susanna, 223
Ring, William, death of, 223
River Humber, 39
River Idle, 8, 21
River Ryton, 8
River Trent, 21, 39
River Witham, 38
Roberts, Thomas, 226
Robinson, John, Pastor, 1, 20, 22-23, 27, 30, 34-35, 43, 45-47, 51, 56, 58-60, 79, 85-86, 113, 115-116, 137-138, 214, 218-219, 221, 256-259
  admits corporal punishment on children is controversial, 257
  arrives in Amsterdam, 42
  as assistant clergyman at Norwich, 21
  as mentor to William Bradford, 22
  as original planner of Plymouth Colony, 175
  death of, 158, 167
  joins Scrooby Separatists, 21
  recommends control of anger, 259
  sends farewell/advise letter to Separatists traveling to America,.... 62
  warns Bradford to beware of Myles Standish, 158
  warns of a childs naturally rebellious nature, 257
  writes letter to Bradford chiding murder of Native Americans, 158
  writes of parental responsibilities, 138-139
Rogers, Joseph, 65, 226
  as Purchaser, 170
Rogers, Thomas, 65, 92
Roman Catholic Church, 13-14, 19, 240, 248, 262

Sabbath
  observation of, 110
  punishment for breaking rules of, 111
Saint Pancraeskerk Church, Leiden, 45
Saint Pieterskerk Church, Leiden, 45
Saint Timothy, 110
Saints and Strangers, G. Willison, 244
Salem, Massachusetts, 3
Samoset, Algonguian sagamore, 124-125, 131
Sampson (Samson), Henry, 65, 170
Sandwich, Massachusetts, 180, 218, 227-229
Schie Canal, 60
school in Plymouth Colony, first discusson of (1670), 32
Scituate, Massachusetts, 180, 183, 218 227, 229
Scrooby Manor House, 17-19, 21, 27, 43, 45
  meeting place of Separatists, 19, 22
Scrooby Separatists, 17, 21, 24, 37, 39, 42, 44-45, 49-50, 64, 129
Scrooby, Nottinghamshire, England, 17, 19
scurvy, 103, 120
Separatism becomes irrelevant, 239
Separatist meeting place, Leiden, purchase of, 46
Separatists (Pilgrims of Plymouth)
  beliefs of, 20, 23
  attitudes towards women, 23, 25, 27, 29, 43
  in England
    betrayal of, 38
    first attempt to leave England, 38
    Gainsborough Separatists, 37
    imprisoned, 39
    movement within Scrooby, 20
    punished for trying to leave England, 38
    second attempt to leave England, 39

seek funding for new life in America, 51
separating from England, 37
talks of moving to America, 47
vote to leave England, 23
women and children left behind, 40
in Holland
concerns of leaving Leiden for America, 56
decide to send families to America, 51
discuss leaving Leiden, 49
first group departs for America, 56, 59
men arrive safely in Amsterdam, 42
women and children sporadically arrive in Amsterdam, 42
women gather supplies for America, 58
in Plymouth
establish complete religious control of Plymouth Colony, 146
womens role in church, 29-30
womens role in family, 43, 56
sewan, wampum as currency, 172-173, 193-194
Seward, William, 262
sexual relations
female orgasm and pregnancy, 86, 114
laws governing, 33
premarital, 81
premarital, punishment for, 33-34, 81
punishment for wrongdoing, 33
shallop, onboard *Mayflower* (ship), 66, 69, 95-97, 99-100, 104, 120, 122, 123, 162
Sharp, Jane, 86
Shaw, Edward, 163
found guilty of stealing, 163
Shaw, John, 136, 188, 204
as Purchaser, 170
Shaw, John Sr., 190
Sherley, James, as undertaker of original debt, 169
Shillingsworth, Thomas, 190
Shurtleff, Nathaniel, 261
silpee, description of, 107
Simonson, Moses, 170
Skiff(e), James, 75-76, 78, 82, 225
as builder of George Clarke home, 77
Smith, Bradford, 90
Smith, John, Captain, 52-53, 75, 101, 161
Smith, Ralph, represents Town of Plymouth as member of Code of Laws review committee (1636), 183

Smyth, John, 19, 37, 43
Snow, Anthony, 190
Snow, Nicholas, as Purchaser, 170
socializing among women, 109
Soule, George, 65, 92
as Purchaser, 170
Southworth, Constant, 149
Southworth, Edward, 63
death of, 149
Southworth, Thomas, 149
Sowther, Nathaniel, 164-165, 222
named Clarke of the Court, 165
Sparrow, Richard, 188, 190
Speedwell (ship), 57, 60-63, 223
arrives in Southhampton, 61
as fishing boat, 169
deemed too unreliable for Atlantic crossing, 63
develops leaks at sea, 62
puts into Dartmouth for repairs, 62
puts into Plymouth, England for repairs, 62
loss of ship for fishing in new land, 63
purchase of, 57
sets sail from Southampton, 62
Sprague, Francis, 163
as Purchaser, 170
Squanto (Tisquantum) Patuxet Native American, 125, 129-131, 153, 168
St. Helena's Church, Austerfield, England, 8, 11, 15
Standish of Standish, J.G. Austin, 263
Standish, Myles, 2-5, 60, 66, 92, 123, 156-158, 161-162, 189, 210, 215-216
and murder of Martha Clark
attends Court of Assistance (1648), 187
attends General Court meeting (October 1648), 189
as caregiver to dying, 126
as Purchaser, 170
as undertaker of original debt, 169
kills Pecksuot, 157
leads exploration into new land, 96
moves from original settlement to Duxbury, 180
returns to Plymouth with Wituwamat's head, 157
takes command of military affairs, 123
takes possession of farm animals, 179
trains militia, 215
Standish, Rose, 60, 66
death of, 123

Stinnings, Richard, 193
Story, Elias, 65
Strangers, (non-Separatists onboard the *Mayflower* (ship)), 61, 65, 67, 88-89, 91, 93, 95
stress in family life, 247
Sturtevant, Samuel, 232
   sued by John Jenney (Jenny), 232
subsistence economy of Plymouth, 135
Succonet, Native American settlement, 156
Sutton, Alice, 231
   birth of, 230
Sutton, Benjamin
   birth of, 231
   death of, 231
Sutton, Damaris (daughter of WS), birth of, 230
Sutton, Damaris Bishop (wife of WS), 166, 187, 199, 209, 224, 226-227, 229-231, 247, 251, 257
   birth of, 166
   death of, 231
   marries William Sutton, 227
   moves to New Jersey, 230
Sutton, Daniel, 231
   birth of, 231
Sutton, George, 229
Sutton, Jane Barnes, marries William Sutton, 231
Sutton, John, birth of, 230
Sutton, Joseph, 231
   death of, 231
Sutton, Judah, birth of, 231
Sutton, Marah "Mary", birth of, 230
Sutton, Richard, birth of, 231
Sutton, Thomas, birth of, 230
Sutton, William, 231
   as Quaker, 227
   birth of, 229
   death of, 231
   fined for theft of Bible, 229
   lives in Meeting House, Piscataway, New Jersey (1713), 231
   marries Damaris Bishop, 227, 229
   marries Jane Barnes, 231
   moves to New Jersey, 230
   proposes Quaker Meeting in Woodbridge, 231
   purchases land in New Jersey (1677), 230
Swan (ship), arrives in Plymouth (1623), 154
Swift, Joan, 34

Sylvester, Dinah, 250
   accuses wife of William Holmes of witchcraft, 250
   apologizes to court, 255

Talbot, Peter, 75
Talby, Dorothy, 3, 249
Taunton, Massachusetts, 164, 180, 218
Taylor, W. L., 263
Thanksgiving Day, 260, 262, 264
thanksgiving, "day of thanksgiving" in Plymouth (1621)
   Native Americans join celebration, 132
   planning of, 132
theft
   cattle, punishment for, 210
   of corn from Native Americans, 97-98, 105, 156
      repayment of, 132
   of Native American household goods, 99
Thomas, William, 189, 210, 216
   attends Court of Assistance (1648), 187
   attends General Court meeting (October 1648), 189
Thompson, Edward, 65
   death of, 99
Tilden, Nathaniel, 229
Tilden, Sarah, 229
Tilley, Ann, 65
Tilley, Edward, 65, 92
Tilley, Elizabeth, 65
Tilley, Joan, 65
Tilley, John, 65
timber available in Plymouth Colony, 148
Times of Their Lives: Life, Love and Death in Plymouth Colony, J. & P. Deetz, 247
Tinker, Thomas, 65, 92
tools
   farm equipment, standard, 82
   woodworking, standard, 83
Tory, Joseph, 189
Tracy, Stephen, 163
   as Purchaser, 170
treaty with Native Americans, 105
Trevor, William, 66, 162
   returns to England, 162
trial, public
   as deterrent to crime, 214
   as tool for redemption, 215
   held in public, 213

352 *Index*

Trotula of Salerno, 250
trousseau, Pilgrim bride's, 84
Turn, Michael, 34
Turner, John, 65, 92
Twelve Years' Truce, 48
Tyndale, William, 13

Undertakers
　agreement with Purchasers, 172, 174
　bring over remaining Separatists, 174
undesirables in Plymouth Colony, 252
United States Senate Special Commission on Aging, 248
Upshall, Nicholas, 242

Victoria, Queen of England, 261
Vincent, Margaret, 268
Virginia Company of London, 53-54, 89
Virginia, Colony of, 55, 90, 147
Vliet Canal, 60
voyage to America as sacred mandate, 66

Wadsworth, Christopher, represents Duxbury as member of Code of Laws review committee (1636), 183
Walker, James, 189
Wallen, Ralph, as Purchaser, 170
Wampanoag, Native American tribe, 125, 132-133, 147
　alerts Pilgrims of ship, 133
　as trading partners, 152
　attend and dance at the Bradford's wedding, 150
　wasting plague among members, 131
Warren, Elizabeth, as Purchaser, 170
Warren, Richard, 66, 92
Warwick Charter, 174
Warwick Patent, 112-113, 175
Warwick, (Robert Neville), Earl of, 112, 174-175
watchfulness, 34-35, 138, 183, 215, 222, 247, 253, 255, 265
Watson, John, 261
weather in Plymouth, 102, 121, 123-124, 127
Wells, Isaac, 189
Wessagussett (Weymouth), Massachusetts, 2, 156
Weston, Thomas, 53-54, 57-58, 61, 65, 89, 134
　abandons settlement and goes to Maine, 157
　alters Pilgrims contract while searching for investors, 57
　recruits common folk to join Separatists in America, 61
　starts settlement in Plymouth, 156
Weymouth, Massachusetts, 156
White, Peregrine, 65, 99, 102
White, Resolved, 65
White, Roger, 158
White, William, 65, 92, 99, 130
widows in Plymouth
　as land owners, 142
　as taxpayer, 143
　freedoms of, 142
　responsibilities of, 141
Wilder, Roger, 64
Williams, Roger, 111, 194
Williams, Thomas, 65, 92
Willis, John, 190
Willison, George, 244
windows in Plymouth homes, 77
Winslow, Edward, Governor, 59, 65, 69, 92, 97, 126, 130, 132-133, 145-146, 183, 199
　arrives in Plymouth aboard *Charity* (ship) 1624, 178
　as author of *New England's Salamander Discovered*, 184
　as Purchaser, 170
　as undertaker of original debt, 169
　brings books to Court, 184
　elected Governor, 181
　marriage of, 130, 145
Winslow, Elizabeth, 65
　death of, 126, 130, 145
Winslow, Gilbert, 65, 92
Winslow, John, 99, 199-200
　arrives in Plymouth (1621), 199
　as Purchaser, 170
　granted land, 200
　takes possession of farm animals, 179
Winslow, Josiah, Sr., 189
Winslow, Mary Chilton "Goodwife", 32, 187-188, 199-200
　arrives in Plymouth, 200
Winslow, Susanna White, 65, 99, 130, 145
Winthrop, John, 176
　argues against death penalty in Massachusetts Bay Colony, 220
　his purpose for forming Massachusetts Bay Colony, 176
　visits Plymouth, 111
witchcraft in Puritan New England, 249
Wituwamat, Neponset, 156-157

Index 353

and Myles Standish, 156-157
death of, 157
women
  attire in Plymouth Colony, 35
  behavior, expectations of, 33, 35-56
    monitoring of, 109, 183
  breastfeeding, 117-118
    as contraception, 118
  childbirth
    dangers of, 114-115
    fear of, 115
    feeding of newborn, 117
    food during, 116
    help during, 115-116
    newborn survival rate, 115
    procedure afterward, 116-117
    procedure during, 115-116
  demeanor of, 35
  economy and trade among, 109
  education of in Plymouth Colony, 31
  family life, women's role in, 30
  in Holland
    women gather supplies for move to America, 58
  in Plymouth
    ability to enter contracts and hire servants, 143
    daily life, 107
    role in entertaining, 133
  in Separatism
    as deaconess, 29
    role in church, 30
  literacy of in Plymouth Colony, 32
  midwives at Plymouth, 115
  miscarriage, rules for avoidance of, 114
  "mother fits," *see* postpartum psychosis depression
  physical appearance of, 36
  reputation, personal value of, 204
  rights and responsibilities, 27, 44
  role in education of children, 140
  role in entertaining, 133
  role in family life, 30
  socializing among women, 109
  widows in Plymouth
    as land owners, 142
    as taxpayers, 143
    freedoms of, 142
    responsibilities of, 141
  work ethic of, 30
Wood, Henry, 189
Wood, Jane, 34
Wood, Stephen, 190
Woodbridge, New Jersey, 231
wool, spinning and weaving, 47
workload, inequal, in Plymouth (1623), 30
World War II, 263
Wright, William, as Purchaser, 170
Wyatt, James, 189
Wyncop, John, 53

Yarmouth, Massachusetts, 180, 218

Interior design by David E. Kane
Cover design by Rick Bickhart
Printed in the United States of America

About the Author

DONNA WATKINS has published articles in magazines, journals, and newspapers, including the Los Angeles Times. Donna has an undergraduate degree in American Studies (CSULA), and she holds graduate degrees in Library and Information Management (USC) and American Studies (CSUF). Alice Bishop, the subject of this book, is her ninth-great-grandmother. Donna's career included work as a librarian at the Pasadena Public Library. After years of helping patrons find books in public libraries, she has turned to writing her own. She resides in Fullerton, California, with her husband in a house full of quilts.

www.ingramcontent.com/pod-product-compliance
Lightning Source LLC
Chambersburg PA
CBHW020048170426
43199CB00009B/204